The Rediscovery of Jesus' Eschatological Discourse

David Wenham

GOSPEL PERSPECTIVES Volume 4

Wipf and Stock Publishers
EUGENE, OREGON

Wipf and Stock Publishers
199 West 8th Avenue, Suite 3
Eugene, Oregon 97401

Gospel Perspectives, Volume 4
The Rediscovery of Jesus' Eschatological Discourse
By Wenham, David
Copyright© January, 1984 The Continuum International Publishing Group
ISBN: 1-59244-286-2
Publication Date: July, 2003
Previously published by JSOT Press, January, 1984 .

Volume 4 in a 6 volume series

PREFACE

This is the fourth volume in the *Gospel Perspectives* series: the first three volumes have been symposia of essays on different topics by many authors; this volume is different in that it is a single monograph by a single author. But like its predecessors it is the product of the Tyndale House Gospels Research Project. I am much indebted to the Tyndale House Council for inviting me to be involved in the Project, and for enabling me to undertake the research that is contained in this book, also to numerous participants in the Research Project and to colleagues at Tyndale House for their comments and advice on various parts of my study.

To mention particular people who have helped and encouraged me is invidious, since I have been assisted by so many. But I would like to mention Professor F. F. Bruce, who initiated me into gospel research, Dr. R. T. France and Dr. Murray Harris, successive wardens of Tyndale House, and Dr. Richard Bauckham, who helped me more than anyone through his expert and detailed comments on parts of the monograph. Dr. G. R. Beasley-Murray and Professor D. A. Hagner kindly read and commented on my whole manuscript. Mr. John Sherriff allowed me access to his own unpublished work on Matthew 24 and 25. Mrs. E. Pilmer typed the manuscript. My wife, Clare, helped with the preparation of the indices of the volume, and has been a constant support during the course of my research.

I would like especially to thank my father for his inspiration and encouragement. He has been keenly interested in the critical issues surrounding the gospels for many years, and I owe much to the stimulus of his ideas. I owe to both my parents my personal interest in the gospels and in the Jesus they portray. Although this book is inevitably a rather dry literary-historical study - quite unlike the gospels themselves! - my hope is that it may contribute in a small way to a greater understanding of the gospels and so ultimately to a greater appreciation of the good news they proclaim.

August 1983
Tyndale House, Cambridge

Abbreviations and acknowledgements

Standard abbreviations are used in the monograph (as in
the *Members' Handbook of the Society of Biblical Literature*,
1980, pp.86-97). References to literature in the footnotes
have been kept deliberately brief, but fuller details of
books and articles consulted will be found in the bibliography.
In addition to the works listed in the bibliography, I have
made constant use of the Greek synopses of A. Huck and K. Aland,
of the Nestle edition of the Greek New Testament and of the
Revised Standard Version of the English Bible. The Greek
text normally reproduced in the monograph is the Nestle-Aland
26th edition.

CONTENTS

INTRODUCTION

1. THE PURPOSE OF THE STUDY

There are perhaps no more difficult chapters in the
gospels than the chapters containing Jesus' eschatological
discourse, i.e. Matthew 24,25, Mark 13, Luke 21. The ordinary
Christian believer finds them difficult: What is to be made of
the 'desolating sacrilege'? What did Jesus mean when he said
that 'all these things' would take place in a generation? Does
the discourse relate to recent developments in the Middle East,
and, if it does, how? And the New Testament scholar finds them
equally difficult: to the layman's questions about the
interpretation of these chapters the scholar will add questions
about the authenticity of the material, about the relationship
of Matthew's, Mark's and Luke's different versions of the
discourse and about the intention and situation of the different
evangelists.

The purpose of this monograph is not to look at all of
these questions, but is to look particularly at the question of
the history of the traditions found in the relevant synoptic
chapters, and even more specifically at the question of the
relationship of the differing Matthean, Markan and Lukan
versions. The findings of the study will have implications for
other questions (e.g. of authenticity and interpretation), but
these will only be alluded to, not explored in depth.

To undertake a review of the relationship of the traditions
of Matthew, Mark and Luke does not necessarily imply a
rejection of the two-source hypothesis; indeed so far as Markan
priority is concerned our conclusions will lend at least some
support to the hypothesis. But the undertaking does imply
(a) that there are questions about the eschatological discourse
that need answering even granting the two-source hypothesis,
e.g. about the relationship of Mk 13:33-37 to the Matthean and
Lukan traditions, and perhaps about the relationship of the 'Q'
eschatological discourse in Luke 17 to the Markan discourse;
(b) that even with the two-source hypothesis the possibility
that Matthew and Luke have primitive non-Markan traditions in
Markan sections must be reckoned with; (c) that the two-source
hypothesis at least needs review and defence in the light of

recent debates. The intention of this study is not to consider
the synoptic problem in general, but the synoptic problem
within a particular passage; and, although it may not unfairly
be argued that to consider the particular apart from the
general is not enough, it may on the other hand be suggested
that the most promising route to the solution of the general
problem may be through detailed analysis of particular
passages.

The sort of study being done here may be considered rather
old-fashioned in the age of redaction criticism. And yet
redaction critics almost invariably build on their assumptions
about source criticism and tradition criticism. This is a
perfectly proper way to proceed: if it is known what sources an
evangelist was using, then the obvious way of identifying that
evangelist's redactional contribution is by examining his use
of those sources. But what this means is that questions of
source and tradition criticism remain fundamental. It is
arguably a fault with some redaction-critical work that simple
solutions to these questions are too easily taken for granted.
This may be excused on the grounds that every critic cannot
reexamine every question and that the redaction critic must
start somewhere. But at a time when there is widespread
questioning concerning the synoptic problem, the person who
builds unquestioningly on one solution of the synoptic problem
is living dangerously. On the other hand, the redaction critic
who tries to build without making source-critical judgments,
though perhaps on safer ground, has much less to build on.
Questions of source and tradition thus remain crucially
important.

2. *THE SCHOLARLY STATE OF PLAY*

Anyone undertaking a study of the eschatological discourse
must be conscious of being inheritor to a vast tradition of
earlier study. The course of the scholarly debates about the
discourse was expertly charted by G. R. Beasley-Murray in his
*Jesus and the Future. An Examination of the Criticism of the
Eschatological Discourse, Mark 13, with Special Reference to
the Little Apocalypse Theory.*/1/ Beasley-Murray's work is
helpful both as a survey of the history of research and as a
critique of many of the arguments that have been used to deny
the discourse to Jesus. But, as the title of his book suggests,

---

/1/ London: Macmillan, 1954.

it is primarily a study of Mark and of the authenticity of the
Markan discourse. Beasley-Murray has useful things to say
about the Matthean and Lukan traditions and about Paul's related
teaching in 1 and 2 Thessalonians,/1/ but he does not explore
the questions raised by those traditions in much detail.

Since the appearance of Beasley-Murray's work in 1954,
there have been several other important studies of the
discourse. Lars Hartman in his *Prophecy Interpreted: The
Formation of Some Jewish Apocalyptic Texts and of the
Eschatological Discourse, Mark 13 par.*/2/ argues that the
synoptic eschatological discourse is an elaboration of a midrash
on the book of Daniel, and he explains the history of the
traditions in terms of this thesis. The result is a study
which is illuminating in showing the heavy dependence of the
eschatological discourse on the OT and on OT themes (even if
Hartman's identification of OT background for certain sayings
seems over-ingenious/3/) and which includes valuable
observations about the history of the traditions and in
particular about the relationship of 1 and 2 Thessalonians to
the synoptic discourse. However, his central thesis concerning
the midrashic origin of the discourse is uncertain: it is quite
as likely that the discourse was originally, as it is now in
the synoptic gospels, a synthesis of material, much of it
derived from the OT, but some of it prophecy and exhortation
without direct OT background. One effect of Hartman's thesis
is that it leads him to concentrate attention on those parts of
the eschatological discourse that may be seen as midrashic;
consequently he does not pay much attention to the hortatory
and parabolic material that concludes the discourse in all
three synoptic gospels, though he recognizes that some of this
material is primitive going back at least to the time of Paul.
His book then is suggestive rather than definitive so far as the
history of the traditions is concerned.

/1/ pp. 226-34
/2/ Uppsala: Gleerup, 1966.
/3/ See, e.g., his conjecture that the use of the verb κολοβοῦν
in Mk 13:20 may be explained on the basis of an emended Hebrew
text of Dan 12:1 (pp. 163,164.) Cf. also the reviews of
Hartman's book by J. Lambrecht, *Biblica* 49 (1968) 254-70 and
M. D. Hooker, *JTS* 19 (1968) 263-65.

The monographs of Jan Lambrecht, *Die Redaktion der Markus-Apokalypse: Literarische Analyse und Strukturuntersuchung*,/1/ and of Rudolf Pesch, *Naherwartungen: Tradition und Redaktion in Mk 13*/2/ are both redaction-critical studies of Mark 13. Lambrecht considers that the Markan discourse is a compilation of originally independent traditions, and Pesch that it is a revision of an earlier apocalyptic tract (that did not derive from Jesus)./3/ Neither author gives much attention to the Matthean or Lukan traditions or to the potentially significant evidence of 1 and 2 Thessalonians./4/ Lambrecht, however, argues perceptively for Mark's use of 'Q' tradition in the persecution sayings (Mk 13:9-13 & par.) and in the closing parabolic material (Mk 13:33-37 & par.).

Two redaction-critical studies of the relevant Lukan traditions appeared in Germany in quick succession, Josef Zmijewski's massive *Die Eschatologiereden des Lukas-Evangeliums. Eine traditions- und redaktionsgeschichtliche Untersuchung zu Lk 21,5-36 und Lk 17,20-37*/5/ and Ruthild Geiger's *Die Lukanischen Endzeitreden*/6/. Both consider the question as to whether Luke used non-Markan traditions and both answer the question in the negative. But their studies do not look much more broadly at the tradition-critical question; they are essentially discussion of Luke in the light of Mark and on the basis of earlier study of Mark.

The most recent book to appear is Fred Burnett's, *The Testament of Jesus-Sophia: A Redaction-Critical Study of the Eschatological Discourse in Matthew*./7/ This study of Mt 24:1-31 takes the two-source hypothesis for granted, and gives very little consideration to questions of tradition- or source-criticism.

/1/ Rome: Pontifical Biblical Institute, 1967.

/2/ Düsseldorf: Patmos, 1968.

/3/ Pesch takes a very much modified line in his later commentary, *Das Markusevangelium*, vol. 2 (Freiburg: Herder, 1977), accepting a substantially dominical core to the discourse.

/4/ Both authors subsequently published studies of the Matthean discourse, Lambrecht in *L'Évangile selon Matthieu* (ed. M. Didier: Gembloux: Duculot, 1972), 309-42, and Pesch in *Bibel und Leben* 11 (1970) 223-238.

/5/ Bonn: Peter Hanstein, 1972.

/6/ Bern: Herbert-Lang, 1973.

/7/ Washington: UP of America, 1981.

All of the books mentioned touch in one way or another on the question of the history of the traditions in the eschatological discourse. But none of them attempts comprehensively to review the source-critical and tradition-critical issues raised by the discourse, and all of them operate within the general framework of the two-source hypothesis. Thus the studies of Mark by Lambrecht and Pesch pay little attention to Matthew and Luke; the studies of Luke by Zmijewski and Geiger pay little attention to the specifically Matthean material; the study of Matthew by Burnett pays little attention to specifically Lukan material. None of these redaction-critical studies looks very carefully at the possibly related eschatological traditions in 1 and 2 Thessalonians and Revelation. Beasley-Murray and Hartman do look more broadly at the evidence and both have particularly suggestive insights; but neither is directly addressing the source- and tradition-critical questions, and neither reviews the evidence thoroughly and comprehensively with that question in view.

As well as the monographs, there have, of course, been many significant articles on the discourse published in recent years, including the particularly valuable studies of Jacques Dupont,/1/ and the discourse has been treated in commentaries and other works./2/ But inevitably articles and commentaries tend to be even more limited in their coverage of source- and tradition-critical issues than the monographs.

There is thus a place for a work addressing these issues in particular. It is arguable that the lack of an adequate and comprehensive study of the relationship and history of the traditions has in various respects hampered the work of the scholars mentioned: had the redaction critics, for example, wrestled more with the Pauline evidence, various of their conclusions might have been different. It may also be suggested that a thorough review of the evidence may help to

---

/1/ For details see the bibliography on pp. 377-90 below.
/2/ L. Gaston's *No Stone on Another* (Leiden: Brill, 1970) deserves special mention, as containing substantial discussion of the eschatological discourse and useful observations on the source-critical questions. For other works see the footnotes to the text that follows (though these have been kept deliberately brief and contain only selected and sometimes abbreviated references) and the bibliography.

remove or reduce the very great differences of opinion among
scholars about the early history of the traditions: may the
bulk of the discourse be traced back to Jesus? Is the discourse
a compilation of different fragments of tradition? Was it
originally a non-Christian tract taken over by the church? Was
it originally a Christian midrash? Although the question of
origins and authenticity is not the specific question being
addressed in this book, at least the survey of the evidence may
help to throw light on the question.

3. THE METHOD OF STUDY

The procedure to be followed in the book is essentially
simple: the differing synoptic traditions in the eschatological
discourse will be compared with each other and with other NT
eschatological traditions, and various explanations of the
relationship of the traditions will be considered and
evaluated. The relevant Greek texts will usually be cited in
the course of the discussion, but the reader will also need to
refer to a synopsis in order to follow the inevitably detailed
argument.

Four more specific points may be made about the method to
be adopted.

3.1. Synoptic relationships

The priority of the Markan form of the tradition will not
be assumed. Although the book will in fact end up concluding
that Mark's gospel was used by the authors of Matthew and Luke,
the possibility that Matthew and Luke have early non-Markan
traditions, even where they overlap with Mark, will be taken
very seriously. The openness in this respect is perhaps the
most distinctive feature of this book. This open approach is
not only demanded because of the current scholarly uncertainty
over the synoptic problem, but it also arises out of the
author's own earlier study of Paul's eschatological teaching
in 1 and 2 Thessalonians, since it was argued there that
Paul knew many of the traditions found in the synoptic
eschatological discourse, including some of the traditions
found only in the Matthean and Lukan versions of the discourse.
/1/ In a real sense this book may be said to be following up

/1/ 'Paul and the Synoptic Apocalypse' in Gospel Perspectives II
(ed. R. T. France and D. Wenham. Sheffield: JSOT, 1981) 345-75.

leads suggested by that article, and much of the contents of the article will be reproduced here. On the other hand, the book does not assume the conclusions of the previous article. It corroborates those conclusions in many respects, but it is first and foremost a study of synoptic texts, and Paul's evidence, though very useful, is not essential to it.

3.2. Identifying tradition and redaction

Seeking to evaluate differing synoptic texts and to decide what is traditional and what is redactional is not always straightforward. One very common criterion used is stylistic: if a particular phrase or expression is untypical of the evangelist, then this is taken to point to its being received tradition; but if the phrase reflects the evangelist's style or interests, then this is taken to indicate that the material is redactional. This criterion sounds useful; but two significant cautions are needed.

On the one hand, the occurrence of unusual vocabulary or unusual ideas in a particular saying in a gospel need not prove that the saying is tradition rather than redaction. All authors use some words infrequently, and, especially when we have a rather small quantity of the particular author's writings and therefore a very limited statistical base to work from - as is the case with the gospels - , it is unwise to build too much on arguments about unusual vocabulary or ideas.

On the other hand, it is equally unwise to jump to the conclusion that signs of an evangelist's style or of an evangelist's special interests necessarily prove that the material concerned derives from the particular evangelist. It is entirely possible that the evangelist has selected material from the tradition that interests him and/or that he has reexpressed a received tradition in his own words and idiom. Even if it can be shown that a particular saying in Matthew or Luke that is not paralleled in Mark contains more characteristically Matthean or Lukan terminology than another saying that is paralleled in Mark, this still does not prove the Matthean or Lukan origin of the saying in question. It is quite possible that Matthew or Luke were more conservative in reproducing traditions from the written gospel of Mark than in reproducing traditions derived from the church's oral tradition or elsewhere.

To point out the limitations of stylistic criteria is not to deny that they have any value. When there is more than one version of a particular tradition, then stylistic arguments may well help one to evaluate the relationship of the versions: if the divergence of the two versions is clearly explicable in terms of the style or interests of one of the authors concerned, then this may be a significant clue in reconstructing the history of the traditions. But where a particular tradition is found only in one gospel, then judgments based solely on stylistic criteria must be recognized as very tentative.

In any case judgments about redaction and tradition are often very fine judgments. It may, for example, be possible to explain all the variations between two traditions in terms of one author's stylistic or theological tendencies. Certainly many treatments of the common material in Matthew and Mark or Mark and Luke start from the assumption that Matthew and Luke are modifications of Mark and succeed more or less in explaining Matthew and Luke on the basis of Mark. But such arguments can be dangerously circular, since the later evangelist's tendencies will often be identified by an examination of the changes made to the earlier gospel by the later evangelist. Such circularity is not a problem, given the correctness of the initial assumption about the relationship of the gospels. But, if a particular relationship is not assumed, then greater caution is needed, and the possibility that a variation may be explicable in terms of one evangelist's tendencies has to be weighed against the possibility that it may be explicable in terms of the other evangelist's tendencies or in terms of independent tradition. And the matter is not even as simple as that, since in a particular passage and even a particular verse several factors may have led to the divergence between the two versions of the tradition: for example, both evangelists may have modified the wording of a common underlying tradition and one may have retained parts of the tradition that the other omits. It is evident that coming to decisions about redaction and tradition involves a delicate weighing of probabilities.

3.3. Agreements and parallels

3.3.1. Agreements of two evangelists against one
It has been suggested that judgments about tradition and redaction are much easier when there are two versions of a tradition than when there is only one. But it is the fact that

there are more than two versions of the material found in the
eschatological discourse which makes much of the following
study possible.

The fact that there are three synoptic versions of much of
the material in question might be of little advantage to us if
Matthew and Luke were exclusively dependent on Mark in their
common tradition. However, even if Markan priority is assumed,
it is a priori probable that from time to time Matthew and Luke
may both have known non-Markan forms of these common traditions,
whether oral or written forms (including perhaps the 'Q'
tradition, if this overlapped with Mark); and it is at least
possible that they may from time to time agree in reproducing
such non-Markan forms. It will be argued in what follows in
this book that this is not only a theoretical possibility, but
that it is an actual probability in a number of places. It is
the agreements of Matthew and Luke against Mark that suggest
this.

The minor agreements of Matthew and Luke have, of course,
been a very controversial topic in NT studies with some
scholars minimizing and others maximizing their importance.
Both extreme positions must be avoided: on the one hand, the
fact that all the agreements can, sometimes with difficulty, be
explained on the assumption that Matthew and Luke had no other
source than Mark should not be taken to mean that such an
explanation is correct or probable; some scholars seem scarcely
to consider other possibilities. On the other hand, care must
be taken not to assume that every small agreement must be
explained in terms of common tradition.

Once again fine judgments of probability have to be made:
a small isolated agreement will prove little by itself, but a
series of agreements or a particularly unusual agreement should
not easily be dismissed as accidental. Serious consideration
should be given in those cases to the possibility that the
agreement does indicate a connection between the agreeing
traditions. If a connection is deemed probable, then further
consideration must be given to the nature of the connection:
was there a direct connection? For example, did Luke use
Matthew? Or was there an indirect connection? For example,
did both Luke and Matthew have access to some non-Markan form of
tradition? And if there was a non-Markan form of tradition,
what was the relationship of that to the Markan tradition? The
questions are evidently quite complex. But too often
agreements are not even noted: commentators explain a

particular variant from Mark in either Matthew or Luke in terms
of Matthean or Lukan theology without even noting that the
variant in question is an agreement against Mark, or at least
without considering what the implications of the agreement
might be.

3.3.2. Parallels in Paul and Revelation

There are not only the three synoptic versions of the
eschatological discourse to be considered. Some of the material
in the discourse is paralleled elsewhere in the NT, notably in
the writings of Paul and in the book of Revelation. The
synoptic problem is thus expanded, since some explanation must
be offered of the relationship between the synoptic traditions
and these other NT parallels. Paul's evidence is of
particular interest, since the Pauline letters in question are
usually reckoned to have been written before the composition of
any of the synoptic gospels.

But there are, of course, several problems in dealing with
the evidence of Paul and Revelation. There is, first, the
question of identifying significant parallels. There are again
two extreme approaches to this: some scholars seem reluctant to
contemplate the thought that shared ideas found in Paul and the
synoptics are related, pointing out perhaps that there is often
OT or Jewish background for the idea in question and suggesting
that this explains the similarity. Others go the opposite way
and seize on every possible parallel as evidence of relatedness.
Deciding between the two approaches in particular instances can
be difficult. But if a shared idea is distinctive enough (and
perhaps untypical of one or other writer) and if it does not
have an obvious OT background, or if an OT text is used in an
unusual or distinctive way by Paul or the author of Revelation
and the synoptic writer, or if there are a series of agreements
between a passage in Paul or Revelation and a synoptic passage,
then the probability of some sort of a link is increased.

But even if a link between the synoptic and the other
tradition is established, this does not solve the question of
the relationship of the traditions concerned. Since Paul is
usually dated before the synoptics, it is possible that some of
the sayings found in the synoptics actually derive from Paul.
And since Revelation is usually dated after the synoptics, it
is possible that the author of Revelation derived his
eschatological material from the synoptics. On the other hand,
it is also possible that Paul derives his material from a form

of the Jesus tradition similar to what we have in the synoptics
and that the author of Revelation also had access to a form of
the tradition independent of the synoptics. Each case and each
possibility has to be weighed carefully.

3.3.3. Uncertain synoptic parallels

Another problem in the sort of study undertaken in this
monograph is that it is not always clear whether two similar
traditions in different gospels are in fact different versions
of the same tradition, or whether they are in fact quite
distinct traditions. This question will be faced at several
points in the discussion that follows.

There is a tendency among some scholars to assume that
almost all even vaguely similar traditions are related and have
a common origin. But this is a dangerous assumption. As
conservative scholars often point out, every teacher repeats
himself or herself, and uses similar or the same teaching on
different occasions, and there is no doubt that Jesus and his
followers did the same. The possibility then that similar
traditions are quite distinct must always be reckoned with.
So must the complicating possibility that originally distinct
traditions may sometimes have been assimilated with other
similar traditions, so that they no longer appear as distinct
as they once were! On the other hand, conservative scholars
tend to assume that traditions that are similar but not
identical (whether in wording or location) must be considered
independent. This assumption is, however, almost as uncertain
as the contrary assumption: if it is recognized, as it must be,
that the evangelists did feel free on occasions to reword and
rearrange gospel traditions, then the possibility that similar
traditions are variant versions of a common tradition must at
least be considered.

There is no simple rule of thumb that enables the student
of the gospels to decide between the possibilities in particular
cases. What can and should be done, however, is to examine the
similar traditions carefully and to consider two things:
(a) Are there particular features in one or both of the two
traditions that are explicable on the assumption that the
tradition in question is a modification of the other tradition,
or on the assumption that both are derived from a common
tradition? For example, is there some discontinuity or
difficulty in the one tradition which is hard to explain purely
in terms of the author's usual - maybe by our standards
unsophisticated - style, but which can be explained as the

result of the author's omission or adaptation of something that
is present in the other tradition? (b) Is it possible to explain
persuasively how and why the one tradition might have developed
out of the other (or how and why both might have developed from
some common ancestor)? If the answer to both those questions is
yes, then there must at least be a good case for considering
that the traditions have a common origin. If the answer is no,
then there is a good case for considering them to be independent.
Once again the judgment may often be a fine one. But in the book
it will be argued that a number of uncertainly related
traditions are in fact related, and it will be shown how the
traditions concerned have evolved and diverged.

3.4. A detailed and cumulative argument

Although the procedure being followed in this study is
essentially simple, the argument is inevitably very detailed.
It is only through such detailed tradition- and source-critical
study that questions which have perplexed scholars over many
years are likely to be resolved.

The argument is also a cumulative one: very many small
pieces of evidence have to be put together for the whole picture
to be clear. This is indeed how the central thesis of this book
- the thesis of an elaborate and substantial pre-synoptic
tradition - emerged. It was not a case of the author looking for
the particular solution that is offered here, but of many
pieces of evidence converging and pointing in one direction.

It is true that with some cumulative arguments the whole
argument is no stronger than its weakest link. But in other
cases - and hopefully with this book - the argument is more like
a cable with many strands, which does not depend on its weakest
strands, than a chain with many links. A slightly different
analogy might be that of a complicated crossword puzzle: the
answer to a certain clue may at first only be tentative, and
there may be alternative possible answers. But if the probable
answers to other clues then fit in with that first tentative
answer, and if that tentative answer leads on to the solution of
other clues, then, as the whole fits together, the originally
tentative answers are seen to be highly probable.

The crossword analogy describes helpfully what this book
seeks to do: in the early stages of the argument various clues
are examined, and provisional answers are reached, often quite
tentatively. But then these provisional and tentative answers
are found to come in useful when other evidence is explored,
and further answers are then obtained which, broadly speaking
at least, fit in with the earlier answers. An increasingly

complete picture is thus built up, and many of the answers that could only be tentative 'possibilities' at first look increasingly like strong 'probabilities'. The crossword analogy may also help to explain the relatively cursory discussion of some issues in the later sections of this book (e.g. in chapters 8 and 9): in these sections we are building on the earlier discussion and conclusions and, as it were, filling in quickly some of the final clues of the crossword.

A danger with this sort of argument is that it may be possible, certainly in synoptic criticism if not with a crossword, to get some of the earlier answers wrong and then to make all the other evidence fit in. That this can happen in scholarly research is suggested by the alarming way in which biblical scholars, apparently with all honesty and conviction, can read the same evidence in thoroughly different ways. There may be no sure way of avoiding this. But in what follows we believe that the key elements in the argument (notably the central arguments of chapters 1-3) are soundly argued, and, although some other things are more speculative, this has been noted and we have tried to avoid forcing evidence to fit into a pattern.

So far as the reader is concerned, an undoubted difficulty with the sort of argument presented in this book is that it is hard to assimilate quickly. We have summarized the argument (on pp. 355-59); but, because of its very detailed nature, it is really not the sort of argument that can be summarized. And because it is a cumulative argument, it is not the sort of argument that can easily be sampled: to feel the force of the converging evidence the reader needs to work carefully through at least chaps. 1-3 and preferably chaps. 4-7 as well.

That is not to say, however, that the arguments in the individual chapters do not stand up by themselves. On the contrary much of the argumentation in the separate chapters could be valid, even if the overall thesis of the book was incorrect, and it is the author's hope that even those who find it hard to accept the overall thesis will find much of the detailed argument persuasive.

But it is also the author's hope that the overall thesis, which is in certain respects quite revolutionary, raising questions for conservative and radical critics alike, will not be prematurely dismissed. It is the very fact that the book does raise basic questions that makes its argument potentially

significant. It is the author's hope that some readers will
have the patience and persistence to examine the book's
arguments in detail and that they will consider that some
progress at least has been made in understanding the history of
the gospel traditions.

4. THE CONTENTS OF THE BOOK

The subtitle of this monograph is 'Studies in the history
of gospel traditions', because the book is in a real sense a
series of individual studies. The chapters do not work through
the eschatological discourse in order; indeed the first
chapters look at the end of the discourse, and the last chapter
looks at the preceding context of the discourse! But there is
some method in the madness, since each chapter does lead on to
the next.

Chapter 1 looks at the parabolic material of Mk 13:34-36
and Lk 12:36-38, exploring the possible relationship of the two
sections and some of the problems in both passages. *Chapter 2*
examines the rest of the parabolic material in Mt 24:42-25:30,
Mk 13:33-37 and Lk 12:35-48, and *chapter 3* completes the study
of the end of the discourse, taking in the sayings about Noah
and Lot that come towards the end of Matthew's discourse
(Mt 24:37-44/Lk 17:26-35) and also the Lukan exhortations of
Lk 21:34-36. *Chapter 4* looks at Lk 17:22-37 and considers how it
relates to the eschatological discourse of Matthew 24/Mark 13/
Luke 21. *Chapter 5* seeks to explain how the Matthew/Mark
description of the desolating sacrilege relates to the Lukan
description of the destruction of Jerusalem. *Chapter 6*
considers the sayings about appearing before the authorities
(Mt 10:17-20/Mk 13:9-11/Lk 12:11,12/Lk 21:12-15) and in
particular the questions raised by Matthew's location of the
sayings in his mission discourse. *Chapter 7* looks more
generally at the section of the eschatological discourse
describing future suffering, i.e. Mt 24:9-14/Mk 13:9-13/
Lk 21:12-15. *Chapter 8* surveys the material in the discourse
not already covered, i.e. the introduction to the discourse
(Mt 24:1-3/Mk 13:1-3/Lk 21:5-7), the opening warnings (Mt 24:4-8/
Mk 13:5-8/Lk 21:8-11), the description of the parousia itself
(Mt 24:29-31/Mk 13:24-27/Lk 21:25-28), and finally the parable of
of the fig tree and the sayings about the time of the end
(Mt 24:32-36/Mk 13:28-32/Lk 21:29-33). *Chapter 9* looks at the
context of the discourse in each of the gospels. The *Conclusion*
seeks to sum up the findings of the preceding chapters and to
note some possible implications.

Chapter 1

THE PARABLE OF THE WATCHMAN: MK 13:34-36, LK 12:36-38

1. INTRODUCTION

It may seem curious to begin a study of the eschatological
discourse with an examination of the end sections of the
discourse. But there are particularly puzzling problems in
these end-sections, and, if a way can be found through those
problems, this may prove the way to understanding the whole
discourse.

The most obvious problem is the sudden divergence of the
three synoptic evangelists: Matthew, Mark and Luke run roughly
parallel through most of the eschatological discourse
(cf. Mt 24:1-36, Mk 13:1-32, Lk 21:5-33): they all describe wars and
other troubles, suffering affecting the disciples, a crisis in
Judea, and then the second coming itself; they all have the
parable of the fig tree, and a solemn assurance that all things
will happen in a generation. But then the evangelists each go
their separate ways: Mark has a short semi-parabolic section of
exhortation to wakefulness (13:33-37); Luke too has a section of
exhortation, but it is quite different from Mark's (Lk 21:34-36);
Matthew has a much longer conclusion consisting largely
of parables (24:42-25:30). This sudden divergence requires
some explanation. If Matthew and Luke are dependent on Mark,
as is usually supposed, why do they follow Mark quite
faithfully up to this point, but now abandon their source?

There are other connected questions: in particular, how
do the divergent endings relate to each other, if at all? Is
it simply a case of Matthew and Luke omitting the Markan
ending and grafting on something else, or is the situation
more complex? The Markan end-section (13:33-37) in fact has some
links with the Matthean end-section (including the Matthean
parable of the talents. See Mt 25:13,14; 24:42 and our
discussion below on pp. 23-29,35-41); it has a very few links with
the Lukan ending (cf. Mark's βλέπετε, ἀγρυπνεῖτε with Lk 21:34,
36 προσέχετε...ἀγρυπνεῖτε); it has other possible links with a
quite different Lukan passage, i.e. Lk 12:36-38, some scholars
considering that a common parable of a watchman lies behind the
Markan and Lukan traditions. Interestingly the Matthean ending
(24:42-25:30) has strong links with the same section in Luke,

i.e. Lk 12:35-48; in both we find eschatological parables,
including the parables of the thief and the steward. To
complicate matters further, Paul's evidence may be mentioned
since in 1 Thessalonians 5 he has in close proximity what
appears to be an echo of the parable of the thief (1 Thess 5:2)
and a possible echo of Lk 21:34-36 (1 Thess 5:3).

Quite apart from the question of relationships, Mark's
ending raises questions of its own: have we a complete
'parable of a doorkeeper' in Mark, or an amalgam of more than
one parable, or what?

It is only necessary to mention these questions for the
complexity of the issues to be apparent. But it is the claim
of the first three chapters of this monograph that a
comprehensive and relatively simple explanation of these things
can be offered, and indeed is demanded by the evidence. But,
although the hypothesis being proposed is essentially simple,
much detailed analysis of texts must be undertaken in order to
establish it. The case is a cumulative one and many different
pieces of evidence must be examined and accounted for.

Attention will be given in the first chapter to the Markan
parable of the doorkeeper of Mk 13:34-36 (if this is correctly
called a parable) and to the Lukan parable of the watching
servants of Lk 12:36-38. Numerous commentators have noticed
the similarity of these Markan and Lukan sections, and some
have claimed that we have in Mark and Luke two different
versions of the same parable. Other scholars, however, have
pointed to the substantial differences of form and wording, as
well as to the totally different location of the sections in
question in the two gospels, and have preferred to regard the
two sections as similar but distinct traditions. Is it
possible to decide between these two scholarly opinions? What
are the arguments?

2. *PRELIMINARY OBSERVATIONS ON THE LINKS BETWEEN MK 13:33-37,*
    LK 12:35-48 AND MT 24:42-25:30

A complicated pattern of links between various of the
synoptic passages that concern us has already been noted. It
was observed (a) that Mk 13:33-37 has a possible link with Lk
12:35-48 - this possible link is what we are investigating - ;
but it was also noted (b) that Mk 13:33-37 has a few links with
Matthew 24 and 25; and (c) that Matthew 24 and 25 have definite
and substantial links with Lk 12:35-48. We thus have this pattern:

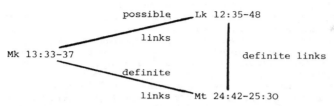

The interesting thing about this for the question of whether
Mk 13:34-36 and Lk 12:36-38 reflect a common parabolic
tradition is that the Markan and Lukan passages are definitely
linked via Matthew. On the two source-hypothesis it may, of
course, be explained that Matthew has conflated the Markan
and the 'Q' (i.e. the Lukan) traditions, and it may even be
argued that Matthew has conflated these traditions precisely
because of their similarity to each other (both passages having
reference to one or more watching servant(s)). It is perhaps a
little curious on this view that Matthew in conflating the
passages should have omitted the parabolic imagery that Mark
and Luke have in common - he has hardly any trace of the
watching servant(s). A quite different possibility is that
Mark and Matthew both knew a form of the tradition which had
the parabolic material of Lk 12:35-48 at the end of the
eschatological discourse. This idea raises all sorts of
difficult questions, but it would account both for the possible
Lukan links with Mark and for Matthew's two-way links (things
that need explaining on any hypothesis). However the
suggestion must be considered quite speculative, unless other
evidence can be found to support it and unless, in particular,
a good case can be made out for identifying the Markan and the
Lukan parables.

3. PRELIMINARY OBSERVATIONS ON THE DIFFICULTIES OF MK 13:33-37

The pattern of links between different passages needs
explaining, and so does the slight awkwardness of Mark 13:33-37.

βλέπετε, ἀγρυπνεῖτε· οὐκ οἴδατε γὰρ πότε ὁ καιρός ἐστιν.
34. ὡς ἄνθρωπος ἀπόδημος ἀφεὶς τὴν οἰκίαν αὐτοῦ καὶ δοὺς
τοῖς δούλοις αὐτοῦ τὴν ἐξουσίαν, ἑκάστῳ τὸ ἔργον αὐτοῦ,
καὶ τῷ θυρωρῷ ἐνετείλατο ἵνα γρηγορῇ. 35. γρηγορεῖτε οὖν·
οὐκ οἴδατε γὰρ πότε ὁ κύριος τῆς οἰκίας ἔρχεται, ἢ ὀψὲ ἢ
μεσονύκτιον ἢ ἀλεκτοροφωνίας ἢ πρωΐ· 36. μὴ ἐλθὼν ἐξαίφνης
εὕρῃ ὑμᾶς καθεύδοντας. 37. ὃ δε ὑμῖν λέγω, πᾶσιν λέγω,
γρηγορεῖτε.

The difficulties of the Markan section are these: (i) in v 34
we have the impression that we are beginning a parabolic story
(like the parable of the talents or the parable of the steward
appointed over his master's house); but then the 'story' does not
develop, and we never hear what happened to the servants or
the watchman, since v 35 takes us straight into hortatory
application. (ii) In v 34 we have the impression that we are
starting a parable about a man going away from home for a long
time and organizing his household accordingly (like the
parables of the talents and the steward);/1/ but in v 35, where
the parabolic imagery persists, we have more the impression
that the master is just out for an evening, during which the
watchman is expected to stay awake for his return./2/ (iii) In
v 34 the focus is first on the master's servants in the plural,
but then it narrows to the doorkeeper in the singular. There
is nothing very difficult about this, but the servants other
than the doorkeeper seem slightly irrelevant, and could have
been left unmentioned without loss. Such superfluous scene-
setting may be hard to parallel in other parables. (iv) The
use of the word 'authority' (ἐξουσία) in v 34 has struck
commentators as odd in the context. The clarificatory 'to
each his work' makes clear that 'authority' is probably to be
understood (unusually) as meaning 'delegated responsibility';
but the very existence of the clarification could possibly
reflect the evangelist's consciousness of the oddity of
ἐξουσία. (v) Commentators have noted the shift of mood from
the participial ἀφείς and δούς to the indicative ἐνετείλατο,
this indicative being preceded surprisingly by καί (v 34).

    The difficulty of these features should not be
exaggerated. It is possible to make sense of the verses as
they stand, and it may be argued that our ideas of consistency,
stylistic comfort and purity of parabolic form may not have

_____

/1/ ἀποδημεῖν often means to go abroad or away from one's
country, although it can be used of a shorter, more local,
absence; here it sounds like something more major that has to
be specially organised in advance.
/2/ The assumption in v 35 seems prima facie to be that the
master will return at night, probably on a known night; this
could hardly be assumed if the master were on a long journey.
The picture seems to be like that of the parable of the virgins
(Mt 25:1-13) and the parable of the watching servants
(Lk 12:36-38): in both the master comes back from a late-night
function.

been shared by the NT writers. On the other hand, it would be
foolish to assume that all biblical difficulties can be
explained as figments of modern scholarly imagination; we must
at least consider whether there may be any alternative and
preferable explanations of things that seem awkward to us.

Perhaps the commonest explanation of the Markan difficulty
is that it is the result of rather inexpert editing of some
earlier traditions. Advocates of Matthean priority have argued
that Mk 13:33-37 is a summary of the fuller Matthean traditions
(e.g. the parables of the talents and of the virgins). This
might indeed explain both the awkwardness and the divergence
from Matthew (if not from Luke), and it could be acceptable not
only to Matthean priorists, but to any who allow that Matthew
might sometimes preserve non-Markan sequences of material
(e.g. from 'Q'). But even those unprejudiced against Matthean
priority find some difficulty in recognizing Mk 13:33-37 as an
amalgam of elements found in Matthew as we know it: Mark's
reference to the 'doorkeeper' does not sound like the parable
of the virgins; if anything it is more like the Lukan parable
of the watching servants (from Lk 12:36-38).

Perhaps then the Markan passage is an amalgam of elements
from Matthew 24, 25 and from Luke 12:35-46. This idea might
sound quite speculative, except that we have already seen that
there are strong links between Matthew 24, 25 and Lk 12:35-46.
It could be that the traditions of Matthew 24, 25 and
Lk 12:35-46 originally belonged together and that Mark reflects
knowledge of such a united tradition. However, the case for
identifying the Lukan parable of the watching servants and the
Markan parable of the doorkeeper would have to be established
if such an explanation were to be cogent.

4. MK 13:34-36, LK 12:36-38 COMPARED

The relevant texts are as follows:

Mk 13:34-36

'Like a man going away,
leaving his house and giving
his servants authority, to
each his work, and to the
doorkeeper he commanded that
he should keep awake. Keep
awake then. For you do not

Lk 12:36-38

'And you be like men awaiting
their master, when he returns
from a (wedding) feast, so that
when he comes and knocks they
may immediately open to him.
Blessed are those servants whom
the master coming shall find

know when the master of the   awake. Truly I tell you that
house will come, whether late   he will gird himself and sit
or at midnight or at cock   them down and coming will serve
crow or early. Lest coming   them. And if in the second or
suddenly he finds you   third watch he comes and finds
sleeping.'   them thus, happy are they ...'

There are obvious differences between the Markan and Lukan
sections: for example, the opening is different; then Luke
appears to have lots of 'watching servants' not one 'doorkeeper',
as in Mark; also Luke has the master reward the wakeful
servants with a feast, and Mark has nothing comparable. But
alongside these significant differences there are similarities:
the central point about the need for wakefulness is the same in
both parables; in both the picture is of servant(s) staying
awake for their master so that they may open the door; in both
there is the suggestion that he may come at any watch of the
night, though Mark enumerates the four watches of the night in
the Roman manner, whereas Luke has the more Hebraic three
watches; and in both there is a phrase about the master 'coming'
and 'finding' them - sleeping (Mk), awake (Lk).

On the basis of this comparison it is impossible to say
anything decisive: there are interesting similarities between
the Markan and Lukan sections, but there are also substantial
differences. Is this then a case of similar, but independent,
traditions - a possibility always to be reckoned with
seriously? Or is this a common tradition utilized differently
in the two gospels? If the latter view is correct, then it
should be possible to offer some plausible explanation of how
the now rather different Markan and Lukan texts evolved from
the common original.

5. *SUGGESTIONS ABOUT THE ORIGINAL 'PARABLE OF THE WATCHMAN'*

Several notable scholars have done detailed work on the
Markan and Lukan traditions, making suggestions about the
original form of 'the parable of the watchman' and about the
evolution of this original into the present Markan and Lukan
forms. Two of the most thorough recent studies by Jacques
Dupont/1/ and Alfons Weiser/2/ come, apparently independently,

---

/1/ La Parabole du Maître qui Rentre dans la Nuit (Mc 13,34-36)'
in *Mélanges Béda Rigaux* (Gembloux: Duculot, 1970) 89-116.
/2/ *Die Knechtsgleichnisse der Synoptischen Evangelien* (München:
Kösel, 1971) especially pp. 123-77.

to similar (though not identical conclusions). They both
endorse several of the earlier conclusions of Joachim
Jeremias./1/

The conclusions of Dupont, Weiser and Jeremias may be
summarized as follows:

1. All are agreed that the original parable was in the
singular, about a doorkeeper who awaited his master's return
from a feast.
2. All agree that the Markan opening to the parable is
not original, being taken from the parable of the talents.
Jeremias thinks that Mark's reference to the giving of
'authority' comes from the parable of the supervising steward
(Mt 24:45-51, Lk 12:42-46).
3. All agree that Mark has modified the ending of the
parable, turning the ending into hortatory application - 'Keep
awake, for you do not know when the master of the house comes
....'
4. All agree that Luke's statement of the watchful
servants' reward in 12:37b, 'Truly I tell you that he will gird
himself and sit them down and coming will serve them' is
incongruous Christian allegorizing. Jeremias and Dupont think
that it breaks an earlier sequence of thought from v 37a to v
38. Weiser and Dupont go further and suspect that the
beatitudes of these Lukan verses were probably not in the
original parable at all.
5. Weiser thus proposes (p. 174) as the original form of
the parable:
> 'It is as when a man leaves his house and instructs
> the doorkeeper to keep awake. He will therefore keep
> awake, because he does not know when the master of the
> house comes, at the first, second or third watch of
> the night, lest he comes suddenly and finds him
> sleeping.'

Each of these conclusions must be considered in turn.

5.1. *An originally singular parable*

If there was an original underlying parable, it does seem

/1/ *The Parables of Jesus* (London: SCM, 1963[2]) 53-55.

likely enough that it was a parable of the doorkeeper - not a
parable of many servants keeping awake. Note: (a) Mark is
evidence for the singular, since he speaks specifically of 'the
doorkeeper' being commanded to keep awake (13:34). It is true
that he has a reference to 'servants' being given authority in
the immediately preceding sentence, and this together with
Luke's reference to 'servants' in the plural could appear to
tell against the originality of the singular. But if the
underlying tradition had all the servants being commanded to
stay awake, why did Mark change from the plural to the singular
in the middle of his v 34? The result of the change is, as has
been seen, that what looks as though it is going to be a parable
about a group of servants turns out to be a parable about only
one servant (with the other servants disappearing from view).
This slightly unexpected state of affairs is explicable if, as
Dupont and Weiser argue, Mark in fact began v 34 with the sort
of scene described in the parable of the talents in mind (i.e.
a master giving responsibility to several servants) and if he
then moved over into a singular parable of a watchman. See
further discussion of this below (pp. 23-29).

(b) It probably makes better sense having one watchman
staying awake all night for the master's return from a feast,
than having all the household waiting to open the door, though
the Lukan picture of a group of servants waiting up is not
intolerable.

(c) It is easy to see how Luke might have slipped into
plurals through his introductory phrase 'You (ὑμεῖς) be like men
awaiting...'. To have preserved the original singular, he
should have had 'You be like a man awaiting his master...'; the
alteration is minor and easily understood. If it seems odd that
Luke should have substituted the parabolically less likely
picture of a group of servants staying awake for the more
original picture of the doorkeeper doing his duty, the
explanation of that is probably that Luke has in mind the
application of the parable to all Christians (so his 'You be
like...', v 36), and he has allowed the application to influence
the wording of the parable.

(d) There are some interesting formal links between Luke's
parable of the watching servants and the following parable of
the steward (12:40-46). Compare especially 12:37 'Blessed are
those servants whom the Lord coming will find.... Truly I say
to you, he will...' with the almost identical 12:43,44. The

major difference in these parallel clauses is that the parable
of the watchman is plural and the parable of the steward
singular. This difference could be original, but could also be
explained if Luke has modified the original singular parable of
the watchman.

**5.2. Mk 13:34 a & b from the parable of the talents, not the
parable of the watchman**

The suggestion that the Markan opening to the parable is
not original but is taken from the parable of the talents may
sound improbable, but is in fact quite plausible. In order to
demonstrate this, it is necessary to note first the close
resemblances between Mt 25:13-15 and Mk 13:32-34.

Mt 25:13-15	Mk 13:32-34

(Mt 25:1-12: parable of
ten virgins)

13. γρηγορεῖτε οὖν, ὅτι
οὐκ οἴδατε τὴν ἡμέραν
οὐδὲ τὴν ὥραν.

14. ὥσπερ γὰρ ἄνθρωπος
ἀποδημῶν ἐκάλεσεν τοὺς
ἰδίους δούλους καὶ
παρέδωκεν αὐτοῖς τὰ
ὑπάρχοντα αὐτοῦ,
15. καὶ ᾧ μεν ἔδωκεν ..
καὶ ᾧ δὲ .. ἑκάστῳ
κατὰ τὴν ἰδίαν δύναμιν.

περὶ δὲ τῆς ἡμέρας ἐκείνης -
ἢ τῆς ὥρας οὐδεὶς οἶδεν ....

33. βλέπετε, ἀγρυπνεῖτε.
οὐκ οἴδατε γὰρ πότε ὁ καιρός
ἐστιν.

34. ὡς ἄνθρωπος
ἀπόδημος ἀφεὶς τὴν οἰκίαν αὐτοῦ
καὶ δοὺς τοῖς δούλοις αὐτοῦ
τὴν ἐξουσίαν ἑκάστῳ τὸ ἔργον
αὐτοῦ....

(Continuous underlining = close similarity; broken
underlining = less close similarity)

The points of resemblance include the following:

(a) The injunction to 'keep awake' is similar, despite
detailed differences of wording. In both Matthew and Mark the
saying is - keep awake for you do not know the time (Matthew
'the day nor the hour', Mark 'when the moment is'). A first
reaction may be to think that this was surely a very common
sort of saying in the early church tradition and that the
similarity is insignificant (so far as relating or
identifying the sayings is concerned). But, although this

sounds plausible enough in the abstract, the actual evidence of
of the gospels is that there are indeed similar sayings
elsewhere, but all of these are quite distinct from Mt 25:13/,
Mk 13:33 in the 'you do not know' clause (though not in the
call to 'keep awake')./1/

It is true, of course, that Matthew has 'you do not know
the day nor the hour' and Mark the slightly different 'you do
not know when the moment is'. However, the fact that the
thought is identical is suggested by Mark's preceding verse
(v 32), where he has the phrase 'concerning that *day or hour* no
one knows'; the juxtaposition of this phrase with the following
phrase in v 33 'not knowing when the moment is' strongly
suggests that the two phrases are understood by Mark in the
same way and, therefore, that Mark's v 33 means the same as
Mt 25:13./2/

(b) Matthew and Mark are strikingly similar in that they
both have parabolic material about a man going away
immediately following the saying about not knowing the time.
It may be coincidence that in the only two places where this
particular form of the saying about 'not knowing' is found the

/1/ Cf. Mk 13:35 'Keep awake then, for you do not know when the
master of the house comes', Mt 24:42 'Keep awake then, for you
do not know on what day your master comes', Mt 24:44 'Because
of this you too be ready, for in the hour you do not expect the
Son of man comes', Lk 12:40 'You too be ready, for in the hour
you do not expect the Son of man comes'.
It must be admitted that the opening of Mt 25:13
γρηγορεῖτε οὖν is more like the opening of Mk 13:35 than the
opening of Mk 13:33. But the substance of the whole saying
resembles Mk 13:33 (whereas Mt 24:42 resembles Mk 13:35). For
an explanation of the differences between the γρηγορεῖτε of
Mt 25:13 and the ἀγρυπνεῖτε of Mk 13:33 see pp. 118-20 below.
/2/ J. Lambrecht, *Redaktion*, 241, argues that Mark's 'moment'
in v 33 must have a different nuance from his 'day or hour' in
v 32; otherwise Mark would be repetitious. But, although we
agree that Mark has probably used the word 'moment' in v 33 so
as not to sound too repetitious, it is not obvious that there
is a substantial difference in meaning. Indeed we shall argue
later that Mark may have placed the saying of v 33 here,
precisely because of its similarity of thought to v 32. (See
below pp. 26,27.)

following material is so similar; but in view of the other
points of contact this seems unlikely.

(c) The opening of the parabolic material in Mt 25:14,
Mk 13:34 is similarly worded and is unparalleled elsewhere in the
gospels. The point is not just that both gospels have the
similar thought of a man going away on a journey; that thought
has several other parallels in the gospel tradition (e.g.
Mk 12:1, Mt 24:45-51/Lk 12:42-46). The point is that the thought
is expressed (to start with) in an almost identical and
unusual way. The form of Matthew's opening to the parable
ὥσπερ γὰρ ἄνθρωπος ἀποδημῶν.. is without parallel in his
gospel;/1/ and similarly the Markan ὡς ἄνθρωπος ἀπόδημος ἀφεὶς
... is without real parallel in Mark./2/ These Matthean and
Markan uses are very similar to each other, and are without
proper parallel elsewhere in the gospel tradition.

(d) After the opening phrase Matthew and Mark diverge,
and only have a few less striking points of resemblance;
compare Matthew's τοὺς ἰδίους δούλους ... with Mark's τοῖς
δούλοις αὐτοῦ, Matthew's παρέδωκεν .. ἔδωκεν... ἑκάστῳ, with
Mark's δοὺς ...ἑκάστῳ.

The combination especially of points (a), (b) and (c)
above make it very hard to avoid the conclusion that the
Matthean and Markan traditions are somehow connected at this
point. But it may be objected that we have conveniently
concentrated on the similarities (notably verbal similarities)
and that we have ignored important differences.

The main differences are:

(a) in the preceding context. The saying about not
knowing the time comes in Matthew at the end of the parable of
the virgins and in Mark after the saying about 'no one knowing
the day or hour' (Mk 13:32). But this difference in context is
not a very weighty argument against identifying the sayings,

/1/ ὥσπερ is a common enough Matthean word, used often in
conjunction with οὕτως. But it is never used to introduce a
parable as here (though see 25:31).
/2/ ὡς is used in parables by Mark, e.g. 4:26,31, but never as
here - with the nominative and participle. Whether Matthew's
ὥσπερ or Mark's ὡς is the more original opening is uncertain.

since it is quite possible that both Matthew and Mark have the
saying in contexts that are not original. (i) So far as
Matthew is concerned, commentators have often argued that
Matthew's 25:13: 'Keep awake, then, for you do not know the day
nor the hour' is rather odd immediately after the parable of the
virgins, since the wise as well as the foolish virgins fall
asleep in the parable; and furthermore in the parable there was
no question of not knowing 'the day', only 'the hour'. It
would be wrong to exaggerate this point and to claim that
Mt 25:13 makes no sense in its present position; it *is* possible
to regard it as a sort of general hortatory refrain which is to
be taken metaphorically and which sums up the teaching of this
whole section of Matthew (including the parable of the virgins),
rather than as a specific application of the one parable.
However, even that is to admit that Mt 25:13 does not have very
obviously strong links with the immediately preceding context,
and that it might once have belonged elsewhere. (ii) As for
Mk 13:33, it is not at all certain that this is in a primitive
context. It is possible to argue that after the forceful 13:32,
'But concerning that day or hour no one knows, not even the
angels in heaven, nor the Son, except the Father', 13:33 is
slightly anticlimactic and repetitive, 'Watch, keep awake, for
(γάρ) you do not know when the moment is' - the explanatory
γάρ clause seems a little unnecessary after v 32! But, whether
or not that is a fair observation, it is certainly possible
that v 33 could have been attached to this context because of
the similarity of theme to v 32. We conclude that neither
Mt 25:13 nor Mk 13:33 is very firmly attached to its preceding
context, and therefore that the difference in preceding
context is not a strong argument against connecting the two
sayings and sections.

    (b) It may be argued against the linking of Matthew and
Mark that, despite the similarity of thought in Mt 25:13,
Mk 13:33, the difference in wording between 'the day nor the hour'
and 'when the moment is' remains considerable. That is true,
but it is an entirely plausible hypothesis that one or other
of the evangelists has changed the original wording of the
saying. If, on the one hand, Matthew knew the Markan 'you do
not know when the moment is' in its Markan context, i.e.
immediately after the saying about 'no one knowing that day or
hour', he might have produced his 'you do not know the day or
the hour' out of the two Markan verses by a sort of process of
conflation. It is admittedly not very obvious why he should

have bothered, since he cheerfully uses the word καιρός
elsewhere in his gospel; furthermore, 'you do not know when the
moment will be' would have been more appropriate than 'you do
not know the day or the hour' after the parable of the ten
virgins, where Matthew places the saying. But the supposed
change is possible, even if not very probable. The opposite
possibility, however, makes simple sense: if Mark knew Matthew's
form of the saying ('you do not know the day or the hour'),
then we have an immediate explanation of Mark's positioning of
the saying after 13:32 - with its reference to 'no one knowing
the day or the hour' - and it is easy to see how, having made
this connection, Mark changed the second 'day or hour' into a
thoroughly Markan phrase 'when the moment will be', in order to
avoid even more acute repetitiousness than we have in his
present text. It would be going too far to say that Mark would
have had to change the Matthean wording, but it is at least
quite intelligible that he should have done so. And so the
argument against the linking of the Matthean and Markan sayings
on the grounds of this difference is insubstantial.

(c) Apparently more substantial is the argument that the
following parabolic material has a quite different thrust in
Matthew: while both agree in portraying a master going away and
giving each of his servants something, in Matthew the something
is property, in Mark it is authority and work. It may be
possible to soften the starkness of this contrast by suggesting
that the giving of the talents was the giving of a task - note
Mt 25:15 'to each according to his ability' (δύναμιν), and
compare Luke's parable of the pounds in 19:13 'Trade until I
come' -, and by noting that the reward was in terms of increased
authority - see Mt 25:21 and especially Lk 19:17 'Because you
were faithful in very little, have authority (ἐξουσίαν) over
ten cities'. But it is not possible to avoid the fact that
Matthew and Mark do go entirely separate ways after the opening
words of the parable, Matthew giving us the parable of the
talents and Mark introducing us to the watchman.

This may seem a major difficulty with the view that
Matthew and Mark are related in the previous verses in the way
we have suggested. If the suggestion is correct, then Matthew
and Mark both began to record the same parable, but one of them
almost immediately abandoned that parable and continued with
another. But, although this sounds a rather odd procedure, it
is not unthinkable.

It could be that Matthew abandoned his Markan source,
precisely because of the uncomfortable flow of thought in
Mark's parabolic material; he was able to produce a much more
coherent parable by expertly welding his parable of the talents
on to the Markan opening. A difficulty with this view is that
it is not very clear on this view why Matthew started to use
Mark at all in his 25:13: v 13 (which on this view Matthew took
from Mark) does not fit particularly well after the preceding
context, as we have seen, and then after a few words in v 14
Matthew abandons Mark and goes his own way. It seems rather
odd, though superbly successful, editing.

The alternative possibility is that Matthew retains the
original sequence (with the reference to the man going away
introducing the parable of the talents), and that it is Mark
who abandons the original parable and introduces us instead to
the doorkeeper. This is the explanation offered by Dupont and
Weiser, and given the preceding arguments about the links
between the Markan and Matthean traditions, the suggestion
cannot be quickly dismissed.

Perhaps the strongest positive argument in favour of this
suggestion is that it helps to account for some of the
awkwardness of Mk 13:33-37 (described above on pp. 17 - 19). In
particular it accounts for the change of forms within v 34 from
the 'servants' of v 34b to the 'doorkeeper' of v 34c, and also
for the fact that v 34 appears to be describing a long journey
and absence, whereas v 35 sounds like a straightforward night
out at a dinner. Of course there are other big questions
remaining, most obviously the question as to why Mark uses the
opening of the parable of the talents and then abandons it.
But it is not very hard to suggest a possible reason for this:
even a cursory reading of Mk 13:33-37 shows that the short
section is dominated by exhortations to keep awake (vv 33,35,37).
If this was the theme Mark had in mind, it is quite easy to see
why Mark picked up from the tradition his v 33, which then led
him into the following parable of the talents, and then why he
abandoned that tradition half-way through v 34, turning to
other parabolic material more relevant to his theme.

Although there are plenty of other questions to be
considered in connexion with the suggestion, the idea that Mk
13:34a and b is from the parable of the talents not from the
postulated parable of the watchman must be considered
plausible. Mark's wording of the exhortation to wakefulness is

probably less original than Matthew's, at least in the οὐκ οἴδατε
clauses and reflects his location of the saying after 13:32.

5.3. Mark's exhortation (13:35,36) secondary?

So far the suggestions of Dupont and Weiser have been
supported. Their view that the Markan exhortation to stay
awake (13:35,36) is a modification of the original ending of
the parable postulated (of the watchman) is much less certain.
Points that may appear to favour the suggestion are: (a) The
exhortation comes in Mark where we would expect a parable
ending. If it is not such an ending, we have no trace of a
parable-ending in Mark. (b) Luke has the references to the
watches of the night and to the master coming *within* (and at the
end of) his parable - 'and if he comes in the second or third
watch and finds them thus, happy are they'./1/   (c) The Markan
application is not just application, but is very much the
continuation of the parabolic imagery - with the reference to
'the lord of the house', etc.

These points are, however, not decisive. (a) It is true
that the Markan verse comes where we might expect a parable
ending; but it is quite possible that Mark, who on this theory
has not reproduced the original parable at all closely, has
omitted the ending and gone straight into the sort of
hortatory application that often follows parables in the gospel
tradition. (b) As for the Lukan evidence, there is some
suspicion that the second Lukan beatitude (v 38) containing
the reference to the night-watches is itself secondary. Luke's
vv 37,38 read as follows: 'Blessed are those servants, whom
the master will find awake when he comes. Truly I tell you that
he will gird himself and sit them down and coming will serve
them. (38) And if in the second or the third watch he comes
and finds them thus, blessed are they.' Following the
climactic beatitude + promise of v 37, Luke's v 38 sounds
like a slight after-thought. It is notable that in the
following rather similar Lukan parable (of the supervising

/1/ If the traditions are related, we may accept with other
commentators that Mark's Roman enumeration of the night watches
is probably secondary to Luke's Hebraic form of expression.
See, e.g. G. R. Beasley-Murray, *A Commentary on Mark 13* (London:
Macmillan, 1957) 117; E. Lövestam, *Spiritual Wakefulness in the
New Testament* (Lund: Gleerup, 1963) 82.

steward) there is only one beatitude (vv 43,44). (c) Although
it is true that the Markan application continues the thought
and imagery of the postulated parable, it is not clear why an
application should not do so! (For partial parallels see Mt 5:16,
Lk 16:9)./1/ It is, of course, commonly assumed that all
or most applications of parables in the gospel tradition are
secondary; but, even were that quite uncertain assumption to
be accepted, we could not automatically in this case assume
that Mark's application was secondary to Luke's beatitude.
Luke could conceivably have created his beatitude out of Mark's
application. Whether he has or has not done so need not be
decided at this stage; but at least a question mark must be put
against the view that the Markan exhortation is secondary.

5.4. Luke's promise (12:37b) secondary?

    A similar question must be raised with regard to the view
that Luke's v 37b is not original. It is true that the picture
of the master sitting his watchman down and feeding him is
remarkable (and somewhat reminiscent of Jesus' own action in
washing his disciples' feet). But it is not clear that the
reference to a generous reward can be dismissed as a secondary
element in the parable. Two things at least tell against this
view: (a) there is the following similar parable of the
supervising steward, where there is also a beatitude + very
generous promise - 'Blessed is that servant whom his master will
will find doing thus. Truly (ἀληθῶς) I say to you that he will
set him over all his possessions' (vv 43,44). Of course, it
might be arguable that Luke has assimilated the parable of the
watchman to what follows, adding in a promise where originally
there was none. But the wording of the promise in the parable
of the watching servant(s) tells against this idea: the promise
there is also introduced by 'Truly I say to you', but the word
for 'truly' is here ἀμήν and ἀληθῶς. An examination of Lukan
usage shows that Luke tends to eliminate ἀμήν when he finds it
in his sources and that he prefers ἀληθῶς; thus predictably in
the beatitude of vv 43,44 he has ἀληθῶς for Matthew's ἀμήν./2/

/1/ Another parallel would be Lk 12:35, if that is recognized
as a conclusion to the parable of the virgins. See chapter 2
below.
/2/ Compare also Lk 7:9,9:27,21:3 etc. with synoptic parallels.
And cf. Weiser, *Knechtsgleichnisse*, 169. Contra C. M. Tuckett,
The Revival of the Griesbach Hypothesis (Cambridge: UP, 1983) 159.
The motif of 'going in' with the master to celebrate is also

It is therefore unlikely that, if he were responsible for the
creation of the earlier beatitude (cf. v 37) by assimilation,
he would have used ἀμήν. The ἀμήν suggests that he is
preserving in v 37 a received tradition, as indeed Weiser
recognizes.

Furthermore, (b), without some description of the
watchman's reward, the parable seems a little lame, or at
least less forceful than it is at present. ·As for the opinion
that the reward described is excessive and unlikely, this seems
a subjective judgment. We might possibly allow that there
could have been some rewording of the original promise; but
still some description of a generous reward makes good sense
within the parable, as well as being paralleled in the
following similar parable./1/

These two points cast doubt on the view that the promise
of Luke's v 37b is secondary. They also cast doubt on the view
that the beatitude form of v 37 is not original. (i) The
evidence of the following parable suggests at least that the
beatitude form goes back to the pre-Lukan tradition; and,
although we cannot exclude the possibility that it was absent
at an earlier stage (in the pre-pre-Lukan tradition!), it must
at least be said that reconstructing the source of a source (as
Weiser does) is a highly speculative operation. (ii) If the
beatitudes are lost, as in Weiser's reconstruction, then the
story of the watchman has no climax; indeed it hardly has a
story-line at all, ending rather disappointingly 'lest he comes
and finds him sleeping'./2/ As for Dupont's contrary feeling
that a beatitude is out of place in this parable but

---

present in the parable of the virgins, which may be seen as a
companion parable to that of the watchman (see chapter 2 below).
/1/ If R. J. Bauckham is correct in linking Rev 3:20 with the
parable of the watching servant (*NTS* 23, 1977, pp. 170-74),
then this may be a further argument for the originality of a
reward clause at least similar to what we have at present in
Luke. But, of course, the author of Revelation might have
known Luke (though he certainly knew non-Lukan eschatological
traditions as well). In *NTS* 29 (1983) 130 Dr Bauckham argues
that Asc. Is. 4:16 may be evidence that the thought of the
master serving goes back to pre-Lukan tradition.
/2/ There is a probable echo of the beatitude in Rev 16:15
μακάριος ὁ γρηγορῶν. Note the proximity of the beatitude to
the 'thief' saying in both Revelation and Luke.

appropriate in the following parable of the supervising
steward,/1/ this seems quite subjective. And equally
unimpressive is Weiser's argument that the beatitude fits well
in the following parable with the balancing warning of judgment
(vv 45,46), but less well here./2/

5.5. *Weiser's reconstruction of the parable of the watching servant*

Weiser's own suggested original form of the parable has
already been criticised to some extent. (a) We have found
unconvincing the arguments for regarding the Markan ending of
the parable as secondary and for seeing Luke's first beatitude
as secondary. (b) We have suggested that the parable as
reconstructed by Weiser has a rather weak story line without a
good climax. (c) To that we may add that his reconstruction
has slightly awkward changes of subject; 'he (the master)
instructs the doorkeeper; he (the doorkeeper) will keep awake,
because he does not know when the master comes ... lest he (the
master) comes and finds him (the doorkeeper) sleeping'.

(d) More seriously we may question whether his method of
isolating of the original parable is entirely sound. For
example, his excluding from Mk 13:34-36 of those elements that
can be explained as a borrowing from elsewhere (e.g. the
parable of the talents) may appear to produce a reasonably
coherent original parable, but it seems a slightly arbitrary
approach. Perhaps the original parable had important things
in common with the parable of the talents, hence the
assimilation of the two parables; Weiser's method excludes such
possible common elements. Is Weiser's exclusion of the words
'his servants', despite the fact that 'servants' are
mentioned in Mk 13:34 *and* Lk 12:37, an example of this?/3/

/1/ 'La Parabole du Maître', p. 105.
/2/ *Knechtsgleichnisse*, 173. As it happens, our later argument
will suggest that in the original parable of the watching
servant the beatitude was followed by a warning. See below, p.48.
/3/ *Knechtsgleichnisse*, 137. Weiser perhaps recognizes the
possibility of overlapping elements at the beginning of the
parable, since he keeps the Markan opening ὡς ἄνθρωπος as part
of the original parable, though it could (perhaps should, on
his view) be explained as a borrowing from ὥσπερ ἄνθρωπος in
the Matthean parable of the talents (25:14).

Or perhaps Mark's process of assimilation of the two parables
forced him to introduce things that were originally in neither
parable. For example, the word 'doorkeeper' could indeed have
been in the original parable, as Weiser suggests; but it would
be quite possible to argue that the original parable (like so
many) had a simple reference to a 'servant', who was to keep
watch, but that Mark's introduction into the parable of
other servants (from the parable of the talents) forced him to
change an original 'servant' to 'doorkeeper' (in order to
differentiate the doorkeeper/watchman from the other servants).
This is only a possible suggestion, given by way of example,
though it so happens that it would tie in with the previous
comment about Weiser's exclusion of the word δοῦλος from the
original parable./1/ Another possible example of Weiser's
method leading him astray is in his ascription of the word
ἀπόδημος to the parable of the talents, but of the phrase
ἀφεὶς τὴν οἰκίαν αὐτοῦ to the original parable of the watchman.
In fact it is arguable that the two phrases belong together,
the one amplifying the other. ἀφεὶς τὴν οἰκίαν αὐτοῦ is not a
very natural phrase to use of going out to an evening dinner
(cf. Weiser's reconstructed original parable); it suggests a
more major expedition, e.g. to a foreign country as in the
parable of the talents./2/

     (e) It is not all that easy on Weiser's hypothesis to
explain the evolution of the present Markan and Lukan forms of
the parable. Mark is supposed to have had a coherent parable
of the doorkeeper, but to have produced something much less
coherent by mixing in elements from another parable. And so
far as Luke is concerned, his version is a quite radical
modification of the original: the modification was done, on
Weiser's view, not only by Luke, but also by his predecessor.
As we have suggested already, this is - at least - complicated.

/1/ The thought of the Lord at the 'doors' was in the context -
v 29.
/2/ The reference to the master 'commanding' the watchman to
stay awake could also reflect the Markan context (where the
master shares out the tasks) rather than the original parabolic
context. Would the master going out for an evening have needed
to command his watchman to stay awake? Maybe.

*5.6. Conclusions on the suggestions of Jeremias, Dupont and
Weiser*

The results of our examination of the suggestions of
Jeremias, Dupont and Weiser may be summed up as follows:
(1) If there was one original parable lying behind the sections
of Mark and Luke being considered, then it was probably a
parable of a watchman (singular). (2) There is plausibility in
the idea that Mark's opening was taken from the parable of the
talents. (3) The view that Mark 13:35,36 is a secondary mix-up
of parable-ending and application is questionable. (4) So is
the view that Luke's beatitude in v 37 (a and b) was secondary.
(5) But it is not unlikely that Luke's v 38 may be secondary.
(6) Weiser's suggested reconstruction of the original parable
was found unsatisfactory: in particular his method was
questionable, and his suggestion did not easily explain the
evolution of the Markan and Lukan forms.

6. AN ALTERNATIVE PROPOSED ORIGINAL

If scholars are unable to offer convincing suggestions
about the hypothetical parable, then the only conclusion may
seem to be that the Markan and Lukan traditions are
independent after all. However in what follows an alternative
suggestion will be made that takes into account the points
already noted.

6.1. Evidence from Luke

The first ingredient in the proposal is the recognition
that Lk 12:35-38 probably contains pre-Lukan tradition./1/ In
favour of this note:

(a) that the section comes in the middle of a block of
Lukan 'Q' material. In the so-called 'Q' sections either side
───────────────
/1/ Some of Weiser's arguments from vocabulary statistics may
strengthen our case. But we confess to some reservation about
basing conclusions (as to whether a word/usage derives from an
evangelist or his source) on word counts, when the statistical
base is so small. We are also uneasy about his quickness to
conclude that hortatory material or material with church
relevance is secondary.

of 12:35-38 Luke agrees quite closely with Matthew, and is thus
being conservative in his editing. Although it is possible
that in vv 35-38 he has a sudden radically creative burst of
writing, it is more likely that he is proceeding in the same
sort of conservative way as before and as afterwards (where he
has further eschatological material, par. Mt 24:42-45).

(b) We have already seen reason for regarding the
beatitude of v 37 as pre-Lukan, particularly because of the
unLukanness of the ἀμήν and because of the need for some such
conclusion in the parable. This is also suggested if 12:35-38
is correctly seen as a companion parable to the following parable
of the supervising servant. (See above pp. 30,31.)

But if these two arguments suggest that the Lukan form of
the parable may in fact be pre-Lukan and that Luke may
therefore give us important clues for the reconstruction of the
original form of the parable, this conclusion must be balanced
by recalling two other points made earlier about respects in
which Luke seems secondary to Mark: (i) in the plurality of
the watching servants; see the arguments on pp.21-23 above. And
(ii) in the beatitude of 12:38, which seems to be tagged on to
12:37 and which could possibly be a modification of the more
original Mk 13:35; see pp. 29,30 above.

6.2. Evidence from Matthew

Matthew does not have a version of the postulated parable
of the watchman but he does have one verse that resembles the
Markan traditions in question. Compare

Mt 24:42,43   with Mk 13:35a,36

(Warning of suddenness   (ἑκάστῳ τὸ ἔργον αὐτοῦ, καὶ
of judgment, one taken   τῷ θυρωρῷ ἐνετείλατο ἵνα
one left, etc.)   γρηγορῇ.)

γρηγορεῖτε οὖν, ὅτι οὐκ   γρηγορεῖτε οὖν, οὐκ
οἴδατε ποίᾳ ἡμέρᾳ ὁ   οἴδατε γὰρ πότε ὁ
κύριος ὑμῶν ἔρχεται.   κύριος τῆς οἰκίας ἔρχεται
                                 ἢ ὀψὲ ἢ μεσονύκτιον ἢ
43 ἐκεῖνο δὲ γινώσκετε   ἀλεκτοροφωνίας ἢ πρωΐ.
ὅτι εἰ ᾔδει ὁ
οἰκοδεσπότης ποίᾳ   36 μὴ ἐλθὼν ἐξαίφνης
φυλακῇ ὁ κλέπτης   εὕρῃ ὑμᾶς καθεύδοντας.
ἔρχεται .....
                                 37 ὃ δὲ ὑμῖν λέγω ....

6.2.1. Mt 24:42 and Mk 13:35 versions of the same saying
     The resemblances between Mt 24:42 and Mk 13:35 are obvious
enough, but the differences are substantial. So it is necessary
to spell out the arguments for identifying the Matthean and
Markan traditions. They are as follows:

     (a) These are the only two 'keep awake' sayings of this
form that refer to the κύριος coming. (See the earlier remarks
on the saying of Mk 13:33 – on pp. 23,24 above).

     (b) Although the different context of the sayings in the
two gospels might appear to tell against the sayings being the
same, it is notable that they have the sayings in broadly the
same context (following the main body of the eschatological
discourse), and furthermore that there is some evidence that
could point to Matthew's knowledge of – and abandonment of – the
the particular preceding context in Mark. The point is this:
Mark's preceding context is the parable (or half-parable) of
the man and his night-watchman, whereas Matthew's is a
description of day-time activities (in the field or mill) being
interrupted by the second coming. The following exhortation,
which we are considering, ties in neatly with the Markan
context, but indifferently in Matthew: (i) the encouragement
to 'keep awake' makes possible sense in the Matthean day-time
context, but more forceful sense in the Markan night-time
context. (ii) Mark's reference to 'the *master of the house*
coming' picks up what immediately precedes in Mark, but
Matthew's '*your master*' is an unparalleled expression in
Matthew and connects with nothing particular in the preceding
context. This observation of the excellence of the Markan
context and the inferiority of the Matthean context may prove
nothing; but a possible explanation is that Mark has retained
(essentially) the original context for the exhortation and
that for some reason Matthew has not.

     (c) The differences of wording between the saying in
Matthew and the saying in Mark might appear to tell against
their identification; but in fact most of the differences are
quite simply explicable. A lot are explained, if our previous
suggestion about Matthew having changed the context of the
saying is correct. Matthew's postulated abandonment of the
watchman-parable context forced him to alter Mark's 'master of
the house' to the unparalleled 'your master'; it forced him to
omit the references to the night-watches (Mk v 35b) and the
reference to him 'coming and finding you sleeping'. Matthew

had to alter these, as his preceding context was a day-time
scene. Presumably also his ποίᾳ ἡμέρᾳ was his day-time
adaptation of a time-reference more applicable to the night
(cf. Mark's πότε)./1/ Other differences are explicable simply
as stylistic changes: note how in the other saying of Mt 25:13/
Mk 13:33 we have the same divergence between Matthew's ὅτι οὐκ
οἴδατε and Mark's οὐκ οἴδατε γάρ, also a Markan πότε for a
different Matthean time-note./2/

(d) The proposal that Matthew may have known the fuller
Markan form of the saying might claim some support from the
following verse in Matthew (v 43, about the thief). The Markan
material which Matthew supposedly omitted included reference to
the watches of the night (Mk 13:35) and ended with a warning
'lest coming suddenly he finds you sleeping'; Matthew's v 43
with its warning about the thief coming in some unknown 'watch'
of the night is very much a continuation of the same thought.
One possibility is that Matthew was influenced by the Markan
form of the saying to place the thief saying at this point.

6.2.2. Mt 24:42 not drawn directly from Mark?
But how does the linking of the Matthean and the Markan
traditions illuminate the question of the original form of the
parable of the watching servant? If Matthew's form of the
saying is explicable on the basis of Mark's and is inferior to
the Markan form, then Matthew's evidence proves nothing.
However, there are a number of considerations that may point to
Matthew having had access to a non-Markan form of the tradition.

(a) It is at least interesting that Matthew has the
concluding exhortation from the Markan parable of the watchman
immediately preceding the parable of the thief and that Luke too
has his parable of the watching servants followed immediately by

---

/1/ The opposite hypothesis, i.e. that Mark altered the Matthean
form of the saying, is not impossible, but would entail a far
more complex editorial process with Mark not only adapting the
Matthean saying, but also creating a preceding context to suit
it - a considerably superior context to that found in Matthew.
/2/ See further on the difference between Matthew's ποίᾳ ἡμέρᾳ
and Mark's πότε below, pp. 39-41.

the parable of the thief.

This may simply reflect Matthew's editorial acuteness: if
he knew the Lukan sequence with the parable of the watching
servants preceding the parable of the thief, he may have
recognized the similarity of the Markan and Lukan parables (of
the watching servant(s)), and so have moved over from the
Markan tradition and continued with the Lukan (i.e. the 'Q')
sequence. Or if Matthew did not know the Lukan parable of the
watching servant(s), he could still have seen that the Markan
parable led well into the 'Q' parable of the thief, and so have
linked the ending of Mark's parable with the 'Q' parables.
Either explanation is possible; but neither is very easy. It
is at least rather odd that Matthew should have been following
the 'Q' tradition (about the days of Noah etc. 24:37-41), that
he should then have picked up only the conclusion of the Markan
parable of the watchman (24:42), necessarily modifying it to
fit his context, and that he should then have been led by the
Markan parable, most of which he has omitted, into a different
'Q' tradition (i.e. 24:43-51).

A much simpler explanation is that the so-called 'Q'
tradition from which Matthew and Luke drew the parables of the
thief and the steward also included the parable of the watching
servant(s), as Luke's evidence would suggest. If this were the
case, then Matthew's form of wording in 24:42 might not be
dependent on Mark's at all; he could simply be picking up the
'Q' tradition, which he carries on, at this point. Matthew
could in this case be a significant witness for the
reconstruction of the postulated parable.

(b) A particular piece of evidence could support this and
also throw light on the original form of the parable. It was
noted above (p. 37) that Matthew's φυλακῇ in his version
of the parable of the thief (v 43) is reminiscent of the
thought, found in the Markan parable of the doorkeeper, of the
master coming at any watch of the night. But, although Mark
has this thought, he does not have the word φυλακή. Luke,
however, has both the thought and also the particular term
φυλακῇ in his parable of the watching servants. The Lukan form
of the parable then goes together particularly well with the
Matthean parable of the thief, and it may well be that Matthew
knew the Lukan form.

But there is a more significant point than this: in the
parable of the thief the wording of the Matthean and Lukan
versions is quite closely parallel, but one small difference
lies in the fact that Luke has ποίᾳ ὥρᾳ ὁ κλέπτης ἔρχεται
ὅτι ᾗ ὥρᾳ οὐ δοκεῖτε..., but Matthew has ποίᾳ φυλακῇ ....
.... ᾗ ὥρᾳ .... The fact that Matthew has φυλακῇ the
first time round, not ὥρᾳ, may be insignificant. His may be
the original wording, and Luke may have altered φυλακῇ to ὥρᾳ
under the influence of the ὥρᾳ in the following verse (though
it is not very obvious why he should have done so, nor why he
should have omitted Matthew's ἐγρηγόρησεν ἄν..). But the
opposite possibility is perhaps more likely, namely that Luke
has the original wording of the thief saying and its original
preceding context (the watchman parable with its emphasis on
'keeping awake' [γρηγορεῖν] at any 'watch' [φυλακῇ] of the
night); Matthew omits the watchman parable (except for the
concluding exhortation), but betrays his knowledge of it by
importing φυλακῇ and perhaps also by adding his ἐγρηγόρησεν ἄν
to the thief saying. Matthew may have felt impelled to draw
out the thought of the thief coming at night, precisely because
of his omission of the originally preceding night-time parable
of the watchman.

The neatness of this explanation of a difference between
Matthew and Luke in a 'Q' saying makes it attractive, and lends
weight to the view that Matthew was aware of and influenced by
something like the Lukan form of the parable of the watchman.

But the argument may be pressed one step further: it is
possible that Matthew gives a clue as to the original wording
of the parable in his phrase ὅτι οὐκ οἴδατε ποίᾳ ἡμέρᾳ ....
Mark here has οὐκ οἴδατε γὰρ πότε .... It was suggested above
that Matthew's ἡμέρᾳ was probably his day-time adaptation of an
original time-reference more applicable to the night, the
possible implication being that Mark's πότε was the more
original form. However, two points put this assumption in
doubt: (i) Mark's πότε would have been perfectly appropriate
for Matthew's day-time context; he did not need to change
Mark's πότε. (ii) In the similar saying found in Mk 13:33
οὐκ οἴδατε γὰρ πότε ὁ καιρός ἐστιν the Markan form was seen to
be less original than Mt 25:13 οὐκ οἴδατε τὴν ἡμέραν οὐδὲ τὴν
ὥραν (see pp. 26-29 above). In view of these considerations
and the earlier observation about the parable of the thief, a
probable explanation of the evidence is that the original form
was ποίᾳ φυλακῇ. Matthew had to change this in his 24:42 to

ποίᾳ ἡμέρᾳ, and Mark also changed it out of stylistic
preference to πότε. But when Matthew came on to the parable of
the thief and to the first ποίᾳ ὥρᾳ here (cf. Lk 12:39) he
altered this to ποίᾳ φυλακῇ - for the reasons already explained.
This change is particularly well-explained, if Matthew had the
phrase ποίᾳ φυλακῇ (rather than Mark's πότε) in his parable of
the watchman, and the proposal makes straightforward sense of
all the differences.

One possible difficulty with this view is that Luke uses
the word φυλακή in a verse (12:38), which seemed of doubtful
originality and possibly a modification of the more original
Markan form (see pp. 29,30 above). But in fact this is not a
real difficulty: (a) although the form of Lk 12:38 may be
suspect, it is probable that, if there was an original
parable, it must have contained a reference to the different
watches of the night, since Mark and Luke both have such a
reference. (b) It is also the opinion of most scholars that
Mark's four Roman-style watches are less original than Luke's
three Hebrew-style watches (see p.29 n.1 above). Given these
considerations, the obvious conclusion is that Mark's form of
the saying, but Luke's wording are original. This is precisely
what the Matthean evidence would suggest, since he has the
form of Mark's exhortation and attests the Lukan word φυλακή.
This dovetailing of evidence is significant.

6.2.3. Summary of the implications of Matthew's evidence

It may be helpful to summarize the argument by setting out
the relevant texts in parallel with a proposed original form:

Mt 24:42-44	Mk 13:35,36	Lk 12:38-40	Proposed pre-synoptic form
(sayings on the day of the Lord)	(parable of watchman)	(parable of watching servants)	
42. γρηγορεῖτε οὖν, ὅτι οὐκ οἴδατε ποίᾳ ἡμέρᾳ ὁ κύριος ὑμῶν ἔρχεται.	35. γρηγορεῖτε οὖν· οἴδατε γὰρ πότε ὁ κύριος τῆς οἰκίας ἔρχεται, ἢ ὀψὲ ἢ μεσονύκτιον ἢ ἀλεκτοροφωνίας ἢ πρωΐ,	38. κἂν ἐν τῇ δευτέρᾳ,κἂν ἐν τῇ τρίτῃ φυλακῇ ἔλθῃ καὶ εὕρῃ οὕτως, μακάριοί εἰσιν ἐκεῖνοι.	γρηγορεῖτε οὖν, ὅτι οὐκ οἴδατε ποίᾳ φυλακῇ ὁ κύριος τῆς οἰκίας ἔρχεται, ἢ ἐν τῇ πρώτῃ ἢ ἐν τῇ δευτέρᾳ, ἢ ἐν τῇ τρίτῃ, μὴ ἐλθὼν ἐξαίφνης εὕρῃ ὑμᾶς καθευδόντας.
43. ἐκεῖνο δὲ γινώσκετε ὅτι εἰ ᾔδει ὁ οἰκοδεσπότης ποίᾳ φυλακῇ ὁ κλέπτης ἔρχεται...	36. μὴ ἐλθὼν ἐξαίφνης εὕρῃ ὑμᾶς καθεύδοντας.	39. τοῦτο δὲ γινώσκετε, ὅτι εἰ ᾔδει. ὁ οἰκοδεσπότης ποίᾳ ὥρᾳ ὁ κλέπτης ἔρχεται....	ἐκεῖνο δὲ γινώσκετε ὅτι εἰ ᾔδει ὁ οἰκοδεσπότης ποίᾳ ὥρᾳ ὁ κλέπτης ἔρχεται...
44. ὅτι ᾗ οὐ δοκεῖτε ὥρᾳ ὁ υἱὸς τοῦ ἀνθρώπου ἔρχεται...		40. ὅτι ᾗ ὥρᾳ οὐ δοκεῖτε ὁ υἱὸς τοῦ ἀνθρώπου ἔρχεται...	ὅτι ᾗ ὥρᾳ οὐ δοκεῖτε ὁ υἱὸς τοῦ ἀνθρώπου ἔρχεται...

The proposed original may be considered a tentative proposal in details at least, but it accounts for many of the points noted already.

Note that (1) Matthew's text is well explained from it: almost all his alterations of the original are the result of his omission of the parable of the watchman (see pp. 36,37 above). In favour of his use of the proposed pre-synoptic form rather than Mark are (a) his agreement in order with Luke, (b) his ποίᾳ ἡμέρᾳ in v 42, which is better explained from the pre-synoptic ποίᾳ φυλακῇ than from Mark's πότε, since Matthew would not have needed to change this, (c) his ποίᾳ φυλακῇ in v 43, which spoils the ὥρᾳ ... ὥρᾳ parallelism within the parable of the thief, but which is explicable if Matthew knew and had to alter the pre-synoptic ποίᾳ φυλακῇ in his v 42 and if he now wished to emphasize the night-time context of the parable of the thief.

(2) Mark's text is simply explained from it. His οὐκ οἴδατε γὰρ πότε represents a minor alteration and is the same alteration that he made in his v 33 (see pp. 39,40 above). Apart from this he substitutes the four Roman-style watches with their names for the more original 'first, second and third' watches.

(3) Luke has reproduced the content of the pre-synoptic exhortation, but has for some reason put it into the form of a beatitude (that form being ready to hand in the immediately preceding conclusion to the parable, i.e. Luke's v 37, and also in the following parable, Lk 12:43). This explains why his v 38 now reads like an afterthought in the parable. The small divergence between Matthew's ἐκεῖνο (v 43) and Luke's τοῦτο (v 39) at the opening of the parable of the thief is also explained. Luke has used ἐκεῖνος at the end of his reworded v 38 (perhaps under the influence of the pre-synoptic opening of the parable of the thief), and so he changes to τοῦτο at the start of v 39 for the sake of variation./1/

/1/ H. Schürmann, *NTS* 6 (1959) 208, notes this link, but proposes the opposite explanation, i.e. that Matthew's ἐκεῖνο is secondary to Luke's τοῦτο and reflects the influence of the form of Lk 12:38. But there is no very obvious reason why Matthew should have made the change, and the evidence for Lk 12:38 being a Lukan construction is strong.

6.3. Further evidence from Mark

In the preceding discussion various points about
Mk 13:34-36 have been noted. But now it is necessary to
consider this Markan material as a whole and to see whether the
evidence points in the same direction as the evidence
previously discussed. Three features of this section need to be
reckoned with: (a) the opening words of the parable in v 34
resemble Matthew's parable of the talents (see pp. 23-29 above);
(b) the reference to the watchman and the possible parallels to
Lk 12:36-38 occur only at the end of Mark's v 34 and especially
in vv 35,36 (see pp. 29,30 above on vv 35,36); and (c) the
difficulties that some commentators have had with this Markan
section have been particularly (i) with the tension between the
talent-like opening and the watchman-like continuation,
(ii) with the actual wording and grammar of v 34 b and c,
i.e. the material between the opening that resembles the talents
and the later material that resembles Luke's watching servant(s)
parable. (E.g. there is the word ἐξουσία and the change from
participle to indicative. On the difficulties see pp. 17-19
above.)

Given these features, one obvious possible explanation of
Mark's text is that he does indeed start out on the parable of
the talents, but then abandons it and continues with the
parable of the watchman: this would account for his beginning,
his ending, the tension between them and the awkwardness of the
material at the point of transition.

How well does this suggestion work when examined more
closely in the light of the text of Mark? In fact it works
well: (i) the beginning, ὡς ἄνθρωπος ἀπόδημος ἀφεὶς τὴν
οἰκίαν αὐτοῦ, is unproblematic, has close links with the
parable of the talents (as we saw), and is explicable entirely
within the framework of thought of that parable. Although
ἀφεὶς τὴν οἰκίαν αὐτοῦ is not in the Matthean parable, it is
intelligible as an explanatory expansion of ἀπόδημος, and is
better taken thus than ascribed to the parable of the watchman.

(ii) The ending, γρηγορεῖτε οὖν. οὐκ οἴδατε γὰρ πότε ὁ
κύριος τῆς οἰκίας ἔρχεται. μὴ ἐλθὼν ἐξαίφνης εὕρη ὑμᾶς
καθεύδοντας, is unproblematic, has links with the Lukan parable
of the watching servant(s), and is explicable entirely within
the framework of thought of that parable.

(iii) The transitional material is different: καὶ δοὺς
τοῖς δούλοις αὐτοῦ τὴν ἐξουσίαν, ἑκάστῳ τὸ ἔργον αὐτοῦ, καὶ τῷ
θυρωρῷ ἐνετείλατο ἵνα γρηγορῇ. This section is problematic, as
we have seen; and, although it has some verbal links with the
parable of the talents (.. τοὺς ἰδίους δούλους καὶ παρέδωκεν
αὐτοῖς τὰ ὑπάρχοντα αὐτοῦ, καὶ... ἑκάστῳ κατὰ τὴν ἰδίαν δύναμιν,
Mt 25:14,15) it does not fit comfortably either within the
framework of the parable of the talents - the giving is of
'authority' and 'work', not property - or within the framework
of the parable of the watchman - the reference to servants
other than the watchman seems superfluous.

All these things are, however, quite simply explained on
the hypothesis that Mark is here performing the rather delicate
manoeuvre of transferring from the one parable to another. We
suggest that in the phrase καὶ δοὺς τοῖς δούλοις αὐτοῦ τὴν
ἐξουσίαν, ἑκάστῳ τὸ ἔργον αὐτοῦ he is still to a considerable
extent following the parable of the talents. The words καὶ
δοὺς τοῖς δούλοις αὐτοῦ carry on the preceding participial
construction (ἀπόδημος ἀφείς), and with their reference to a
plurality of servants they could well have been taken unaltered
from Mark's version of the parable of the talents. (Compare Mt
25:14,15: ... τοὺς ἰδίους δούλους καὶ παρέδωκεν αὐτοῖς τὰ
ὑπάρχοντα αὐτοῦ, καὶ ..ἑκάστῳ κατὰ τὴν ἰδίαν δύναμιν . But
whereas the parable of the talents spoke of giving property or
money to the servants - to each of them - Mark speaks of them
being given 'authority', to each his work'. Here we see the
beginning of Mark's change of direction: he is still following
the form of the parable of the talents, but these two new words
'authority' and 'work' indicate the switch to a parable about a
servant with a responsibility (i.e. the watchman). This switch
of direction, which at first leads to a modification of the
wording of the talents, next leads to a radical break with that
parable: Mark's καὶ τῷ θυρωρῷ ἐνετείλατο ἵνα γρηγορῇ
represents a grammatical jump (from participle to indicative)
and a jump of focus from the group of servants to the watchman
- a jump from the old parable to the new one.

This explanation of the transitional section is
attractively simple. The only thing that is perhaps a slight
continuing mystery is Mark's use of the word ἐξουσία. Why,
when replacing a reference to the giving of property (as in the
talents) with a reference to the giving of a job (the
watchman's), did he use the word ἐξουσία? One suggestion is
that this word reflects the influence of the parable of the

supervising steward (Mt 24:45-51, Lk 12:42-46); but the word is
not found in the 'Q' version of the parable, and it in any case
complicates life if we have to postulate the influence of a
third parable as well as the parables of the talents and the
watchman,/1/ though, if the parables of the watchman and the
supervising steward were a parable pair, it is perhaps
conceivable that Mark's thought could have touched on both.
However, it is probably simpler to seek an explanation that
does not involve the third parable.

Given the Markan context, we have little option but to
understand ἐξουσία as meaning 'delegated responsibility',
unusual though the sense may be when speaking of tasks being
given to a group of servants. One possibility is that Mark
chose it in this transitional passage precisely because it
could cover the thought (from the parable of the talents) of the
servants being given the master's property to trade with
('according to his own ability')/2/ and the thought of the
watchman being given the responsibility of watching. Yet
another possibility is that Mark has slipped into
allegorization here, and that he has in mind the 'authority'
given by Jesus to his disciples; cf. 6:7./3/ More mundanely we
may suggest that, if Mark was following a form of the parable
of the talents which spoke of the master 'giving to his
servants his property, to each ...', and if he was looking for

---

/1/ R. J. Bauckham's hint in *NTS* 23(1977)166 that the whole of
the opening of Mk 13:34 could derive from the parable of the
supervising servant (rather than the talents) is contradicted
by the evidence we have produced for a link with the talents.
Also neither Matthew nor Luke show traces of such an opening
for the parable of the supervising servant; we would therefore
be thinking of a pre-Q stage of transmission. Furthermore, the
plurality of servants in Mk 13:34 is not explained on this
view.
/2/ On the other hand, Matthew's 'to each according to his
ability' could be explained on the basis of Mark's ἐξουσίαν
and/or on the basis of Mark's 'to each his work' (cf. R. H.
Gundry, *Matthew A Commentary on His Literary and Theological
Art* [Grand Rapids: Eerdmans, 1982] 503). But the Matthean
phrase hardly needs explanation given the context of his parable.
/3/ So Pesch, *Naherwartungen*, 198. But this, as Dr Bauckham has
pointed out to me, could contradict the strong Markan emphasis
on *all* being called to watch.

some replacement words for the property references, the
combination 'authority ... work' would have fitted neatly after
the verb to give.

But perhaps the most ingenious suggestion of all is that
Mark's form of the parable of the talents read καὶ δοὺς τοῖς
δούλοις τὴν οὐσίαν αὐτοῦ, ἑκάστῳ .... Given such an
original text, Mark's ἐξουσίαν represents an easy change; the
alteration moved the parable in the new direction in which Mark
was going, though the new sense was awkward enough to perplex
modern scholars! There is no independent evidence of this
suggested wording in the parable of the talents. But it is
quite conceivable that Matthew could have known it, changing
τὴν οὐσίαν αὐτοῦ into his more familiar τὰ ὑπάρχοντα αὐτοῦ (cf.
Mt. 19:21 and especially the preceding 24:47 which could have
influenced his wording in 25:14; and for οὐσία used in this
sort of sense see Lk 15:12,13./1/).

Whether the last suggestion is correct or not, we may at
least say that the slightly incongruous ἐξουσίαν is not a
serious objection to our explanation of the so-called
transitional material; there are various possible explanations
of it. Our overall conclusion is that the view of Mark 13:34-
36 as beginning with the parable of the talents but then
switching over to the parable of the watchman works remarkably
well in explaining the text as we have it, including the
tensions that have so often bothered scholars.

Two possible objections remain: (1) Are we not now
advocating what we earlier criticized in Weiser's theory, namely
the idea that Mark had a perfectly good parable of the watchman
but that he spoiled its coherence by adding in bits from the
parable of the talents? The answer to that is: No. Weiser
assumes that Mark jumped to and fro between the parable of the
watchman and the parable of the talents: ὡς ἄνθρωπος may come
from either parable; ἀπόδημος comes from the talents; ἀφεὶς τὴν
οἰκίαν αὐτοῦ comes from the watchman; δούς from the talents -
why does Mark revert to the parable that doesn't suit his
purposes well? -; καὶ .. ἐνετείλατο comes from the watchman.
Our suggestion is much simpler than this: Mark does not go to

---

/1/ On whether this suggestion throws light on the original form
of the parable of the talents see below in chapter 2, pp. 74,75.

and fro between the two parables; he starts with the one (the
talents) and then transfers to the other (the watchman).

But (2) still another objection remains: why ever did Mark
start the one parable and then awkwardly jump into another?
The answer to that, as we have already hinted, lies in the
theme of this whole Markan section, 13:33-37: from beginning to
end the emphasis is on 'wakefulness'. That theme comes out in
the saying of v 33. But the saying of v 33 (as we saw on
pp. 23-29 above) was probably found in the pre-Markan tradition
immediately before the parable of the talents. So we can
understand how Mark was led into the talents (v 34a). However,
that parable was not very relevant to the theme of wakefulness,
and so, almost before he has got into the parable, he changes
direction in favour of the parable of the watchman, which was
much more suitable for his purpose. So by the end of v 34 and
in what follows we are firmly back into exhortations to
wakefulness. It is not accidental that in this whole section
Mark has three exhortations to 'keep awake'.

It might be objected to this that it is rather
unsatisfactory to suggest that Mark inadvertently got into the
parable of the talents and then had to extricate himself from
it: Mark is made out to be a rather inefficient editor, and
could surely have done better./1/ But on almost any view of
this rather difficult section Mark might have done better, and
in fact there is no insuperable difficulty in the idea that
Mark began the parable and then thought better of it. However,
the matter may perhaps be slightly differently and better
understood: it may not be that Mark began the one parable and
then regretted it, but that he intended all along to take us to
the exhortation of vv 35,36 (which concluded the parable of the
watchman). His vv 33-37 are exhortation through and through,
and he quite probably had no desire to reproduce the parable of
the watchman here. But he *had* to introduce vv 35 and 36 with a
very brief parabolic setting. In setting the scene in v 34 he
uses the language of the parable of the talents (which was
naturally in his mind after the saying of v 33), but he is
using the language for his own purposes, turning it into an
introduction for vv 35,36.

/1/ Would Mark's readers have known the traditions in question
and so have understood his complicated form? This is possible
but may be to assume too much.

The hypothesis that Mk 13:34-36 is a blend of material
taken, first, from the parable of the talents and then from the
parable of the watchman has been seen to make good sense of
Mark's text; and, if it is correct, the hypothesis has obvious
relevance for our quest for the original form of the parable of
the watchman. (1) It means that the beginning of Mark's
parabolic material (v 34a) will probably be of no use to us,
since that was taken from the parable of the talents. (2) It
means also that the rest of v 34 must be of doubtful value.
It was suggested that the whole of v 34 could be a Markan
introduction to the exhortations of vv 35 and 34; but in any
case v 34 b and c are transitional material, leading us over
from the echo of the parable of the talents into the parable of
the watchman. It was suggested above that the words ἐξουσία
and ἔργον mark the beginning of the transition to the new
parable, and with καὶ τῷ θυρωρῷ ἐνετείλατο ἵνα γρηγορῇ Mark
takes a big and decisive jump. It is possible that in this
material we have elements taken from the parable of the
watchman, but it is equally possible that most of what we have
here is Markan bridge-work reflecting his bringing together of
elements from the two different parables. For example, as we
noted before, the specific reference to a 'doorkeeper' could
have replaced an original 'servant', the change being made
necessary by the preceding reference to 'his servants' in
general. Similarly the 'commanding' of the doorkeeper to keep
awake could be an original part of the parable of the watchman.
But it could quite as well be a reflection of the parable of
the talents with its picture of the master with his servants
before him 'giving them' things: Mark adapts this, replacing
the giving of talents with the giving of tasks. The only thing
then that may reasonably confidently be deduced about the
parable of the watchman from v 34 is that it was originally a
parable about one watching servant. (3) It is only when we get
to vv 35,36 that we are safely over 'the bridge' into the new
parable and certainly out of the framework of the parable of
the talents. So it is in these Markan verses that we might
most expect to find the original parable of the watchman,
though the prima facie impression given by Mark is that we have
here hortatory application of the parable, not the parable
itself./1/

/1/ J. Lambrecht, *Redaktion*, 249, notes the flowing structure
and chiasmus of vv 35-36 - you keep awake/master coming/coming/
you sleeping.

6.4. A proposed original parable of the watching servant

The evidence of Luke, Matthew and Mark has been examined, and the whole picture can now be put together. Luke's parable of the watching servants was seen to contain pre-Lukan tradition, and the only things that seemed possibly or probably secondary were the plurality of servants and the form of the second Lukan beatitude (12:38). Matthew's evidence confirmed that the exhortation form of Mark 13:35 was probably to be preferred to the beatitude form of Lk 12:38, but pointed to the greater originality of Luke's wording of the reference to the different watches.   Mark's evidence yielded few clear clues as to the wording of the body of the parable of the watchman, except to indicate that it was probably a parable about *one* watchman, not about watching servants; but the hortatory application of the parable in Mk 13:35,36 had a much greater claim to originality (a finding that coheres with the finding about Matthew's evidence).

On the basis of this evidence the following proposal of an original form of the parable may be made:

> (It is) like a man waiting for his master, when he will return from a (wedding) feast, so that when he comes and knocks he may immediately open to him. Blessed is that servant whom the master shall find watching, when he comes. Truly I tell you, he will gird himself and sit him (his servant) down and serve him.
> So then keep awake. For you do not know in what watch the master of the house comes, whether in the first, or in the second or in the third, lest coming suddenly he finds you sleeping.

This reconstruction may not be correct in all its details, but it does satisfactorily account for all the evidence that has has been examined.

Luke has most nearly preserved the original parable – a conclusion that fits in with his evident editorial conservatism in the two 'Q' parables that follow. He has changed the singular servant to the plural for reasons already explained, and also the final exhortation into his second beatitude. Despite this last change (which will later be seen to be paralleled by Luke's avoidance of exhortations to wakefulness elsewhere – see pp. 57-60 below), Luke has retained the original reference to the 'watches' of the night.

Mark has not, according to this reconstruction, retained
the wording of the parable to any significant extent, though he
may be credited with preserving the singularity of the
watchman! What he has preserved is the concluding exhortation
to the parable with insignificant modifications. His procedure
is explicable in terms of his evident overriding interest in
vv 33-37, which is to encourage wakefulness. Matthew has not
preserved the parable at all, but does have a version of the
concluding exhortation, which has had to be drastically
modified because of the omission of the parable. But still
Matthew preserves one original word (ποίᾳ), which neither Mark
nor Luke preserve, and he gave important clues for the
reconstruction of the original parable.

Not only is it possible to explain each of the synoptic
versions on the basis of the proposal without straining the
evidence; but the proposal also illuminates a whole range of
problems that need resolving: it explains the similarities and
differences between the Matthean and Markan injunctions to
wakefulness in Mt 24:42 and Mk 13:35; and between the parables
of Mk 13:34-36 and Lk 12:36-38 and between Mt 24:42,43 and
Lk 12:38,39. It explains the rather unusual ὁ κύριος ὑμῶν in
Mt 24:42 and the much more problematic content and form of
Mk 13:34. It explains the anticlimactic beatitude of Lk 12:38.

It is because the hypothesis 'solves' such teasing problems
that it must be considered probable. On the other hand, the
hypothesis has also raised issues that must be pursued, for
example concerning the parable of the talents and concerning
the parables of the thief and steward. Before proceeding to an
examination of these questions in the next chapter, it is worth
noting straightaway how potentially significant the findings of
this chapter have been, pointing to a pre-synoptic tradition
known to all three evangelists and used differently by each of
them. The importance of this conclusion makes it all the more
imperative to see whether other evidence supports or contradicts
it.

Chapter 2

A PRE-SYNOPTIC PARABLE COLLECTION (MT 24:42-25:30,
MK 13:33-37, LK 12:35-48)

1. INTRODUCTION

It was noted at the beginning of chapter one that there
are various links or possible links between Mk 13:33-37,
Mt 24:42-25:30 and Lk 12:35-48

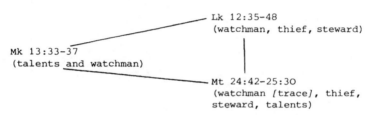

Lk 12:35-48
(watchman, thief, steward)

Mk 13:33-37
(talents and watchman)

Mt 24:42-25:30
(watchman [trace], thief,
steward, talents)

Chapter one explored several of those links, and the emerging
picture is interesting as well as complex. (a) Mk 13:33-37 was
seen to contain an echo of the parable of the talents (which is
found also in full form in Mt 25:14-30) and also a rather more
substantial extract from the parable of the watching servant
(which is found also in Lk 12:36-38 with a trace in Mt 24:42).
In neither case does Mark give the relevant parable in full; it
seems as though his interest was more in the exhortations
attached to the parables than in the parables themselves. Mark
has no parable of the thief, though it was observed that his
vv 35-36 contain a similar thought. (b) Lk 12:35-48 contains the
parable of the watching servant(s) (cf. Mk 13:34-36, Mt 24:42)
and the parables of the thief and the steward (which are found
also in Mt 24:43-51). (c) Mt 24:42-25:30 has only a trace of
the parable of the watchman, but has the parables of the thief
and the steward (which are found also in Luke 12) and the
parable of the talents (which is echoed in Mark 13).

Given this complicated pattern of links and the argument of
the previous chapter about the three evangelists' independent
knowledge of a pre-synoptic form of the parable of the watchman,

the possibility that must suggest itself is that the three
evangelists not only knew a pre-synoptic version of the parable
of the watchman, but also a pre-synoptic collection of parables
including the watchman, the thief, the steward and the talents.

Can this hypothesis be shown to be probable? There are
obvious problems: Luke does not have the parable of the talents
in his chapter 12 (but has his parable of the pounds in 19:11-27
+ a slightly similar parable about disobedient servants in
12:47,48). Mark does not have the parables of the thief and
the steward; but then he does not retain much of the parables
of the talents or the watchman either, and so his omission of
other parabolic material may not occasion surprise. But can
positive arguments for an underlying parable collection be
adduced?

2. THE PARABLE OF THE THIEF

Mt 24:43,44   Lk 12:39,40

ἐκεῖνο δὲ γινώσκετε ὅτι εἰ   τοῦτο δὲ γινώσκετε, ὅτι εἰ ᾔδει
ᾔδει ὁ οἰκοδεσπότης ποίᾳ φυλακῇ   ὁ οἰκοδεσπότης ποίᾳ ὥρᾳ ὁ
ὁ κλέπτης ἔρχεται, ἐγρηγόρησεν   κλέπτης ἔρχεται, οὐκ ἂν
ἂν καὶ οὐκ ἂν εἴασεν διορυχθῆναι   ἀφῆκεν διορυχθῆναι τὸν οἶκον
τὴν οἰκίαν αὐτοῦ. 44. διὰ τοῦτο   αὐτοῦ.
καὶ ὑμεῖς γίνεσθε ἕτοιμοι, ὅτι ᾗ   40. καὶ ὑμεῖς γίνεσθε ἕτοιμοι,
οὐ δοκεῖτε ὥρᾳ ὁ υἱὸς τοῦ   ὅτι ᾗ ὥρᾳ οὐ δοκεῖτε ὁ υἱὸς τοῦ
ἀνθρώπου ἔρχεται.   ἀνθρώπου ἔρχεται.

2.1. Findings so far

There is good reason for thinking that both Matthew and
Luke knew a tradition containing the parable of the watching
servant and the parable of the thief together. This emerged in
chapter one, where it was observed (a) that Matthew and Luke
both have the parable of the watchman (or in Matthew's case a
trace of that parable) immediately before the parable of the
thief; (b) that Matthew's ποίᾳ φυλακῇ in his v 43 is probably
his modification of Luke's more original ποίᾳ ὥρᾳ. Matthew had
omitted the nocturnal parable of the watchman, only retaining an
adapted day-time conclusion in his v 42; now in the parable of
the thief he wishes to suggest a nocturnal setting, and so he
alters the 'hour' of the parable to 'watch', picking up the
phrase ποίᾳ φυλακῇ from the parable of the watchman (see pp. 39,
40 above); (c) that Luke's τοῦτο in his v 39 is probably his

substitute for Matthew's more original ἐκεῖνο. Luke had used
ἐκεῖνο in his own reformulated conclusion to the parable of the
watchman (12:38), and so here he varies the pronoun.

2.2. Matthew's additional ἐγρηγόρησεν ἄν

The only other substantial difference between Matthew's
and Luke's versions of the parable is that Matthew has the
additional phrase ἐγρηγόρησεν ἄν in his v 43. It is possible
that this phrase is original and was omitted by Luke./1/ But
it seems more likely that Matthew added the phrase, whether to
bring out again the night-time context of the thief parable or
in order to reinforce the message of the parable about
wakefulness.

It has been argued that Matthew's introduction of
ἐγρηγόρησεν ἄν into the parable of the thief complicates or
threatens to complicate the simpler Lukan picture. In Luke the
main point of the parable at least is about the 'unknownness'
of the hour of someone's coming' (note the similar phrases in
12:39a and 12:40). By introducing the thought of the
householder 'keeping awake' Matthew may be thought to imply that
the householder is an example to the Christian; but this is
complicated, since the situation of the householder who would
have stayed awake if he had known the time of the thief's
coming is different from the situation of the Christian who is
to stay awake because he does not know the time of the Lord's
coming./2/ Has Matthew then introduced something incongruous?

Two things may be said on this: (a) it is not certain
that the addition of the one word proves that Matthew saw the
householder as an example to Christians. The addition may
simply be filling out the picture of the parable and
emphasizing the nocturnal scene. (b) It is not certain that the
idea of the householder being an example is absent from Luke's
version. It is evident that for Matthew and Luke the main

/1/ J. Jeremias, *Die Sprache des Lukasevangeliums* (Göttingen:
Vandenhoeck & Ruprecht, 1980), 220, claims that Luke dislikes
the verb γρηγορεῖν, because it was rather vulgar Greek. This
may be so, though he uses the verb in 12:37; and Luke could
surely have found a substitute expression, had he wished to do
so.
/2/ Cf. H. Gollinger, *Bibel und Leben* 11 (1970) 243,244.

point of comparison concerns the unpredictability of the hour,
but it is possible that they both have the subsidiary thought
that what the householder would have done is what the Christian
should do, i.e. get ready. If this is intended, then there is
a slight incongruity between parable and application (neither
the householder nor the Christian know the hour: so the
householder does not get ready and the Christian should get
ready...); but it is the sort of incongruity that would bother
a scholar more than the ordinary listener!/1/

The argument that Matthew's phrase is incongruous is thus
uncertain; but it remains probable that it is a Matthean
addition.

Apart from this Matthean addition, the Matthean and Lukan
parables are closely parallel, and there is little doubt that
they have a common tradition. Normally this would be regarded
as a 'Q' tradition. The possible complication for the 'Q'
hypothesis is that the evidence points to the thief parable
being linked to the parable of the watchman in the tradition.
There is, however, no great problem with the idea that 'Q'
contained both parables. The unanswered question then is:
did Mark know this version? The fact that the parable of the
thief fits well after the parable of the watchman is no proof
that they were thus connected in Mark's tradition.

2.3. *The evidence of 1 Thess 5:2-6*

It is possible that Paul's evidence in 1 Thess 5:2-6 may
help us:

v 2 αὐτοὶ γὰρ ἀκριβῶς οἴδατε ὅτι ἡμέρα κυρίου
     ὡς κλέπτης ἐν νυκτὶ οὕτως ἔρχεται......
v 4 ὑμεῖς δέ, ἀδελφοί, οὐκ ἐστὲ ἐν σκότει,
     ἵνα ἡ ἡμέρα ὑμᾶς ὡς κλέπτης καταλάβῃ .....
v 6 ἄρα οὖν μὴ καθεύδωμεν ὡς οἱ λοιποί, ἀλλὰ
     γρηγορῶμεν καὶ νήφωμεν.

Paul here gives the impression that the comparison of
the coming of the day of the Lord to the coming of a thief is
an early tradition known to the Thessalonians. It is not
possible to prove that he knew the parable of the thief in
anything like its 'Q' form (or indeed in parable form at all);

/1/ See also p. 61 n. 2 below.

but it is possible that his rather unusual phrase αὐτοὶ γὰρ
ἀκριβῶς οἴδατε ὅτι is an echo of the opening of the parable
ἐκεῖνο δὲ γινώσκετε ὅτι..../1/   And Paul connects the parable
with a call 'not to sleep' but to 'keep awake', using the
verbs καθεύδειν and γρηγορεῖν. Both words are quite unusual in
the Pauline corpus,/2/ and Paul could here be betraying his
acquaintance with the preceding context of the parable of the
thief, i.e. of the parable of the watchman with its warning
against sleeping (καθεύδειν) and its concluding call to
γρηγορεῖτε. Another phrase in the Pauline passage could
reflect that parable: Paul's comments that the Thessalonians
are not in the dark ἵνα ἡ ἡμέρα ὑμᾶς ὡς κλέπτης καταλάβῃ.
This could be connected with the Markan γρηγορεῖτε μὴ ἐλθὼν
ἐξαίφνης εὕρῃ ὑμᾶς καθεύδοντας, since εὑρίσκειν and
καταλαμβάνειν can be equivalents (both translating אצמ in the
LXX). If Paul did know the parable, he has understandably
avoided the comparison of the Lord to the thief, substituting
the less personal 'day'; it may be that this change led on
to the substitution of καταλαμβάνειν for the more personal
εὑρίσκειν.

    This combination of Pauline evidence is interesting, but
hardly decisive of anything by itself. All that can be said
is that Paul could have known both the parables of the
watchman and of the thief, and that, if he did, he linked them
together. This could reflect his awareness of a link in the
tradition. /3/

2.4. The evidence of Revelation

    To the Pauline evidence may be added the evidence of
Rev 3:3 and 16:15. Rev 3:3b reads: ἐὰν οὖν μὴ γρηγορήσῃς, ἥξω ὡς
κλέπτης, καὶ οὐ μὴ γνῷς ποίαν ὥραν ἥξω ἐπὶ σέ. The opening
ἐὰν οὖν μὴ γρηγορήσῃς could be taken as an echo of the
peculiarly Matthean phrase ἐγρηγόρησεν ἄν in the parable of the
thief (Mt 24:43). But it is at least as plausibly linked to
the conclusion of the parable of the watchman, since then we
get a parallel sequence of thought:

/1/ On the unusualness of οἶδα with an adverb see my 'Paul and
the Synoptic Apocalypse', p. 347.
/2/ καθεύδειν is found in Eph 5:14 (apart from in
1 Thessalonians 5), and γρηγορεῖν in 1 Cor 16:13, Col. 4:2.

Mt 24:42	keep awake	Rev 3:3	unless you keep awake,

43   parable of thief   I will come like a thief,

44   ... you do not   and you will not know
      realize at what   at what hour I will
      hour the Son of   come to you.
      man comes

The evidence of Rev 16:15 also suggests that the author of
Revelation knew the parables of the thief and the watchman
together, since it reads: ἰδοὺ ἔρχομαι ὡς κλέπτης· μακάριος
ὁ γρηγορῶν ..... The second phrase here is distinctly
reminiscent of Lk 12:37 μακάριοι οἱ δοῦλοι .. οὓς ... εὑρήσει
γρηγοροῦντας; Revelation has the singular μακάριος, which
corresponds to what we saw to be the original form of the
parable of the watchman. (It will be recalled that Rev 3:20 is
a possible allusion to the same verse in Lk 12:37; see p. 31
above. Again Revelation uses a singular ἐάν τις ... ἀνοίξῃ.)
This probable linking of the parables of the thief and of the
watchman may prove nothing, since the author of Revelation
could have known and used Luke (and Matthew); but his singular
μακάριος could be a small hint that he is familiar with the
pre-synoptic tradition./1/

2.5. Conclusion

     The conclusion on the parable of the thief is that this
was very probably connected with the parable of the watchman
in a tradition known to Matthew and Luke. It is possible, but
unprovable, that Paul and the author of Revelation were
familiar with the combination.

     The original wording of the parable was probably

       ἐκεῖνο δὲ γινώσκετε, ὅτι εἰ ἤδει
       ὁ οἰκοδεσπότης ποίᾳ ὥρᾳ ὁ κλέπτης
       ἔρχεται, οὐκ ἂν εἴασεν/ἀφῆκεν
       διορυχθῆναι τὴν οἰκίαν/τὸν οἶκον αὐτοῦ.
       (διὰ τοῦτο) καὶ ὑμεῖς γίνεσθε ἑτοιμοι,
       ὅτι ᾗ οὐ δοκεῖτε ὥρᾳ ὁ υἱὸς τοῦ
       ἀνθρώπου ἔρχεται.

/1/ The 'thief' tradition is also found in 2 Pet 3:10 and in
Gospel of Thomas sayings 21 and 103. See further in my 'Paul
and the Synoptic Apocalypse', pp. 347,366.

3. THE SAYINGS OF LK 12:41 AND MK 13:37

3.1. The two sayings related

Immediately after the parable of the thief, Luke has Peter
ask κύριε, πρὸς ἡμᾶς τὴν παραβολὴν ταύτην λέγεις ἢ καὶ πρὸς
πάντας; (12:41). This question is strikingly reminiscent of
Jesus' saying in Mk 13:37 ὃ δὲ ὑμῖν λέγω, πᾶσιν λέγω, γρηγορεῖτε.
This similarity has surprisingly been overlooked by most
commentators, and the two verses concerned have regularly been
dubbed as Lukan and Markan redaction. But there is reason to
believe that they are related sayings./1/

This is suggested not only by the closely similar wording,
but also by the similar order of sayings in the two gospels.

Mark has:	the parable of the watchman.	Luke has:	the parable of the watching servants
			the parable of the thief
	"What I say to you I say to all, keep awake."		"Lord, do you say this parable to us, or also to all?"

Since we have seen reason to identify Mark's parable of the
watchman and Luke's parable of the wátching servants, it is very
hard to avoid the conclusion that these so strongly similar
sayings that follow that parable are related.

3.2. How are the sayings related?

If the two sayings are related, what is the nature of the
relationship?

3.2.1. Luke dependent on Mark?

Various scholars have suggested that the Lukan question
(whether it is based on Mk 13:37 or not) was formulated by Luke

---

/1/ So also A. H. McNeile, The Gospel according to St. Matthew
(London: Macmillan, 1915) 358; J. Schmid, Das Evangelium nach
Lukas (Regensburg: Pustet, 1960) 223.

to lead into the following parable of the steward./1/ It is
certainly striking that in that parable, where Matthew has
reference to a plain δοῦλος and to his συνδούλους, Luke refers
to an οἰκονόμος and to the παῖδας and παιδίσκας. The
formulation of the question and the Lukan wording of the parable
could both reflect a Lukan desire to differentiate between
church leaders and ordinary church members and a deliberate move
away from Mark's democratic emphasis in the saying 'What I say
to you I say to all'.

Whether this argument has any plausibility so far as Luke's
version of the parable of the steward is concerned will be
considered in due course. So far as the preceding Lukan
question is concerned, the argument is distinctly problematic:
in the first place it is not at all obvious that Luke would
have rejected the Markan suggestion that *all* should keep awake
- surely Lk 21:36 applies to all Christians - and it seems
rather odd that he should have used the Markan words to make a
contrary point./2/ Secondly - and more significantly - the
suggestion that Luke created the question in order to lead into
the parable is problematic, since the exact force of the
question is not very clear; and, despite the Lukan changes in
the following parable (if that is what they are), the parable
does not answer the question at all clearly - *was* the parable of
thief addressed to the disciples or to all? Luke's supposed
editorial creativity has thus been quite unsuccessful; as T. W.
Manson comments, 'Editorial glosses are usually more transparent
than this'./3/ A third observation on this view that the Lukan
question is an adaptation of Mk 13:37 is that it seems
improbable that in a section where Luke is quite independent of
Mark - in the parables of the watchman, the thief and the
steward - he should have inserted a saying from Mark 13. If the
suggestion is to be at all plausible, then it must be assumed
that the Markan saying was also in the non-Markan tradition
being used by Luke. This is quite possible, but to admit that

---

/1/ E.g. Schmid, *ibid*; W. Michaelis, *Die Gleichnisse Jesu*
(Hamburg: Furche, 1956) 72-74; E. Schweizer, *The Good News
according to Matthew* (London: SPCK, 1976) 460,461.
/2/ Cf. W. Bussmann, *Synoptische Studien II* (Halle: Waisenhauses,
1929) 95,96.
/3/ T. W. Manson, *The Sayings of Jesus* (London: SCM, 1949) 118.

Luke was not dependent on Mark is to admit that there may be
other ways of explaining the relationship between the Markan
and the Lukan sayings. Mark could, for example, be dependent
on the Lukan form, though that is probably even more difficult
to imagine than the opposite.

3.2.2. Mark and Luke dependent on a common source

The preferable explanation of the relationship is that Mark
and Luke have both drawn on a common tradition, and that Luke
has preserved the question 'Lord, do you say this parable to us
or to all?' and Mark the answer 'What I say to you I say to all,
keep awake'./1/

In favour of this suggestion note: (a) Mark and Luke were
seen to have independent access to a common tradition in the
preceding parable of the watchman, and so it is reasonable to
explain their similarities here in the same way, especially as
it is unlikely that Luke derived his 12:41 from Mk 13:37 (see
above).

(b) The Lukan question provides an excellent context for
the Markan saying. In Mark, as we have it, v 37 may be said to
strike a rather unexpected note: why does Mark suddenly
introduce this thought of a differentiation between the
disciples and others? It may be, as some have argued, that Mark
at the end of the discourse is applying the discourse to the
readers of his gospel (though the view that the verse is wholly
Markan is put in question by the Lukan evidence). But the
hypothesis suggested offers a simpler (though not necessarily
contradictory) explanation.

(c) Mark's omission of the Lukan question and his retention
of the hortatory answer are only what might be expected on the
basis of our earlier arguments about Mk 13:33-36, since it was
seen that Mark's interest in this section is in exhortation to
wakefulness, not in parables. In any case if Mark found the
Lukan question after the parable of the thief, which he had
omitted, he could hardly have retained the question about 'this
parable' (but see further on this below).

(d) Luke's question is very clearly and directly answered
by the Markan saying, whereas it is not clearly answered in the

----

/1/ So H. B. Swete, *The Gospel according to St Mark* (London:
Macmillan, 1909[3]) 319.

Lukan parable of the steward. If the pre-synoptic sequence was
(i) the Lukan question, (ii) the Markan answer, (iii) the
parable of the steward, then everything fits well together. We
have Peter's question about the disciples and 'all', followed
by a direct answer to the question which explains that all are
to keep awake and then a further answer, which, at least as
Luke probably understood it, looks particularly at the position
of the disciples - as responsible stewards.

(e) It may seem mysterious that Luke omits the direct
answer of Mk 13:37, leaving an inferior sequence of thought in
Lk 12:41-42. But in chapter 1 (above) it was argued that Luke
for some reason changed the hortatory conclusion of the parable
of the watchman (Mk 13:35,36) into a beatitude (Lk 12:38). It
seems probable that the same reason provoked him to omit the
next exhortation to wakefulness in his source, i.e. Mk 13:37.
The two arguments converge and confirm each other. And the
existence of such a Lukan tendency is confirmed by the evidence
of the Gethsemane story, since Luke there omits all three of the
Matthean/Markan references to keeping awake (cf. Mt 26:38,40,41,
Mk 14:34,37,38 and Lk 22:39-46)./1/

These different arguments add up to a strong case and a
very significant case, since it is now established that Mark
did not only know the pre-synoptic parable of the watchman, but
also the following pre-synoptic dialogue.

3.3. Did Mark know the parable of the thief?

The obvious inference from this conclusion must be that
Mark also knew the parable of the thief, which precedes the
dialogue in Luke, and probably the parable of the steward,
which follows it. However, some scholars have felt that the
Lukan question (cf. 12:41) would fit better after the parable of

---

/1/ Cf. Jeremias, *Sprache*, 220, who explains that as a Greek
purist Luke did not like the term γρηγορεῖν, using it only in
12:37, Acts 20:21. Whether this is an adequate explanation of
Luke's omissions is at least debatable. See C. L. Holman,
Studia Biblica et Theologica III (1973) pp. 19,20, for the
suggestion that Luke faced a particular problem with false
teachers.

the watching servants (12:35-38) than after the parable of the
thief (12:39-40)./1/ Perhaps Mark knew such a sequence.

Against this must be said: (a) The Lukan question κύριε,
πρὸς ἡμᾶς λέγεις; may well be picking up the immediately
preceding καὶ ὑμεῖς γίνεσθε ἕτοιμοι of the parable of the
thief (Lk 12:40, Mt 24:44). (b) It is possible that the brief
parable of the thief could be seen as a sort of additional
comment on the previous parable of the watchman rather than as
a completely separate parable. Then v 40 might be considered
a summary of the whole of the preceding parabolic section, and
the question of v 41 would indeed be picking up v 40 and the
parable of the watchman./2/ (c) Since Mark and Luke have been
seen to have common tradition where their relationship can be
tested and since Mark's omission of the parables and his
retention of the exhortations to wakefulness are what we have
come to expect in this section, it seems completely unnecessary
to postulate a significant difference in their sources.
(d) Some possible arguments for the early association of the
parables of the watchman and of the thief (e.g. based on the
evidence of Paul and of Revelation) were noted above
(pp. 54-56).

Added together these points make it probable that Mark
knew the Lukan sequence - watchman, thief, dialogue ....

3.4. Conclusions

The case for the probable connection of Lk 12:41 and Mk
13:37 in the pre-synoptic tradition is strong, explaining the
similarity of the traditions and resolving various questions
posed by the two gospels. The case is significant, since it
points to a pre-synoptic parable collection known to all the

/1/ E.g. I. H. Marshall, *The Gospel of Luke* (Exeter:
Paternoster, 1978) 540.
/2/ Perhaps this suggestion that the exhortation of v 40 is not
just application of the thief parable would alleviate the
problems that some have seen about the compatibility of the
exhortation with the parable. (See pp. 53,54 above and the
discussion there of Matthew's ἐγρηγόρησεν).

evangelists./1/ The wording will have been approximately:

εἶπεν δὲ ὁ Πέτρος· κύριε, πρὸς ἡμᾶς τὴν
παραβολὴν ταύτην λέγεις ἢ καὶ πρὸς πάντας;
καὶ εἶπεν ὁ κύριος (ὁ 'Ιησοῦς)· ὃ ὑμῖν λέγω,
πᾶσιν λέγω, γρηγορεῖτε.

4. THE PARABLE OF THE STEWARD   MT 24:45-51, LK 12:42-46

Mt 24:45-51

τίς ἄρα ἐστιν ὁ πιστὸς δοῦλος
καὶ φρόνιμος ὃν κατέστησεν ὁ
κύριος ἐπὶ τῆς οἰκετείας αὐτοῦ
τοῦ δοῦναι αὐτοῖς τὴν τροφὴν
ἐν καιρῷ; 46. μακάριος ὁ δοῦλος
ἐκεῖνος ὃν ἐλθὼν ὁ κύριος αὐτοῦ
εὑρήσει οὕτως ποιοῦντα· 47. ἀμὴν
λέγω ὑμῖν ὅτι ἐπὶ πᾶσιν τοῖς
ὑπάρχουσιν αὐτοῦ καταστήσει
αὐτόν. 48. ἐὰν δὲ εἴπῃ ὁ κακὸς
δοῦλος ἐκεῖνος ἐν τῇ καρδίᾳ
αὐτοῦ· χρονίζει μου ὁ κύριος,
49. καὶ ἄρξηται τύπτειν τοὺς
συνδούλους αὐτοῦ, ἐσθίῃ δὲ καὶ
πίνῃ μετὰ τῶν μεθυόντων,
50. ἥξει ὁ κύριος τοῦ δούλου
ἐκείνου ἐν ἡμέρᾳ ᾗ οὐ προσδοκᾷ
καὶ ἐν ὥρᾳ ᾗ οὐ γινώσκει, καὶ
διχοτομήσει αὐτόν, καὶ τὸ μέρος
αὐτοῦ μετὰ τῶν ὑποκριτῶν θήσει·
ἐκεῖ ἔσται ὁ κλαυθμὸς καὶ ὁ
βρυγμὸς τῶν ὀδόντων.

Lk 12:42-46

τίς ἄρα ἐστὶν ὁ πιστὸς
οἰκονόμος ὁ φρόνιμος, ὃν
καταστήσει ὁ κύριος ἐπὶ τῆς
θεραπείας αὐτοῦ τοῦ διδόναι ἐν
καιρῷ [τὸ] σιτομέτριον;
43. μακάριος ὁ δοῦλος ἐκεῖνος,
ὃν ἐλθὼν ὁ κύριος αὐτοῦ
εὑρήσει ποιοῦντα οὕτως.
44. ἀληθῶς λέγω ὑμῖν ὅτι ἐπὶ
πᾶσιν τοῖς ὑπάρχουσιν αὐτοῦ
καταστήσει αὐτόν. 45. ἐὰν δὲ
εἴπῃ ὁ δοῦλος ἐκεῖνος ἐν τῇ
καρδίᾳ αὐτοῦ· χρονίζει ὁ
κύριός μου ἔρχεσθαι, καὶ
ἄρξηται τύπτειν τοὺς παῖδας
καὶ τὰς παιδίσκας, ἐσθίειν τε
καὶ πίνειν καὶ μεθύσκεσθαι,
46. ἥξει ὁ κύριος τοῦ δούλου
ἐκείνου ἐν ἡμέρᾳ ᾗ οὐ προσδοκᾷ
καὶ ἐν ὥρᾳ ᾗ οὐ γινώσκει, καὶ
διχοτομήσει αὐτόν, καὶ τὸ
μέρος αὐτοῦ μετὰ τῶν ἀπίστων
θήσει.

/1/ Matthew, of course, has no trace of the dialogue and has
presumably omitted it as superfluous. His knowledge of the
pre-synoptic tradition, however, has already been established.

4.1. The parable in the pre-synoptic collection

If, as has been suggested, there was a pre-synoptic parable collection, then this very probably included the parable of the steward. Matthew and Luke both place this parable after the parables of the watchman and of the thief, both of which they probably derived from the pre-synoptic collection. There can be little doubt that they derived this parable from the same source. Mark does not record the parable, but in the preceding sections, including the immediately preceding dialogue between Peter and Jesus, he appears to be following the same tradition as Matthew and Luke; so it is probable that he too was familiar with the parable. It was observed earlier that there are certain similarities between the parable of the watchman and the parable of the steward (see pp. 30, 31 above); this could also suggest that they belonged together at an early stage.

It is possible that Paul knew the parable, since in 1 Cor 4:1-5 he describes himself and Apollos as ὑπηρέτας...καὶ οἰκονόμους, of whom it is required ἵνα πιστός ... εὑρεθῇ. He goes on to speak of the coming unknown moment of judgment when 'the Lord comes'. The Lord will expose the hidden things of darkness (which, to judge from other strikingly similar Pauline passages, include drunkenness: cf. Rom 13:11-13, 1 Thess 5:6,7, Eph 5:12-18), and each will receive his praise from God. The language and thought is closely similar to that found in the parable of the steward, and it may be that in 1 Corinthians 4 (and indeed in the other passages mentioned, where the theme of 'sleeping' is prominent) Paul is echoing this parabolic collection. However, to balance this, it must be said that, given the existence of 'stewards' in the ancient world, the ideas expressed are fairly obvious, and there need be no link between Paul and the synoptic tradition.

4.2. The Matthean and Lukan forms of the parable

There are a number of minor differences between the Matthean and the Lukan versions of the parable. Is it possible to say anything about the probable original form? The interesting divergence between Matthew's δοῦλος + τοὺς συνδούλους αὐτοῦ and Luke's οἰκονόμος + τοὺς παῖδας καὶ τὰς παιδίσκας has already been mentioned. Has Luke here introduced a distinction between the disciples (or church leaders in general) as 'stewards' and other ordinary Christians, perhaps

under the influence of the preceding question of Peter about
'us' and 'all'?

There does seem to be a case for regarding Matthew's
δοῦλος ... συνδούλους as more original than Luke's wording:
(a) Although Luke begins with οἰκονόμος in v 42, he has δοῦλος
throughout the rest of the parable. (b) The preceding
parable of the watching servant, which is formally parallel to
this, probably referred to a δοῦλος rather than to a θυρωρός
(see chapter 1 above). (c) There may be something in the
argument that the 'servant' of the parable is not properly
called a 'steward' at the outset of the parable; he is only
made a steward, at least in the full sense, after proving
himself faithful./1/ But this is at best a fine point, since
the servant is made a sort of acting steward at the beginning
of the parable.

But, although Luke may well have made these changes, it
is not clear that there is any subtle significance in them.
It may simply be a case of Luke painting the picture a little
more clearly and spelling out that this servant's job was to be
a kind of steward, just as in Mk 13:34 Mark spells out that the
'watching servant' was a 'gatekeeper'. It may be that Luke
sees the parable as a parable about the role of disciples or
church leaders, following up the preceding question of Peter.
But if the question was in the pre-synoptic tradition, as has
been suggested, then this may well also have been the original
sense: Jesus tells Peter that all, not only the disciples, are
to be kept awake, but then proceeds with a parable about a
servant whose position is like that of the disciples, since he
has responsibility for the care of other servants./2/

/1/ Cf. Michaelis, *Gleichnisse*, 73,74; Schweizer, *Matthew*,
460,461.
/2/ Note that the reward of the faithful steward is to be set
over all the master's possessions. Compare this with the
promise to the disciples that they will judge the tribes in
Mt 19:28, Lk 22:28-30. See further below, pp. 128-134.

The other divergences are minor: Matthew has οἰκετείας ...
τὴν τροφὴν for Luke's θεραπείας..... σιτομέτριον. Matthew
speaks of the unfaithful steward being put with 'the
hypocrites', a favourite term of his, where Luke has 'the
unfaithful', which perhaps fits the parable better. At the end
of the parable Matthew adds - or Luke omits! - the typically
Matthean 'Then there will be weeping and gnashing of teeth'.

4.3. The ending of the parable

The parable of the watchman ended with an appropriate
exhortation to wakefulness. The parable of the steward, which
is formally similar to that of the watchman, has no such
ending in either Matthew or Luke. But at the end of his next
parable (of the virgins) Matthew has an ending that would make
an excellent conclusion to the parable of the steward, i.e. his
25:13. If we append this verse to the parable, the point is
clear. Compare:

<u>parable of watchman</u>   and   <u>parable of steward</u>

                                      '... the master will come in
                                      a day you do not expect and in
                                      in an hour you do not
                                      recognize ....'

'Keep awake, then, for you   (25:13) 'Keep awake, then,
do not know in what watch   for you do not know the day
the master of the house   nor the hour.'
comes, whether ....'

Two things are clear from this comparison: (a) Mt 25:13 has
the thought of the unknown 'day' and 'hour', in common with the
parable of the steward./1/   (b) Mt 25:13 is exactly the sort
of ending we might expect in a parable that is parallel to the
parable of the watchman.

/1/ There is no thought of literally 'keeping awake' in the
parable of the steward, though the steward was metaphorically
'awake'. As with the exhortation at the end of the parable
of the thief, the *main* point of comparison lies in the second
'for' clause.

The obvious difficulty with the suggestion that Mt 25:13
is the original conclusion to the parable of the steward is
that neither Matthew nor Luke has it as such. However, Luke's
omission is no surprise, since he omitted the previous similar
exhortation (i.e. the saying of Mk 13:37) and he has an
apparent aversion to such exhortations to 'keep awake'. So far
as Matthew is concerned, the implication of the suggestion
would be that Matthew has put his parable of the virgins
between the parable of the steward and its conclusion. This
may seem odd. And yet we have already observed that many
commentators have felt that Mt 25:13 is a rather unhappy
conclusion to the parable of the virgins (see pp. 25,26
above); although that point should not be pressed too far, it
must at least be said the saying would fit much better after
the parable of the steward.

4.4. Conclusion

It seems very probable that the parable of the steward
was in the pre-synoptic tradition and not improbable that its
conclusion is preserved in Mt 25:13. But this last conclusion
raises some problems, notably to do with Matthew's positioning
of the parable of the virgins, which must be explained.

The wording of the parable may have been approximately:

τίς ἄρα ἐστιν ὁ πιστὸς δοῦλος καὶ φρόνιμος ὃν κατέστησεν ὁ
κύριος ἐπὶ τῆς οἰκετείας/θεραπείας αὐτοῦ τοῦ δοῦναι αὐτοῖς
τὴν τροφήν/σιτομέτριον ἐν καιρῷ; μακάριος ὁ δοῦλος ἐκεῖνος
ὃν ἐλθὼν ὁ κύριος αὐτοῦ εὑρήσει οὕτως ποιοῦντα· ἀμὴν λέγω
ὑμῖν ὅτι ἐπὶ πᾶσιν τοῖς ὑπάρχουσιν αὐτοῦ καταστήσει αὐτόν.
ἐὰν δὲ εἴπῃ ὁ (κακὸς) δοῦλος ἐκεῖνος ἐν τῇ καρδίᾳ αὐτοῦ·
χρονίζει μου ὁ κύριος, καὶ ἄρξηται τύπτειν τοὺς
συνδούλους αὐτοῦ, ἐσθίῃ δὲ καὶ πίνῃ μετὰ τῶν μεθυόντων,
ἥξει ὁ κύριος τοῦ δούλου ἐκείνου ἐν ἡμέρᾳ ᾗ οὐ προσδοκᾷ
καὶ ἐν ὥρᾳ ᾗ οὐ γινώσκει, καὶ διχοτομήσει αὐτόν, καὶ τὸ
μέρος αὐτοῦ μετὰ τῶν ἀπίστων θήσει· (ἐκεῖ ἔσται ὁ κλαυθμὸς
καὶ ὁ βρυγμὸς τῶν ὀδόντων.) γρηγορεῖτε οὖν ὅτι οὐκ οἴδατε
τὴν ἡμέραν οὐδὲ τὴν ὥραν.

5. THE PARABLE OF THE TALENTS AND THE PARABLE OF THE DISOBEDIENT SERVANTS

Mt 25:13-30	Mk 13:33,34	Lk 19:12-27	Lk 12:47,48
γρηγορεῖτε οὖν, ὅτι οὐκ οἴδατε τὴν ἡμέραν οὐδὲ τὴν ὥραν. 14. ὥσπερ γὰρ ἄνθρωπος ἀποδημῶν ἐκάλεσεν τοὺς ἰδίους δούλους καὶ παρέδωκεν αὐτοῖς τὰ ὑπάρχοντα αὐτοῦ, 15., καὶ ᾧ μὲν ἔδωκεν πέντε τάλαντα, ᾧ δὲ δύο, ᾧ δὲ ἕν, ἑκάστῳ κατὰ τὴν ἰδίαν δύναμιν....	οὐκ οἴδατε γὰρ πότε ὁ καιρός ἐστιν. 34. ὡς ἄνθρωπος ἀπόδημος ἀφεὶς τὴν οἰκίαν αὐτοῦ καὶ δοὺς τοῖς δούλοις αὐτοῦ τὴν ἐξουσίαν, ἑκάστῳ τὸ ἔργον αὐτοῦ, καὶ τῷ θυρωρῷ ἐνετείλατο ἵνα γρηγορῇ.	εἶπεν οὖν· ἄνθρωπός τις εὐγενὴς ἐπορεύθη εἰς χώραν μακρὰν λαβεῖν ἑαυτῷ βασιλείαν καὶ ὑποστρέψαι. 13. καλέσας δὲ δέκα δούλους ἑαυτοῦ ἔδωκεν αὐτοῖς δέκα μνᾶς, καὶ εἶπεν πρὸς αὐτούς· πραγματεύσασθε ἐν ᾧ ἔρχομαι. 14.οἱ δὲ πολῖται αὐτοῦ ἐμίσουν αὐτόν, καὶ ἀπέστειλαν πρεσβείαν ὀπίσω αὐτοῦ λέγοντες· οὐ θέλομεν τοῦτον βασιλεῦσαι	ἐκεῖνος δὲ ὁ δοῦλος ὁ γνοὺς τὸ θέλημα τοῦ κυρίου αὐτοῦ καὶ μὴ ἑτοιμάσας ἢ ποιήσας πρὸς τὸ θέλημα αὐτοῦ δαρήσεται πολλάς. 48. ὁ δὲ μὴ γνούς, ποιήσας δὲ ἄξια πληγῶν, δαρήσεται ὀλίγας. παντὶ δὲ
21. ἔφη αὐτῷ ὁ κύριος αὐτοῦ· εὖ, δοῦλε ἀγαθὲ καὶ πιστέ, ἐπὶ ὀλίγα ἦς πιστός, ἐπὶ πολλῶν σε καταστήσω....		17. καὶ εἶπεν αὐτῷ· εὖ γε, ἀγαθὲ δοῦλε, ὅτι ἐν ἐλαχίστῳ πιστὸς ἐγένου, ἴσθι ἐξουσίαν ἔχων ἐπάνω δέκα πόλεων....	ᾧ ἐδόθη πολύ, πολὺ ζητηθήσεται παρ' αὐτοῦ, καὶ ᾧ παρέθεντο πολύ, περισσότερον αἰτήσουσιν αὐτόν.
29. τῷ γὰρ ἔχοντι παντὶ δοθήσεται καὶ περισσευθήσεται· τοῦ δὲ μὴ ἔχοντος καὶ ὃ ἔχει ἀρθήσεται ἀπ'αὐτοῦ. 30. καὶ τὸν ἀχρεῖον δοῦλον ἐκβάλετε εἰς τὸ σκότος τὸ ἐξώτερον· ἐκεῖ ἔσται ὁ κλαυθμὸς καὶ ὁ βρυγμὸς τῶν ὀδόντων .		26. λέγω ὑμῖν ὅτι παντὶ τῷ ἔχοντι δοθήσεται, ἀπὸ δὲ τοῦ μὴ ἔχοντος καὶ ὃ ἔχει ἀρθήσεται. 27. πλὴν τοὺς ἐχθρούς μου τούτους τοὺς μὴ θελήσαντας με βασιλεῦσαι ἐπ' αὐτοὺς ἀγάγετε ὧδε καὶ κατασφάξατε αὐτοὺς ἔμπροσθέν μου.	

5.1. The parables of the talents and of the disobedient servants in the pre-synoptic tradition

The suggestion that Mt 25:13 may be the pre-synoptic conclusion to the parable of the steward was not proved, but seemed plausible; and it is worth seeing if the suggestion makes sense of other data. One effect of the suggestion would be to bring the parable of the talents into the parable source, since the saying of Mt 25:13 has a parallel in Mk 13:33 and both Matthew and Mark link the saying to the opening of the parable of the talents. (This was argued at some length in chapter 1 (pp. 23 - 29) and the arguments need not be repeated here.) But can the idea that the pre-synoptic source contained the parable of the talents after the parable of the steward be verified in any way? Mark's evidence may appear not to support the idea, since he has the relevant material before his other extracts from the pre-synoptic source. Luke's evidence may also seem negative, since he does not have the parable of the talents in his chapter 12 at all; his partial equivalent is the parable of the pounds in Lk 19:12-27.

However, a number of observations tell in favour of the
idea.

5.1.1. Approximately the same location in Matthew and Mark

Although Matthew and Mark do not have the parable of the
talents in precisely the same position, they do both have it in
approximately the same location and they both link it with
other parabolic material that, as has been shown, belonged
together in the pre-synoptic tradition. Since Matthew and
Mark appear to have been drawing independently on the pre-
synoptic tradition in question, it seems not improbable that
the talents belonged somewhere in this context in that tradition.

5.1.2. Mark's precise location probably secondary

It has already been argued that Mark's positioning of his
vv 33 and 34 is probably not original. (See chapter 1 above,
pp. 25-29.) V 33 seems slightly anticlimactic and repetitive
after v 32, and it seems quite likely that Mark attached the
saying of v 33 to v 32 because, especially in its more original
form preserved by Matthew referring to 'not knowing the day or
the hour', it picked up the thought of v 32 – 'of that day or
hour knows no one..'. It has been noted that Mk 13:33-37 is
essentially a collection of exhortations to wakefulness, and,
given v 32 as a starting-point, it is easy to see why Mark began
his concluding section of exhortations with the saying of v 33.
These observations mean that Mark's location of his vv 33 and 34
is not a substantial argument against the view that they
belonged after the parable of the steward in the pre-synoptic
source. Matthew may have the more original position (except
that he has the parable of the virgins in between the steward
and the talents).

5.1.3. Links between the parables of the steward and the talents

There are some interesting similarities between the parables
of the steward and of the talents, and they go well together.
Both are parables about a master going away and giving his
servants responsibility; both portray faithful (πιστός) and
unfaithful servants; both have the faithful servants who are
faithful in little rewarded with greater responsibility: compare
Mt 24:47 / Lk 12:44 ἐπὶ πᾶσιν τοῖς ὑπάρχουσιν αὐτοῦ καταστήσει
αὐτοῦ with Mt 25:21 ἐπὶ πολλῶν σε καταστήσω./1/

/1/ Lk 19:17 has ἴσθι ἐξουσίαν ἔχων ἐπάνω δέκα πόλεων, a form
reflecting the distinctive emphasis of his parable of the pounds
on the king and his citizens. See below for further discussion.

A small additional point emerges from our discussion in
chapter 1: it was proposed there that the original opening of
the parable of the talents may have spoken of the master giving
his servants τὴν οὐσίαν αὐτοῦ. Matthew, however, has τὰ
ὑπάρχοντα αὐτοῦ. This Matthean alteration, if it is such,
would be especially well-explained if in the pre-synoptic
tradition the parable of the talents was immediately preceded
by the related parable of the steward with its reference to
τοῖς ὑπάρχουσιν αὐτοῦ. Matthew's substitute for Mark's phrase
was ready to hand.

5.1.4. Luke's evidence and his parable of the disobedient servants

Luke does not have the parable of the talents following
the parable of the steward. But he does have some curiously
similar sayings in precisely the right place: 'That servant
who knew his master's will and did not prepare or do his will
will be beaten with many stripes ... '(Lk 12:47). This
description is very reminiscent of the description of the
unfaithful servant in the parable of the talents who knew his
master's will and who was punished for his disobedience.
Lk 12:48 continues to speak of the servant who did not know, who
will receive few stripes, and then Luke has his saying παντὶ δὲ
ᾧ ἐδόθη πολύ, πολὺ ζητηθήσεται παρ' αὐτοῦ, καὶ ᾧ παρέθεντο
πολύ, περισσότερον αἰτήσουσιν αὐτόν. This saying is
reminiscent of the parable of the talents with its
differentiation of the amount given to and earned by the
different servants (contrast Luke's parable of the pounds where
each is given the same amount); it is also reminiscent of,
though not identical with,/1/ the comment in the parable of the
talents τῷ γὰρ ἔχοντι παντὶ δοθήσεται καὶ περισσευθήσεται. τοῦ
δὲ μὴ ἔχοντος καὶ ὃ ἔχει ἀρθήσεται ἀπ' αὐτοῦ (Mt 25:29
cf. Lk 19:26).

These similarities are striking and can hardly be thought
accidental, especially when the preceding arguments about the
pre-synoptic tradition known to Matthew and Luke are recalled.

/1/ The parable of the unfaithful servants has a distinctive
emphasis on the question of knowing/not knowing. Cf. P.
Fiedler, *Bibel und Leben* 11 (1970) 272.

Matthew has: watchman   Luke has: watchmen
               thief   thief
               steward   steward
               (virgins)
               talents   disobedient servants

How are the similarities to be explained? One possibility is
that Luke has retained the original pre-synoptic form and that
Matthew, recognizing the similarity of the parable of the
talents and of the parable of the disobedient servants located
the parable of the talents here: but this then leaves us
entirely in the dark about the original location of the parable.
Another possibility is that Luke knew the parable of the talents
here and for some reason substituted his parable of the
disobedient servants for it; but it is not obvious why Luke
should have wished to make such a substitution, and it seems out
of keeping with his conservative editing in this section. The
third possibility, which seems in all ways preferable, is that
in the pre-synoptic source the parable of the talents was
followed by the parable of the disobedient servants. The latter
parable makes good sense understood thus, picking up and
developing a point from the preceding parable. It is perhaps a
debatable point as to whether what we have called the parable of
the disobedient servants is in fact a parable in its own right,
or whether it is a sort of supplement to the parable of the
talents. But it is a distinct unit of tradition and it may be
regarded as a sort of mini-parable (not entirely dissimilar from
the preceding parable of the thief). In any case it fits even
better after the parable of the talents than it does
immediately after the parable of the steward, where Luke has it:
it is true that there is a verbal link between Lk 12:46 and 47
in the phrase 'that servant', but Luke could have made this link,
and there are other links with the parable of the talents. In
addition to those already noted above, it may be suggested that
the comment in Lk 12:47 about the servant 'not preparing' sounds
more like the parable of the talents than that of the steward.

On the hypothesis proposed Matthew has omitted the parable
of the disobedient servants, which is not very remarkable in
view of what was said about the parable seeming a sort of
supplementary 'mini-parable'; and Luke has omitted the parable
of the talents. Why he did so can only be guessed: it is
possible that his entirely predictable omission of the
immediately preceding exhortation (of Mt 24:13) led on to the
omission of what followed (though that did not happen in the

case of his omission of Mk 13:37). It may more simply be that
Luke did not wish to include a long parable, such as the
talents, here. It may be that Luke already had it in mind to
put his parable of the pounds in the context of the end of
Jesus' ministry - note the distinctive introduction to that
parable in 19:11 - and that he therefore decided to omit the
similar parable of the talents here. Whatever the reason,
there is nothing very hard about the idea that Luke knew and
omitted the parable in his chapter 12, and the hypothesis that
he knew a pre-synoptic tradition containing the parable of the
talents and the parable of the unfaithful servants is probable.

5.1.5. Conclusion
Although the evidence is not decisive, the few strands of
evidence considered add up to a strong case for the parable of
the talents being part of the pre-synoptic tradition.

5.2. The wording of the parable in the pre-synoptic tradition

If the talents was in the pre-synoptic tradition, is it
possible to say anything about the probable pre-synoptic
wording? This is not of crucial importance for the thesis
being propounded, but is at least of interest.

5.2.1. The Lukan parable of the pounds
The first and obvious thing to be said is that much will
depend on whether the Lukan parable of the pounds is considered
to be a version of the parable of the talents or a separate but
similar parable. This question cannot be fully explored here,
but the issues may be briefly summarized. The main
similarities and differences between the Lukan and Matthean
parables are these: (a) At the beginning (Lk 19:11-12), at the
end (19:27) and at one point in between (19:14,15a) Luke has
material that is without parallel in Matthew; these verses
describe a nobleman going to get a kingdom for himself and the
objections of his subjects to his rule. (b) When that material
is taken out, what is left in Luke is very similar to the
Matthean parable in substance and even in some of the wording:
servants are called and given money to trade with; they are
called to account; two of them have traded well and are
rewarded by being given greater responsibility; one of them has
done nothing, and complains of his master's harshness; he is
condemned with his own words, and his money is taken and given
to the faithful one with 10 talents/pounds; and the explanation
given in both the Matthean and Lukan parables is:'To everyone who

has will be given; from him who has not will be taken even what
he has.' (c) Within that similar material there are some
differences between Matthew and Luke: (i) In Matthew three
servants are given 5, 2 and 1 talents respectively, and when
the master returns they have 10, 4 and 1 talent respectively;
in Luke ten servants are given 1 mina each; but when the
master returns and the accounting takes place, only three
servants are mentioned who now have 10, 5 and 1 minas
respectively. (ii) In Matthew the faithful servants are
rewarded with the words: 'You have been faithful over few
things; I will appoint you over many things. Enter the joy of
your Lord.' In Luke the promise is: 'You were faithful in
very little; have authority over 10/15 cities.' (iii) In
Matthew the unfaithful servant digs a hole for his one talent
in the ground; in Luke he wraps it in a cloth. (iv) In Matthew
the unworthy servant is cast out into outer darkness. Luke has
no equivalent of this; but at the comparable point in the
parable he has the description of the killing of the king's
enemies.

Faced with this evidence, some scholars note the
differences and consider that the Matthean and Lukan parables
are two distinct, but similar, parables. And there is
certainly no reason why Jesus should not have used variations
on a common theme on different occasions./1/ Other scholars
believe that the parables have a common original and that they
have been transmitted differently by the two evangelists; an
obvious possibility is that Luke has elaborated an original
parable of a master and his servants with material about a
nobleman going to get a kingdom. The fact that the non-
Matthean material in the Lukan parable of the pounds can (for
the most part) be so easily separated off from the Matthean
material, and that the Lukan parable starts with ten servants
but then refers only to three are among the points that favour
this second view. A variation of this point of view is the
suggestion that Luke has merged together two originally
separate parables - a parable of the pretender to the throne
(the title employed by M. Zerwick in an interesting and

/1/ If the Matthean and Lukan contexts of their respective
parables are thought original, then Jesus gave two very similar
parables to much the same audience within a short space of
time.

persuasive article/1/) and the parable of the talents. It is
possible that Luke, having for some reason omitted the parable
of the talents in his chapter 12, wished to incorporate it
later and so put it here, though that would not in itself
explain why he conflated the two parables. Perhaps he
conflated them because they were both parables comparing Jesus
to someone going away on a long journey and returning to settle
accounts, and because he considered that the teaching of both
could be conveniently expressed through one composite parable.
Perhaps he considered the parable of the pretender to the
throne to be by itself a rather negative and incomplete
description of Jesus and his return.

The choice between these explanations will depend on
various considerations, not least on one's estimate of Luke's
editorial technique elsewhere. Would he have performed the
rather curious operation of welding one parable on to the
other? Later in this study evidence will be forthcoming which
suggests that Luke is conservative in preserving the contents
of his traditions, but that he sits quite lightly to the
original context of these traditions and that he does make some
perhaps surprising connexions. (For example, it will be argued
that the parables of Lk 12:35-48 belong properly in the
eschatological discourse, but Luke has used them out of
context.) This conclusion would tend to favour the view that
Luke has merged two parables./2/ However, at this stage in the
argument, that view can only·be considered one of several
possibilities, and too much cannot therefore be built on a
comparison of Matthew's and Luke's wording./3/

/1/ Zerwick, 'Die Parabel vom Thronanwärter', *Biblica* 40 (1959)
654-74. Others who consider that Luke (or his source) has
merged two parables include Jeremias, *Parables*, 59 and Weiser,
Knechtsgleichnisse, 227.
/2/ P. Fiedler, *Bibel und Leben* 11 (1970) 267, cannot envisage
a Sitz im Leben for the postulated parable of the pretender to
the throne. But if it is possible that Jesus spoke (a) of his
own going and returning, (b) of the destruction of Jerusalem,
there is no difficulty in envisaging a Sitz im Leben in Jesus'
ministry.
/3/ For detailed comparison of the Matthean and Lukan parables,
see S. Schultz, *Q Die Spruchquelle der Evangelisten* (Zürich:
Theologischer, 1972) 288-93, Weiser, *Knechtsgleichnisse*, 226-
258, Marshall, *Luke* 701-709, Lambrecht, *Parables of Jesus*
(Bangalore: Theological Publications in India, 1978) 243-64.

5.2.2. Other evidence

Even without building much on the evidence of Luke, it is possible to reach some tentative conclusions about the pre-synoptic wording of the parable on the basis of evidence noted earlier.

(a) The opening of the parable. Compare

Mt 25:14,15	Mk 13:34	Lk 19:12,13
ὥσπερ γὰρ ἄνθρωπος ἀποδημῶν ἐκάλεσεν τοὺς ἰδίους δούλους καὶ παρέδωκεν αὐτοῖς τὰ ὑπάρχοντα αὐτοῦ. 15. καὶ ᾧ μὲν ἔδωκεν πέντε τάλαντα, ᾧ δὲ δύο, ᾧ δὲ ἕν, ἑκάστῳ κατὰ τὴν ἰδίαν δύναμιν....	ὡς ἄνθρωπος ἀπόδημος ἀφεὶς τὴν οἰκίαν αὐτοῦ καὶ δοὺς τοῖς δούλοις αὐτοῦ τὴν ἐξουσίαν, ἑκάστῳ τὸ ἔργον αὐτοῦ....	ἄνθρωπός τις εὐγενὴς ἐπορεύθη εἰς χώραν μακρὰν λαβεῖν ἑαυτῷ βασιλείαν καὶ ὑποστρέψαι. 13 καλέσας δὲ δέκα δούλους ἑαυτοῦ ἔδωκεν αὐτοῖς δέκα μνᾶς....

The Matthean and Markan texts were discussed at some length in chapter 1, and it seems probable that the pre-synoptic form of the parable is reflected in Matthew and Mark. The most interesting suggestion to emerge was the idea that the pre-synoptic parable may have spoken of the master giving his servants τὴν οὐσίαν αὐτοῦ, which Matthew, perhaps under the influence of the preceding parable of the steward, rendered τὰ ὑπάρχοντα αὐτοῦ. If this suggestion is correct, then Luke's 'ten minas' of 19:13 was not part of the parable of the talents. Furthermore if the original parable did describe a man dividing up his whole estate, then the large amounts of money described in Matthew make sense (the Matthean talent being far more valuable than the Lukan mina), as does the giving of differing amounts of money to the different servants, since a man sharing out his whole estate might be expected to apportion it to his servants κατὰ τὴν ἰδίαν δύναμιν (so Mt 25:15) rather than to give equal amounts to many servants (as in the Lukan parable). These considerations suggest that Matthew has retained the original shape of the parable of the talents, and that Luke has either modified it or is using a different tradition./1/

/1/ Luke may have known a parable of the pretender to the throne, which described the pretender giving ten minas to the servants. His merging of such a parable with the parable of the talents would be the more easily intelligible.

Where Matthew has τὰ ὑπάρχοντα αὐτοῦ,(15) καὶ ᾧ μὲν ἔδωκεν πέντε τάλαντα, ᾧ δὲ δύο, ᾧ δὲ ἕν, ἑκάστῳ κατὰ τὴν ἰδίαν δύναμιν, Mark has τὴν ἐξουσίαν ἑκάστῳ τὸ ἔργον αὐτοῦ. Did Mark know a version of the parable that read τὴν οὐσίαν αὐτοῦ, ἑκάστῳ ....? If so, did his version suggest that 'each' was given the same amount? This does not follow. Mark may have known something like Matthew's v 15, but he omits the references to the giving of amounts to each servant because it does not suit his purpose. Or Mark could have known a version reading τὴν οὐσίαν αὐτοῦ, ἑκάστῳ κατὰ τὴν ἰδίαν δύναμιν· ᾧ μὲν ἔδωκεν πέντε.... Had Mark known such a wording with the expressions τὴν οὐσίαν and κατὰ τὴν ἰδίαν δύναμιν in immediate proximity to each other, his substituting of the word ἐξουσίαν might be the more easily explicable. But Matthew's reordering of the phrases would then need to be explained.

If Luke is using the same tradition as Matthew, then he supports Matthew against Mark in his omission of the phrase ἀφεὶς τὴν οἰκίαν αὐτοῦ (which we in any case recognized as possibly Markan. See p. 42 above) and in referring to the servants being 'called by the master', as well as in the use of the aorist (παρ) ἔδωκεν . Even without the Lukan evidence it would be a reasonable surmise that Matthew's form of words was more original than Mark's; e.g. in the opening ὥσπερ for ὡς and in ἀποδημῶν for ἀπόδημος (cf. Luke's ἐπορεύθη εἰς χώραν μακράν) and then in what follows:

(b) The rewards of the servants

Matthew has the master congratulate the faithful servants with the words 'You have been faithful over few things, I will set you over many', whereas Luke has 'You have been faithful over very little, have authority over .. cities'. And Matthew has the wicked servant cast out into outer darkness, and where there is weeping and gnashing of teeth. Luke has no equivalent, but has the king order the execution of the rebellious citizens. There is good reason here for believing that Matthew is closer to the original parable of the talents. In the first place the rewards for faithful in his version are closely similar to the rewards in the parable of the steward, which we have seen to belong with the parable of the talents. Matthew might, of course, have assimilated the parable of the talents to that of the steward (though he has separated them by the parable of the virgins), but he might in that case have been expected to have more similar wording at least so far as the

punishment of the unfaithful servant is concerned. And in any
case - in the second place - Luke's wording in both instances
reflects his parable of the pretender to the throne, if there
was such a parable, and has little claim to be the original
form of the parable of the talents.

(c) The evidence of Lk 12:48

If the earlier argument about Luke's parable of the
disobedient servants following on from the parable of the
talents was correct, then the wording of Lk 12:48b 'From
everyone to whom much is given much will be required and from
him to whom they commit much they will demand the more' may
well be seen as picking up the thought of the parable of the
talents about the three servants being given differing amounts.
This may be further support for the Matthean form of the
parable.

5.2.3. Conclusions on the pre-synoptic wording

No attempt has been made to examine the whole of the
parable of the talents; the limited selection of evidence
looked at points to Matthew having preserved to a considerable
extent the form of the pre-synoptic parable. This conclusion
stands whether Luke's parable of the pounds is thought to be
related to Matthew's parable or not.

The pre-synoptic wording of the parables of the talents
and the disobedient servants probably included approximately:

ὥσπερ ἄνθρωπος ἀποδημῶν ἐκάλεσεν τοὺς δούλους αὐτοῦ καὶ
ἔδωκεν αὐτοῖς τὴν οὐσίαν αὐτοῦ. καὶ ᾧ μὲν ἔδωκεν πέντε
τάλαντα, ᾧ δὲ δύο, ᾧ δὲ ἕν, ἐκάστῳ κατὰ τὴν ἰδίαν
δύναμιν.....

.... ἔφη αὐτῷ ὁ κύριος αὐτοῦ, εὖ, δοῦλε ἀγαθὲ καὶ πιστέ,
ἐπὶ ὀλίγα ἧς πιστός (or ἐν ἐλαχίστῳ πιστὸς ἐγένου) ἐπὶ
πολλῶν σε καταστήσω ....

τῷ γὰρ ἔχοντι παντὶ δοθήσεται καὶ περισσευθήσεται.
τοῦ δὲ μὴ ἔχοντος καὶ ὃ ἔχει ἀρθήσεται ἀπ'αὐτοῦ ......

ἐκεῖνος δὲ ὁ δοῦλος ὁ γνοὺς τὸ θέλημα τοῦ κυρίου
αὐτοῦ καὶ μὴ ἑτοιμάσας ἢ ποιήσας πρὸς τὸ θέλημα αὐτοῦ
δαρήσεται πολλάς· ὁ δὲ μὴ γνούς, ποιήσας δὲ ἄξια πληγῶν,
δαρήσεται ὀλίγας. παντὶ δὲ ᾧ ἐδόθη πολύ, πολὺ ζητηθήσεται
παρ' αὐτοῦ, καὶ ᾧ παρέθεντο πολύ, περισσότερον αἰτήσουσιν
αὐτόν.

6. *THE PARABLE OF THE VIRGINS AND LK 12:35*

6.1. *Introduction*

The argument so far has pointed to a pre-synoptic parable collection containing the following elements:

1. Parable of watchman

2.   "   " thief

3.   "   " steward

4.   "   " talents

5.   "   " disobedient servants

Matthew shows knowledge of the first four parables; Luke in his chapter 12 has all the parables, except the talents. The probability is that both evangelists knew all five parables together in their tradition.

But both Matthew and Luke have additional material: Matthew has the parable about the wise and foolish virgins with their lamps between the parable of the steward and that of the talents. Luke has the saying of 12:35 'Let your loins be girded and your lamps burning' at the very start of the parabolic section (before the parable of the watchman). The remarkable thing about these Matthean and Lukan additions is that the additional material in both gospels speaks of 'lamps burning'. This could be accidental; but in view of the close connections between the relevant Matthean and Lukan sections this seems unlikely.

It is true that Matthew and Luke have their 'lamp' sayings differently placed in their respective sections; but it has already been suggested that Matthew's parable of the virgins is misplaced in Matthew and indeed that it interrupts the sequence between the parable of the steward and the original conclusion to that parable, i.e. Mt 25:13. The hypothesis, then, that suggests itself is that Luke has the more original order and that the Matthean parable of the virgins belonged originally at the start of this parable section, where it preceded the parable of the watchman; Matthew will then have moved it into its present location within his gospel. This hypothesis is immediately appealing (a) because it fits in with the observations about the parable of the virgins being an interpolation in its present Matthean context and (b) because

it means that all the Matthean and Lukan parabolic material
(including the parable of the virgins) is explicable from the
pre-synoptic parable collection. It is as though the last
piece of the jig-saw has been fitted in. But to say that may
be prematurely optimistic, since there are several difficult
questions involved in the hypothesis which need answering.

6.2. The Matthean and Lukan pictures the same?

First, there are several possible objections to
the suggestion that the Matthean parable and the Lukan saying
should be associated.

6.2.1. The wakefulness of Lk 12:35 incompatible with the with the sleep of the virgins?

In the first place it can be argued that the reference to
'girded loins and lighted lamps' in Lk 12:35 suggests people
staying awake, and that the saying therefore fits the parable
of the watchman better than the parable of the virgins, where
the wise as well as the foolish fall asleep. But this point is
hardly substantial. The girded loins and burning lamps in fact
fit the parable of the virgins well: the virgins in the story
do not go to bed and lay aside their garments; rather they nod
off (νυστάζειν) because of the delay, but they are ready (they
hope) for immediate action. The wise virgins' readiness lies
in the fact that their lamps are burning (cf. Lk 12:35
καιόμενοι), whereas the foolish exclaim in alarm αἱ λαμπάδες
ἡμῶν σβέννυνται (Mt 25:8). The Lukan saying is not explicitly
a call to 'wakefulness' (contrast other similar exhortations)
any more than is the parable of the virgins, though both the
saying and the parable may, of course, be seen as calls to
spiritual wakefulness. The Lukan saying would, it is true, be
an appropriate exhortation for a watchman; and yet in the Lukan
parable of the watching servants there is nothing explicit said
about girding loins or burning lamps. The point in that
parable is about not falling asleep and about staying awake, a
point not explicit in the saying of Lk 12:35. The saying is
then less obviously connected with the parable of the watching
servant(s) than with the parable of the virgins.

Before leaving this point, it may be worth commenting
briefly on the expression 'girding up the loins'. This is
frequently taken to refer to the action of someone who is
wearing a belt and who then tucks up his cloak into his belt to
allow himself freedom of movement when doing a manual task.

This may be the sense in Lk 12:37, where the master girds
himself to wait at table. But the phrase may also and more
simply refer to the action of putting one's belt on, this being
a normal part of getting dressed at the beginning of a day's
work. Examples of this sense may be Acts 12:8 (ζῶσαι RSV
'Dress yourself') and probably Eph 6:14, where the command to
gird oneself with the belt of truth means simply - put on the
belt of truth. (For a metaphorical reference to a woman
girding herself with a belt see Prov 31:17; we are not dealing
with a purely male activity!)/1/ The injunction in Lk 12:35
'to have your loins girded' is probably to be taken in this
sense: 'the disciples must not take off their girdles and
devote themselves to the repose of the night'./2/ It is thus
very similar to the injunctions to 'keep awake' that are found
with other parables. But, given the context of the parable of
the virgins (who are not to be blamed for falling asleep),
'have your loins girded' is more appropriate than 'keep awake'.
Note that the injunction is a double one 'Let your loins be
girded and your lamps burning' - the foolish virgins
presumably were girded, but their lamps went out.

This interpretation of 'let your loins be girded' may
perhaps claim support from - and cast light on - the rather
mysterious verse in Rev 16:15 'Blessed is he who stays awake
and keeps his clothes, lest he go naked'. This passage has two
clear links with Lk 12:35-40 in the 'blessed is he who stays
awake' (cf. Lk 12:37) and in the reference to the coming of the
thief (cf. Lk 12:39); and our suggestion is that the phrase
'Blessed is he who .....keeps his clothes, lest he go naked'
could well be linked to the Lukan command to 'let your loins be
girded'. Commentators have been puzzled by the 'keeping' of
the clothes in the verse from Revelation: they have plausibly
suggested a link with Rev 3:18, but this does not fully explain
the phrase. Some commentators have drawn attention to the
practice of the Jerusalem temple captain, who apparently took
the clothes of sleeping guards and set them on fire, but this
seems a rather esoteric interpretation. More likely is the
suggestion that the picture is the familiar one (in the ancient
world) of men who have their clothes on (wrapped round them,
ready for action) - not laid aside for sleeping. (The use of

/1/ Cf. G. Dalman, *Arbeit und Sitte in Palästina* V (Hildesheim:
Georg Olms, 1964) 319.
/2/ So Lövestam, *Spiritual Wakefulness*, 94. Cf. P. Joüon, *RSR*
30 (1940) 367.

the word 'keep' is admittedly a little odd, but it is a word to
which the author of Revelation is partial, when speaking of
the saints' good conduct.) This is the sense we have proposed
for the Lukan saying about having one's loins girded, and it is
reasonable to use the Lukan and Revelation texts to illuminate
each other.

Whether or not this suggestion about Revelation is
correct, the general appropriateness of linking Lk 12:35 to the
parable of the virgins is not in question.

6.2.2.   The lamps of Lk 12:35 different from the virgins'
lamps?
A particular discrepancy between the Lukan saying and the
Matthean parable is that Luke uses the word λύχνος for lamp and
Matthew the word λαμπάς. It has been argued by J. Jeremias
that the Matthean word should be translated 'torch', and that
the picture is of long sticks with quick-burning oil-soaked
rags tied around them, which would be carried, blazing, by the
girls in the wedding procession and then in festal dances./1/
If this is correct, then there is a significant difference
between this and the Lukan word, which suggests a domestic oil
lamp. This might tell against the linking of the Matthean
parable and the Lukan saying, though it is quite possible to
suppose that one or other of the evangelists has modified the
picture slightly.

However, Jeremias' interpretation of λαμπάς in the parable
of the virgins is quite dubious. The word could by the New
Testament period be used of a lamp, not only of a torch (cf.
Dan 5:5θ, Jdt 10:22, Acts 20:8 and possibly Rev 4:5, P. Oxy.
XII, 1449, 19), and the sense of Matthew's parable makes it
probable that this was his meaning: this is suggested (a) by
the emphasis in the parable on the master's delay, which fits
the picture of oil lamps burning up their oil over a period of
hours, but not Jeremias' picture of torches that were lit at
the master's coming and that burned for a short time; (b) by
the cry of the foolish virgins 'our lamps σβέννυνται', which is
naturally taken to mean 'are going out' or 'have gone out',
whereas Jeremias has to take it as the virgins' realisation at

---

/1/ ZNW 56 (1965) 196-201. Translated in Soli Deo Gloria: New
Testament Studies in Honor of William Childs Robinson (Richmond:
John Knox, 1968) 83-87.

the time of lighting the lamps that they have not enough oil to
keep the lamps burning for all the festivities - their lamps,
they realise, 'will go out'. (Surely on Jeremias' view the
foolish might have thought of their failure to bring enough oil
while they waited and before they fell asleep!); (c) perhaps by
the reference to the virgins 'trimming' their lamps (κοσμεῖν),
which is probably better taken of adjusting lamps after a long
period of burning rather than as preparing and lighting torches
for the first time. Jeremias' view has the advantage of
offering a realistic explanation of the role of the virgins
within the pictured wedding ceremony (though the idea of the
virgins waiting with oil lamps does not seem difficult, even if
it is hard to parallel/1/); but his suggestion that the virgins
are with the bride at the start of the parable, helping her to
dress, and that their task after the bridegroom's coming is to
perform a wedding dance, rather than to participate in the
wedding feast, is without support in the text./2/

     The conclusion again is that the Lukan saying fits the
Matthean parable. The different word used for 'lamp' is a
minor matter and may reflect nothing more than different
authors' stylistic preference (though see on for further
discussion)./3/

*6.3. The relationship of the Matthean parable and the Lukan
saying*
     To show the compatibility of the Matthean parable and the
Lukan saying is not to resolve the question of their precise
relationship. If they are related, there would seem to be at

/1/ Cf. Lövestam, *Spiritual Wakefulness*, 109,110; also E.
Linnemann, *Parables of Jesus* (London: SPCK, 1966) 124,190.
/2/ On the use of the words for 'lamp' see R. H. Smith's
important article in *Biblical Archaeologist* XXIX (1966) 2-27,
in which he links Lk 12:35 and Mt 25:1-12 and in which he
interestingly suggests that λαμπάς in Rev 8:10 may have a
double meaning 'lamp' and 'torch'. Cf. also A. Oepke, *TDNT* IV,
16,17 on λαμπάς.
/3/ Weiser, *Knechtsgleichnisse*, 163, claims that the picture of
burning lamps used to illustrate the thought of keeping awake
and ready is found only in OT and NT in Lk 12:35 and Mt 25:1-
13. The rarity of this metaphorical usage may support the case
for associating the two passages, though Weiser himself finds
difficulty with the differing words used for 'lamp'.

least three possibilities: one possibility is that the parable
of the virgins is a Matthean composite parable, created out of
the Lukan exhortation and the parable of the watching
servants(s), both of which Matthew omits. But this presupposes
a complex editorial process in the middle of a section where
Matthew seems to be reproducing other traditions without
radical alteration; and in this supposed composite parable
Matthew curiously loses the idea of keeping awake, even though
this was the point of the parable of the watchman./1/ Another
possibility is that Lk 12:35 is a Lukan summary of the Matthean
parable. But it is not very obvious why Luke should have
produced such a summary (unless it was simply for brevity; but
why then did he include it at all?); the evidence of the rest
of Lk 12:35-48 points to rather conservative editing on Luke's
part in this section of his gospel.

The third and most likely possibility is that the Lukan
saying was the pre-synoptic conclusion to the parable of the
virgins. In favour of this suggestion are the following
points:

(a) It does not involve either Matthew or Luke in any
complicated editing-process; both the evangelists on the view
proposed have drawn differently on the pre-synoptic tradition.
This argument might not seem very weighty, were it not for the
fact that their editing in the rest of the parabolic material
in Matthew 24,25 and Luke 12 has been seen to be similarly
conservative.

(b) The saying of Lk 12:35 would be an eminently suitable
conclusion to the parable of the virgins similar to the
hortatory applications that probably concluded the parables of
the watchman (Mk 13:35,36) and the steward (Mt 25:13). If
the parable of the virgins did precede those parables in the
pre-synoptic tradition, we would expect it to have some sort of

---

/1/ Gundry, *Matthew*, 497-99, argues that the parable of the
virgins is a Matthean composition created out of Mk 13:33-37,
Lk 12:35-38 and Lk 13:25-28. This suggestion is implausible
for the reasons mentioned, and there are simpler explanations
of the synoptic traditions in question, as is shown elsewhere
in this chapter.

appropriate conclusion. Mt 25:13 is the present Matthean
conclusion to the parable of the virgins; but we saw reason to
suspect that it originally belonged with the parable of the
steward. In any case Lk 12:35 makes a much better conclusion
to the parable of the virgins than does Mt 25:13.

(c) To this may be added the observation that, unless Lk 12:35
is viewed as we have suggested, it is something of an odd man
out in Lk 12:35-48. It is an isolated parabolic saying in the
company of several proper parables, and it does not have a very
obvious function. Perhaps it could be seen as a lead into the
following parable of the watching servant(s); but it has
already been argued that it has less obvious connections with
the parable of the watchman than with the parable of the
virgins. Furthermore, it is not very closely linked by Luke
with what follows: his καὶ ὑμεῖς ὅμοιοι in 12:36 sounds like
the beginning of a new thought. Maybe 12:35 can be seen as an
introduction to the whole of the following section; but we
might expect a more general and less figurative introduction.
On the other hand, if the Lukan saying is recognized as a
conclusion to the parable of the virgins, it is not an oddity
in the context and its function is clear.

(d) Although Lk 12:35 seems better linked to the parable of the
virgins than to the parable of the watchman, our proposal
would mean that it came originally between the two parables.
In that position it will have served - like the Markan
conclusion to the parable of the watchman which led on very
well into the parable of the thief - as a conclusion to the one
parable and as a preparation for the following parable.

It has been seen already how the parables we have been
discussing were closely connected with each other in the pre-
synoptic source. For example, the parable of the steward leads
well into the talents which leads well into the unfaithful
servants. This would also be the case if the parable of the
virgins preceded that of the watching servant(s): both are
parables about people waiting at night for their 'lord' to come
and both have a possible 'wedding' connexion./1/ The two
parables fit eminently well together with the saying of
Lk 12:35 in between.

/1/ γάμοι in Lk 12:36 is ambiguous, and could mean simply
'feast'.

All of this evidence is not of equal weight. But the
cumulative weight of the arguments in favour of viewing
Lk 12:35 as a conclusion to the parable of the virgins is such
as to make the case probable. The one thing still needing to
be explained is why Matthew and especially Luke used the pre-
synoptic tradition in the way suggested.

6.4. Matthew's divergences from the pre-synoptic tradition

Matthew on the hypothesis proposed moved the parable of
the virgins from its pre-synoptic location before the parable
of the watchman to its present Matthean position after the
parable of the steward. In the process he dropped the pre-
synoptic conclusion to the parable of the virgins (i.e. the
saying of Lk 12:35).

6.4.1. Matthew's omission of the saying of Lk 12:35
This last omission is not altogether surprising, since
Matthew has inserted the parable into the tradition
immediately before the exhortation of Mt 25:13. Had he
retained the saying of Lk 12:35 at the end of the parable of
the virgins, he would either have had to omit Mt 25:13 (which
led into the following parable) or he would have had the two
exhortations of Lk 12:35 and Mt 25:13 side by side. He opts
instead for omitting the saying of Lk 12:35.

6.4.2. Matthew's removal and relocation of the parable of virgins
More mysterious than this is his removal of the parable of
the virgins from its original context. Why did he omit the
parable from a context where it fitted well and insert it in a
seemingly less satisfactory context later? It is impossible to
answer this question with certainty. But four observations
can be made:

(a) His omission of the parable of the virgins at the
beginning of the section is not an isolated phenomenon, since
we have already argued for his knowledge and omission of the
parable of the watchman from the same context. It is not, then,
altogether surprising to find the immediately adjacent and
thematically similar parable of the virgins omitted too.

(b) It may be that Matthew's omission has something to do
with the emphasis on 'not knowing' the time of the second
coming that runs through Mt 24:36-25:13. Thus we find in 24:36
'Of that day and hour knows no one'; 24:39 'And they did not

know until the flood came' (Note that in the Lukan parallel the
words 'they did not know' are not found - Lk 17:27.); 24:42 'You
do not know in what day ...'; 24:43,44 'If the householder had
known ... in the hour you do not think ....'; 24:50 'the lord of
that servant will come in a day he does not expect and an hour
he does not know'; 25:13 'you do not know the day nor the
hour'./1/ To recognize that this theme runs strongly through
this Matthean section does not necessarily explain Matthew's
omission of the parable of the virgins, since that is after all
thematically similar and Matthew in any case includes the
parable towards the end of the section. However, note: (i) the
parable of the virgins does not bring out explicitly the thought
of 'not knowing', and its probable hortatory conclusion
(i.e. Lk 12:35) does not spell out the thought. Matthew may
therefore have decided to skip the parable and that of the
watchman in order to get on to a saying explicitly on the theme,
i.e. his v 42. The theme is certainly very strong in vv 42-44.
(ii) It is true that Matthew later decides to include the
parable of the virgins; but it may be significant that he
includes it between the parable of the steward and its
conclusion (about not knowing the day or the hour) and that he
omits the original conclusion to the parable of the virgins. By
making these changes to the pre-synoptic order and form Matthew
could perhaps intend to make more explicit the 'not knowing'
theme.

(c) A different possibility is suggested when it is
observed that the effect of Matthew's relocation of the parable
of the virgins is that he has three parables that speak of the
delay of the parousia together: the parables of the steward and
of the virgins both speak similarly of the returning master
delaying (cf. Mt 24:48 and 25:5), and the parable of the talents
also speaks of the master going away for 'a long time' (25:19).
It is possible that Matthew's omission of the virgins from the
pre-synoptic context was due to a deliberate desire to have
these parables grouped together: Matthew focuses first on the
theme of the unknownness of the hour (e.g. the parable of the
thief), but then, alongside that thought, he introduces the idea
of the master's long delay./2/

/1/ I am indebted to Dr Craig Blomberg for drawing my attention
to these connections.
/2/ I am grateful to Mr John Sherriff for alerting me to this
point. Note that, if Matthew's interest in this section of his
gospel was particularly in (a) the unknownness of the time of

(d) A less likely possibility is that Matthew is
developing a deliberate 'day-hour' pattern in the section
24:36-25:13: at each end the thought is about not knowing 'the
day and/or the hour' (24:36, 24:50 and 25:13), and in between
there is one saying about not knowing 'the day' (24:42) and
another about not knowing 'the hour' (24:44). If this
arrangement (day/hour, day, hour, day/hour) is deliberate, then
Matthew's omission of the nocturnal parables of the virgins and
the watchman and his rewording of v 42 could be the consequences
of this; but v 42 can be otherwise explained, and Matthew's
φυλακῇ in his v 43 perhaps indicates that he is not trying to
bring out the thought of the 'hour' here.

Whether Matthew moved the parable of the virgins from its
pre-synoptic position for any of the reasons proposed is not
certain. Perhaps the explanation is much more mundane: Matthew
might, for example, have wanted to abbreviate his source, but
then have thought better of his omission of the parable of the
virgins. In any case there are several possible explanations,
and the suggestion that Matthew did move the parable in the
way suggested is not difficult.

6.5. *Luke's use of the pre-synoptic tradition*

Luke's editing is at first sight more mysterious than
Matthew's, since, although he does not move or alter anything
substantially on the hypothesis suggested, he does omit the
parable of the virgins, while retaining its conclusion and using
that to introduce the following section of material. Why does
he do so? It should not be supposed that we will always be able
to fathom the mind of an ancient author, nor that we need do so;
but it would clearly strengthen the hypothesis if some
plausible explanation of Luke's editing can be offered.

The key to such an explanation is probably the preceding
context in Luke 12, where the injunction to 'make for
yourselves purses that do not grow old, unfailing treasure in
heaven, where thief does not come near nor moth destroy...' is
found (12:33). One possibility is that this parabolic
exhortation to prepare now for the future caused Luke to recall

the parousia and (b) the master's long absence, this may help
explain his omission both of the dialogue 'Do you say this
parable to us or to all? Etc.' and of the parable of the
disobedient servants; neither tradition illustrated the points
that concerned Matthew.

another parabolic exhortation 'Let your loins be girded and
your lamps burning'; so he picked up the eschatological
tradition we have been considering at that point - after the
parable of the virgins./1/ This suggestion would fit in with
the widely held view (for which we shall see further arguments
later) that the so-called Lukan travel narrative is in part at
least a Lukan compilation of miscellaneous teaching of Jesus.

    But there is another possible explanation of Luke's
editing at this point, also arising out of the preceding
context. The material there about laying up treasure in heaven
has a parallel in Matthew's Sermon on the Mount; indeed the
whole of the preceding section from Lk 12:22-34 (on the subject
of earthly cares and riches) has a parallel in Matthew 6.
There are many verbal differences between the Matthean and
Lukan parallels, but substantially Matthew and Luke are very
close, and the probability is that we have the same material
here. One possibility is that Jesus himself used the same
material twice; the other possibility is that we have one
tradition of Jesus used differently by the evangelists./2/
Whichever possibility is correct, the striking thing is that in
Matthew 6 the saying about laying up treasure is followed
immediately by a saying about a lamp; and it seems very
possible that this is the clue to Luke's use of 12:35.

    We may compare

Mt 6:21 ὅπου γάρ ἐστιν   and Lk 12:34 ὅπου γάρ ἐστιν
         ὁ θησαυρός σου,   ὁ θησαυρὸς ὑμῶν,
         ἐκεῖ ἔσται καὶ   ἐκεῖ καὶ
         ἡ καρδία σου.   ἡ καρδία ὑμῶν ἔσται.

    22   ὁ λύχνος τοῦ   35   ἔστωσαν ὑμῶν
         σώματός ἐστιν ὁ...   αἱ ὀσφύες.
                                              περιεζωσμέναι καὶ
                                              οἱ λύχνοι καιόμενοι.

/1/ We should probably make nothing of the occurrence of the
word 'thief' in both the 'laying up treasure' saying and in the
following eschatological material (the thief in the night
saying), though this could conceivably have encouraged the
association of the two passages.
/2/ Perhaps Luke was prompted to place the material here by the
immediately preceding parable of the rich fool.

A first reaction may be that the agreement of Matthew and
Luke in having a 'lamp' saying immediately after the 'treasure'
saying is probably a curious coincidence, especially as the
'lamp' sayings in the two gospels are so different. However,
we believe that their agreement in this may be the key to
several matters. We suggest that Luke was using a tradition
like, or the same as Matthew 6, in which the treasure saying
was followed by the saying about the lamp of the body
(cf. Mt 6:20-22); but when he came to this lamp saying, he
declined to reproduce it, having already used it, or something
very like it, in 11:34 in connection with other lamp sayings. He
therefore broke off from the tradition he was using at this
point, and his mind went over to a different 'lamp' saying,
i.e. the exhortation to keep 'your lamps burning' from the end
of the parable of the virgins, which happened to fit in quite
well with the preceding theme of the treasure saying.

The strength of this apparently rather speculative
suggestion is that it helps explain not only (a) Luke's
omission of the parable of the virgins, but retention of its
conclusion (the conclusion being the link to the preceding
treasure tradition), but also (b) Luke's location of the
eschatological traditions of 12:35-48 at this particular point
in his gospel, and perhaps also (c) Luke's use of λύχνος
instead of λαμπάς, the word which Matthew uses for 'lamp' in
the parable of the virgins. If the original conclusion of the
parable urged that λαμπάδες be kept burning, then Luke might
well have altered this under the influence of the saying
attested in Mt 6:22, where the word for 'lamp' is λύχνος./1/
(On the other hand, if the original wording in the parable and
in its following saying - or even only in the following saying
- was λύχνος, then it is that much easier to see how Luke might
have jumped from one lamp saying [i.e. the lamp of the body
saying] to the other lamp saying [i.e. the keep lamps burning
saying].)

/1/ R. Bauckham, *NTS* 29 (1983) 131-32, notes that Epiphanius
Haer. LXIX. xliv. 1 reads αἱ ὀσφύες ὑμῶν περιεζωσμέναι, καὶ αἱ
λαμπάδες ὑμῶν ἐν ταῖς χερσὶν ὑμῶν, and considers that
Epiphanius may have had access to tradition independent of the
synoptics.

The preceding argument about the two lamp sayings gives
a plausible solution to the one remaining problem with the view
that Lk 12:35 be considered the pre-synoptic conclusion to the
parable of the virgins. It also tells in favour of the view
that the Lukan verse be explained in that way, rather than as a
Lukan summary of the parable: for Luke to jump from the one
tradition to the other and at the same time to summarize and
paraphrase the second tradition would be a much more
complicated operation than for him to transfer simply from the
one tradition to the other.

*6.6. Conclusion on the place of the parable of the virgins and
Lk 12:35 within the pre-synoptic tradition*

The conclusion of a rather complicated argument is not
complicated: Matthew's parable of the virgins probably belonged
in the pre-synoptic tradition (before the parable of the
watchman), and it concluded with the saying preserved by Lk 12:35.
This hypothesis explains the similarity and differences of
Matthew and Luke, and certain of the problems in both gospels.

6.7. Possible confirmation from Paul

It has already been suggested that Paul could show his
knowledge of the parable of the thief and perhaps of the
parable of the watchman in 1 Thessalonians 5. In the
immediately preceding verses there are possible echoes of the
parable of the virgins: (a) In 1 Thess 4:14 Paul speaks of God
'bringing with him' (σὺν αὐτῷ) those who have fallen asleep
with Jesus. And in 1 Thess 4:17 it said that we shall all be
'with him'. The picture is not unlike that of the parable of
the virgins, where the wise go into the marriage μετ'αὐτοῦ./1/
(b) the 'shout of command' and the 'voice of the archangel'
(1 Thess 4:16) are a little reminiscent of the 'cry' in the
parable of the virgins - 'Behold the bridegroom, come out to
meet him' (Mt 25:6); (c) the phrase εἰς ἀπάντησιν is found in
1 Thess 4:17 and Mt 25:6 and only twice elsewhere in the NT
(though it is common enough in the Septuagint)./2/

_____

/1/ Cf. also Rev 3:20.
/2/ Cf. J. B. Orchard, *Biblica* 19 (1938) 19-42.

The occurrence of these three possible echoes of the
parable of the virgins in three verses of 1 Thessalonians may
be significant. W. Schenk in an interesting article has argued
that Paul is drawing on a version of the parable of the virgins
to answer the Thessalonians' anxieties about Christians who
have died before the parousia. He maintains that this version
described five virgins falling asleep (representing the dead)
and five staying awake (representing the living); but it had all
ten virgins entering the feast at the bridegroom's coming./1/
The parable, as reconstructed by Schenk, would very directly
have answered the Thessalonians' problem. But his
reconstruction is improbable: it means that the original
parable had no note of judgment and division, though this is so
typical of the eschatological parables; it involves Matthew in
very radical redaction, though in other parables in Matthew 24
and 25 he appears quite conservative; it also builds on the
assumption that Matthew has drawn on the saying of Lk 13:25 in
the parable, whereas it is more likely that Luke is the
dependent one. (On this see below.)

However, although his reconstruction of the original
parable is unlikely, his suggestion that Paul may be drawing on
the parable of the virgins remains feasible. Paul could very
well have known the parable in approximately its Matthean form
and have seen the five wise virgins, who 'fell asleep' and who
then 'arose' (ἠγέρθησαν) and went into the wedding feast 'with
him', as helping to provide an answer to the Thessalonians'
worries about believers who had 'fallen asleep'. Paul assures
the Thessalonians that their dead will rise (ἀναστήσονται) and
that God will bring them 'with him', i.e. with Christ. If this
hypothesis is correct, then it may be at least a partial
solution to the much debated problem of the 'word of the Lord'
in 1 Thess 4:15: Paul is here referring to a tradition of the
sayings of Jesus (cf. 1 Cor 7:25; also 7:10,12; 11:23, 15:2),
not to a word of Christian prophecy; but he is expounding the
tradition freely rather than quoting it verbatim./2/

/1/ *NovT* 20 (1978) 278-299.
/2/ For further discussion of this text see my 'Paul and the
Synoptic Apocalypse', pp. 367,368, though I do not there bring
out the suggestion concerning the parable of the virgins.
Probably Paul was drawing on several traditions in
1 Thess 4:15-18, including Mt 24:30,31 and parallels,
but especially the parable of the virgins.

To find these possible echoes of the parable of the
virgins in close proximity to the possible echoes of the
parables of the thief and of the watchman is interesting and
may be seen as supporting the view that the parable of the
virgins was in the pre-synoptic tradition. But it must be said
that the echoes are not very striking, and it would be unwise
to build much on this evidence.

*6.8. The pre-synoptic wording of the parable and the evidence
of Lk 13:25*

If the hypothesis proposed is correct, then the
probability must be that Matthew has preserved the pre-synoptic
form of the parable of the virgins, since he has been seen to
be a generally conservative editor in the parabolic material in
question. One possible complication with this assumption is
the possibly related saying of Lk 13:25 ἀφ' οὗ ἂν ἐγερθῇ ὁ
οἰκοδεσπότης καὶ ἀποκλείσῃ τὴν θύραν, καὶ ἄρξησθε ἔξω ἑστάναι
καὶ κρούειν τὴν θύραν λέγοντες· κύριε, ἄνοιξον ἡμῖν, καὶ
ἀποκριθεὶς ἐρεῖ ὑμῖν· οὐκ οἶδα ὑμᾶς πόθεν ἐστέ.

Some have considered that this Lukan saying lies behind
Matthew's parable. But it seems more probable that we have in
Luke a fragment/echo of the parable of the virgins inserted
into his context than that Luke has the more original form of
the saying and that Matthew has incorporated it into his
parable. This is suggested by a number of things, e.g. (a) by
the fact that Lk 13:25 is a rather obscure parabolic allusion as
it stands: who is the 'master' who is suddenly referred to?
Where does he get up from? What does the 'door' lead to?;
(b) by the slight incongruities of sequence between v 25 and
the preceding and following verses: v 24 suggests, at first
sight, that one must struggle through the door because it is
narrow, but v 25 suggests that the problem (admittedly not
necessarily unrelated!) is that the door will soon be shut.
V 25 speaks of a 'master' of a house, and v 26 of one who taught
'in our streets'; (c) by the comparison of Lk 13:23-27 with
the similar, but different, Mt 7:13,14 and 21-23.

Cf. also Hartman, *Prophecy Interpreted,* 181-90 and R.F. Collins
in J. Lambrecht, *L'Apocalypse johannique et l'Apocalyptique
dans le Nouveau Testament* (Gembloux: Duculot, 1980) 331,332.

Compare Mt 7:13,14,21-23   and Lk 13:23-27

13. εἰσέλθατε διὰ τῆς
στενῆς πύλης· ὅτι πλατεῖα
ἡ πύλη καὶ εὐρύχωρος ἡ
ὁδὸς ἡ ἀπάγουσα εἰς τὴν
ἀπώλειαν, καὶ πολλοί εἰσιν
οἱ εἰσερχόμενοι δι'αὐτῆς
14. ὅτι στενὴ ἡ πύλη καὶ
τεθλιμμένη ἡ ὁδὸς ἡ
ἀπάγουσα εἰς τὴν ζωήν καὶ
ὀλίγοι εἰσὶν οἱ
εὑρίσκοντες αὐτήν. ...
21. οὐ πᾶς ὁ λέγων μοι κύριε
κύριε, εἰσελεύσεται εἰς τὴν
βασιλείαν τῶν οὐρανῶν, ἀλλ'
ὁ ποιῶν τὸ θέλημα τοῦ
πατρός μου τοῦ ἐν τοῖς
οὐρανοῖς. 22. πολλοί ἐροῦσίν
μοι ἐν ἐκείνῃ ἡμέρᾳ· κύριε
κύριε, οὐ τῷ σῷ ὀνόματι
ἐπροφητεύσαμεν, καὶ τῷ σῷ
ὀνόματι δαιμόνια
ἐξεβάλομεν, καὶ τῷ σῷ
ὀνόματι δυνάμεις πολλὰς
ἐποιήσαμεν; 23. καὶ τότε
ὁμολογήσω αὐτοῖς· ὅτι
οὐδέποτε ἔγνων ὑμᾶς·
ἀποχωρεῖτε ἀπ' ἐμοῦ οἱ
ἐργαζόμενοι τὴν ἀνομίαν.

23. εἶπεν δέ τις αὐτῷ· κύριε,
εἰ ὀλίγοι οἱ σῳζόμενοι; ὁ δὲ
εἶπεν πρὸς αὐτούς·
24. ἀγωνίζεσθε εἰσελθεῖν
διὰ τῆς στενῆς θύρας, ὅτι
πολλοί, λέγω ὑμῖν, ζητήσουσιν
εἰσελθεῖν καὶ οὐκ ἰσχύσουσιν.
25. ἀφ'οὗ ἂν ἐγερθῇ ὁ
οἰκοδεσπότης καὶ ἀποκλείσῃ
τὴν θύραν, καὶ ἄρξησθε ἔξω
ἑστάναι καὶ κρούειν τὴν
θύραν λέγοντες· κύριε,
ἄνοιξον ἡμῖν, καὶ ἀποκριθεὶς
ἐρεῖ ὑμῖν· οὐκ οἶδα ὑμᾶς
πόθεν ἐστέ. 26. τότε ἄρξεσθε
λέγειν· ἐφάγομεν ἐνώπιόν σου
καὶ ἐπίομεν, καὶ ἐν ταῖς
πλατείαις ἡμῶν ἐδίδαξας·
27. καὶ ἐρεῖ λέγων ὑμῖν· οὐκ
οἶδα (ὑμᾶς) πόθεν ἐστέ·
ἀπόστητε ἀπ'ἐμοῦ πάντες
ἐργάται ἀδικίας.

The probable explanation of these points is that Luke 13
and Matthew 7 reflect common traditions (whether these
traditions were used on one or more occasions). These
traditions consisted (1) of an exhortation to enter into the
narrow gate/door, pointing out that many enter the broad gate
and few the narrow gate; (2) of a saying about many seeking
entry to the kingdom – saying 'Lord, lord' and claiming
fellowship with the Lord – but being disowned by him. Luke
has conflated these two different traditions together, and
introduced into his conflated version an allusion to the
strikingly similar parable of the virgins.

More precisely, Luke's procedure was as follows: (a) In
v 24a Luke reproduces the narrow gate/door tradition: '(Strive to)
enter through the narrow door'. (b) But in v 24b he replaces
the original description of the broad and narrow gates and of
the many and few going in with his brief 'for many, I tell you,
will seek to go in and will not be able'. This phrase
expresses a subtly different thought from the more original
Matthean form: in Matthew there is no suggestion that 'many'
people seek to enter the narrow gate, being somehow thwarted;
the thought (which incidentally corresponds well to the opening
Lukan question 'Lord, are there few that are saved?') is more a
statement of fact - that many go through the broad gate and few
the narrow gate to life. The Lukan form of expression may be
simply Luke's summary paraphrase of what the longer Matthean
form adds up to, picking up especially the final Matthean
phrase 'And few there be that find it'. But it may also be
that Luke is here looking ahead to the next tradition about
entering the kingdom: 'Not everyone who says to me "Lord, lord"
will enter....many will say to me "Lord,lord"..' (Mt 7:21,22),
and that his reference to 'many seeking to go in and not being
able' is a conflation of the thought in these verses with the
thought of the few finding the way through the narrow gate to
life.

(c) Whatever the explanation of the Lukan change, he has
introduced a slight complication into his v 24: it is not clear
why the 'narrowness' of the door should stop many who want to
get in from doing so. Surely all that the narrowness of the
gate would mean is that they might have to queue! The answer
to that point, which Luke proceeds to supply in v 25, is that
the door will be shut. But this does complicate things: if
the problem is that the door is going to be shut, the width of
the door is not a very decisive factor - a wider door could
also be shut! Or, if the thought is of a crowd of genuine
seekers, queuing before the narrow gate, some of whom happen to
get into the kingdom and some who don't, depending on their
position in the queue, this is a decidedly odd and
unsatisfactory picture. The explanation of this situation, we
have suggested, is that Luke has merged the picture of the
broad and narrow gates with the quite distinct picture of a
closed door with people outside asking to come in. This
hypothesis helps explain Luke's v 25: having slipped over from
the metaphor of the narrow door to the metaphor of the door
which people cannot get through, evidently because it is shut
(e.g. having moved from the thought of Mt 7:13-14 to that of

7:21), Luke introduces an echo of the parable of the virgins in order to make explicit the point that the door is shut. The parable of the virgins came readily to mind, having the thought of a door and of people saying 'Lord, lord', but being shut out. (Perhaps it is misleading to say that Luke introduces part of the parable of the virgins into his context, if this gives the impression that he actually wishes to recall that parable. It may simply be a case of using traditional language [from that parable] for editorial purposes.)

(d) The reason for the inclusion of the echo of the parable of the virgins - to explain the thought of the closed door and of people unable to get through it - explains the form of the echo. Luke does not refer to the bridegroom, the virgins, their lamps, etc., all of which would have been peripheral to the point; instead he refers generally and briefly (and hence slightly obscurely) to 'the master' 'getting up' (a verb used of the virgins in Mt 25:7), and 'shutting the door'. That is all he needs to say. The slight grammatical oddity of the verse (notably the καί in v 25c καί ἀποκριθείς ἐρεῖ) is also explained: Luke explains the scene with the long ἀφ' οὗ clause of v 25a, and then slips into the sequence of thought and the form of words found in Mt 25:12 '"Lord, (lord), open to us;" and (Luke καί Matthew δέ) he will say to you, "I don't know you".' Luke integrates the echo of the parable of the virgins into his context by maintaining the second person (as used in his previous verse) 'You will begin to stand outside...', where Matthew has the third person of the virgins.

(e) The echo of the parable of the virgins in v 25 ends up with people saying 'Lord, lord' and being disowned by the Lord, and this leads Luke naturally back to the tradition preserved also in Matthew 7:21-23. Luke reverts to this in his v 26, using the phrase τότε ἄρξεσθε λέγειν (including his favoured word ἄρχεσθαι) as a bridge back. The exact relationship of the claims to fellowship with Jesus in Lk 6:46 and Mt 7:22 need not be explored here (though note Justin Mart. Apol. 1.16,11-12 and Dial.7b, 4-5).

(f) In v 27 Luke differs from Matthew having καί ἐρεῖ λέγων ὑμῖν οὐκ οἶδα (ὑμᾶς) πόθεν ἐστέ for Matthew's καί τότε ὁμολογήσω αὐτοῖς· ὅτι οὐδέποτε ἔγνων ὑμᾶς (7:23). This is now simply explicable as due to the influence on Luke of the similar phrase from the parable of the virgins ὁ δὲ ἀποκριθείς εἶπεν· ἀμὴν λέγω ὑμῖν, οὐκ οἶδα ὑμᾶς (Mt 25:12), a phrase

which Luke has already echoed in his v.25. Not only is the
difference between Matthew and Luke explained, but so is
(i) Luke's repetition of the phrase - he uses it once in v 25
in his echo of the parable of the virgins and again in v 27 in
his parallel to Matthew 7:23; (ii) Luke's rather odd
combination ἐρεῖ λέγων ὑμῖν, the redundant λέγων being an echo
of εἶπεν ἀμὴν λέγω ὑμῖν (Mt 25:12). (But note the strong
textual evidence for reading λέγω not λέγων in Luke, which
would only reinforce the argument.)

The hypothesis offered above leaves certain questions
unanswered: e.g. were the traditions of Mt 7:13,14 and of
7:21-23 originally immediately adjacent to each other? (Not
necessarily.) How does Lk 6:46 fit in? (Perhaps as an
allusion to the fuller Matthean form of tradition.) But its
ability to explain the peculiarities of the Lukan text and the
relationships of the Matthean and Lukan texts suggests its
probability./1/

The preceding rather extended digression into Luke 13 and
Matthew 7 suggests that Luke knew the parable of the virgins,
but that Lk 13:25 is unlikely to help us establish the pre-
synoptic wording of that parable. We are left with the
Matthean wording, and there is no good reason for supposing
that the pre-synoptic wording differed much from Matthew,
though we suppose that the pre-synoptic parable was followed
by the exhortation of Lk 12:41.

7.   THE PRE-SYNOPTIC PARABLE COLLECTION: CONCLUDING
     OBSERVATIONS

7.1. Observations about the parable collection

In chapter 1 it was argued that all three evangelists knew
a pre-synoptic form of the parable of the watching servant. In
this chapter the other parables (and allusions to parables) in
Mt 24:42-25:30, Mk 13:33-37 and Lk 12:35-48 have been examined
one by one. In each case the evidence has pointed to the
evangelists having known a pre-synoptic form of the tradition

---

/1/ For an important discussion of Lk 13:23-28, that
anticipates various of the points made above and considers
others, see P. Hoffman *ZNW* 58 (1967) 188-214. See also my
review article in *Trinity Journal* 4 (1983) forthcoming.

concerned and, even more significantly, to a pre-synoptic
collection of parables. Not all the evidence has been
equally strong; but the convergence of so many different lines
of evidence all pointing in the same direction makes for a very
strong cumulative argument.

The postulated pre-synoptic source contained:

A.   Parable of virgins   )
B.   Parable of watchman   )
C̄.   Parable of thief
     (Peter's question and Jesus' reply)

B.   Parable of steward   )
A.   Parable of talents   )
C̄.   Parable of disobedient servants

        There are several interesting observations to make about
this:

(a) The whole section consists of parousia parables, all of
which teach the need to be ready for the Lord's return at an
unknown time. But it divides into two groups of three, the
first group focusing on the unknown hour and the need for
alertness at every moment, the second group portraying a long
absence (hence the reference in the parable of the steward not
just to the unknown 'hour' but to the unknown 'day or hour') and
emphasizing the need to fulfil one's responsibilities and the
master's will.

        (b) The three parables within each group dovetail into
each other; the parable of the virgins leads well into the
parable of the watchman, and that in turn leads into the
parable of the thief; then the parable of the steward has links
with that of the talents, and the parable of the talents with
that of the disobedient servants. (For all these points see
discussion above.)

        (c) There are also links between the two groups. Both
groups (i) have a long parable about wise and foolish
servants, i.e. the virgins and the talents (A - A); (ii) have
a medium-length parable about a servant with a task, i.e. the
watchman and the steward (B - B), and these two parables have
a similar structure, including a beatitude and an ἀμήν promise
in the middle; (iii) have a small subsidiary parable with a

negative point, i.e. the thief and the disobedient servants
(C - C), both of which open with the word ἐκεῖνος, and both of
which refer to being 'prepared' (ἐτοῖμος in Mt 24:44 / Lk 12:40,
ἐτοιμάζειν in Lk 12:47).

(d) It is possible to detect a careful structure in the
whole section with the major parables of the virgins, the
watchman, the steward and the talents in a steadily developing
sequence (each parable leading on to the next) and in a
chiastic relationship (AB x BA) and with the two subsidiary
parables of the thief and the disobedient servants appended to
the end of each section.

Whether all of these observations are significant or not
is uncertain and not very important; but it is still clear that
the reconstructed form of the pre-synoptic discourse has
considerable coherence and that the different sections fit
together remarkably well. The fact that they fit together so
well could lead one to suspect that the pattern is an in
ingenious schema artificially imposed on the material,
especially as each of the evangelists has to a greater or
lesser degree lost it. However, the pattern has emerged
incidentally, one might say, from the preceding detailed
analysis; and, although the whole pattern is not attested in
any one gospel, all the postulated links are attested in at
least one gospel. Given these observations, the coherent
structure of the reconstructed pre-synoptic collection of
parables cannot but impress, and it is not unreasonable to
regard this result of our earlier analysis as probable
confirmation of that analysis.

7.2. Summary of findings in relation to each gospel

7.2.1. The pre-synoptic form
The preceding analysis suggests that the pre-synoptic
tradition included the following parables and exhortations:

1. Parable of virgins
2. Gird up loins, keep lamps burning
3. Parable of watchman
4. Keep awake, you do not know in which watch the lord
    of the house comes...
5. Parable of thief
6. So be ready
7. a Peter: to us or all?
    b Jesus: to all I say keep awake

8. Parable of steward
9. Keep awake; you do not know day/hour
10. Parable of talents
11. Parable of disobedient servants

7.2.2. Matthew's use of this tradition

If, as we suppose, Matthew knew and used the pre-synoptic
tradition, he omitted the first three sections, perhaps for
thematic reasons (see pp. 84-86 above). But he uses the
exhortation (no. 4) in his Mt 24:42, modifying it to fit his
preceding context. He then follows the pre-synoptic source,
only omitting sections 7 and 11 (quite probably for the sake of
brevity) and adding in the parable of the virgins between
sections 8 and 9.

The hypothesis provides an answer for the following
questions raised by the Matthean text: (a) How does the
parable of the virgins relate, if at all, to the saying of Lk
12:35? The answer is that the Lukan saying is the pre-synoptic
conclusion to the parable. (b) How do the sayings about
keeping awake for the lord's coming in Mt 24:42 and Mk 13:35
relate? The answer is that they both go back to a common
original, which has been modified by both evangelists. (c) How
is the slight inappropriateness of the present Matthean
conclusion to the parable of the virgins (i.e. Mt 25:13) to be
explained? The answer is that Matthew has inserted the parable
between the parable of the steward and that parable's
conclusion. (d) How do Matthew's parable of the talents and
the preceding exhortation relate to the similar sounding
Mk 13:33,34? The answer is that Mark knows something very like
the Matthean text, but he has deliberately omitted the parable
of the talents, using its opening for his own purposes.

7.2.3. Mark's use of the tradition

Essentially what Mark has done is to extract from the
original tradition the exhortations to wakefulness; apart from
that he hardly preserves anything. He begins with the
exhortation preceding the parable of the talents (i.e. no.
9 above), probably because that referred to 'not knowing the
day or hour' and so connected well with Mk 13:32 'Of that day
or hour no one knows...'; but to reduce repetitiveness he
alters 'day or hour' to 'when the moment is' in his v 33. Mark
then has an echo of the next section in the pre-synoptic
tradition (i.e. section no. 10, the parable of the talents); but
he is not interested in retaining the parable and he simply uses

its opening wording to lead into another of the pre-synoptic
exhortations to wakefulness, i.e. no. 4, the conclusion
to the parable of the watchman. From there he moves, not
surprisingly, to the next similar pre-synoptic exhortation,
i.e. to the second half of no. 7. It turns out that Mark's
redaction in 13:33-37 is simply explicable: he is governed at
each step by the desire to emphasize the call to wakefulness,
and he is not concerned to preserve the parabolic material –
hence the fragmentary allusions to the parables of the talents
and the watchman.

   The hypothesis answers all sorts of questions raised by
the Markan text: we have already seen (in considering Matthew)
that it explains the relationship of Mk 13:33,34 and Mt 25:13,
14 and also the relationship of Mk 13:35 and Mt 24:42. In
addition it explains (a) the problems of grammar and sense in
Mk 13:34, including the slightly odd ἐξουσίαν, which is
probably Mark's adaptation of an original οὐσίαν in the pre-
synoptic version of the talents (cf. Matthew's τὰ ὑπάρχοντα
αὐτοῦ). It explains also (b) the relationship of Mark's
parable of the watchman and Luke's parable of the watching
servants of Lk 12:36-38, both being derived from a common
original, and (c) the relationship of the saying of Mk 13:37
'What I say to you I say to all keep watch' to the Lukan
question of 12:41 'Lord, do you say this parable to us or to
all?', the saying being the pre-synoptic answer to the
question.

7.2.4. Luke's use of the tradition

   Luke's procedure is even simpler to explain than that of
Matthew or Mark. He starts to use the pre-synoptic source with
the exhortation that concluded the parable of the virgins in
his 12:35 (i.e. section no.2).He starts at this point because
the tradition he has been following in 12:22-34 has a saying
about a 'lamp' immediately following 12:34 (cf. Mt 7:21 and
22), and Luke has already used this saying. He therefore picks
up the saying about 'girding up your loins and keeping your
lamps burning' in his 12:35 and then continues to follow the
pre-synoptic tradition. He follows it faithfully right
through, except that (1) he avoids exhortations to 'keep awake',
changing no. 4 into a beatitude and omitting nos. 7b and 8
altogether; (2) he leaves out the parable of the talents.

   Several questions from Luke's text are explained by this
hypothesis: we have already seen that it explains the

relationship of Lk 12:35 and Matthew's parable of the virgins
and of Luke's parable of the watching servants and Mark's
parable of the watchman. It explains the anticlimactic
beatitude of Lk 12:38 and the lack of a direct answer to
Peter's question in Lk 12:41. The question of Luke's parable
of the pounds (Lk 19:11-27) and of its possible relationship to
the talents was not resolved decisively; but if Luke put the
traditions of 12:35-48 into their present context because of
the suggested 'lamp' link, then this suggests something about a
possible editorial tendency to associate and link similar but
originally separate traditions; and it could support the view
that the Lukan parable of the pounds is a conflation of the
parable of the talents with another parable.

7.3. Conclusion

    The preceding summary, though it is only a summary and not
a catalogue of all the detailed evidence, shows that the
proposed hypothesis of a pre-synoptic parable source makes
sense of all the present synoptic texts and resolves many of
the difficulties in those texts that have perplexed scholars.
The hypothesis must then be considered very probable. If it is
probable, then it is of evident significance. But there are,
of course, further questions to be considered: in particular
there is the question of the relationship of the pre-synoptic
parable collection to the eschatological discourse, which will
be considered in the next chapter. /1/

/1/ The arguments presented in the preceding chapters tell in
various ways against the thesis of M.D.Goulder in his *Midrash
and Lection in Matthew* (London: SPCK, 1974). For example,
(a) with regard to the thief in the night analogy, Goulder
believes that Matthew was dependent on Paul (cf. 1 Thess 5:2-4)
and Luke on Matthew. (p.166). But we have seen that Luke's form of the
thief parable is more original that Matthew's in certain
respects (see pp. 38-41 above). Also Paul is more likely
dependent on something like the synoptic tradition in
1 Thess 5:2-4 (as elsewhere in 1 and 2 Thessalonians) than
vice versa. See my 'Paul and the Synoptic Apocalypse', 346 and
passim. (b) Goulder improbably considers that Matthew's parable
of the virgins is the link between Mark's parable of the
doorkeeper and Luke's parable of the watching servants, Matthew
being dependent on Mark and Luke on Matthew (pp. 438-40). But
we have seen substantial evidence for thinking that Matthew, Luke
and Mark had a shared pre-synoptic tradition at this and other points.

Chapter 3

THE PRE-SYNOPTIC CONCLUSION TO THE ESCHATOLOGICAL DISCOURSE

1. *THE PARABLE COLLECTION THE PRE-SYNOPTIC CONCLUSION TO THE DISCOURSE?*

It has been demonstrated in the preceding two chapters that Matthew, Mark and Luke knew the pre-synoptic collection of parables, which we have reconstructed. Matthew and Mark both use material from that collection to conclude Jesus' eschatological discourse. It is possible that the one evangelist was influenced by the other in this respect; and yet Matthew and Mark seem to be thoroughly independent of each other in their use of the parabolic collection, and so it seems quite possible that the parables were attached to the discourse in their tradition. It is true that Luke has the parables elsewhere; but his evidence hardly weighs against the suggestion, since, if our argument about Lk 12:35 was correct, (a) Luke's location of his 12:35-48 is not original - he placed the material in this context because of a verbal and/or thematic link -; and (b) Luke's 12:35-48 is an extract out of some larger context, which included at least the preceding parable of the virgins. It is quite possible that this context was that found in Matthew and Mark. But can a positively convincing case be made out for this suggestion?

2. *THE EVIDENCE OF MT 24:37-41*

Although it is true that both Matthew and Mark have their parabolic material at the end of Jesus' eschatological discourse, they do not have it in exactly the same context. Mark has his material immediately after the saying 'of that day knows no one ... ' (Mk 13:32); Matthew, on the other hand, has that saying followed by the 'Q' passage that compares the time of the parousia to the days of Noah and that speaks of 'one being taken and one left' (Mt 24:37-41). Only after this does Matthew start to draw on the parable collection. At first sight this evidence may appear to complicate the case for regarding the parables as the pre-synoptic conclusion to the eschatological discourse; it does not after all seem to be a simple case of Matthew and Mark

having the same order, since Matthew has a substantial section
of 'Q' material interpolated, material which Luke has in a quite
different context (in his Lk 17:26-35). If Matthew attached
that material to the eschatological discourse, he may well have
done the same with the parable collection.

However, there is a quite different possibility, and that
is that the Matthean 'interpolation' from 'Q' is not an
interpolation at all. It is possible that the pre-synoptic
tradition was like Matthew in having the eschatological
discourse followed by the sayings concerning the days of Noah
(etc.) and then by the parable collection. This may seem an
unlikely speculation. But (a) we saw that the so-called 'Q'
parables in Matthew 24,25 were in the pre-synoptic tradition
known to all the evangelists; it seems quite possible that the
immediately preceding 'Q' section (the days of Noah, etc.) was
also part of that tradition. (b) We saw that Lk 12:35-48 is
placed by Luke in a secondary context, and that Matthew's
context has a more probable, though as yet uncertain, claim to
originality; it seems quite possible that the same applies to
the Noah sayings, which Luke has in his 17:26-35. (c) It is
true that Mark has no trace of the Noah sayings after the saying
about no one knowing the day or the hour; but we saw that
Mk 13:33-37 is a collection of exhortations to wakefulness,
culled from the parable source and attached to the saying of
13:32. Given Mark's evident redactional interests here, his
omission of the Noah sayings is not surprising at all.

Even given these three observations, the idea that
Mt 24:37-41 is in its original pre-synoptic position is far from
being established; and the hypothesis that the pre-synoptic
tradition contained the eschatological discourse + those verses
+ the parable collection is only a possibility.

3. THE EVIDENCE OF LK 21:34-36

Luke's conclusion to the eschatological discourse is very
different from Matthew's and Mark's. It reads:

προσέχετε δὲ ἑαυτοῖς μήποτε βαρηθῶσιν ὑμῶν αἱ καρδίαι ἐν
κραιπάλῃ καὶ μέθῃ καὶ μερίμναις βιωτικαῖς, καὶ ἐπιστῇ ἐφ'
ὑμᾶς αἰφνίδιος ἡ ἡμέρα ἐκείνη 35. ὡς παγίς· ἐπεισελεύσεται
γὰρ ἐπὶ πάντας τοὺς καθημένους ἐπὶ πρόσωπον πάσης τῆς γῆς.
36. ἀγρυπνεῖτε δὲ ἐν παντὶ καιρῷ δεόμενοι ἵνα κατισχύσητε
ἐκφυγεῖν ταῦτα πάντα τὰ μέλλοντα γίνεσθαι, καὶ σταθῆναι
ἔμπροσθεν τοῦ υἱοῦ τοῦ ἀνθρώπου.

The fact that Luke diverges so markedly here from Matthew and
Mark may seem to show fairly decisively that Luke did not know
a pre-synoptic form of the eschatological discourse that ended
as do Matthew and Mark. It may seem probable that the
eschatological discourse ended with the statement that 'all
these things will happen' within a generation (Mt 24:34,
Mk 13:30,31, Lk 21:32,33), and that the different evangelists
have each appended different hortatory sections after the body
of the discourse. This, however, does not necessarily follow:
the fact is that all three evangelists do conclude the
discourse with exhortation (including exhortation to
wakefulness). And it is perfectly possible to explain Luke's
divergence from Matthew and Mark as due to Luke's desire to
avoid repetition: he had used nearly all that we find in
Mt 24:37-25:30 and in Mk 13:33-37 earlier in his gospel, and now
he uses other material in his 21:34-36. If this is the correct
explanation, the question remains as to where Luke derived this
other material. Perhaps the most obvious explanation is that
that Luke himself created his 21:34-36, drawing slightly on
Mark (cf. the word ἀγρυπνεῖτε in Mk 13:33 and Lk 21:36) and on
other Christian traditions./1/ If he did so, then he has been
remarkably innovative and creative for an author who kept
reasonably close to Matthew and Mark in the earlier sections of
the discourse (and who seemed a quite conservative editor in
Lk 12:35-48). Another possibility is that Luke's 21:34-36 were
in the pre-synoptic tradition along with the Matthean and
Markan material. This may seem quite unlikely; but there is
substantial evidence that points that way.

4. THE COMBINED EVIDENCE OF LK 21:34-36 AND MT 24:37-41

    The crucial observation is this: the Lukan section in
question consists (i) of a warning not to be embroiled in other
things and to be caught off one's guard by the sudden day of
the second coming (21:34,35), (ii) of a call to keep awake so
as to stand before the Son of man (21:36). The second part,
the call to wakefulness, is reminiscent of the eschatological
parabolic material that has already been discussed, though it
is not exactly parallel to anything yet studied; the first
part, the warning against embroilment, is quite different.
However, the first part, as numerous scholars have noted, is
reminiscent of Mt 24:37-41, the passage before the
eschatological parables where the time of the parousia is
compared to the days of Noah - it will come suddenly on people

---

/1/ Cf. J. Zmijewski, *Eschatologiereden*, 291-294.

in the middle of everyday life. The striking thing about this
is that in exactly the same context (immediately after the body
of the eschatological discourse) we have in both Matthew 24 and
Luke 21 exactly the same development of thought: (i) a negative
warning against worldly unpreparedness for the sudden second
coming, (ii) a positive call to wakefulness.

In Matthew we have:	In Luke we have:
(a) As in days of Noah ... in that day two in field, one taken ... etc.	(a) Take care lest hearts weighed down in carousing, worldly cares ...
(b) Parables of wakefulness	(b) But keep awake at every moment ...

This similarity of thought and sequence may very well be
explained as due to the use by Matthew and Luke of a common
underlying tradition in which there was a section of warning
about the sudden second coming followed by a section of
exhortation to wakefulness.

But if the Matthean and Lukan traditions are related, can
it be shown more specifically how they are related, and/or how
they fit together? One possibility is that Luke knew something
like the Matthean form of the tradition, and that Lk 21:34-36 is
his summary of that form. That is a relatively complicated
possibility: (a) Despite the similarity of thought, the verbal
links between the Matthean and Lukan traditions are few, and
(b) there is reason to believe that Lk 21:34-36 contains
primitive pre-Lukan traditions,/1/ so that we would have to
envisage Luke producing his loose summary of the Matthean form
of the tradition with the aid of these other traditions. A much
simpler possibility is that the Lukan exhortations were drawn,
roughly as they are, from the pre-synoptic tradition. But how
will they have fitted into the pre-synoptic tradition? The
Lukan exhortation to wakefulness (21:36) is reminiscent of some
of the Matthean/Markan parable conclusions, and so it is
tempting to see if it would fit after any of the parables. But
it does not very obviously fit, nor is it needed after any of
the parables on the theme of wakefulness. In any case that
would leave vv 34,35 unaccounted for, and also perhaps rather
unbalanced (vv 34,35 being the negative and v 36 the positive

---

/1/ See my 'Paul and the Synoptic Apocalypse', 353-359; and
further discussion below on pp. 109-117.

exhortation)./1/ The preferable and probably correct
explanation is that the Lukan exhortations in 21:34-36 belonged
in the original tradition *between* on the one hand the passage
about the days of Noah and the suddenness of the second coming
and on the other hand the parables of wakefulness (the first of
which was originally the parable of the virgins). The original
order was:

1. Mt 24:36-41/Lk 17:26-end	As in the days of Noah, so in the day of the Son of man ... two in a field .. one taken, one left.	
2. Lk 21:34,35	Take care of yourselves, lest your hearts weighed down in carousing, worldly cares, and that day come suddenly .. on all earth.	
3. Lk 21:36	But keep awake (ἀγρυπνεῖτε) at every moment (καιρῷ), pray .. to stand before the Son of man.	
4. Mt 25:1-13 etc.	Parables of virgins, watchman, thief ...	

What are the arguments that support this suggestion?

4.1. A simple explanation of Mt 24:37-41 and Lk 21:34-36

First, the suggestion fits in well with the observations
made in sections 2 and 3 (above): to ascribe Mt 24:37-41 to the
same pre-synoptic tradition as the parabolic material is
evidently simpler than ascribing the two sections to different
sources, and to ascribe Lk 21:34-36 to the same tradition means
that no complex editing was involved on his part (though there
may well have been some redactional rewording here and there).
A comparison with Mark suggests that Matthew and Luke were
by and large conservative in their editing of the main body of
the eschatological discourse and our study of the parabolic
collection showed that they were distinctly conservative in
their editing there; exactly the same sort of editing is pre-
supposed on the suggestion that Mt 24:37-44 and Lk 21:34-36
belonged together in the pre-synoptic tradition.

/1/ The Pauline evidence suggests that vv 34,35 belonged with
v 36 in the tradition. See my 'Paul and the Synoptic
Apocalypse', 353-359.

4.2. A good sequence of thought

The proposed sequence of thought is good: the first section compares the 'days' of Noah (and Lot) and the 'day' when Noah went into the ark with the 'days' and the 'day' of the Son of man,/1/ and it speaks of sudden judgment coming on people in the midst of their worldly affairs. This leads very well into the negative warning against worldly embroilment of Lk 21:34-35 with its reference to 'that day' coming suddenly on all the earth./2/ This is then balanced by the following positive call to wakefulness 'at every moment .... that you may be able ... to stand before the Son of man', which in turn leads very well into the following parables of the virgins, the watchman and the thief, where the emphasis is on readiness at any moment (though not on literal wakefulness in the parable of the virgins). Lk 21:34-36 turns out to be very similar to the other exhortations in the postualted pre-synoptic tradition, e.g. Mk 13:35,36, in that it applies what precedes and leads into what follows.

The argument about the satisfactory sequence may perhaps be extended if the saying of Mt 24:36/Mk 13:32 is brought into the picture: this speaks of no one knowing 'the day or the hour'; if this was part of the pre-synoptic tradition, we then get this pattern:

'Of that *day* or *hour* knows no one ...'

Sayings about the *day*(s) of Noah and the *day*(s) of the Son of man

The Lukan exhortation which speaks of the *day* (v 34)

/1/ Matthew in this section refers to the 'days' and the 'day' of Noah, but to the 'parousia' of the Son of man. But his 'parousia' is probably less original than Luke's 'day(s)'. See discussion of this and of other points relating to Mt 24:37-41 and Lk 17:26-37 in chapter 4 below.

/2/ The thought of 'drunkenness, carousing and worldly cares' in Lk 21:34 gives a rather more negative picture than the picture of eating, drinking, marrying etc. in the Noah/Lot traditions. It is possible that Luke has reexpressed the original form of the exhortation. But the change of emphasis is not very significant, and is perhaps only to be expected in the change from comparison to exhortation.

and of being ready at every *moment*

Parables that speak about being alert every *moment/hour*
   (virgins, watchman, thief)

(The dialogue between Peter and Jesus)

Parable that speaks about being ready for the *day* or *hour*
   (steward)

This symmetrical arrangement – day/hour ... day, day, moment,
moment ... day/hour – may be accidental, but may be deliberate.

   The proposal explains satisfactorily the thematic
similarity of the exhortations of Lk 21:34-36 to the sayings
about the days of Noah; to see Lk 21:34-36 as a Lukan version or
distillation of the Noah sayings is less simple. On the other
hand, it must be admitted that the link between the respective
passages could be even less direct than we have suggested,
since we are dealing with common apocalyptic themes.

4.3. *The evidence of Luke 17 and 18*

   Perhaps the most obvious objection to the view proposed is
that the passage about the day(s) of Noah is used by Luke in a
quite different context in his chapter 17. It may seem
improbable that Luke, if he had known the material in question
in the context of the eschatological discourse (which he has
in chapter 21) would have extracted a substantial section of it
and used it in a quite different and earlier context.

   However (i) this is exactly what Luke appears to have done
in Luke 12, where he uses an extract from the eschatological
discourse out of context (see preceding discussion). (ii) A
strong case can in fact be made out for seeing all of Lk 17:22-
37 as an extract from the eschatological discourse. This will
be explored in the next chapter. (iii) We may anticipate part
of the argument of the next chapter by observing that the
evidence of Luke 17 may in fact be cited as positive support
for the suggestion that in the pre-synoptic tradition the
material about the days of Noah etc. (Mt 24:37-41) was followed
by the exhortation of Lk 21:34-36 about 'keeping awake at every
moment praying', since in Luke the sayings about the days of
Noah etc. are followed in Lk 18:1 by 'He told them a parable

that they should *always pray and not grow weary*.....' The full
picture is therefore this:

Mt 24	Lk 17	Lk 21
Passage about Noah and suddenness of parousia (vv 37-41)	Passage about Noah and suddenness of parousia (vv 26-35)	
	(saying about body and eagles. v 37)	
		Take care lest hearts weighed down in cares etc. and that day come suddenly (vv 34, 35)
Call to keep awake + parables about keeping awake (vv 42ff)	He told them a parable that they should always pray and not grow weary + parable about praying for coming of Son of man (18:1ff.)	But keep awake at every moment praying .. to stand before Son of man (v 36)

The combination of similarities and differences in the sequence
of ideas is striking. It could be coincidence that Matthew and
Luke have the sayings about the days of Noah (and Lot; Luke)
followed by encouragement to 'keep awake' (Mt 24:42)/'not to grow
weary' (Lk 18:1) + parabolic material. It could be coincidence
that Matthew has this material at the end of the eschatological
discourse and that Luke has rather similar material at the same
point in his eschatological discourse (Lk 21:34-36). It could
be coincidence that Luke has the Noah passage followed by a
reference to 'praying always and not growing weary' in his
chapter 17 and that he has in chapter 21 a call not to be
embroiled in worldly distractions (cf. the people of Noah's day)
followed by a call to wakefulness and prayer./1/ But the

/1/ Few scholars seem to have noticed the parallel sequence of
ideas in Luke 17/18 and Luke 21. But ·see W. Ott, *Gebet und Heil*
(München: Kösel, 1965) pp. 19,20,71-73 and C. L. Holman,

combination of coincidences is very unlikely, and the simple
explanation of all the evidence is that the pre-synoptic
tradition was as suggested, and that Matthew and Luke have
drawn on that tradition in Matthew 24, Luke 21 and also Luke 17.

In that case the probable explanation of Lk 17:26-18:1 is
that Luke follows the pre-synoptic tradition about the day(s)
of Noah and the suddenness of the parousia (17:26-36); he
inserts the saying of v 37 (see further discussion of this in
chapter 4 below); he then continues with the thought of the
pre-synoptic tradition about prayer and wakefulness (18:1). He
does not, however, carry on with the parables found in the pre-
synoptic tradition (which he has already drawn on extensively
in his chapter 12), but has instead an eschatological parable
about prayer, i.e. 18:2-8. It may be significant that not only
is the introduction to that parable reminiscent of the
eschatological discourse, but so also is its conclusion 'But
when he comes will the Son of man find faith on earth?' (v 8b:
compare the wording here with Mk 13:36 and the thought with
Lk 21:35,36)./1/ It is not unreasonable to suppose that Luke's
train of thought here is still with the eschatological
discourse; he has introduced the eschatological parable of the
unjust judge into this context, but has put it within the
framework of thought of the eschatological discourse./2/

If this explanation of Luke chapters 17 and 18 is correct,
then far from contradicting the idea that Lk 21:34-36 belongs
with the Noah sayings, the evidence adduced seems to confirm
it.

_____

*Eschatological Delay in Jewish and Early Christian Apocalyptic
Literature* (University of Nottingham, Ph.D. thesis, 1982) 313,314.
I am grateful for the author's permission to cite this study.
/1/ Holman, *Eschatological Delay*, 314, notes that v 8b
envisages a future time of overwhelming apostasy and of major
trials. This is a theme of the eschatological discourse, most
notably in Mt 24:9-14.
/2/ Ott, *Gebet*, 72, sees Lk 18:1 and 8 as Lukan redaction;
others have seen 18:8b as such (e.g. Linnemann, *Parables*, 187-
89). Were either view correct, this would fit in with the
suggestion that Luke is here incorporating the parable into the
framework of thought of the eschatological discourse.

4.4. Paul's evidence

4.4.1. The evidence for Paul's knowledge of the traditions of Lk 21:34-36./1/

a. Lk 21:34,35 related to 1 Thess 5:3

In Luke 21:34,35 the Lord warns of being weighed down by carousing, drunkenness (μέθη) and worldly cares, καὶ ἐπιστῇ ἐφ' ὑμᾶς αἰφνίδιος ἡ ἡμέρα ἐκείνη ὡς παγίς· ἐπεισελεύσεται γὰρ ἐπὶ πάντας ... ἀγρυπνεῖτε δὲ .... ἵνα κατισχύσητε ἐκφυγεῖν.. . In 1 Thess 5:3, having spoken of the coming of the ἡμέρα κυρίου, Paul says ὅταν λέγωσιν· εἰρήνη καὶ ἀσφάλεια, τότε αἰφνίδιος αὐτοῖς ἐφίσταται ὄλεθρος ὥσπερ ἡ ὠδὶν τῇ ἐν γαστρὶ ἐχούσῃ, καὶ οὐ μὴ ἐκφύγωσιν. He goes on to urge γρηγορῶμεν καὶ νήφωμεν and contrasts those who sleep and get drunk (μεθύουσιν) (vv 5,6).

The parallelism in idea and wording here is unmistakable: αἰφνίδιος occurs only in these two places in the NT. ἐφιστάναι, though common in Luke/Acts, occurs only three times in Paul (the two others being in the Pastorals), and ἐκφεύγειν occurs only twice in Paul and three times in Luke/Acts. In addition to these parallels note how in the sentence regarding the sudden coming of judgment day Paul's αὐτοῖς corresponds to Luke's ἐφ' ὑμᾶς and his ὥσπερ ἡ ὠδίν to Luke's ὡς παγίς. We have then this situation:

Luke   ἐπιστῇ ἐφ' ὑμᾶς αἰφνίδιος ... ὡς παγίς .... ἐκφυγεῖν

1 Thess αἰφνίδιος αὐτοῖς ἐφίσταται ... ὥσπερ .... ἐκφύγωσιν

All these verbal and structural parallels, together with the agreement in meaning, make it very probable that there is a common tradition here./2/

/1/ This section is from my 'Paul and the Synoptic Apocalypse', pp. 353-358. See there for a somewhat fuller discussion.
/2/ The punctuation found in some MSS ὡς παγίς γὰρ ἐπελεύσεται ..., favoured by Ott, Gebet, 73, would give a slightly poorer parallelism. Another textual variant, also followed by Ott, καταξιώθητε for κατισχύσητε would give a new verbal link with the Thessalonian epistles (2 Thess 1:5). On both points see Marshall, Luke, 782,783.

b. The differences point to Lukan originality

The similarity between the Pauline and Lukan tradition is especially close, where Luke has ἐπιστῇ ἐφ᾽ ὑμᾶς αἰφνίδιος ἡ ἡμέρα ἐκείνη ὡς παγίς and Paul has .... τότε αἰφνίδιος αὐτοῖς ἐφίσταται ὄλεθρος ὥσπερ ἡ ὠδὶν τῇ ἐν γαστρὶ ἐχούσῃ. There are, however, two substantial differences, an examination of which confirms the idea of a common tradition, but also throws light on the history of the tradition: (1) Paul has ὄλεθρος for Luke's ἡ ἡμέρα ἐκείνη. The difference here in sense is slight: Paul in the immediately preceding verse has referred to the 'day of the Lord', and so the coming of the ὄλεθρος is the coming of that day. As for whether the Lukan or the Pauline wording is original, it is possible that Luke put 'that day' for 'destruction' to fit his context and perhaps under the influence of Mark 13:32; but it is probably simpler to suggest that, having just referred to the 'day of the Lord' in the previous saying, Paul substitutes ὄλεθρος (a term he uses elsewhere) for a further reference to 'the day' for the sake of variation. Either way, there is no difficulty in postulating one form of words behind the two traditions.

(2) Paul has ὥσπερ ἡ ὠδίν ... for Luke's ὡς παγίς. The variation in this case may seem more surprising, but there are in fact several possible explanations. L. Hartman, following earlier writers, has proposed an explanation of this difference on the basis of Hebrew/Aramaic, since in Hebrew and Aramaic the word חבל/חבלא (with slightly different pointings) can mean either 'rope' (hence 'trap') or 'birth-pangs'; the suggestion is therefore that we have a translation variant here in Paul and Luke./1/

This idea has some plausibility. Although חבל is not the most obvious Hebrew/Aramaic word for 'trap', Greek παγίς, it is sometimes used with that sense (e.g. Job 18:10, Ps 119:61, 140:6 Prov 5:22); and it is possible that an original כחבל might have been understood by one translator to mean 'like a rope/ trap' and by another to mean 'like pangs'. The idea of sudden trouble would be conveyed by both translations. Interestingly, we find a similar sort of variation in translation with the Hebrew phrase חבלי שאול, this being taken in the LXX to mean 'the pangs of death', but by modern commentators as 'the cords

---

/1/ Hartman, *Prophecy*, 192.

of death'./1/ Even more remarkably, the Hebrew phrase may be
taken both ways in neighbouring contexts in the Hymn Scroll of
Qumran ('pangs' 1 QH 3:7f., 'cords' 3.28)./2/

But, although the idea is possible, it loses a lot of its
attraction when it is realised that the difference between Paul
and Luke may also be well explained on the basis of a common
Greek text. In the first place, it may be noted that the two
terms ὠδίν and παγίς are not completely unconnected, even in
the LXX: both are found in OT eschatological contexts that
describe the day of the Lord (e.g. Isa 13:6,7: 24:17), and in
Ps 18:6 LXX the two words are found in close parallelism. So
even without the hypothesis of a Semitic original, it is
possible to conceive of a New Testament writer substituting the
one term for the other.

But secondly and more specifically it may be plausibly
argued that the Lukan form of the saying 'like a snare' is the
original text and that Paul has changed this to 'like pangs'./3/
In favour of this is (1) the fact that two of the ideas
present in 1 Thessalonians 5 and Luke 21, the idea of the
unexpectedness of the day of the Lord and the thought of
'escaping', both fit slightly better with the Lukan 'snare'
than the Pauline 'pangs', and (2) that the Pauline alteration
of Luke can be well explained from Isa 13:6,7 'Wait, for the
day of the Lord is near; as destruction from the Almighty it
will come ... Pangs and agony will seize him; they will be in
anguish like a woman in travail'. This OT passage on the day
of the Lord was of obvious relevance to NT eschatology: verses
9,10 of the same chapter are echoed in Mt 24:29 (and parallels;
cf. Rev 6:12), and several possible links may be shown with
1 Thessalonians 5; (a) Paul's use of ὄλεθρος, where Luke has ἡ

/1/ Ps 18:5,6, the parallel 2 Sam 22:6, and Ps 116:3. Cf.
Acts 2:24.
/2/ But translators and commentators are not unanimous on 3:28,
some taking it there as 'pangs'.
/3/ The opposite possibility cannot be excluded. J. Plevnik,
Biblica 60 (1979) 82, argues that γαστήρ is not a Pauline term,
which might appear to tell against the view that Paul's wording
is his modification of the Lukan form. But the word is rare
throughout the NT, and the point is hardly substantial.

ἡμέρα ἐκείνη, may, we suggested, have been for the sake of
variation; but his particular choice of word may be explained
from Isa 13:6, 'the day of the Lord is near; as *destruction*
from the Almighty it will come' (though the LXX on this
occasion does not translate שׁד with ὄλεθρος). (b) The
references to pangs and the 'woman with child' obviously
connect the two passages, though Paul speaks of a 'woman with
child' and the onset of labour whereas Isaiah speaks of a
'woman giving birth' and the experience of labour. (c) Paul's
reference to people saying 'peace and security' when judgment
comes has been linked by commentators with Jer 6:14.
Interestingly Jer 6:14 is followed in 6:24-26 by a passage
portraying judgment in terms very similar to Isaiah 13. It seems
possible that Paul (or his tradition) has been influenced by
these two related OT traditions./1/

        Since this suggested explanation of the divergence
between Luke 21 and 1 Thessalonians 5 is possible on the basis
of the Greek text, and since several of the other vocabulary
links between Luke 21 and 1 Thessalonians point to a connexion
at the level of Greek tradition, the hypothesis of a Semitic
original becomes unnecessary, though still not impossible. But
with or without a Semitic original, our investigations have
made the idea of a common tradition here the more plausible and
have pointed to the Lukan form of the tradition being the
earlier form and to Paul (or his tradition) having modified
it./2/

        One further phenomenon that would be accounted for by this
explanation is the unPauline style of 1 Thess 5:3. Best,
following Lightfoot, notes (i) the impersonal λέγωσιν, (ii)
the unusual words ἀσφάλεια, αἰφνίδιος, ἐφιστάναι./3/

/1/ I am indebted to Dr R. J. Bauckham for drawing my
attention to the possible importance of these OT texts.
/2/ If it is thought that Paul and Luke are here using a
tradition purporting to come from Jesus, then it is not
surprising that Paul would feel more free to modify the wording
in his free allusion than Luke in his direct citation.
/3/ E. Best, *A Commentary on the First and Second Epistles to
the Thessalonians* (London: Black, 1972) 207. Cf. also, Plevnik,
Biblica 60, p. 82. The argument from word usage must not be
pressed too far. For example, ἀσφάλεια is not paralleled
elsewhere in Paul; but it only occurs twice elsewhere in the
whole NT. Perhaps Paul is thinking of Jer 6:14, but prefers not

Most of these untypical features may be explained from the
postulated underlying tradition, also attested in Luke, or from
the OT passages, whose influence has been detected in Paul's
version of the tradition.

c. Luke 21:36 related to Ephesians 6

As well as resembling 1 Thessalonians 5, Luke 21:34-36 also
resembles Ephesians 6. Thus Luke 21:36 reads ἀγρυπνεῖτε δὲ ἐν
παντὶ καιρῷ δεόμενοι ἵνα κατισχύσητε ἐκφυγεῖν ταῦτα πάντα τὰ
μέλλοντα γίνεσθαι καὶ σταθῆναι ἔμπροσθεν τοῦ υἱοῦ τοῦ ἀνθρώπου.
In Ephesians 6 Paul calls his readers to take the armour of God
πρὸς τὸ δύνασθαι ὑμᾶς στῆναι ... (v 11). Paul goes on ἵνα
δυνηθῆτε ἀντιστῆναι ἐν τῇ ἡμέρᾳ τῇ πονηρᾷ καὶ ἅπαντα
κατεργασάμενοι στῆναι· στῆτε οὖν... (vv 13,14a). He continues a
few verses later διὰ πάσης προσευχῆς καὶ δεήσεως, προσευχόμενοι
ἐν παντὶ καιρῷ... καὶ εἰς αὐτὸ ἀγρυπνοῦντες ἐν πάσῃ
προσκαρτερήσει καὶ δεήσει.·(v 18)./1/

The parallels here are less striking than those between
1 Thessalonians 5 and Luke 21, especially when it is recalled
that exhortations to 'stand' and to 'pray always' are found
quite often in Paul's writings and may have been a common part
of the early church's parenesis./2/ However, the close
similarity of wording in Luke 21 and Ephesians 6, notably in
the use of ἀγρυπνεῖν (found only here in Paul), does suggest
some specific link between the traditions, not just that they
both drew on the general stock of early Christian parenesis;
none of Paul's other injunctions to 'stand', 'to watch' or 'to
pray' come so close to Luke 21.

Against this conclusion it might be argued that one of the
key words in common, to 'stand', is used differently in the two
contexts - Luke 21 of 'standing' in divine judgment, in
Ephesians 6 of 'standing' in battle. But this point should not
be given too much weight: both in Luke 21 and Ephesians 6 the
picture is of getting through a dangerous situation (from the
devil and the evil day in Ephesians, from coming events in

---

to have the repetitious 'Peace, peace', and so uses the
relatively rare ἀσφάλεια. For the combination of ἀσφάλεια and
εἰρήνη, G. Friedrich, in ZTK 70 (1973) 293, compares Lev 26:5f.
and Pss.Sol. 8:16f.
/1/ I am assuming the basic Paulinicity of Ephesians; the
argument might stand even without that assumption.
/2/ The similarity is less if καταξιωθῆτε is read in Luke 21:36
rather than κατισχύσητε. See note 2 on p. 110.

Luke), and the final 'standing' after the battle referred to at
the end of Eph 6:13 is not dissimilar to the 'standing' before
the Son of man in Luke 21. One possibility is that Paul has
incorporated a traditional, non-military exhortation to 'stand'
into the context of the warfare metaphor, thereby giving it
military overtones. In favour of this may be (a) the fact that
non-military exhortations to stand are found elsewhere in Paul
in contexts that could be related to Ephesians 6;/1/ (b) the
multiplication of references to 'standing' in Eph 6:11-14 (twice
'being able to stand'). This repetitiousness could be partly
explained if Paul is working with a traditional 'standing'
motif, which he elaborates in verse 12 and then again in the
description of the armour in verses 14-18. It is interesting
that the description of the armour is immediately followed by a
slightly repetitious call to unceasing prayer, being paralleled
in Luke 21:36. Is Paul here reverting to his tradition, having
wandered from it? If so we have, as with 1 Thessalonians 5, a
significant connexion between a Lukan and Pauline tradition,
Paul's version showing most signs of modification.

    d. The connexion between Luke 21:34,35 and 21:36
    Even if the last suggestions about Ephesians 6 are too
speculative to build on, we still have come to the probable
conclusions (a) that the exhortation of Luke 21:34,35 is related
to 1 Thessalonians 5, and (b) that the exhortation of Luke 21:36
is related to Ephesians 6. The two Lukan exhortations form a
pair, one being the negative exhortation to get rid of evil
'lest ....', the other being the positive encouragement to
prayer and faithfulness 'so that .....'. We are reminded of
similar balancing exhortations in the epistles. Luke's
particular combination of sayings might be judged secondary in
the light of the Pauline parallels; but, since we have seen some
reason to think Luke's form of the sayings more primitive than
Paul's, it is quite possible that his ordering of them is also
primitive./2/

/1/ E.g. 1 Cor 16:13 combines the call to 'stand' with a call
to wakefulness - cf. Luke 21:36 - and with a call to strength -
cf. Eph 6:10-18. 2 Thess 2:15 has a call to stand followed by a
call to prayer (3:1) rather similar to Eph 6:18,19.
/2/ If the exhortation form of Luke 21:34,35 is primitive, it
seems likely that there would have been a balancing positive
exhortation. If there was, then it is simpler to suppose that
Luke has retained it (in his verse 36) than to suppose that he
displaced it with a substitute saying.

This suggestion receives rather striking support from the observation that, quite apart from their relationship to Luke 21, 1 Thessalonians 5 and Ephesians 6 seem to be related to each other, and also to Romans 13 (another eschatological passage with some similarity to Luke 21)./1/ These three Pauline passages all have a call to 'wakefulness' and an injunction to don the Christian armour,/2/ and it can be reasonably argued that Paul is drawing in all three passages on an early catechetical tradition, a tradition that was originally strongly eschatological, but which in Ephesians has lost some of its eschatological flavour (though not all of its eschatological vocabulary, e.g. ἀγρυπνεῖν, also the reference to standing 'in the evil day'). The internal Pauline evidence by itself may be considered by some insufficient to establish the case for this sort of catechetical tradition; but when Luke 21:34-36 with its clear links with two of the three passages and possible links with the third is considered and also the probability that Luke 21:34,35 is primitive material, then the cumulative case is strong, and the possibility that all Luke 21:34-36 is based on primitive tradition becomes a probability./3/

The conclusion of this slightly complex argument is that Paul very probably knew the traditions of Lk 21:34-36./4/

/1/ Compare Rom 13:11,12 with Luke 21:28,31; Rom 13:13 with Luke 21:34.
/2/ The parallels are the more striking if we include with Ephesians 6 the talk of light/dark in Eph 5:8-21. Note too the parallel between 1 Thess 5:16 and Eph 6:18 in the call to unceasing prayer; cf. Luke 21:36.
/3/ On the question as to how and why this tradition got combined in the Pauline tradition with the 'light/dark' 'put on /off' and 'armour' motifs see my 'Paul and the Synoptic Apocalypse', p. 372. With regard to the 'armour' motif, note that several of the Lukan terms in Lk 21:34-36, e.g. κατισχύειν (a verb used in the LXX of victory), ἐκφεύγειν and ἱστάναι, could all be taken to suggest a battle scene (and could perhaps be linked to the references to 'being strong' in Eph 6:10).
/4/ If this primitive tradition existed, then it may be possible to trace other elements in the Thessalonian epistles back to it. Note that the references to 'standing' and 'praying' in 2 Thess 2:15, 3:1 come in a context rather similar to 1 Thess 5:9,10; is Paul echoing the one tradition in both contexts?

But this does not by itself further the case for considering
those traditions to have been part of the eschatological
discourse.

4.4.2. Paul's linking of the traditions of Lk 21:34-36 with the parable collection

What is, however, of interest is that in 1 Thessalonians 5
Paul has the traditions of Lk 21:34-36 sandwiched between his
two uses of the 'thief in the night' analogy (5:2 & 4). Paul's
analogy is no doubt connected in some way with the parable of
the thief; so in 1 Thessalonians 5 Paul brings together
traditions which Matthew and Luke place at the end of their
respective versions of the eschatological discourse. This
could be coincidence. But it is desirable not to postulate
coincidences unnecessarily; and the preferable explanation is
that Paul was familiar with the postulated pre-synoptic
tradition which had the Lukan ending and the Matthean parables
together.

Given these two hardly mistakable links between
1 Thessalonians 5 and the pre-synoptic tradition, other possible
links become probable: (a) There are the possible links
between 1 Thess 4:15-18 and the parable of the virgins, i.e. the
'shout of command', the phrase 'to meet him' and the references
to being 'with him'. (See chapter 2 above, pp. 89-91.)
Perhaps also the reference to the living being 'snatched up' to
meet the Lord in the air may be linked to the sayings of
Mt 24:40,41 about one being taken and one being left. (b) There
are possible echoes of the parable of the watchman in
1 Thessalonians 5, i.e. in the references to 'sleeping' and
'waking' and in the phrase ἵνα ἡ ἡμέρα ὑμᾶς ... καταλάβῃ (5:4).
(See chapter 2 above, pp. 54,55.)

This agglomeration of links between 1 Thessalonians 4 and
5 and the postulated pre-synoptic tradition seems unlikely to
be accidental. The evidence does not add up to proof that Paul
knew the pre-synoptic tradition as reconstructed, and it would
be unwise to place too much weight on it. Nevertheless Paul's
evidence points in the same direction as other evidence, and
confirms the probability of the hypothesis that Lk 21:34-36
belonged with the parabolic collection./1/

/1/ If Paul is drawing on the pre-synoptic tradition in
1 Thessalonians 4 and 5, then he may well be doing so also in
1 Cor 4:1-5 (where there are the possible echoes of the parable

4.5. Mark's evidence

The hypothesis that Lk 21:34-36 belonged in the pre-
synoptic tradition receives some perhaps rather surprising
support from Mark's gospel. It was argued in chapter 1 above
(pp. 23 - 29) that Mk 13:33 βλέπετε, ἀγρυπνεῖτε· οὐκ οἴδατε γὰρ
πότε ὁ καιρός ἐστιν was the Markan equivalent of Mt 25:13
γρηγορεῖτε οὖν, ὅτι οὐκ οἴδατε τὴν ἡμέραν οὐδὲ τὴν ὥραν. Mark,
it was suggested, altered Matthew's more original τὴν ἡμέραν
οὐδὲ τὴν ὥραν to avoid repetitiousness (after his v 33). But
no explanation was given for the difference between Matthew's
γρηγορεῖτε and Mark's ἀγρυπνεῖτε, nor for Mark's opening
βλέπετε.

No explanation might seem to be necessary: βλέπετε could
be a Markan addition, and the difference in the words for
'keeping awake' may not seem significant. Perhaps Mark's
ἀγρυπνεῖτε should be preferred, since Mark evidently has no
objection to the verb γρηγορεῖτε (vv 35 and 36) and ἀγρυπνεῖν
is relatively rare in the NT. On the other hand, Matthew seems
to have the more original wording in the following clause about
'not knowing', and so he may have some claim to originality in
the 'keep awake' clause. The difference may then seem
explicable either way.

However, Luke's evidence casts a new light on the question,
since in Lk 21:34 we find προσέχετε δὲ ἑαυτοῖς ... which is a
rough equivalent of Mark's βλέπετε, and in Lk 21:36 we find
ἀγρυπνεῖτε, the same unusual word as is found in Mk 13:33.
Luke then agrees with Mark at exactly those points where Mark
differs from Matthew.

---

of the steward), 1 Cor 16:13, Eph 5:8-21 and 6:10-18 (where,
among other things, the reference to 'girding your loins' in
6:14 could be an echo of Lk 12:35, which has acquired military
connotations in Ephesians), 2 Thess 2:15-3:1, and Rom 13:11-12.
It would be foolish to suppose that every parallel of theme or
vocabulary must be significant: but the links between these
passages and between these passages and the synoptic traditions
mean that the suggestion is not fanciful.

This evidence might seem to show decisively that Mark's
is the most original wording in the saying of Mk 13:33. But
the matter is by no means as simple as it may look at first.
Luke may indeed agree with Mark in having equivalents to the
two Markan terms in question; but he agrees with Mark in almost
nothing else! Furthermore it has been demonstrated that Luke
21:34-36 is not a Lukan adaptation of Mark, but is based on
other primitive tradition. What then are to be made of Luke's
agreements with Mark? They could be accidental, though it is a
remarkable accident that both evangelists should use the rather
rare ἀγρυπνεῖτε. Or it could be that Luke used basically the
primitive non-Markan tradition, but that he was influenced
slightly by Mark and so added in the opening προσέχετε δὲ
ἑαυτοῖς and then the ἀγρυπνεῖτε. But it seems odd, to say the
least, that Luke should have taken the first two words of
Mk 13:33 and then used them separately to introduce his vv 34 and
36. In any case Luke's ἀγρυπνεῖτε was probably in his non-
Markan source (cf. Eph 6:18 and the discussion above on pp. 114-
117). The third and most likely explanation of the agreements
between Mark and Luke is that Luke has the relevant terms in
their original contexts and that Mark has been influenced by
the Lukan form, not vice versa. In other words, Luke 21:34-36
(including the terms προσέχετε ἑαυτοῖς and ἀγρυπνεῖτε) belonged
in the pre-synoptic tradition and Luke derived these verses from
that tradition, not from Mark. Mark knew the same pre-synoptic
tradition, and his βλέπετε, ἀγρυπνεῖτε in his v 33 are a
reflection of that tradition.

In favour of this are the following points:

(a) We have already seen that in his 13:33-37 Mark has
collected together the exhortations to wakefulness found in the
pre-synoptic parable collection. If the parables were preceded
in the pre-synoptic tradition by the exhortation of Lk 21:34-
36, as has been argued, then we would expect Mark to make use
of it, since it too contains a call to keep awake. The
hypothesis is entirely consistent with what has been seen of
Mark's redactional concerns, and it means that Mark has drawn
on *all* the exhortations to wakefulness found in the pre-
synoptic tradition (though he has merged the Lukan exhortation
with the exhortation paralleled in Mt 25:13, taking the
ἀγρυπνεῖτε from the Lukan exhortation and the explanatory 'you
do not know' clause from the other saying).

(b) Mark's extracting of the imperatives βλέπετε, ἀγρυπνεῖτε
from the much fuller Lukan (i.e. pre-synoptic) exhortation is
also consistent with what we have seen of his editing in this
section: in this section he omits almost all the parabolic
material, retaining only the exhortations to wakefulness. It
is, therefore, no surprise that he omits most of the content of
Lk 21:34-36, while keeping the imperatives. The alternative
possibility, i.e. that Luke built up his fuller section out of
the Markan imperatives, is, as has been seen, a much more
complicated possibility. The similarities and differences
between Mark and Luke are thus neatly explained.

(c) The difference between the wording of Mt 25:13 γρηγορεῖτε
οὖν, ὅτι οὐκ οἴδατε τὴν ἡμέραν οὐδὲ τὴν ὥραν and Mark's
βλέπετε, ἀγρυπνεῖτε. οὐκ οἴδατε γὰρ πότε ὁ καιρός ἐστιν is now
wholly explained. Matthew's is the pre-synoptic form of the
conclusion to the parable of the steward; Mark's is a hybrid:
his opening imperatives are taken from the exhortation of
Lk 21:34-36,/1/ but he then tacks on the 'you do not know... '
clause from the other exhortation to wakefulness (i.e. the
saying of Mt 25:13), since this is the train of thought that he
wishes to develop after the saying of Mk 13:32 about no one
knowing the day and the hour. He modifies the wording of the
'you do not know' clause, referring to the καιρός rather than
to the 'day or hour', to avoid sounding repetitious; it may
not be accidental that the word καιρός is found in the
exhortation of Lk 21:34-36. Mark's merging of different
exhortations may seem a little odd; but it is not at all odd in
the light of our earlier observations about Mk 13:33-37.

(d) We have assumed that Mark's βλέπετε is an equivalent of
Luke's προσέχετε ἑαυτοῖς. This equivalence is suggested by the
evidence of several other verses where Mark has βλέπετε for
Matthew's and/or Luke's προσέχετε: compare Mk 8:15 with
Mt 16:6 and Lk 12:1, Mk 12:38 with Lk 20:46, Mk 13:9 with
Mt 10:17. (See chapter 6 below for further discussion,
especially pp. 229,230).

The conclusion on the basis of Mark's evidence must be
that Mark knew the sayings of Luke 21:34-36 in the context of
the parable collection.

/1/ Lambrecht, Redaktion, 242,243, may well be correct in
thinking that the original Markan text was ἀγρυπνεῖτε καὶ
προσεύχεσθε, this being the majority manuscript reading.

4.6. Conclusion on Mt 24:37-41 and Lk 21:34-36

The preceding five arguments for considering Mt 24:37-41
and Lk 21:34-36 to have been part of the same pre-synoptic
tradition as the already reconstructed parable collection add
up to a strong case. The resulting picture of the tradition is
set out in table 1 (pp.122,123 below). Each of our gospels is
explicable on the basis of this reconstruction.

4.6.1. Matthew
Matthew has the opening two sections of the pre-synoptic
tradition (though he omits the reference to Lot/1/). He then
omits sections 3-6 altogether, going on to section 7, perhaps
because of his interest in the 'not knowing' theme or for other
reasons. He has to modify section 7 because of his preceding
omission; but he then follows the pre-synoptic order quite
faithfully, making minor omissions and bringing back the
previously omitted parable of the virgins.

4.6.2. Mark
After the saying of 13:32 about no one knowing the day or
the hour, Mark goes through the pre-synoptic tradition picking
out the exhortations to keep awake and omitting everything else
he can. He picks out the imperatives from section 3, then
jumps on to the exhortation of section 12; then he goes via
section 13 back to sections 6 and 7, the latter being an
exhortation; finally he rounds the section off with the
exhortation of 10b.

4.6.3. Luke
Luke uses a large chunk of the pre-synoptic tradition,
i.e. most of sections 5-14, in his chapter 12. He uses section
2 in his chapter 17 and perhaps section 13 in his chapter 19.
He is as a result left with very little when he comes to
chapter 21; but he has here the exhortation of sections 3a and
3b.

4.6.4. Paul
In 1 Thessalonians 4 and 5 Paul has a lot of possible or
probable echoes of sections 3-9. In addition to those already
discussed, he may perhaps have an echo of section 2 in his
4:17. And in view of all the other links the suggestion that
1 Thess 5:1 περὶ δὲ τῶν χρόνων καὶ τῶν καιρῶν may be an echo of
section 1 περὶ δὲ τῆς ἡμέρας ἐκείνης ἢ τῆς ὥρας cannot be

/1/ On this see below in chapter 4, pp. 152-59.

Table 1: *Proposed reconstruction of the pre-synoptic discourse conclusion*

			Mt	Mk	Lk	
1.	'of that day/hour no one knows ... except the Father.'	*Key statement*	/ Mt 24:36	/ Mk 13:32		/
2.	'For as in the days of Noah ... Lot ... so it will be in the day of the Son of man. In that day two will be ...... one taken, one left.'	*Illustrations of unknowness of day*	/ Mt 24:37-41		/ Lk 17:26-35	/
3a.	'Take care lest hearts weighed down in carousing and worldly cares, and that day come suddenly on you like snare'	*Exhortation applying preceding teaching about day, and ....*		/ (Mk 13:33) βλέπετε	/ Lk 21:34,35	/
3b.	'But keep awake (ἀγρυνεῖτε) at every moment (καιρῷ) praying... to stand before Son of man'	*leading into parables on being ready any moment for the coming Lord*		/ (Mk 13:33) ἀγρυπνεῖτε (καιρός)	/ Lk 21:36 (cf. 18:1)	/
4.	'The kingdom shall be like ten virgins ......'	*Parable of virgins*	/ Mt 25:1-12			/
5.	'(So) let your loins be girded and lamps burning'	*Exhortation of application and transition*			/ Lk 12:35	/
6.	'(You be) like a man awaiting his master ... blessed is that servant (found) awake. Truly I tell you he ... will serve him.'	*Parable of watching servant*		/ (Mk 13:34b) '.. and to the doorman he ordered that he stay awake'	/ Lk 12:36,37	/
7.	'Keep awake then, for you do not know in what watch the lord of the house comes, whether first, second, third, lest ... he finds you sleeping'	*Exhortation of application and transition*	/ Mt 24:42 '... you do not know in what day your lord comes.'	/ Mk 13:35,36 '... you do not know when the lord of the house ... whether late ... or ... lest he .. finds you ......'	/ (Lk 12:38) 'And if he comes in the second .. in the second third watch and finds them thus, ... lest he .. blessed are they.'	/

		Mt	Mk	Lk
8. 'Know this that if the householder knew in what hour the thief comes, he would not have allowed his house to be broken into.'	*Parable of thief*	/ Mt 24:43 '.. in what watch ... he would have stayed awake and not allowed..'	/	/ Lk 12:39 '.. in what hour ... he would not have allowed..' /
9. 'So you be ready for in the hour you do not suppose the Son of man comes'	*Exhortation of application*	/ Mt 24:44	/	/ Lk 12:40 /
10a. 'And Peter said: Lord, do you say this parable to us or also to all? And the Lord said.'	*Exchange concluding preceding section & leading into*	/	/	/ Lk 12:41,42a /
10b. 'What I say to you I say to all: keep awake.'	*parables on responsibility*	/	/ Mk 13:37	/
11. 'Who then is the faithful servant/steward? ... blessed that servant ... truly I tell you ... But if he says ... his master will come at a day and hour he does not know and ..'	*Parable of steward*	/ Mt 24:45-51	/	/ Lk 12:42-46 /
12. 'So keep awake, for you do not know the day nor the hour.'	*Exhortation of application*	/ Mt 25:13	/ Mk 13:33 '.. for you do not know when the moment (καιρός) is.'	/
13. 'Like a man going away and giving to his servants his property (οὐσίαν).. to each ... to everyone who has will be given ....'	*Parable of talents*	/ Mt 25:14-30 '...he gave them τὰ ὑπάρχοντα αὐτοῦ ...'	/ Mk 13:34a '...and giving to his servants ἐξουσίαν, to each his work ...'	/ (Lk 19:12-27) /
14. 'That servant who knew ... and did not prepare ... shall be beaten ... Everyone to whom much is given, from him ....'	*Parable of disobedient servants*	/	/	/ Lk 12:47 /

regarded as impossible, though it is hardly necessary. /1/

4.6.5. The Didache
It is possible that the author of the Didache knew the
pre-synoptic tradition, since in Did. 16:1 there is a curious
patchwork of sayings./2/

γρηγορεῖτε ὑπὲρ τῆς ζωῆς ὑμῶν·
οἱ λύχνοι ὑμῶν μὴ σβεσθήτωσαν,
καὶ αἱ ὀσφύες ὑμῶν μὴ ἐκλυέσθωσαν,
ἀλλὰ γίνεσθε ἕτοιμοι·
οὐ γὰρ οἴδατε τὴν ὥραν, ἐν ᾗ ὁ κύριος ἡμῶν ἔρχεται

This patchwork is not particularly well explained on the basis
of our gospel texts, but it is explicable from the postulated
pre-synoptic tradition. Thus (a) 'Keep awake for the sake of
your life' may be an echo of sections 3a and 3b - προσέχετε
ἑαυτοῖς ... ἀγρυπνεῖτε. But the Didache uses the common
γρηγορεῖτε, and the echo could be of the other 'keep awake'
sayings. (b) 'Don't let your lamps be quenched and your loins
go loose' may be a conflation of sections 4 and 5 (the
Matthean parable of the virgins + the Lukan exhortation): the
form is that of the Lukan exhortation, but the placing first of
the lamps (before the loins) and the reference to 'quenching'
may reflect the influence of Matthew's parable./3/ (c) 'Be
ready, for you do not know the hour in which our Lord comes' is
section 9, the exhortation following the thief, except that
'our Lord' has replaced 'the Son of man', presumably because
the writer wishes to avoid the title Son of man and probably
under the influence of Mt 24:42 ('your Lord', the Matthean form
of section 7).

In the light of these observations, it seems quite
possible that the author of the Didache knew the pre-synoptic
tradition; and, rather like Mark, he has put together a number
of the exhortations from the tradition, omitting the related
parables but for the most part following the order of the

/1/ Cf. 'Paul and the Synoptic Apocalypse', p. 366 n. 10.
/2/ Cf. R. J. Bauckham, *NTS* 23 (1977) 169.
/3/ R. Glover, *NTS* 5 (1958-59) 22, considers that *Did.* 16:1 is
probably taken from 'Q' tradition. He does not think that it
could be taken from Luke's gospel, since the Didache does not
elsewhere contain echoes of 'L' material, as might be expected
if Luke's gospel was a source.

pre-synoptic source. The evidence for the Didache would not by
itself suggest this explanation; but, given the probability of
the pre-synoptic tradition, this explanation of the Didache is
at least attractive.

4.6.6. *Final remarks*
The observations about the Didache are at best a small
extra point to add to a case that is already strong. The
ability of the proposal concerning the pre-synoptic tradition
to explain each of the synoptic accounts and many of the
synoptic differences and difficulties (as well as the Pauline
evidence) suggests that the proposal is correct.

5. *BUT WHY A PRE-SYNOPTIC CONCLUSION TO THE ESCHATOLOGICAL DISCOURSE?*

To establish the thesis that Mt 24:37-41 and Lk 21:34-36
belonged with the eschatological parables in the pre-synoptic
tradition is not to prove that this pre-synoptic eschatological
tradition was originally attached to a preceding eschatological
discourse. However, (a) the fact that all three evangelists
use the pre-synoptic tradition to conclude their respective
versions of the eschatological discourse points very strongly
in this direction, especially as the evangelists are so
obviously independent of each other in their use of the
tradition. (b) It is obvious that the tradition as it has been
reconstructed must have had some preceding context. Since the
reconstructed tradition is full of exhortation about the
parousia, it seems entirely probable that the preceding context
will have contained a description of the parousia. (c) If Paul
is indeed drawing on the reconstructed pre-synoptic tradition
in 1 Thessalonians 4, he mixes it with description of the
second coming that resembles the description in the
eschatological discourse: for example, in both we find
reference to the lord coming from heaven, to angel(s), clouds,
the trumpet. It is quite possible then that Paul's pre-
synoptic tradition contained this sort of description of the
parousia together with the parabolic and hortatory material.

Of these arguments the first one is the decisive one. It
must at least be concluded that the burden of proof is on
anyone who wishes to deny that the reconstructed pre-synoptic
tradition was originally the conclusion to a pre-synoptic
eschatological discourse. But the positive case for regarding
it as such will be strengthened if evidence can be produced for

the existence of a pre-synoptic form of the earlier sections of
the discourse. This evidence will be produced in subsequent
chapters.

6. ADDITIONAL NOTES: MT 25:31-46 AND MT 19:28

6.1. The sheep and the goats

Before finally leaving the conclusion of the eschatological
discourse, some consideration must be given, if only for the
sake of completeness, to Matthew's description of the final
judgment in Mt 25:31-46. Was this part of the pre-synoptic
discourse conclusion? There is a substantial weight of
scholarly opinion behind the idea that the material is to a
greater or lesser extent pre-Matthean,/1/ but this would not
necessarily indicate that it belonged with the reconstructed
conclusion to the eschatological discourse.

However, (a) since everything else in Matthew's discourse
conclusion can be traced back to pre-synoptic tradition, and
since Matthew seems to be following this tradition quite
faithfully, there is some a priori likelihood that the sheep
and the goats belonged there too.

(b) There is no problem at all with Mark's omission of the
sheep and goats tradition; and Luke's omission is hardly
surprising either, given his rearrangement of other material at
the end of the discourse.

(c) It was noted (in chapter 2 above, pp. 95-97) that the
parables in the discourse conclusion seem to be symmetrically
arranged. It is arguable that the sheep and the goats passage
might fit the structure of the conclusion balancing the opening
description of the days of Noah and of Lot and of the one being
taken and the other left (i.e. section 2 in the reconstruction
above in table 1). Not only is the theme of separation in both
passages, but the passages are similar in being illustrated
descriptions of the day of judgment, not parables or
exhortation, such as make up the rest of the conclusion of the
discourse.

/1/ See among others J. A. T. Robinson, *NTS* 2 (1955-56) 225-37;
I. Broer, *Bibel und Leben* 11 (1970) 273-95; J. Friedrich, *Gott
im Bruder* (Stuttgart: Calwer, 1977); D. Catchpole, *BJRL* 61 (1978-
79) 355-97; Lambrecht, *Parables*, 281-333.

(d) C. L. Holman has observed that there are some
vocabulary links between Lk 21:34-36 and the Matthean
description of the sheep and the goats, notably between the
last phrase of Lk 21:36 σταθῆναι ἔμπροσθεν τοῦ υἱοῦ τοῦ
ἀνθρώπου and Mt 25:32 συναχθήσονται ἔμπροσθεν αὐτοῦ
καὶ στήσει τὰ μὲν πρόβατα.../1/ It is unwise to make much of
agreements in the use of common terminology of this sort; but
it would be entirely consistent with what we have seen so far
of the pre-synoptic tradition if Lk 21:36 were looking forward
to (or picked up by) the sheep and the goats section.

(e) A small further point which might possibly support the
view that the sheep and the goats tradition belongs with the
pre-synoptic parables is noted by D. Catchpole./2/ He notes
that the word ἐλαχίστος is used both in the Lukan parable of
the pounds (Lk 19:17) and in Matthew's sheep and goats section
(Mt 25:40,45). The word is not used particularly frequently
in the New Testament, and its occurrence in two sections that
may have been adjacent in the pre-synoptic tradition could be
significant: it could be that Luke's wording of the parable of
the pounds at this point is secondary to Matthew's and that
Luke was influenced by the wording of the sheep and goats
section, or (as Catchpole thinks) that Luke's wording of the
parable is in this respect original and that Matthew's wording
of the sheep and the goats section has been influenced by the
preceding parable; or it could be that the word was in both
contexts in the pre-synoptic tradition, in which case the most
that can be said is that there is some continuity of thought
with both passages emphasizing the value of the very smallest
service.

These five points are not very weighty, but there is at
least a good possibility that the sheep and the goats section
was part of the pre-synoptic discourse conclusion.

/1/ See his *Eschatological Delay*, 307.
/2/ *BJRL* 61, p. 393.

6.2. The saying of Mt 19:28/Lk 22:28-30

6.2.1. Catchpole's suggestion
A further fascinating possibility is suggested in
Catchpole's significant article on the sheep and the goats
section./1/ He suggests that the saying about the twelve
judging the tribes of Israel (Mt 19:28, Lk 22:28-30) may have
belonged in the 'Q' tradition after the parable of the talents.
If the reasoning is sound, it should - on our hypothesis - have
belonged in the pre-synoptic tradition.

Catchpole's case depends (a) on the observation that
Mt 19:28 has very similar wording to Mt 25:31 - the opening of the
sheep and the goats section which comes immediately after the
parable of the talents; (b) on the observation that Luke's
version of the saying about the apostles (22:28-30) is the next
'Q' material in Luke after Luke's parable of the pounds (19:11-
27). These two things put together add up to the conclusion
that in Q the saying belonged after the parable of the talents/
pounds.

Various aspects of Catchpole's argument seem insecure,
in particular his argument from Luke's order. Already in this
monograph we have seen reason to believe that Luke is quite
free in his arrangement of the pre-synoptic tradition, and
also that in Luke's pre-synoptic source the parable of the
talents was followed by the parable of the disobedient servants
(Lk 12:47,48), not by the saying concerning the twelve
apostles./2/

/1/ BJRL 61, 355-97.
/2/ There is also possible evidence of other common Matthew/
Luke tradition between the parable of the pounds in Luke 19 and
Lk 22:28-30. For example, there are agreements between Matthew
and Luke in the ordering and wording of the description of the
entry into Jerusalem and the cleansing of the temple (notably
their omission of Mark's 'for all nations', 11:17, but others
as well). Also compare Mt 21:15,16 and Lk 19:39,40. (See
further on this in chapter 9 below, p. 346.)

But it is still possible that Catchpole's suggestion is on
the right lines so far as explaining the similarity of Mt 19:28
and Mt 25:31 is concerned.

6.2.2. Observations on the Matthean/Lukan texts
The relevant texts are

Mt 19:27,28	Lk 22:28-30	Mt 25:31
τότε ἀποκριθεὶς ὁ	ὑμεῖς δέ ἐστε οἱ	ὅταν δὲ ἔλθῃ ὁ
Πέτρος εἶπεν αὐτῷ	διαμεμενηκότες μετ'	υἱὸς τοῦ ἀνθρώπου
... τί ἄρα ἔσται	ἐμοῦ ἐν τοῖς	ἐν τῇ δόξῃ αὐτοῦ
ἡμῖν;	πειρασμοῖς μου·	καὶ πάντες οἱ
28. ὁ δὲ 'Ιησοῦς	29. διατίθεμαι	ἄγγελοι μετ'αὐτοῦ
εἶπεν αὐτοῖς· ἀμὴν	ὑμῖν καθὼς διέθετό	τότε καθίσει ἐπὶ
λέγω ὑμῖν ὅτι ὑμεῖς	μοι ὁ πατήρ μου	θρόνου ....
οἱ ἀκολουθήσαντές	βασιλείαν,	
μοι, ἐν τῇ	30. ἵνα ἔσθητε	
παλιγγενεσίᾳ, ὅταν	καὶ πίνητε ἐπὶ τῆς	
καθίσῃ ὁ υἱὸς τοῦ	ἐπὶ τῆς τραπέζης μου	
ἀνθρώπου ἐπὶ θρόνου	ἐν τῇ βασιλείᾳ μου,	
δόξης αὐτοῦ,	καὶ καθήσεσθε ἐπὶ	
καθήσεσθε καὶ ὑμεῖς	θρόνων τὰς δώδεκα	
ἐπὶ δώδεκα θρόνους	φυλὰς κρίνοντες τοῦ	
κρίνοντες τὰς δώδεκα	'Ισραήλ.	
φυλὰς τοῦ 'Ισραήλ.		

The following points are notable:

(a) Mt 19:28 and Lk 22:28-30 are closely parallel at the
beginning and at the end: 'You that have..... me..... you
shall sit....'./1/ But between these points of agreement Luke
has Jesus promising the disciples a kingdom and that they
should eat and drink from his table 'in my kingdom'. Matthew
has no equivalent of these distinctive Lukan elements - with
one exception: he does have an equivalent of the phrase 'in my
kingdom' in his fuller 'in the new world, when the Son of man
shall sit on his glorious throne'.

/1/ F. W. Burnett, JSNT 17 (1982) 63 fails to note the
similarity at the beginning.

What is the relationship between the Matthean and Lukan
sayings? It could be a case of two similar but quite distinct
sayings. If, however, the traditions are related it is much
easier to see how the Matthean form could be derived from
something like the Lukan form than vice versa. Matthew took
the opening phrase of the saying 'You that have followed/
stayed with me ... ', and then jumped on almost to the last
sentence, i.e. to the phrase 'in my kingdom ... you will sit
..'. He paraphrased the phrase 'in my kingdom' with his 'in
the new world, when the Son of man shall sit on his glorious
throne'; but otherwise kept quite close to Luke. The opposite
possibility is much harder to envisage, since it would involve
Luke not only in adding in extra material, but also in
substituting his 'in my kingdom' for the more expansive
Matthean phrase and incorporating that phrase into his
additional material.

(b) The suspicion that Matthew's phrase 'in the new world, when
the Son of man shall sit on his glorious throne' is a Matthean
paraphrase of Luke's 'in my kingdom' may perhaps be supported
by the evidence of Mt 25:31, since the wording here - 'when the
Son of man comes in his glory .... then he will sit on a
throne' - is very similar to the wording of the suspect phrase
in Mt 19:28. One possible explanation of the similarity of the
two texts is that we are dealing in both places with Matthean
redaction and phraseology, in which case the Lukan 'in my
kingdom' will have the greater claim to originality. Another
possibility is that in the pre-synoptic tradition the saying
about the twelve apostles followed the parable collection (cf.
Catchpole's suggestion) and immediately preceded the sheep and
goats section, which opened very much as Matthew suggests.

6.2.3. A proposed pre-synoptic text
More precisely we suggest that the pre-synoptic tradition
may have been approximately as follows:

parable of the talents

parable of the disobedient servants

question from Peter: 'What then about us?'

Jesus' reply:
'You that have followed (or stayed with) me, I covenant
to you as my father covenanted to me a kingdom. You

will eat and drink at my table in my kingdom, and you will
sit on thrones judging the twelve tribes.

But when the Son of man comes in his glory and all the
angels with him, then he will sit on a throne ....'

(sheep and goats)

In favour of this proposal, note

(a) it explains Mt 19:27,28 well. There is little doubt that
the saying about the twelve apostles judging the tribes is an
insertion in its Matthean context: this is suggested by its
absence from the parallel Markan/Lukan context, by the
observation that in Matthew we have two rather different
responses of Jesus to the disciples' remark of Mt 19:27 (i.e.
Mt 19:28 + 19:29),/1/ and also (less certainly) by the different
location of Lk 22:28-30 (if this is indeed the same saying).
And it is easy to see how the saying came to be inserted in its
present Matthean context, especially if the original opening
had ὑμεῖς οἱ ἀκολουθήσαντες (rather than the Lukan
διαμεμενηκότες), since this neatly picks up the preceding
ἠκολουθήσαμεν of Mt 19:27. It seems possible that Peter's
question in Mt 19:27 τί ἄρα ἔσται ὑμῖν, which is not paralleled
in Mark, belonged with and introduced the inserted sayings./2/

In inserting the saying Matthew abbreviates it, omitting
the verses about the covenanted kingdom and about eating and
drinking in the kingdom, perhaps for the sake of brevity,
perhaps because they could have seemed slightly incongruous in
the Matthean context. It may be that his omission led Matthew
next to paraphrase the original 'in my kingdom' with the more
explicit 'in the new life, when the Son of man shall sit on his
glorious throne'. Much of the phraseology used here by Matthew
is borrowed from the opening of the sheep and goats section,
which followed on in the pre-synoptic tradition from the saying
about the twelve apostles and the tribes. It is thus neatly
explained why Matthew has precisely this phrase - with a
reference to the 'Son of man' that is perhaps a little
surprising in the context of Matthew 19:28-29 - at this point.

/1/ So Burnett, *JSNT* 17, p. 63.
/2/ This question is too easily dismissed by Dupont as Matthean
(*Biblica* 45, p. 356). Τίς ἄρα may be a Matthean form of
expression, but at least in 18:1 & 19:25 Matthew is only
rephrasing tradition, not creating sayings.

(b) It explains Lk 22:28-30 satisfactorily, though there
is not all that much to explain since Luke has retained the
original form of the pericope to a considerable extent. He
has, however, found a new location for the material. In view
of Luke's other rearrangement of the eschatological discourse
(with material from the discourse found in Luke 12, 17 and
perhaps 19 as well as in 21) it is not at all surprising that
the sayings of Lk 22:28-30 have become separated from the
discourse. Nor is it surprising that Luke should have located
them in the Last Supper narrative: the sayings refer to
'covenanting' and to 'eating and drinking' at Jesus' table in
the coming kingdom, and so apparently fit into the Last Supper
context with its similar eschatological ideas (cf. Lk 22:15-18),
and they also have a loose thematic link with the discussion of
greatness and servanthood found in Lk 22:24-27.

(c) The proposed pre-synoptic sequence (with the sayings
about the twelve coming between the parable of the disobedient
servants and the description of the sheep and the goats) works
remarkably well. Note the following points:

1. It is suggested that the sayings were introduced by a
question from Peter (or another disciple) 'What then about us?'.
This question would be quite a natural question after the
preceding gloomy parable about the disobedient servants who got
beaten with few or many strokes; Peter looks for some more
hopeful word, and indeed he gets it. The question would also
be rather similar to the earlier Petrine question in the pre-
synoptic tradition. 'Lord is it to us that you tell this
parable or to all?' (cf. Lk 12:41); we have then two
structurally parallel interventions from Peter.

2. The two promises made to the twelve (a) that they shall eat
and drink at Jesus' table and (b) that they shall rule over the
twelve tribes are curiously reminiscent of the rewards for
faithfulness figuratively described (a) in the parables of the
virgins and the watchman: the virgins go into the *feast* with
the bridegroom, and the watching servant is sat down and
feasted by the returning master, (b) in the parables of the
steward and the talents: the faithful steward and servants are
given *authority* over the master's affairs. There is no problem
in supposing that the same rewards might have been promised to
the disciples in two quite unconnected contexts; and yet the
fact that the Lukan saying has exactly the same rewards in the
same order as the parable collection makes the postulated

linking of the two the more attractive./1/

3. Not only would the saying about the twelve fit in well after
the preceding parable collection; it would also fit well
before the section about the sheep and the goats, which at
present lacks any introduction. Note particularly (a) how the
thought of Jesus having a kingdom from his father is picked up
in the sheep and the goats section, where the Son of man is
described as king; (b) how the thought of the disciples being
promised a kingdom and authority as judges is picked up in the
promise to the righteous to 'inherit the kingdom prepared for
you from the beginning of the world'; (c) how the saying about
the twelve would provide a context for understanding the phrase
'the least of these my brethren' in Mt 25:40. Matthean
references to 'little ones' and 'brothers' elsewhere strongly
suggest that this phrase is a reference to Jesus' followers,/2/
as many have recognized, but in the immediate context of
Matthew 25 it is unexplained. The proposal concerning the
saying on the twelve would supply the explanation.

Against the suggestion that the saying about the twelve
belongs in this context it may be argued (a) that the saying
introduces an alien note (discussion of the reward of the
twelve) into the context, which has been emphasizing duty not
promising rewards. But this is not at all a decisive point,
since the thought is not an unnatural development from the
preceding sayings with their emphasis on reward and punishment.
(b) It may perhaps seem complicated to have first a reference
to the apostles judging the twelve tribes and then a
description of the Son of man judging the nations. But this is
not a great complication: if 'my brethren' in the sheep and the
goats section are (in the first instance) the twelve, then that
section is continuing the thought, introduced in the previous
saying, about the significant role of the twelve - they are to

---

/1/ If there is anything in this argument, it tells against
Catchpole's view that the clause about 'eating and drinking' at
Jesus' table was not in the 'Q' form of the saying. In any
case, it seems probable that it was the presence of this clause
in the saying that encouraged Luke to place the saying in the
Last Supper context. See above.

/2/ There is no need to see a subtle distinction between μικροί
and ἐλάχιστοι in Matthew; the dramatic point in Mt 25:40,45
determines the use of the superlative.

judge Israel and to be the criterion of judgment in the
judgment of the nations. And it is perhaps possible to find
some sort of parallels to the idea of a double judgment (of
Israel and the nations): thus in Revelation 7 the 144,000 of
the tribes of Israel are described first, then the international
numberless multitude; in Revelation 20 there is first the rule
on heavenly 'thrones' of 'those to whom judgment was committed'
who will reign with Christ (i.e. the resurrection of true
believers, 20:4-6); then there is the judgment of all by the
one on the great white throne (20:11-15). It may be that the
book of Revelation reflects here the postulated pre-synoptic
sequence with the apostles judging the twelve tribes (God's
people) and the Son of man judging the nations.

6.3. Final observations

The case for including the saying of Mt 19:28/Lk 22:28-30
in the pre-synoptic eschatological discourse is not
implausible,/1/ and, if that saying belonged there, then the
sheep and the goats tradition, which in my case has a claim to
be included, must also have been part of the discourse. But it
must be emphasized in conclusion that the main argument of this
chapter in no way depends on the suggestions made in the
additional notes on the sheep and the goats section and on the
saying about the twelve. The suggestion about the saying in
particular is speculative insofar as there is no direct
evidence for its location in the context of the eschatological
discourse. The earlier arguments, on the other hand,
concerning the conclusion of the discourse were based on
substantial direct and indirect evidence.

/1/ Note that in the 'saying' of 2 Tim 2:11-13 we find 'If we
endure with him' - possibly to be connected with the saying of
Mt 24:13 & par. - together with 'we shall reign with him' -
possibly to be connected with the saying we have discussed.

Chapter 4

LUKE 17:22-37:   AN EXTRACT FROM THE ESCHATOLOGICAL DISCOURSE

In the preceding chapter it was argued that the sayings
about the sudden coming of the Son of man in Mt 24:37-41/
Lk 17:26-35 were part of the original conclusion of the
eschatological discourse. But if those verses were part of the
pre-synoptic eschatological discourse, what about the other
eschatological material found in Lk 17:22-37, some of which is
also paralleled in Matthew 24? It is commonly supposed that the
eschatological material of Luke 17 is quite distinct from the
Markan eschatological discourse and that Matthew has conflated
the Markan and the 'Q' traditions. But the evidence of
Lk 17:26-35 tends to point in the opposite direction and to
suggest that Matthew has retained an original unity, which Luke
has split up. This chapter will explore this possibility
further and will argue that nearly all of Lk 17:22-37 is to be
seen as an extract from the pre-synoptic eschatological
discourse.

1.   *THE PRINCIPAL ARGUMENTS FOR SEEING LK 17:22-37 AS AN EXTRACT
     FROM THE ESCHATOLOGICAL DISCOURSE*

1.1.   *The overlap between Lk 21:34-36 and Lk 17:26-18:1*

There is no need to repeat the arguments presented in the
preceding chapter for linking Lk 21:34-36 and Lk 17:26-18:1
(pp. 107-09 above). If those arguments were correct, then they
show that a substantial part of Lk 17:22-37 was material taken
from the eschatological discourse and used out of context by
Luke in his chapter 17.

1.2.   *The overlap between Lk 17:20-23 and Mt 24:21-26,'
       Mk 13:19-23*

The first part of Lk 17:22-37 was also probably taken from
the eschatological discourse. Compare:

Mt 24:21-26	Mk 13:19-23	Lk 17:20-23
		ἐπερωτηθεὶς δὲ ὑπὸ τῶν φαρισαίων πότε ἔρχεται ἡ βασιλεία τοῦ θεοῦ, ἀπεκρίθη αὐτοῖς καὶ εἶπεν· οὐκ ἔρχεται ἡ βασιλεία τοῦ θεοῦ μετὰ παρατηρήσεως, 21. οὐδὲ ἐροῦσιν· ἰδοὺ ὧδε ἢ ἐκεῖ· ἰδοὺ γὰρ ἡ βασιλεία τοῦ θεοῦ ἐντὸς ὑμῶν ἐστιν. 22. εἶπεν δὲ πρὸς τοὺς μαθητάς· ἐλεύσονται ἡμέραι
ἔσται γὰρ τότε θλῖψις μεγάλη, οἷα οὐ γέγονεν ἀπ' ἀρχῆς κόσμου ἕως τοῦ νῦν οὐδ' οὐ μὴ γένηται. 22. καὶ εἰ μὴ ἐκολοβώθησαν αἱ ἡμέραι ἐκεῖναι, οὐκ ἂν ἐσώθη πᾶσα σάρξ· διὰ δὲ τοὺς ἐκλεκτοὺς κολοβωθήσονται αἱ ἡμέραι ἐκεῖναι. 23. τότε ἐάν τις ὑμῖν εἴπῃ· ἰδοὺ ὧδε ὁ χριστός, ἢ ὧδε, μὴ πιστεύσητε· 24. ἐγερθήσονται γὰρ ψευδόχριστοι καὶ ψευδοπροφῆται, καὶ δώσουσιν σημεῖα μεγάλα καὶ τέρατα, ὥστε πλανῆσαι, εἰ δυνατόν, καὶ τοὺς ἐκλεκτούς. 25. ἰδοὺ προείρηκα ὑμῖν. 26. ἐὰν οὖν εἴπωσιν ὑμῖν· ἰδοὺ ἐν τῇ ἐρήμῳ ἐστίν, μὴ ἐξέλθητε· ἰδοὺ ἐν τοῖς ταμείοις, μὴ πιστεύσητε.	ἔσονται γὰρ αἱ ἡμέραι ἐκεῖναι θλῖψις, οἷα οὐ γέγονεν τοιαύτη ἀπ' ἀρχῆς κτίσεως ἣν ἔκτισεν ὁ θεὸς ἕως τοῦ νῦν καὶ οὐ μὴ γένηται. 20. καὶ εἰ μὴ ἐκολόβωσεν κύριος τὰς ἡμέρας, οὐκ ἂν ἐσώθη πᾶσα σάρξ· ἀλλὰ διὰ τοὺς ἐκλεκτοὺς οὓς ἐξελέξατο ἐκολόβωσεν τὰς ἡμέρας. 21. καὶ τότε ἐάν τις ὑμῖν εἴπῃ· ἴδε ὧδε ὁ χριστός, ἴδε ἐκεῖ, μὴ πιστεύετε· 22. ἐγερθήσονται γὰρ ψευδόχριστοι καὶ ψευδοπροφῆται καὶ δώσουσιν σημεῖα καὶ τέρατα πρὸς τὸ ἀποπλανᾶν, εἰ δυνατόν, τοὺς ἐκλεκτούς. 23. ὑμεῖς δὲ βλέπετε· προείρηκα ὑμῖν πάντα.	ὅτε ἐπιθυμήσετε μίαν τῶν ἡμερῶν τοῦ υἱοῦ τοῦ ἀνθρώπου ἰδεῖν καὶ οὐκ ὄψεσθε.

23. καὶ ἐροῦσιν ὑμῖν· ἰδοὺ ἐκεῖ, ἰδοὺ ὧδε· μὴ ἀπέλθητε μηδὲ διώξητε. |

1.2.1. Agreement about days of distress

It is immediately obvious that there is overlap between the references in Lk 17:21 and 23 to people saying: 'behold here ...there' and the similar reference in Mk 13:21; but before looking at this more closely, note the similarity in the immediately preceding context in both gospels. Mark has a reference to 'days' of unparalleled distress affecting even the elect; Luke also has a reference to coming 'days' when 'you will long to see one of the days of the Son of man and will not see it'.

Luke does not spell out explicitly what period he is describing. But a comparison with the following parable of the unjust judge (18:1-8), which speaks of the 'elect' crying day and night for vindication and which refers to the Lord's coming, suggests that what is being referred to in 17:22 is a period of distress for the elect, which will be brought to an end by the coming of the Son of man. It seems likely that the much-debated phrase 'one of the days of the Son of man' is a reference to the period of the second coming and of the final kingdom, the plural 'days' probably being an echo of the later reference to 'the days of Noah' and 'of Lot' (vv 26,28, on which see discussion below). This is suggested by the preceding context (v 20), where 'the kingdom' (as often in Luke) probably refers to the final coming of the kingdom, and by the following v 23 'Behold there ... here' and the subsequent discussion of the second coming, as well as by the parable in 18:1-8./1/

If this is at least an approximately correct understanding of Luke's thought, then the sense in Luke is very similar to that found in Mk 13:19,20, since we seem in those verses to have moved beyond the thought of a local disaster in Jerusalem

---

/1/ Cf. Marshall, *Luke*, 658,659. Luke's later reference to the 'days of the Son of man' in v 26 may have a slightly different sense if the reference is to the period before the second coming. (Cf. B. Rigaux, 'La petite apocalypse de Luc (XVII, 22-37)', in *Ecclesia a Spiritu Sancto edocta à Mgr G. Philips* [Gembloux: Duculot, 1970] 410-412). But it is arguable that there Luke's source had 'the day' (singular; see discussion below), and in both vv 22 and 26 the rather vague plural phrase of Luke may be paraphrased by some such phrase as 'the period of the Son of man's parousia'. If the plural 'days' in v 26 is Lukan, then the same phrase in v 22 may also be Lukan.

(found in the preceding vv 14-18) to something bigger which
will affect the whole of humanity and which will be brought to
an end by divine intervention through the coming of the Son of
man. (On the interpretation of the Markan passage see further
in chapter 5 below). The thought in Mk 13:20 'because of the
elect ... he shortened the days', is very similar to that of
Lk 18:7,8, where the response to the crying of 'the elect' is
that 'he will produce his vindication speedily'; and it may
possibly be significant that the word 'elect' is used by Mark
only in this context (13:20,22,27) and by Luke only twice in
the whole of Luke/Acts (in Lk 18:7 and 23:35).

Although the sense in Lk 17:22 seems similar to that in
Mk 13:19,20, it is quite differently worded in the two gospels,
and this could weigh against any suggestion that they are
connected. But it is not unreasonable to see the Lukan verse as
Luke's replacement for the Markan verses./1/ Luke in taking up
the eschatological discourse at this point would have had to
modify the Markan words, since he has not the preceding
Markan context which makes Mark's 'those days will be ...'
intelligible; he therefore substitutes for it his favourite
'days will come'. Then he avoids a general description of the
distress of those days, as this would not have been
particularly pertinent to the train of thought that he is
developing (about false expectation, cf. 17:21,23); and he
speaks instead of the particular aspect of the distress that
was relevant to his theme, i.e. of people's longing for the
coming of the Son of man. The actual phraseology used here by
Luke is partly explicable from later parts of the discourse -
for the phrase 'days of' see Lk 17:26,28 and for the 'seeing'
of the 'Son of man' compare Mt 24:30/Mk 13:26/Lk 21:27; but
Luke may possibly also have been influenced by the formulation
of the quite different saying of Mt 13:17/Lk 10:24 'Many ...
have desired (Mt ἐπεθύμησαν, Lk ἠθέλησαν) to see what you see
and did not see ...'./2/

/1/ It is possible that the Lukan and the Markan verses could
have been combined in the underlying pre-synoptic source; but
it is not easy to see how they would have been combined or why
Mark and Matthew would have omitted the Lukan words.
/2/ So Schürmann, NTS 6 p. 199. For the view that Lk 17:22 is
a transitional verse see Rigaux, 'La petite apocalypse', 412.

That this verse was seen by Luke as an equivalent of
Mark's description of the great distress may perhaps be
confirmed by the fact that in Luke 21 Luke omits not only the
Markan reference to false prophets saying 'here', 'there', but
also the preceding description of the 'great distress': it is
explicable that he omits both in Luke 21 because he has used
the substance of both here in chap. 17. But this argument is at
best tentative, and the question of the relationship of
Mk 13:14-23 and Lk 21:20-24 will be taken up in chapter 5. In the
meantime the most that can be said is that Lk 17:22 has
interesting similarities of Mk 13:19,20, and could be related;
whether they are actually thought to be related will depend on
whether the sayings on false prophecy found in both contexts
(i.e. Lk 17:23, Mk 13:21) seem to be connected.

1.2.2. Agreement about the false prophecy
a. The Markan and 'Q' traditions

Can the case for Lk 17:22-23 and Mk 13:19-21 being taken
from one underlying form of tradition be supported by an
examination of the saying about the false prophets who say
'here' 'there' in Mk 13:21 and Lk 17:23? The usual
explanation is that Lk 17:23 is basically 'Q' tradition
(distinct from the Markan tradition), which Matthew also
preserves in his 24:26. In favour of this note the third
person plural ἐροῦσιν (Lk) εἴπωσιν (Mt), the double use of ἰδού
in both Luke and Matthew, where Mark has ἴδε, the order 'there'
'here' in Luke, paralleling Matthew's 'in the wilderness' 'in
the chambers' and contrasting with Mark's 'here' 'there',/1/
and the double prohibition μὴ ἀπέλθητε μηδὲ διώξητε paralleling
Matthew's μὴ ἐξέλθητε ... μὴ πιστεύσητε and contrasting with
Mark's single μὴ πιστεύετε.

However, there are some differences between Lk 17:23 and
Mt 24:26 which need explanation: (a) Whereas Luke has μὴ
ἀπέλθητε μηδὲ διώξητε, Matthew has μὴ ἐξέλθητε ... μὴ
πιστεύσητε. It seems likely that Matthew's asymmetric μὴ

/1/ Note that a substantial number of texts have the order
'here' 'there' in Luke. It is not certain which reading is
correct, but it is probably simpler to suppose that 'there'
'here' has been altered to 'here' 'there' under the influence
of Mk 13:21 and Lk 17:21 than vice versa. Cf. Marshall, *Luke*,
659,660.

πιστεύσητε is assimilation to the Markan wording and that Luke
here retains the original 'Q' (to use the conventional
terminology) in his διώξητε./1/   (b) Where Luke has ἐκεῖ ...
ὧδε Matthew has ἐν τῇ ἐρήμῳ ... ἐν τοῖς ταμείοις. (c) Whereas
Luke has ἰδού ... ἰδού ... μή ... μηδέ, Matthew has ἰδού ... μή
ἰδού ... μή. The key to the explanation of these last two
differences probably lies in the fact that in both cases Luke's
divergence from Matthew is an agreement with Mark 13:21, since
Mark has the words ὧδε ... ἐκεῖ and has the form ἴδε ... ἴδε
... μή. Given this evidence, two possible conclusions could be
drawn: *either* Luke's 'Q' wording is the more original, and
Matthew has made it less like Mark in order to avoid
repetitiousness (since he has just recorded the Markan saying);
one point telling against this is that Matthew's μὴ πιστεύσητε
in v 26 is most probably assimilation to the Markan saying,
which we would not expect if Matthew were consciously trying to
avoid repetition. *Or* Matthew has the original 'Q' wording, and
Luke has mixed the 'Q' and the Markan forms. The latter seems
the simpler hypothesis./2/

     It seems probable then that the 'Q' saying was
approximately as follows:

        ἐὰν οὖν εἴπωσιν ὑμῖν/ἐροῦσιν ὑμῖν ἰδοὺ (ἐκεῖ) ἐν τῇ ἐρήμῳ
        ἐστίν, μὴ ἐξέλθητε ἰδοὺ (ὧδε) ἐν τοῖς ταμείοις, μὴ
        διώξητε./3/

Both Matthew and Luke have drawn on this tradition (in Mt 24:26
and Lk 17:23) and both have altered the wording slightly under
the influence of the similar Markan saying (Mk 13:21).

     b. Two 'behold here ... there' sayings known to Matthew
and Luke
     But to reach this conclusion in no way proves that the 'Q'
tradition and the Markan tradition are to be linked or that
both were derived from a common pre-synoptic source. There is,

_____

/1/ Cf. Geiger, *Endzeitreden*, 61.
/2/ A good case can be made out for the originality of the
Matthean wording. Cf. G. R. Beasley-Murray, *A Commentary on
Mark 13* (London, Macmillan, 1957) 84,85. J. Lambrecht,
Biblica 47 (1966) 341; contra Geiger, *Endzeitreden*, 63.
/3/ Similarly Lambrecht, *Biblica* 47, p. 341, Zmijewski,
Eschatologiereden, 410,411.

however, further evidence to be considered, in that Luke has
not only got one 'behold here, there' saying (in 17:23); but two
verses previously (in the exchange with the Pharisees about the
coming of the kingdom of God) he has another, 'The kingdom of
God does not come with watching, nor will they say, "Behold
here or there"' (17:20,21). When the two Lukan 'behold here,
there' sayings are compared with Mt 24:23,26 and Mk 13:21,
various interesting points emerge:

Compare

Lk 17:21   Mt 24:23   Mk 13:21

οὐδὲ ἐροῦσιν ἰδοὺ   ἐάν τις ὑμῖν εἴπῃ   ἐάν τις ὑμῖν εἴπῃ
ὧδε ἢ ἐκεῖ   ἰδοὺ ἢ ὧδε ὁ Χριστός, ἴδε ὧδε ὁ χριστός,
                     ὧδε, μὴ πιστεύσητε   ἴδε ἐκεῖ, μὴ πιστεύετε

Lk 17:23   Mt 24:26

καὶ ἐροῦσιν ὑμῖν   ἐὰν οὖν εἴπωσιν ὑμῖν·
ἰδοὺ ἐκεῖ ἰδοὺ ὧδε   ἰδοὺ ἐν τῇ ἐρήμῳ
μὴ ἀπέλθητε μηδὲ   ἐστίν, μὴ ἐξέλθητε·
διώξητε   ἰδοὺ ἐν τοῖς
                    ταμείοις, μὴ
                    πιστεύσητε.

Three things are immediately notable: (1) Luke and Matthew both
have a pair of similar, but slightly different, 'behold here
..there' sayings in close proximity to each other. This might
not seem significant since the respective contexts are not
parallel. But (2) the first saying in Luke and the first
saying in Matthew both have an ἰδοὺ ... ἢ construction,/1/
whereas Mk 13:21, Lk 17:23 and Mt 24:26 all have an ἰδοὺ (ἴδε)
.... ἰδοὺ (ἴδε) construction. The first saying in Luke and the
first saying in Matthew also agree in that the first words
ascribed to the false prophets are ἰδοὺ ὧδε - in this they agree
with Mk 13:21 - whereas in the second saying in both Matthew and
Luke ἰδοὺ ἐκεῖ / ἐν τῇ ἐρήμῳ comes first and ἰδοὺ ὧδε/ἐν τοῖς
ταμείοις comes second. (3) The second saying in Luke and the
second saying in Matthew have several agreements against Mk 13:21,
as was noted above, and also against their own first sayings

/1/ Some MSS have ἢ ἰδοὺ ἐκεῖ in Lk 17:21, which reduces the
distinctive similarity of Lk 17:21 and Mt 24:23. But the
reading is probably an assimilation to the form of Lk 17:23.

(e.g. the double use of ἰδού, the order 'there ... here', the
command 'do not go out', the use of two verbs).

It is very hard to see how these three observations about
the parallel structure of Matthew and Luke can be satisfactorily
explained on the two-source hypothesis. They can, however, be
quite simply explained if all three evangelists are drawing on
a pre-synoptic form of the eschatological discourse, which was
rather similar to our Matthew and which included the two
'behold here ... there' sayings. Such a hypothesis would also
account for other points already noted - for the common
sequence of thought in Lk 17:22,23 and in Mt 24:21-23/Mk 13:19-21
(with a description of coming distress preceding a warning
of false prophecy) and for the assimilation of the two 'behold
here ... here' sayings, though that hardly needs explanation.
The hypothesis also fits in with the earlier argument about
Lk 17:26-35/Mt 24:37-41, since that so-called 'Q' material was
also ascribed to the pre-synoptic eschatological discourse.

       c. The pre-synoptic form and the synoptic texts
       If we wish to reconstruct precisely the form of the pre-
synoptic tradition that supposedly explains so much, there
are a number of possibilities which would account for the
evidence. But probably the most straightforward view is that
the pre-synoptic tradition contained two sayings very similar
to those that we now have in Matthew, except that the first
clause had ὧδε .. ἐκεῖ not ὧδε ... ὧδε and the second clause
had μὴ διώξητε not μὴ πιστεύσητε.

It will then have been approximately as follows:

ἐάν τις ὑμῖν εἴπῃ ἰδού/ἴδε ὧδε ὁ Χριστός, ἢ ἐκεῖ, μὴ
πιστεύσητε/πιστεύετε

ἐάν οὖν εἴπωσιν ὑμῖν/ἐροῦσιν ὑμῖν ἰδού (ἐκεῖ) ἐν τῇ
ἐρήμῳ ἐστίν, μὴ ἐξέλθητε, ἰδού (ὧδε) ἐν τοῖς ταμείοις, μὴ
διώξητε....

Each of our present gospel texts is explicable from this: Matthew
has retained the pre-synoptic tradition with little alteration.
But he has spoiled the original chiasm 'here' (A) ... 'there'
(B) .... 'in the desert' (B)... 'in the chambers' (A), by
putting two ὧδεs in the first sentence. (It is not obvious why
Matthew should have made this change. It is not impossible
that his ὧδε ... ὧδε is original and that Mark and Luke have

introduced variation.) And he has altered the final διώξητε to
πιστεύσητε under the influence of the first saying.

Mark has only retained the first saying, but he betrays
his knowledge of the form of the second saying by having a
repeated ἴδε ... ἴδε instead of the original ἴδε/ἴδου...ἤ.

Luke has been the most radical in his editing, no doubt
because he has used the sayings out of context. The first
saying (17:21a) he uses in the middle of the dialogue with the
Pharisees about the coming of the kingdom of God. It may seem
rather improbable that Luke should have taken this saying out
of its pre-synoptic context and have inserted it in an entirely
different context. But (a), even apart from our hypothesis,
there is a possible case for regarding v 21a as an addition to
the context, since it may be said to interrupt the logical and
grammatical flow from v 20 to v 21b./1/ Note the following
points: (i) vv 20 and 21b go very well together. (ii) V 21a
introduces an unexplained impersonal 'they'. (iii) The thought
of people saying 'Behold here or there' about the coming of the
kingdom is perhaps a little strange, and it certainly makes
more sense of the coming of the Son of man (which we suppose
to have been the original reference). (iv) Luke's repetition
of the subject 'kingdom of God' in vv 20,21b is explicable, if
v 21a is seen as an interpolation that originally applied to
the coming of the Son of man. After the interpolated comment
Luke brings us back to the 'kingdom of God' theme by repeating
the expression in v 21b. (b) It is not hard to see that Luke
could have seen the saying that he inserts in 17:21a as
pertinent in this context: he may well have felt that v 20b,
'the kingdom of God does not come with observation'
(παρατηρήσεως), needed explanation, and the saying of 17:21a
came conveniently to mind. It is true that the saying was
originally about the coming of the Son of man not about the
coming of the kingdom; but Luke elsewhere associates the coming
of the kingdom with the coming of the Son of man (e.g. Lk 21:27
and 31, Acts 1:6 and 11), and even here in chap. 17 he follows
these sayings about the kingdom (vv 20,21) with an extended
discussion of the coming of the Son of man (vv 22-37). More
particularly, of course, he follows the 'behold here ... there'
kingdom-saying of 17:21a with the 'behold there .. here'

/1/ Others have recognized the clause as an addition. Cf.
Marshall, *Luke*, 652-54.

Son-of-man-saying of 17:23, and, although the link could be
verbal not substantial, it would seem quite probable that the
two texts should be taken as describing the same experience,
and therefore that for Luke the coming of the kingdom and the
coming of the Son of man go inextricably together./1/ In any
case it is not hard to see how and why Luke might have used the
first 'behold here ... there' saying in the context of Lk 17:20,
21. In placing it here and using it as a commentary on οὐκ
... μετὰ παρατηρήσεως he naturally omits the original μὴ
πιστεύετε clause.

Having used this saying from the pre-synoptic
eschatological discourse in his 17:21a, Luke not surprisingly
returns to the discourse in his 17:22 and begins to reproduce
it at length, starting at that point in the discourse where the
'behold here ... there' sayings are found. He indicates the
transition from the previous tradition - the dialogue with the
Pharisees - to the eschatological discourse by his phrase
εἶπεν δὲ πρὸς τοὺς μαθητάς, giving to the eschatological
material that follows the same setting as Matthew and Mark give
to the eschatological discourse (Mt 24:3 / Mk 13:3)./2/ After
this phrase, he has to find his way into the eschatological
discourse editorially, and so in 17:22 we have a very free
paraphrase of Mt 24:21,22/Mk 13:19,20 (see previous discussion,
pp. 137-39). This then leads into 17:23, the second of Luke's
'behold here ... there' sayings; this is basically the second
of the two pre-synoptic sayings, though Luke has in fact
conflated this and the preceding saying and produced a
composite form.

A number of questions are left unanswered by this
argument: in particular, if the pre-synoptic tradition included
the two sayings, how were they connected and in what context
were they found? Luke is unlikely to help us with this, since
he uses the first saying in a new context. But it is quite

/1/ This might perhaps, though not necessarily, favour the view
that Luke understood the saying of 17:21b futuristically of the
parousia.
/2/ It is interesting that in Luke 21 Luke does not spell out
that the disciples were addressed in the eschatological
discourse, but here he shows his knowledge of the Matthew/Mark
setting.

probable that Matthew preserves - at least approximately - the
original pre-synoptic order in his 24:23-26./1/ Luke would
have omitted the sayings of Mt 24:24-25 as inappropriate in his
context, and one result of this is that Luke's ἐροῦσιν (17:23
cf. v 21) - the future tense ἐρῶ is characteristically Lukan -
lacks any subject and is thus a generalizing 'they', whereas
Matthew's parallel εἴπωσιν has an implied subject in the
preceding 'false Christs and false prophets'. One obvious
implication of this whole proposal is that Mt 24:26 is not 'Q'
material tacked on to a Markan ending (Mt 24:25/Mk 13:23), but
it belongs with the preceding material. The question of the
apparent ending of Mt 24:25 / Mk 13:23 will be considered
further below (pp. 167-70).

Although there are further questions to be explored, the
explanation offered for the similarities and differences
between the relevant synoptic texts is simpler and more
comprehensive than other possible explanations./2/ We conclude

-----

/1/ Tuckett, *Revival*, 170,171, argues that Matthew's vv 23-25,
that speak of the 'wrong people appearing in the right way', do
not fit well with his vv 26-28, that speak of 'people appearing
in the wrong way'. But, although there is a development in the
sequence of ideas - with the first warning about false
Messianic expectation being backed up with a general comment
that there will be false Christs (vv 23,24) and the second
warning about false Messianic expectation being backed up with
instruction about how/where the Christ will appear (vv 26,27) -,
there is no incompatibility in these two warnings, and we
might indeed expect some development of thought within the
passage rather than the repetition of the same ideas. (See
also the discussion of Mt 24:25 and 28 below, p. 170.)
Tuckett's view that v 26 with its Messianic connotations does
not cohere well with the later references to the Son of man's
coming would surely equally impugn Matthew's v 23 (cf.
Mk 13:21), and is hardly a cogent argument for the shorter
Lukan form.
/2/ The other possibilities include (a) that Luke has preserved
something nearer the original of the two sayings, and that
Matthew has conflated the form of Lk 17:21 with the quite
separate (but notably similar) Mk 13:21 and that he has altered
Lk 17:23 quite considerably making it more similar to Mark in
some respects (i.e. in the ἐάν construction and the πιστεύσητε),
but less similar in others (hence his alteration of 'here..

then that Luke is drawing on the pre-synoptic eschatological
discourse in 17:21-23. If he is doing so at the start of the
eschatological section in his chapter 17 as well as at the end,
then there is a strong case for suspecting that the whole
section comes from the eschatological discourse and that
Matthew has preserved the so-called 'Q' material in the original
context.

1.3. The analogy of Lk 12:35-48 and parallels

The arguments put forward concerning Lk 12:35-48 in
chapters 1-3 (above) lend some plausibility to the view of
Lk 17:22-37 being proposed. Note the following points: (a) It
may seem improbable to us that Luke would split up a unified
pre-synoptic discourse using some of it in chap. 17 and some
in chap. 21. But this is precisely the sort of thing that
Lk 12:35-48 suggests that he did with the eschatological
discourse; it was argued that Lk 12:35-48 is an extract from the
eschatological discourse. (b) Lk 12:35-48 is usually
considered 'Q' material, which Matthew combined in his chaps.
24,25 with Markan material. But in fact, it was argued,
Matthew (and the other evangelists) were all drawing on a
common source in which the supposed 'Q' and Markan materials
were already joined; Matthew preserved the original unity
which Luke broke. If that is the correct explanation of one
supposed Q-Mark combination in Matthew 24,25, economy of

---

there' and his dividing of the material into two distinct ἰδού
... μή clauses); (b) that Luke has preserved the original form
of the first clause and that Matthew has conflated it with Mark,
but that Matthew has preserved the original form of the second
clause and that Luke has conflated this with Mark. But both
these possibilities are relatively complicated, and do not
explain the relationship of Mk 13:21 to the two Q sayings. H.
Schürmann's suggestion, *BZ* 7 (1966) 248, that Matthew knew
Lk 17:20f. in his Q and that he has transformed the idea of an
invisible coming into the idea of a visible 'sign of the Son of
man' (Mt 24:30) and the idea of people longing for the days of
the Son of man into the idea of people mourning at his coming
(Mt 24:30) is ingenious, highly speculative and involves a much
more radical and complex editorial procedure than our
hypothesis.

hypothesis would favour the same explanation of other supposed
Q-Mark combinations. (c) The eschatological material comes
quite abruptly in Lk 17:22 and is not obviously in an original
context. It seems quite likely that Luke has located the
material at this point because of the thematic link with the
preceding Lk 17:20,21. The analogy of Lk 12:35 would support
this supposition, since there too we have an abrupt change of
direction explicable via a verbal/thematic link (see earlier
discussion of λύχνος/λαμπάς, pp. 86-89 above). (d) Not only
do we get a rather abrupt transition in 12:35 and 17:22, but we
may also suspect that these verses have lost some preceding
context; our hypothesis supplies such a preceding context in
both cases. It may seem rather surprising that Luke should
start his extract from the eschatological discourse here in
chapter 17 with the warning of false prophets at the time of the
eschatological desolating sacrilege (Lk 17:22,23/Mk 13:19-21/
Mt 24:21-23); but in chapter 12 he starts equally surprisingly
with the conclusion to the parable of the virgins. In both
cases the explanation is in terms of a thematic/verbal link
with what precedes.

     The analogy, then, of chapter 12 lends plausibility to the
proposal that Lk 17:22-37 be seen as an extract from the
eschatological discourse.

2. THE PRE-SYNOPTIC TRADITION IDENTIFIED

     But can this thesis of Lk 17:22-37 as an extract from a
pre-synoptic form of the eschatological discourse be defended
in more detail? Can we explain how the relevant sections of the
supposed pre-synoptic discourse will have looked, and how our
present synoptic texts can be explained from it?

2.1. General comparison of Luke 17 and Matthew 24

     An obvious starting point for answering these questions is
Matthew's gospel: since Matthew has retained the so-called 'Q'
material within the eschatological discourse, it is at least
worth considering whether he has preserved the original form
and order of the discourse. A comparison of Mt 24:21-41 and
Lk 17:22-end looks as follows:

     1. Mt 24:21,22/Mk 13:19,20   Lk 17:22

         There will be great   You will long to see ....
         distress......

2. Mt 24:23-26/Mk 13:21-23,   Lk 17:23 (cf. 17:21)
    And then if anyone says to   And they will say to you
    you 'Behold here...'   'Behold there ....'
    False prophets will arise
    ... Behold I have told
    you before. If they say
    to you, 'Behold in the
    desert..' don't go out...   don't go out.....

3. Mt 24:27   Lk 17:24
    For like the lightning....   For like the lightning.....
    so the parousia of the Son   so the Son of man
    of man

4. Mt 24:28   cf. Lk 17:36
    Where the body, there the
    eagles

5. Mt 24:29-36 & par.   -
    The parousia and its
    timing

6.   -   Lk 17:25
                                 But first the Son of man
                                 must suffer

7. Mt 24:37-39   Lk 17:26-27
    As the days of Noah, so   As in the days of Noah, so
    the parousia of the Son of   in the days of the Son of
    man   man

8.   -   Lk 17:28-30
                                 As in days of Lot .... so
                                 in the day when Son of man
                                 revealed

9. cf. Mt 24:17 & par.   Lk 17:31-33
                                 He who is on the house ...
                                 he who is in the field ...
                                 + other sayings

10. Mt 24:40,41   Lk 17:34-35
    Two in the field one   Two in a bed one taken ....
    taken....
    Two at mill ......   Two at mill ....

From this comparison it is evident that Luke in chapter 17 has
some equivalent to all of Mt 24:21-42, except for the central
section on the parousia and its timing in Mt 24:29-36. And
Luke has the common material in the Matthean order, except for
the saying about the body and the eagles. Luke also has a
little additional material in 17:25, 17:28-30, 17:31-33.

Given this evidence, can Matthew plausibly be thought to
have preserved the pre-synoptic order and form on which Luke
drew? The answer to that is yes, though Luke occasionally may
have the more original wording. The probability is that Luke
included this extract from the eschatological discourse at this
point in his gospel because of the thematic link with Lk 17:20,
21. Luke's emphasis in those verses was on the unpredictability
or suddenness of the coming of the kingdom - it was this that
led him to introduce the clause about people saying 'Here,
there' from the eschatological discourse into 17:21 itself;
and this thematic interest leads him on to use more of the
discourse in what follows. This thematic concern of Luke's
explains (for the most part at least) his use of Mt 24:21-42:
he goes through the section in order (except for Mt 24:28/Lk 17:37)
using the material that illustrates the unpredictability
theme; he leaves out Mt 24:29-36, the description of the
parousia and the following discussion of the time of the end,
since this was eminently unsuitable for this thematic purpose.
(He was not interested in the signs and time of the end, but in
the lack of chronological signs!) The only substantial things
unexplained by this hypothesis are (a) Luke's three insertions
- 17:25 the saying about the Son of man suffering, 17:28-30 the
sayings about the days of Lot, and 17:31-33 the group of three
sayings about saving one's life; (b) his alteration of the
position of the body/eagles saying, and (c) his replacement of
Matthew's saying about two in a field with his saying about two
on a bed.

These differences and the other small differences can,
however, all be explained on the suggested hypothesis, as will
be demonstrated by a systematic examination of the Lukan
material and of the parallel material in Matthew and Mark.

2.2.   *Detailed explanation of Lk 17:22-37 on the basis of the
        postulated pre-synoptic discourse*

2.2.1.   *Lk 17:21-23/Mt 24:21-26/Mk 13:19-22*
This section has already been studied in some detail
above, and it is not necessary to discuss it further here.

2.2.2. Lk 17:24/Mt 24:27
The texts here are as follows:

Mt 24:27   Lk 17:24

ὥσπερ γὰρ ἡ ἀστραπὴ ἐξέρχεται   ὥσπερ γὰρ ἡ ἀστραπὴ ἀστράπτουσα
ἀπὸ ἀνατολῶν καὶ φαίνεται ἕως   ἐκ τῆς ὑπὸ τὸν οὐρανὸν
δυσμῶν, οὕτως ἔσται ἡ παρουσία   εἰς τὴν ὑπ' οὐρανὸν λάμπει,
τοῦ υἱοῦ τοῦ ἀνθρώπου.   οὕτως ἔσται ὁ υἱὸς τοῦ
                                     ἀνθρώπου ἐν τῇ ἡμέρᾳ αὐτοῦ.

a. Preliminary consideration of the differences
There are slight differences here between Matthew and Luke
in wording, construction and sense. It is not possible to be
certain whose version is more original on the basis of a simple
comparison of wording and construction: Matthew could perhaps
be thought to have used the verb ἐξέρχεσθαι under the influence
of the previous saying (v 26 μὴ ἐξέλθητε) and φαίνεσθαι because
it is a favourite word of his, ἀπὸ ἀνατολῶν ... ἕως δυσμῶν
could be a simplification of Luke's slightly obscure ἐκ τῆς
ὑπὸ τὸν οὐρανὸν εἰς τὴν ὑπ' οὐρανόν. And his ἡ παρουσία τοῦ
υἱοῦ τοῦ ἀνθρώπου is almost universally regarded as his own
wording (cf. his later vv 37,39).

On the other hand, Luke's participial construction
ἀστράπτουσα ... λάμπει could be thought less original than
Matthew's parataxis: one result of Luke's change, if it is
such, is to leave us a little unclear how to construe ἐκ τῆς
ὑπὸ τὸν οὐρανὸν εἰς τὴν ὑπ' οὐρανόν: do the phrases go with
ἀστράπτουσα, or with λάμπει, or one with each, or both with
both?   His combination ἀστραπὴ ἀστράπτουσα is typically
Lukan,/1/ and it is he who uses the verb ἀστράπτειν on the only
other occasion it appears in the NT (24:4).   The verb λάμπει
could well be his alteration of Matthew's φαίνεται, since he
never uses φαίνειν in this sense in Luke-Acts, whereas Matthew
has no apparent aversion to λάμπειν (5:15,16; 17:2). Luke's
ἐκ τῆς ὑπὸ τὸν οὐρανὸν εἰς τὴν ὑπ' οὐρανόν could be his
replacement for the less comprehensive description of lightning
going from East to West;/2/ it is just possible that the actual

/1/ So A. Harnack, The Sayings of Jesus (London: Williams and
Norgate, 1908), 106. Cf., for example, Lk 2:8, 22:15, 23:46
etc.
/2/ Cf. Lk 13:29/Mt 8:11 and Harnack, Sayings, 106.

choice of phrase could have been influenced by the saying in
the eschatological discourse on the gathering of the elect -
ἐκ τῶν τεσσάρων ἀνέμων ἀπ' ἄκρων οὐρανῶν ἕως ἄκρων αὐτῶν
(Mt 24:31)/ἀπ' ἄκρου γῆς ἕως ἄκρου οὐρανοῦ (Mk 13:27)./1/ As for
Luke's οὕτως ἔσται ὁ υἱὸς τοῦ ἀνθρώπου (ἐν τῇ ἡμέρᾳ αὐτοῦ),/2/
this could be Luke's deliberate replacement for the term
'parousia', a term that is not found at all in Luke; Luke could
have altered the saying in line with the later sayings about
the day of the Son of man (17:26-30).

b. Matthew's version dynamic, Luke's static
From the points noted already the balance of probability
seems to lie with Luke's version being the less original, at
least in the first half of the saying about the lightning. But
the argument is not decisive, and in any case the most
important difference, which may be the key to several of the
other verbal differences, has not yet been noted. The
difference is this: Matthew's picture is of lightning crossing
the sky from East to West (ἐξέρχεται ἀπό.... καὶ φαίνεται ἕως),
and that is an appropriate comparison for the dramatic *coming/*
parousia of the Son of man; Luke, on the other hand, seems to
emphasize the brightness of the lightning more than its motion
(ἀστράπτουσα ἐκ .. εἰς ... λάμπει), and this is an appropriate
comparison for the *person* of the Son of man. The difference in
meaning is negligible - Matthew, as much as Luke, wishes to
emphasize the visibility of the parousia/3/ - , and yet it is
a real difference of emphasis, Matthew focusing more on the
event and Luke more on the person. And several of the verbal
differences in both halves of the saying are explicable in terms
of this difference.

/1/ On the other hand, the influence could have been the other
way around. See further discussion below on p. 324.
/2/ The last phrase ἐν τῇ ἡμέρᾳ αὐτοῦ is omitted in significant
MSS and may be a scribal gloss.
/3/ Cf. Tuckett, *The Revival*, 170. He later suggests, p. 172,
that this idea of visibility may not have been original and
that the original emphasis may have been on suddenness only.
But the combined evidence of Matthew and Luke is against this.
The fact that Lk 17:26-30 stress suddenness, not visibility, in
no way requires that the earlier verses be interpreted
exclusively in that way. Both sets of verses stress the
unpredictability of the parousia, but they do so in different
ways.

As for whose emphasis is more original, that is not
immediately obvious. Luke's picture is perhaps less clear than
Matthew's: he appears to be comparing the *person* of the Son of
man to the brightness of lightning, and yet, given the
preceding context (v 23) and the wording ὥσπερ ἡ ἀστραπή ἐκ ...
εἰς ... , the thought of the parousia *event* being like lightning
flashing across the sky is not far away. It is at least
possible that Luke's slight ambiguity on this point is the
result of his modification of the less ambiguous Matthean form.
But this is not at all a decisive point, and Matthew could be
thought to have simplified the Lukan picture.

A more promising line of argument arises out of a
comparison of Matthew's and Luke's second clause: οὕτως ἔσται ἡ
παρουσία τοῦ υἱοῦ τοῦ ἀνθρώπου (Mt), οὕτως ἔσται ὁ υἱὸς τοῦ
ἀνθρώπου (ἐν τῇ ἡμέρᾳ αὐτοῦ) (Lk). Since the difference here -
Matthew speaks of the event, Luke of the person - may be
connected with the differences in the preceding clause, it may
help us to reach a verdict about the whole verse if we can
explain the relationship here.

c. The combined evidence of Mt 24:27,37-39 and Lk 17:24,
26-30
This question cannot be considered apart from the question
of the later verses Mt 24:37,38-39 and Lk 17:26,30, where
rather similar phrases are found. Compare:

Mt 24:27	24:37	24:38,39
ὥσπερ γὰρ ἡ ἀστραπὴ ἐξέρχεται ἀπὸ ἀνατολῶν καὶ φαίνεται ἕως δυσμῶν, οὕτως ἔσται ἡ παρουσία τοῦ υἱοῦ τοῦ ἀνθρώπου.	ὥσπερ γὰρ αἱ ἡμέραι τοῦ Νῶε, οὕτως ἔσται ἡ παρουσία τοῦ υἱοῦ τοῦ ἀνθρώπου.	ὡς γὰρ ἦσαν ἐν ταῖς ἡμέραις (ἐκείναις) ταῖς πρὸ τοῦ κατακλυσμοῦ τρώγοντες καὶ πίνοντες, γαμοῦντες καὶ γαμίζοντες, ἄχρι ἧς ἡμέρας εἰσῆλθεν Νῶε εἰς τὴν κιβωτόν, 39. καὶ οὐκ ἔγνωσαν ἕως ἦλθεν ὁ κατακλυσμὸς καὶ ἦρεν ἅπαντας, οὕτως ἔσται (καὶ) ἡ παρουσία τοῦ υἱοῦ τοῦ ἀνθρώπου.

Lk 17:24	17:26,27	17:28-30
ὥσπερ γὰρ ἡ ἀστραπὴ	καὶ καθὼς ἐγένετο	ὁμοίως καθὼς ἐγένετο
ἀστράπτουσα ἐκ τῆς	ἐν ταῖς ἡμέραις	ἐν ταῖς ἡμέραις Λώτ·
ὑπὸ τὸν οὐρανὸν εἰς	Νῶε, οὕτως ἔσται καὶ	ἤσθιον, ἔπινον,
τὴν ὑπ·οὐρανὸν	ἐν ταῖς ἡμέραις τοῦ	ἠγόραζον, ἐπώλουν,
λάμπει, οὕτως ἔσται	υἱοῦ τοῦ ἀνθρώπου·	ἐφύτευον, ᾠκοδόμουν·
ὁ υἱὸς τοῦ ἀνθρώπου	27. ἤσθιον, ἔπινον,	29. ᾗ δὲ ἡμέρᾳ ἐξῆλθεν
ἐν τῇ ἡμέρᾳ αὐτοῦ.	ἐγάμουν, ἐγαμίζοντο,	Λὼτ ἀπὸ Σοδόμων,
	ἄχρι ἧς ἡμέρας	ἔβρεξεν πῦρ καὶ θεῖον
	εἰσῆλθεν Νῶε εἰς	ἀπ·οὐρανοῦ καὶ
	τὴν κιβωτόν, καὶ	ἀπώλεσεν πάντας.
	ἦλθεν ὁ κατακλυσμὸς	30. κατὰ τὰ αὐτὰ ἔσται
	καὶ ἀπώλεσεν πάντας.	ᾗ ἡμέρᾳ ὁ υἱὸς τοῦ
		ἀνθρώπου ἀποκαλύπτεται.

The following points may be noted on these parallels:

(1) Mt 24:27 and Lk 17:24 (the saying about the lightning) are very similar in structure, and the only big difference is that Matthew concludes οὕτως ἔσται ἡ παρουσία τοῦ υἱοῦ τοῦ ἀνθρώπου and Luke concludes οὕτως ἔσται ὁ υἱὸς τοῦ ἀνθρώπου ἐν τῇ ἡμέρᾳ αὐτοῦ, though a significant group of MSS omits the final phrase ἐν τῇ ἡμέρᾳ αὐτοῦ.

(2) Matthew has two verses describing the days of Noah, whereas Luke only has one. Matthew's first verse on the days of Noah (24:37) is structured rather like his previous saying about the lightning with ὥσπερ + nominative (with verb ἦσαν presumably implied) + οὕτως ἔσται etc.; it only has in common with Lk 17:26 the phrase 'the days of Noah'. Matthew's second verse on the days of Noah, here called 'the days before the flood' (for variation perhaps), is structured much more like the Lukan saying with ὡς .... ἦσαν (Luke ἐγένετο) ἐν ταῖς ἡμέραις ... ἄχρι ἧς ἡμέρας εἰσῆλθεν .... , but then reverts to Matthew's regular οὕτως ἔσται ἡ παρουσία .... construction.

(3) Whereas Matthew's refrain 'So will be the parousia of the Son of man' fits well in 24:27 ('As the lightning ... so the parousia'), it fits less well in 24:37 ('As the days of Noah, so will be the parousia') and in 24:38,39 ('As they were in the days before the flood, so will be the parousia'). The event of the parousia is more aptly compared to lightning - a dramatic event - than to a period of days or to the people living them. Not that there is any problem about the meaning in vv 37-39:

Matthew clearly intends to compare what happened in the days of
Noah with what will happen at the time of the parousia; but,
although the point is clear, it is not very felicitously
expressed.

(4) Matthew's vv 38 and 39 are rather cumbersome and awkward
with the parousia being compared first to the days of Noah and
then to the condition of the people in Noah's time and with the
final refrain 'So will be the parousia ....' having a slightly
redundant ring after the previous use in v 37./1/

(5) Luke's first saying (17:24, on the lightning) is notably
different from his second and third sayings (17:26,28-30 on the
days of Noah and Lot); it has ὥσπερ + nominative + verb,
whereas the others have καθὼς + ἐγένετο + ἐν ταῖς ἡμέραις ...
The difference is the more notable if the phrase ἐν τῇ ἡμέρᾳ
αὐτοῦ .. in 17:24 is not part of the original text./2/

(6) Luke's second and third sayings on the days of Noah and Lot
are very similar in structure. They speak of 'the days of Noah
/Lot' and then of the fateful 'day', when Noah went in and Lot
went out. But they differ in the refrain, 17:26 saying 'so
will it be in the *days* (plural) of the Son of man' and 17:30 'so
will it be in the *day* (singular) when the Son of man is
revealed'. It is notable that the thought in 17:30 of 'the Son
of man being revealed' is somewhat similar to the thought in
17:24 of the Son of man 'shining'.

(7) Luke's refrain 'so will it be in the day(s) of the Son of
man ...' fits well in his second saying (17:26:   'As it was in
the days of Noah....') and in his third saying (17:28-30:   'As
it was in the days of Lot...'). But in the first saying (in
17:24) we have a certainly different and perhaps less
comfortable comparison with 'So will be the Son of man (in his
day)...' following 'As the lightning shines...'. The possible
discomfort lies in the slight ambiguity in the Lukan comparison
already noted: is the point of comparison purely between the
brightness of lightning and the Son of man, or also between the
event of lightning and the event of the parousia?

/1/ Cf. H. Gollinger, *Bibel und Leben* 11 (1970) 240.
/2/ Zmijewski, *Eschatologiereden*, p. 449, supposes that
originally all three sayings had ὥσπερ; but he underestimates
the difference between the different sayings.

How is all this evidence to be explained? At the risk of making premature judgments on certain points, we suggest that the following was the approximate form of the original:

1. The lightning saying   ὥσπερ ἡ ἀστραπὴ ἐξέρχεται.... οὕτως
                                      ἡ παρουσία τοῦ υἱοῦ τοῦ ἀνθρώπου

2. The days of Noah   καθὼς ἐγένετο ἐν ταῖς ἡμέραις Νῶε,
                                    οὕτως ἔσται ἐν τῇ ἡμέρᾳ τοῦ υἱοῦ τοῦ
                                    ἀνθρώπου. ἦσαν γὰρ τρώγοντες καὶ
                                    πίνοντες, γαμοῦντες καὶ γαμίζοντες
                                    ἄχρι ἧς ἡμέρας εἰσῆλθεν Νῶε εἰς τὴν
                                    κιβωτόν, καὶ ἦλθεν ὁ κατακλυσμὸς καὶ
                                    ἀπώλεσεν/ἦρεν πάντας.

3. The days of Lot   ὁμοίως καθὼς ἐγένετο ἐν ταῖς ἡμέραις
                                    Λώτ, οὕτως ἔσται ἐν τῇ ἡμέρᾳ τοῦ
                                    ἀνθρώπου. ἦσαν γὰρ ἐσθίοντες ....
                                    ἄχρι τῆς ἡμέρας ἐξῆλθεν Λώτ ἀπὸ
                                    Σοδόμων, καὶ ἔβρεξεν πῦρ καὶ θεῖον
                                    ἀπ' οὐρανοῦ καὶ ἀπώλεσεν πάντας./1/

How does this proposal satisfy the evidence noted above?

(1) In the lightning saying Matthew has preserved the original wording of the pre-synoptic tradition in his οὕτως ἡ παρουσία ... form. Luke has avoided the word παρουσία and substituted the simple ὁ υἱὸς τοῦ ἀνθρώπου (ἐν τῇ ἡμέρᾳ αὐτοῦ ....). As noted before, Matthew's comparison of the parousia event to the lightning event fits well, whereas Luke's comparison of the Son of man to lightning leaves the reader slightly uncertain as to whether Luke is only comparing the person of the Son of man with the brightness of lightning, or also the event of the coming of the Son of man with the flashing of lightning across the sky. This ambiguity in Luke is explicable on the proposal that has been made: Luke has indeed changed the focus of the comparison from the event to the person, not only by altering the reference to the parousia, but also by changing the original 'as the lightning comes out ...' (Mt 24:27) to the participial 'as the lightning flashes/ gleams....'; but he has not radically rewritten the saying, and

---

/1/ For a rather similar reconstruction see Gaston, *No Stone on Another*, 351, and his discussion on pp. 350, 351.

so the older Matthean sense of the comparison has not
completely disappeared. This suggestion then explains both the
Lukan ambiguity, and also the divergence of Matthew and Luke in
the two clauses.

As for why Luke makes the alteration, perhaps one factor
is simply that he wished to avoid the word παρουσία, which must
have been familiar enough to him and to his church, but which
he never uses in Luke-Acts./1/ But perhaps it also reflects a
Lukan interest in the person of the returning Son of man, since
in the third saying about the days of Lot he alters a simple
saying about the day of the Son of man and speaks of the day
when the Son of man 'is revealed' (see on). It is, of
course, commonly supposed that Matthew is secondary here and
that he has introduced the term 'parousia'./2/ But there is
not very strong evidence for Matthean partiality to this word
- it only occurs once in Matthew apart from these three verses -
and there is strong evidence for the word being part of early
Christian eschatological vocabulary (see Paul's use of it in
1 and 2 Thessalonians). It is thus entirely possible that this
was in the pre-synoptic tradition, and indeed that it was the
influence of this tradition (comparing lightning and the
parousia) that led Matthew to introduce the phrase rather
awkwardly into the following sayings about the days of Noah.

(2) In the saying about the days of Noah, Luke has not
diverged from the pre-synoptic tradition substantially. But he
has probably changed the singular 'thus shall it be in the day
of the Son of man' into a plural 'in the *days* of the Son of man'
to produce a better balance with the preceding reference to the
'days of Noah'. The plural 'days' could be original;/3/ but

/1/ Cf. Harnack, *Sayings*, 106,107. If ἐν τῇ ἡμέρᾳ αὐτοῦ was
part of the original text of Luke, then it seems probable that
he took the phrase from the following sayings about the days of
Noah and Lot; he has assimilated this first saying in the light
of the later sayings.
/2/ Cf. Marshall, *Luke*, 661.
/3/ H. Gollinger, *Bibel und Leben* 11 (1970) 240, argues that
Matthew has made the *day* of the Son of man's coming the point
of comparison in place of Luke's more original emphasis on the
behaviour of people at the time of judgment, and he explains
that Matthew omitted the story of Lot because it had the wrong
emphasis. But this Matthean intention is not very clear, nor
is it obvious that the Lot story was less suitable for an
emphasis on the 'day' than the Noah story.

against this note: (a) it is easy to see how the singular could
have got changed to the plural. (For Luke's liking for the
plural see v 22.) (b) In the following saying about Lot Luke
retains the singular 'day' (v 30, cf. v 31 and perhaps v 24).
There he avoids the apparent imbalance of 'as in the days ... so
in the day' by separating the two clauses (see discussion below).
(c) It is probably slightly simpler to see Matthew's reference
to 'the parousia' as a replacement for the singular 'day' rather
than for the plural 'days'.

Matthew's changes to the pre-synoptic tradition about the
days of Noah have been more substantial. He has in v 37
assimilated the form of the tradition to the form of the
lightning saying (his v 27) - hence the ὥσπερ + the nominative
and then the refrain οὕτως ἔσται ἡ παρουσία ... . But, having
altered the pre-synoptic construction in v 37, he proceeds to
use the pre-synoptic construction in what follows (vv 38,39)
and so we find: 'As it was (Matthew: they were) in the days of
Noah .....so....'. The result is somewhat repetitious and
ungainly (contrast Luke). It is probable that Matthew's καὶ
οὐκ ἔγνωσαν ἕως... is Matthew's addition to the tradition,
necessitated by his rearrangement of the material/1/ and
perhaps reflecting his particular concern in this block of
material. (See discussion in chap. 2 above, especially pp. 84,85.)

(3) Luke is the only one of the evangelists to retain the
saying about the days of Lot, which, according to the
hypothesis being proposed, was in the pre-synoptic tradition./2/
But, according to the proposed hypothesis Luke has in this case
separated the two clauses of the opening sentence, so that
καθὼς ἐγένετο ἐν ταῖς ἡμέραις Λώτ comes at the beginning of the
section and οὕτως/κατὰ τὰ αὐτὰ ἔσται ἐν τῇ ἡμέρᾳ comes at the
end. This separation is rather similar to what is found in

/1/ So W. Bussmann, *Synoptische Studien* II, p. 39.
/2/ It is just possible that Matthew's repetitiousness in
vv 37-39 - with the double comparison and the two οὕτως ἔσται
clauses - might have been encouraged by knowledge of the
original double comparison. Cf. Marshall, *Luke*, 662.
Lambrecht, *Biblica* 47, p. 344, suggests with some plausibility
that Matthew omits the Lot material because of his rewriting of
the Noah material, especially v 39.

Matthew 24:37-39; in Luke's case the explanation of the
separation may have been that he felt that the two halves of the
saying 'As in the days .....so in the day' did not balance very
well. In the preceding 17:26 he dealt with this by having a
plural 'so in the days of the Son of man'; here he deals with it
by separating the two unbalanced clauses and by placing the
description of the days of Lot and of the judgment of Sodom
in-between.

But whatever the reason for Luke's modification of the
pre-synoptic form, the suggestion that he has done this may be
confirmed by the fact that it explains a number of things about
the Lot sayings that are otherwise hard to explain. Most
important there is the observation that, whereas the preceding
saying about the days of Noah was essentially a comparison of
people's *situation* up to the time of Noah's flood and people's
situation at the time of the second coming (rather than a
comparison of the coming of the flood and the second coming),
the saying about the days of Lot is less clear. In Luke's v 28
it looks as though a similar comparison is going to be made
between the situation at the time of Lot's exit and the
situation at the second coming; but in vv 29 and 30 the
comparison seems more to be between the *day* of judgment on
Sodom and the *day* of the parousia./1/ This ambiguity in the
Lot saying and also this difference between the Lot saying and
the preceding Noah saying are explicable as the result of
Luke's moving the 'so it will be ....the day of the Son of man
...' clause after the reference to 'the day' when Lot left
Sodom. Luke has created the rather confusing impression that
the comparison is between the day of Lot's exit from Sodom and
the day of the Son of man (not between the days before Lot's
exit and the time of the second coming). He has done this by
moving the clause in question, but also (a) by replacing the
original ἄχρι ἧς ἡμέρας clause with a ᾗ δὲ ἡμέρᾳ ... clause, so
that the reference to the day of Lot's escape is no longer
secondary to the main point of comparison, and (b) by
assimilating the form of the original 'so will it be ἐν τῇ
ἡμέρᾳ τοῦ υἱοῦ τοῦ ἀνθρώπου' to the form of reference to the day
of Lot's escape. Compare ᾗ δὲ ἡμέρᾳ ἐξῆλθεν Λώτ .... (v 29)
with 'so will it be ᾗ ἡμέρᾳ ὁ υἱὸς τοῦ ἀνθρώπου ἀποκαλύπτεται'
(v 30). Several of the differences between the Lukan
description of the days of Noah and the Lukan description of
the days of Lot are thus explained - differences that are
otherwise not very readily explained.

/1/ Cf. Zmijewski, *Eschatologiereden*, 442,443.

The proposed reconstruction of the pre-synoptic tradition
of the three 'as ....so.....' sayings in Luke 17/Matthew 24 has
been seen to account satisfactorily both for the differences
between Matthew and Luke and also for problematic features in
both the Matthean and Lukan texts; in the absence of any other
equally satisfactory explanation, it may be considered probably
correct. This has important implications, confirming, for
example, that the Lot sayings are pre-Lukan, not Lukan creation.
(Luke would hardly have created a saying so similar to the Noah
saying, yet so curiously different.) These implications will be
considered further later. So far as the immediate question of
the ending of Lk 17:24/Mt 24:27 goes, the conclusion is that
Matthew's comparison of the lightning to the 'parousia' is
probably more original than Luke's wording; Matthew's paratactic
construction with its reference to the lightning 'coming out' is
also probably to be preferred to Luke's participial and less
dynamic form of words.

2.2.3. Lk 17:25
The text here is:

πρῶτον δὲ δεῖ αὐτὸν πολλὰ παθεῖν καὶ ἀποδοκιμασθῆναι ἀπὸ
τῆς γενεᾶς ταύτης.

This Lukan verse about the suffering and rejection of the
Son of man has no parallel in the Matthean or Markan versions of
the eschatological discourse, and it fits rather uneasily into
the Lukan context of discussion about the suddenness and
unpredictability of the second coming. The form of the saying
is very similar to that of Lk 9:22 (and parallels) δεῖ τὸν υἱὸν
τοῦ ἀνθρώπου πολλὰ παθεῖν καὶ ἀποδοκιμασθῆναι ἀπὸ τῶν
πρεσβυτέρων... Its difficulty in the context of Luke 17 could be
an argument in favour of the originality of this context, and it
would not be hard to explain why Matthew and Mark omit it; but
it is quite as likely that we have here a brief Lukan cross-
reference to the earlier verse, partly provoked by the reference
to 'the Son of man (in his day)' and partly by Luke's
theological interests. Luke reminds us, as he does elsewhere in
his gospel (e.g. 24:26,46) that the Son of man who will be
glorious in the heaven must first suffer./1/ The insertion of

/1/ Cf. J. Schmid, Das Evangelium nach Lukas (Regensburg: Puslet,
1960) 276; R. Schnackenburg, Schriften zum Neuen Testament
(München: Kösel, 1971) 230; R. Geiger, Endzeitreden, 76-84. But
see also Marshall, Luke, 661,662. Is there a slightly similar

what we might regard as a sort of footnote would have been the
easier at this point, since, to judge from Matthew, Luke was in
any case breaking off from his pre-synoptic source at this
point: Luke omits here all the description of the parousia, and
this saying, as it were, fills a gap.

The view that the verse is an insertion within the context
may appear to weigh against the broader hypothesis that in chap.
17 Luke has selected material on the unpredictability/
suddenness theme: if this was Luke's thematic interest in this
section, why do we suddenly find a verse that does not fit the
theme? Two replies to this are possible: either the
selection of material on the theme of unpredictability from the
eschatological discourse found in Luke 17 could be a pre-Lukan
selection; Luke has taken it over and added in some editorial
additions. Or the more probable answer is that Luke, though
following a general theme in this section, is quite capable of
allowing himself asides that occur to him (and that confuse the
modern scholar!).

2.2.4. Lk 17:26-30/Mt 24:37-39
This section has already been considered above (pp.152-159),
and it was argued that Luke is here drawing on a pre-
synoptic form of the tradition. Luke has made a number of
alterations, notably rearranging the Lot saying.

2.2.5. Lk 17:31-33
The text here is:

ἐν ἐκείνῃ τῇ ἡμέρᾳ ὃς ἔσται ἐπὶ τοῦ δώματος καὶ τὰ σκεύη
αὐτοῦ ἐν τῇ οἰκίᾳ, μὴ καταβάτω ἆραι αὐτά, καὶ ὁ ἐν ἀγρῷ
ὁμοίως μὴ ἐπιστρεψάτω εἰς τὰ ὀπίσω. 32. μνημονεύετε τῆς
γυναικὸς Λώτ. 33. ὃς ἐὰν ζητήσῃ τὴν ψυχὴν αὐτοῦ
περιποιήσασθαι, ἀπολέσει αὐτήν, καὶ ὃς ἂν ἀπολέσει,
ζωογονήσει αὐτήν.

---

train of thought in Lk 21:11,12, where Luke's thought moves to
the parousia and the heavenly signs, but then he checks himself
with πρὸ δὲ τούτων πάντων .... + a description of sufferings
that the disciples will face? A. Schlatter, *Das Evangelium
des Lukas* (Stuttgart: Calwer, 1931) 394, suggests that Luke is
writing for a suffering church; he therefore makes sure that
the passion prediction is not forgotten in the midst of a
vision of future victory.

After the saying about the days of Noah, Matthew goes straight on to the saying about 'two in a field, one being taken and one left'. Luke, however, has the saying about the days of Lot, then a group of sayings about not trying to preserve one's life on that day, the first of them (about 'he who is on the house' etc.) being paralleled earlier in the eschatological discourse in Matthew and Mark; then Luke has a saying about two in a bed (*not* in a field, as Matthew). How is this situation to be explained?

The following points should be noted: (a) As it has already been suggested, the three Lukan sayings (i.e. vv 31-33) seem thematically out of place in the context, just as the earlier saying about the Son of man's suffering (17:25) seemed out of place. Although this could explain why Matthew and Mark omitted them there, there is still the problem of the oddity in Luke's text to be explained.

(b) The first Lukan saying about the person on the house not collecting his belongings etc. seems a little strange (though not impossible) in the Lukan context of reference to the parousia,/1/ and certainly easier where Matthew and Mark have it within the context of the call to flee from Jerusalem.

(c) The fact that this saying has a close parallel in Matthew and Mark in a different context compels us to consider whether the identical saying was used in different contexts and ways by Jesus, or whether either or both of the present synoptic contexts is secondary.

(d) A close comparison of the wording of the saying in the three synoptists shows an interesting range of agreements and disagreements:

/1/ But see Lambrecht, *Redaktion*, 158.

Mt 24:17,18	Mk 13:15,16	Lk 17:31,32
ὁ ἐπὶ τοῦ δώματος	ὁ (δὲ) ἐπὶ τοῦ	ἐν ἐκείνῃ τῇ ἡμέρᾳ ὃς
μὴ καταβάτω ἆραι	δώματος μὴ	ἔσται ἐπὶ τοῦ δώματος καὶ
τὰ ἐκ τῆς οἰκίας	καταβάτω μηδὲ	τὰ σκεύη αὐτοῦ ἐν τῇ οἰκίᾳ,
αὐτοῦ, 18. καὶ	εἰσελθάτω ἆραι τι	μὴ καταβάτω ἆραι αὐτά, καὶ
ἐν τῷ ἀγρῷ μὴ	ἐκ τῆς οἰκίας	ὁ ἐν ἀγρῷ ὁμοίως μὴ
ἐπιστρεψάτω ὀπίσω	αὐτοῦ, 16. καὶ ὁ	ἐπιστρεψάτω εἰς τὰ ὀπίσω.
ἆραι τὸ ἱμάτιον	εἰς τὸν ἀγρον μὴ	32. μνημονεύετε τῆς
αὐτοῦ.	ἐπιστρεψάτω εἰς	γυναικὸς Λώτ.
	τὰ ὀπίσω ἆραι τὸ	
	ἱμάτιον αὐτοῦ.	

These agreements and disagreements will be investigated in the
next chapter of the book;/1/ here it is only necessary to say
that the only distinctively Lukan elements in Luke's form of
the saying (that have no obvious basis in the Matthew/Mark
traditions) are (a) his opening ἐν ἐκείνῃ τῇ ἡμέρᾳ, and perhaps
(b) the construction ὃς ἔσται ἐπὶ τοῦ δώματος ... where
Matthew/Mark have ὁ ἐπὶ ...; Luke, significantly, switches to
the Matthew/Mark construction in his next clause καὶ ὁ ἐν ἀγρῷ.

     (e) Luke's v 34 is rather odd: 'I tell you, in this night
there will be two on one bed ...' The sudden solemn reference
to 'this night' without previous explanation or context has
perplexed scholars./2/ It is easy enough to see why Matthew
might have changed this, if it were original, but it is not
very easy to explain the Lukan wording in the first place.

     How is this evidence to be accounted for? Distinguished
scholars have defended the view that 'Q' contained the Lukan
verses in question and that Matthew omitted them. This view
has some attractions: if Matthew knew and omitted the preceding
Lot saying, as was argued, it might seem reasonable to suppose
that the same applies to the following sayings which continue
the Lot theme. It may also be argued that Matthew changed the
original Lukan 'two in a bed' into his 'two in a field' saying
under the influence of Lk 17:31 (Mk 13:16, Mt 24:18) 'he who is
in the field'./3/ But, although it is indeed quite easy to see
why Matthew, had he known something like Luke, would have
changed it, this hypothesis leaves the oddities of Luke and

/1/ On these texts and Lk 21:21 see below, pp. 189-192.
/2/ Cf. Zmijewski, *Eschatologiereden*, 492-94; Geiger,
Endzeitreden, 136-37.
/3/ Cf. R. H. Gundry, *Matthew*, 494, and for a survey of opinions
see Marshall, *Luke*, 667.

also the question of the relationship of Mark 13:15 to the 'Q'
saying unexplained. It is, as will be shown, simpler and more
satisfactory to explain the Lukan verses as further Lukan
asides, like Lk 17:25.

What seems probable is that the pre-synoptic tradition was
as follows:

Pre-synoptic tradition	Compare: Mt 24:37-40	Lk 17:26-31	Lk 17:34
Days of Noah ...day of Son of man	Days of Noah ... Parousia	Days of Noah ... days of Son of man	
Days of Lot ... day of Son of man		Days of Lot.... Son of man in day	

	40	31	λέγω ὑμῖν,
ἐν ἐκείνῃ τῇ	τότε	ἐν ἐκείνῃ τῇ	ταύτῃ τῇ νυκτὶ
ἡμέρᾳ ἔσονται	ἔσονται	ἡμέρᾳ ὃς ἔσται	ἔσονται δύο
δύο ἐν τῷ ἀγρῷ,	δύο ἐν τῷ ἀγρῷ,	ἐπὶ τοῦ δώματος	ἐπὶ κλίνης
εἷς	εἷς	.. καὶ ὁ ἐν	μιᾶς, ὁ εἷς
παραλάμβανεται..	παραλάμβανεται..	ἀγρῷ ὁμοίως	παραλη`μφθήσεται

Mt 24:17/Mk 13:15
ὁ ἐπὶ τοῦ δώματος
....

Matthew according to this proposal has followed the pre-
synoptic tradition quite closely. He omits the passage about
the days of Lot and alters the references to 'the day of the
Son of man' to 'the parousia of the Son of man'; he also alters
the ἐν ἐκείνῃ τῇ ἡμέρᾳ ... opening of the saying about two in a
field to his favourite τότε, partly perhaps because he has lost
the preceding strong emphasis on 'the day' of the Son of man.

Luke in 17:31 starts with the pre-synoptic wording ἐν
ἐκείνῃ τῇ ἡμέρᾳ. That this was originally the opening of the
saying about two men in a field (not the opening of the saying
about the person on the house) may be suggested (a) by the fact
that Matthew and Mark have no equivalent of this particular
phrase in their versions of the saying about the person on the
house (see above); this does not of itself prove much, but this
peculiarity of Luke's version of that saying could be explained
if Luke knew the postulated pre-synoptic form of the saying

about the men in a field in this context - he took the phrase
from this saying; (b) by the fact that when Luke comes to his
equivalent of the saying about the two men in a field, i.e. his
saying about two men in a bed, he has an equivalent phrase
ταύτῃ τῇ νυκτί; (c) by the excellent coherence of this phrase
with the pre-synoptic context (both backwards to the sayings of
Luke 17:29,30 and also forwards to Lk 21:34-6 - see the
'day' references and p. 106 above); (d) by the fact that
Matthew's τότε is well explained as a substitute for it.

    Luke's next two words ὃς ἔσται ἐπί .. are, as was noted, a
slight problem. The Matthean version of the saying about the
person on the house has ὁ ἐπί ...... and Luke himself falls
into this construction in the second sentence καὶ ὁ ἐν ἀγρῷ ...
One explanation of this anomaly will be suggested in the more
detailed discussion of the verse in our next chapter (pp.189-
192); but it is also possible that Luke is influenced by the
construction of the pre-synoptic saying about two men in a
field (which belongs here); compare ἔσονται ... ἐν τῷ ἀγρῷ ....
with ἔσται ἐπὶ τοῦ δώματος. (He is influenced in this way,
even though he is about to record a different saying. Compare
his opening ἐν ἐκείνῃ τῇ ἡμέρᾳ). But why does he introduce the
other saying here at all? It is not very easy on any hypothesis
to explain the positioning of Lk 17:31; but it seems most
likely that it is another Lukan aside, not dissimilar from
17:25, and that Luke may have been influenced in his
introduction of it here (a) by the reference at this point in
the pre-synoptic tradition to δύο ἐν τῷ ἀγρῷ.. Luke's mind goes
over from this saying to the other saying about ὁ ἐν τῷ ἀγρῷ
(found only a little earlier in the eschatological discourse),
and more significantly (b) by the verbal and thematic
associations of the saying with the story of Lot, which has
just been referred to. Note how the description of the
destruction of Sodom (Lk 17:29) echoes Gen 19:24,25; the warning
not to turn back in Lk 17:31 has a verbal echo of Gen 19:17
(μὴ περιβλέψῃς εἰς τὰ ὀπίσω); the reference to Lot's wife in
Lk 17:32 echoes the same passage in Genesis 19; and the saying about
losing and saving one's life in Lk 17:33 has thematic links with
the same story (cf. Gen 19:19-21)./1/

/1/ On the history of the tradition in v 33 see Marshall, *Luke*,
666,667. It is probably not significant that before this saying
(Lk 17:33, Mt 10:39) both Matthew and Luke have a saying containing the word ὀπίσω (Lk 17:31, Mt 10:38) - used quite
differently. But it is a remote possibility that Luke knew and
was influenced by the Matthean context.

The conglomeration of sayings reminiscent of the Lot story
in Lk 17:31-33 suggests that not only is v 31 a Lukan aside, but
that the whole of vv 31-33 are a digression on the same theme./1/
Luke's introduction of material out of context for
thematic reasons hardly occasions surprise in view of his
editorial procedures elsewhere (e.g. in Lk 12:35-48, discussed
above).

2.2.6. Lk 17:34,35/Mt 24:40,41
The texts are:

Mt 24:40,41

τότε ἔσονται δύο εν τῷ ἀγρῷ,
εἷς παραλαμβάνεται καὶ
εἷς ἀφίεται· 41. δύο ἀλήθουσαι
ἐν τῷ μύλῳ, μία παραλαμβάνεται
καὶ μία ἀφίεται:

Lk 17:34,35

λέγω ὑμῖν, ταύτῃ τῇ νυκτὶ
ἔσονται δύο ἐπὶ κλίνης μιᾶς, ὁ
εἷς παραλημφθήσεται καὶ ὁ ἕτερος
ἀφεθήσεται· 35. ἔσονται δύο
ἀλήθουσαι ἐπὶ τὸ αὐτό, ἡ μία
παραλημφθήσεται, ἡ δὲ ἑτέρα
ἀφεθήσεται.

We have already given some attention to these sayings, and
it was suggested that the opening words in the pre-synoptic
tradition were ἐν ἐκείνῃ τῇ ἡμέρᾳ (as in Lk 17:31). Matthew has
substituted τότε for this, and Luke has ταύτῃ τῇ νυκτὶ. If this
suggestion is correct, then Matthew's 'there will be two in a
field' must be preferred to Luke's 'there will be two on one
bed', since the Lukan wording evidently corresponds to his 'in
this night'. In any case the Lukan form might be thought less
original, since the reference to 'in this night' comes rather
unexpectedly, and Matthew's pair of sayings - two men in a
field, two women at the mill - seem to fit more naturally
together than Luke's pair - two men in a bed (or is it a man
and a woman?), two women at the mill. One possibility is that
Matthew's is an improvement of Luke's form; but then the oddity
of Luke's pairing would be unexplained. The more likely
possibility is that the imbalance of the Lukan pair is the

/1/ It is an interesting question as to whether Luke in putting
this aside here still has the original meaning of v 31 in mind
(and the context of the fall of Jerusalem), or whether he sees
broader relevance in that originally local command and applies
it to every Christian's need to prepare resolutely for the
parousia.

result of his substituting the 'bed' for the 'field' saying./1/
A further point in favour of this is that the Matthean
reference to 'two in a field' may help to explain the Lukan
aside of 17:31 (see discussion above).

But why, on this view, does Luke replace the 'field' with
the 'bed'? It is not easy to explain this. But it may be
partly because he had just had one saying about a 'field'; he
could have considered it slightly confusing to have the one
saying about the one in a field not turning back and then
another saying about one being taken from the field and one
left. Or perhaps Luke wished to have a contrast between v 31,
which starts 'on that day' and speaks of people outside the
house - on the roof or in the field - , and v 34 which speaks
of 'this night' and speaks of people inside the house - in bed
and at the mill. This last suggestion would explain why we
have the otherwise rather unexpected 'in this night'./2/

Apart from the major divergence just discussed, Matthew
and Luke are very close to each other in the sayings concerned:
for example, they both refer first to two masculines, one being
taken and one left, and then to two feminines (milling), one of
whom is taken and the other left. In the remaining minor points
of divergence Luke is probably secondary: he has substituted

/1/ Tuckett, *Revival*, 174, says that we would expect Luke to
have written ἐν ταύτῃ τῇ νυκτί. However, this argument does not
seem to be supported by Luke's other uses of this sort of
phrase. See 12:20, Acts 27:23, 12:6, 23:11.
/2/ Zmijewski, *Eschatologiereden*, 498, following Harnack,
Sayings, 108, thinks that Luke had a particular interest in
giving a night-time setting to the parousia; but the evidence of
Lk 9:28-37, 12:16-21 hardly establishes this. Whatever the
explanation of Luke's alteration, it is not necessary to suppose
that he invented the 'bed' saying. It is possible that in the
pre-synoptic tradition all three sayings - field, bed, mill -
were found, or that the 'bed' saying comes from another context
and that Luke assimilated its form to this context. (Perhaps
the λέγω ὑμῖν derived from the other context? Against T. W.
Manson's defence of the TR 'bed..mill...field' (*Sayings of Jesus*
146) see Marshall, *Luke* 668.)

his favourite ἕτερος/ἕτερα for Matthew's εἷς ... μία ;/1/ and
his ἐπὶ τὸ αὐτό (where Matthew has ἐν τῷ μύλῳ) is a Lukan
phrase./2/   It is more difficult to be sure about Luke's opening
λέγω ὑμῖν and his future tenses 'will be taken ... left'; but it
again seems quite likely that Matthew is to be preferred./3/

   2.2.7. *Lk 17:37/Mt 24:28*
   The texts are:

          Mt 24:28   Lk 17:37

ὅπου ἐὰν ᾖ τὸ πτῶμα, ἐκεῖ   καὶ ἀποκριθέντες λέγουσιν αὐτῷ·
συναχθήσονται οἱ ἀετοί.   ποῦ, κύριε; ὁ δὲ εἶπεν αὐτοῖς·
                                    ὅπου τὸ σῶμα, ἐκεῖ καὶ οἱ ἀετοὶ
                                    ἐπισυναχθήσονται.

   The saying about the body and the eagles is the one saying
in the so-called 'Q' material of Lk 17:22-37 that is positioned
differently in Matthew and Luke. Luke has it at the end of the
section, and Matthew has it just after the comparison of the
parousia to lightning in his 24:28. In neither position is it
very easy to interpret. The saying seems to be an echo of
Job 39:30, where God uses the hawk as one illustration of the
mysterious marvels of his ways./4/ In the Matthean context the

---

/1/ εἷς...εἷς is never found in Luke-Acts (cf. Lk 23:33/
Mt 27:38/Mk 15:27). But ἕτερος is frequent in Luke-Acts, and the
combination εἷς ... ἕτερος is found in distinctively Lukan
material (e.g. 7:41, 18:10, Acts 23:6). It is also found in the
so-called 'Q' tradition, e.g. 16:13, but Jeremias is hardly on
safe ground in ascribing the usage here to pre-Lukan tradition.
(*Sprache*, 270.)
/2/ Cf. Acts 1:15, 2:1,44,47; 4:26. Note that the phrase gives
a prepositional balance with Luke's preceding ἐπὶ κλίνης.
/3/ Zmijewski, *Eschatologiereden* 499,500, argues that Luke's
preceding context leads him to add λέγω ὑμῖν. He sees the
Matthean form of the saying as more primitive than Luke's.
/4/ The verse in Job comes in a section in which God has been
asking Job ποῦ, 'where', he was (38:4). Cf. the ποῦ of
Lk 17:37.

point of the saying may be that the second coming will be
unmistakable when it comes; in Luke the point may be that
judgment (which has just been described) will be universal.

But is it possible to decide about the probable original
context and form of the saying? The main formal difference is
that Luke introduces the saying with the disciples asking
'Where, Lord?', whereas Matthew does not. It is commonly
assumed that Luke has added the question in line with his
practice elsewhere. But three things may make us hesitate
before accepting this assumption: (a) the question is remarkably
obscure if it is a Lukan link and introduction to what follows.
/1/ We immediately wonder: where what?!/2/ (b) The historic
present λέγουσιν is relatively unusual in Luke, as noted by
Rehkopf./3/ (c) We noted in chapter 2 (above) that one other
supposedly Lukan question (12:41) was actually part of the
tradition. It is at least worth considering if this is another
similar case.

So far as positioning is concerned, the argument in the
previous chapter (pp.103-108) about Lk 17:26-18:1 would
suggest that the saying is not in its original context in Lk
17:37. It was argued that the sequence of thought in Lk 17:26-
35 + 18:1 parallels and fits in with Lk 21:34-36. The saying
about the body and the eagles would interrupt the flow of
thought from Mt 24:40,41/Lk 17:34,35 to Lk 21:34-36.
Furthermore, Matthew's placing of the saying in the context of
the warning about false prophets, who say 'here' 'there',
makes more obvious sense than Luke's positioning, and could be
original. But the case for Matthew's position is not very
strong; and, if the Lukan introductory question 'where?' is
original, this would not seem to fit very well in the Matthean
position after the saying about the parousia being like

/1/ Cf. Schmid, *Lukas*, 278; Marshall, *Luke*, 669.
/2/ Zmijewski's observation that Luke had to create some
introduction for the saying (*Eschatologiereden* 507,508) does
not explain why he created such an obscure introduction. And
it does not help very much to suggest that this 'where?'
balances the earlier 'when?'.
/3/ F. Rehkopf, *Die Lukanische Sonderquelle* (Tübingen: Mohr,
1959) 99. Cf. Zmijewski, *Eschatologiereden*, 507.

lightning shining from one side of heaven to the other. We may
then have to content ourselves with being uncertain about the
original pre-synoptic positioning of the saying; if either the
Matthean or the Lukan positioning of the saying is correct,
then we have to recognize that the saying fits rather loosely
into context.

However, an alternative possibility may be suggested,
namely that the saying with the introductory question from the
disciples belonged in the pre-synoptic tradition between
Mt 24:25 and the following verse, 26. This gives a good sequence
of thought: (a) Jesus warns of false prophets who say 'here'
'there' and explains that they are deceivers. 'Behold, I have
told you beforehand' (24:25). (b) The disciples, however, are
not satisfied with a negative warning about people who say
'here' 'there', and so they ask 'Where, Lord?', i.e. 'Where
then will the Christ be seen?'. (c) Jesus then replies first
with the saying 'Wherever the body is, there the eagles will be
gathered'. This is an enigmatic way of saying that the second
coming will be unmistakable when it comes. Then Jesus goes on
with a clear explanation: 'If then they say to you: Behold
in the desert .....for like the lightning... './1/

It may seem irresponsible to suggest that a saying found
in two different places in Matthew and Luke has been moved from
another and more original context by both evangelists.
However, three things can be said in defence of the suggestion:
(1) the question and answer fit well in the suggested position.
(2) It is not difficult to see why both Matthew and Luke might
have moved it: given his editorial rearrangement of material in
Lk 17:23,24, Luke could not have had the question and answer
between his vv 23 and 24, or indeed anywhere else in this
section of chap. 17; so he leaves it to the end.   Matthew
could have retained the question and answer in its original
position; but we saw earlier that he eliminated another Lukan
question (Lk 12:41 cf. Mt 24:44,45, see chap. 2 above) and it
is quite likely that he did not wish to break up the Lord's
words here with interjections; but once he had omitted the

/1/ Less probably one might take the 'where?' of the disciples'
question to mean 'Where will the false prophets be?' and the
saying about the vultures to be a reference to those false
prophets. Cf. Geiger, *Endzeitreden*, 76.

question, he had to move the saying; so he moves it a little
further on in the context where it belongs. (3) The saying of
Mark 13:23 'You watch out; I have told you all things before
beforehand' sounds rather like the end of a section (which
indeed it is so far as Mark is concerned), and it almost
invites a reply from the disciples. Our proposal supplies the
reply! This is not a decisive point, but it is true that the
interjection from the disciples would fit in well./1/ More
significant, however, is the evidence of Matthew: at present he
has a warning of false Christs and false prophets (vv 23,24),
then the saying 'Behold I have told you beforehand' (v 25),
then a further warning of people speculating about the
whereabouts of the Son of man (vv 26,27). It is hard to avoid
the feeling either that Matthew's v 25 is something of a
hiccough between the preceding and following verses, or that
v 26 is a slightly repetitious after-thought that picks up the
theme of vv 23,24 again. This evidence from Matthew is
explicable on the traditional Mark/Q hypothesis, since Matthew
is supposed here to be tacking a bit of 'Q' on to Mark (slightly
ineptly perhaps!); but we have already seen reason to question
the Mark/'Q' hypothesis as an explanation of this passage, and
to think that the double reference to the false prophets was in
the pre-synoptic tradition (see pp. 139-46 above). The
Matthean evidence is, however, well accounted for through the
suggestion that the exchange between Jesus and his disciples
came in the pre-synoptic tradition at this point and has been
omitted by Matthew./2/

/1/ C. Perrot, *RSR* 47 (1959) 491-95, finds the link between
Mark's v 23 and his v 24 'fort inhabile'. Mark seems to have
finished, but then goes on. Perrot's solution is to relocate
Mark's vv 21-23 after v 32; but he has some difficulty in
explaining this transposition (p. 509), and in any case there
is Pauline evidence that suggests the primitiveness of the
position of vv 21-23. See chapter 5 below, pp. 176-80
/2/ Zmijewski, *Eschatologiereden*, 510, plausibly suggests that
the original wording of the saying may have been ὅπου τὸ πτῶμα,
ἐκεῖ (ἐπι)συναχθήσονται οἱ ἀετοί ..... ; cf. Geiger,
Endzeitreden, 70. ὅπου ἐάν may well be Matthean; cf. Mt 15:14,
24:26; so Geiger, *ibid*. The suggestion made about Mk 13:23
contradicts the common opinion that this verse is Markan, but
does not exclude the possibility that some of the phraseology
(e.g. βλέπετε, πάντα) might be Markan.

3. CONCLUSION

Not all the arguments put forward in this chapter have been of equal weight; but the total argument adds up to make it probable that Lk 17:22-37 is an extract from the eschatological discourse. The pre-synoptic form of the material will have been approximately as follows:

1. A description of   Mt 24:21,22   /Mk 13:19,20   /Lk 17:22
   days of distress

2. 'Then if anyone   Mt 24:23,24   /Mk 13:21,22   /Lk 17:21
   says..behold here
   the Christ or
   there, do not
   believe... For
   false Christs will
   arise....the elect.
   Watch out! I have
   told you in
   advance.'

3a Disciples' ques-   Mt 24:28   /   /Lk 17:37
   tion: 'Where
   Lord?'

3b Jesus' answer: /   /Lk 17:37
   'Whereever the body
   ..'

4. 'For if they say   Mt 24:26   /   /Lk 17:23
   Behold he is in
   the desert...
   don't go out ...
   don't pursue....'

5. 'For as the light-   Mt 24:27   /   /Lk 17:24
   ning goes from
   East/under heaven and
   shines to West/ under
   heaven, so will be
   the parousia of
   the Son...'

(6. Description of parousia leading to 'Of that day or hour knows no one....'	Mt 24:36	/Mk 13:32	/)/1/
7. 'For as it was in the days of Noah, so will it be in the day of the Son of man. They were eating... until the day when Noah entered.. and the flood came and destroyed all .....'	Mt 24:37-39	/	/Lk 17:26,27
8. 'Likewise as it was in the days of Lot, so will it be in the day of the Son of man. They were eating....until the day when Lot went out... and it rained fire and brimstone and destroyed them all....'		/	/Lk 17:28-30
9. 'In that day there will be two in a field, one will be.... two at the mill, one ...'	Mt 24:40,41	/	/Lk 17:34,35
(10 'Take heed to yourselves... lest ...that day	(Mt 24:42) keep awake	/(Mk 13:33)	/Lk 21:34-36 (18:1)

/1/ For discussion of this saying and the description of the
parousia see below, pp. 330-32 and 304-23.

come upon you
suddenly ... keep
awake at every
moment praying
....'   )/1/

The detailed arguments for this proposal have been
presented above, and it is only necessary to add the
observation that the sequence of thought, notably in sections
6-10, is very good. If the proposal is correct, then the
situation is similar as in the conclusion of the eschatological
discourse (see chapters 1-3 above). There was a pre-synoptic
form of the tradition; Matthew has preserved the tradition in
its original context and often with its original wording; Luke
has preserved some of the tradition that Matthew omits (i.e. the
Lot sayings), but he has not preserved the original context;/2/
Mark has again omitted several sections of the tradition - his
omissions perhaps illustrate a tendency, also very much evident
in the discourse conclusion, to omit the illustrative or
parabolic and to retain what he presumably saw as the essential
meat of the discourse.

It might appear to be a problem that our hypothesis in this
chapter and the previous chapter has Mark omitting from the full
pre-synoptic form of the tradition those parts of the tradition
that Luke uses, supposedly out of context, in his chaps. 12 and
17. It could be argued that this agreement of Mark and Luke to
omit these sections from the eschatological discourse suggests
that the sections concerned were not in the pre-synoptic form
of the discourse, and so that it supports something like the
'Q' hypothesis./3/ But in fact it is not entirely accurate to

/1/ See discussion of this saying above, pp.102-20.
/2/ If Luke has attached his 17:22-37 to the preceding logia of
vv 20,21, then this confirms that Lk 17:20,21 are essentially
pre-Lukan material, even if some of the present wording is
Lukan. (E.g. παρατηρήσεως may be a Lukan word).
/3/ W. R. Farmer, *The Synoptic Problem* (London: Macmillan, 1964)
273,274, argues against the Augustinian hypothesis on these
sorts of grounds. A proponent of that hypothesis, J. Chapman,
Matthew, Mark and Luke (London: Longmans, 1937) 167,168
explained that Luke quite deliberately kept material from Mark
separate from other material. Perhaps this argument could be
used to defend the hypothesis of a pre-synoptic tradition: if

say that Mark omits these sections: he retains the warning
against false prophecy in his 13:21-23, albeit slightly
abbreviated, and in 13:33-37 he also retains an abbreviated form
of the parabolic material that Luke has in 12:35-48.
Furthermore, it is not altogether surprising if those parts of
the discourse that Mark could most easily omit in his
abbreviated version of the discourse were precisely the parts
that Luke could most easily use out of the context of the
discourse.

What is true is that most of the material that has been
discussed in this chapter is found only in Matthew and Luke,
and that many of the arguments about the pre-synoptic form would
be as relevant on the 'Q' hypothesis as on our hypothesis. But,
although that may commend the chapter to some readers, the case
for the pre-synoptic tradition explained at the beginning of the
chapter is a good one, and the subsequent discussion of detail
has in no way favoured the 'Q' hypothesis rather than the pre-
synoptic hypothesis, if anything the reverse.

The arguments of chapters 1-3 and of this chapter point in
the same direction and reinforce each other. And the
significance of the conclusions of this chapter is that they
confirm that the pre-synoptic conclusion to the discourse
reconstructed in chapters 1-3 really was a conclusion to the
eschatological discourse in the pre-synoptic stage; it was not
an entirely separate collection of eschatological material
(particularly parables) that came to be attached to the
discourse. The pre-synoptic tradition included the central
section of the eschatological discourse (drawn on in Lk 17:22-
37) + the concluding section of exhortation and parables. This
is not surprising: the exhortatory conclusion may be felt to
need some description of the eschatological events and times
preceding it.

Luke had that tradition and Mark (which seems probable), he
could have determined to keep his Markan material as a unity
and have felt free to use the non-Markan pre-synoptic tradition
elsewhere. However, the presence of the non-Markan Lk 21:34-36
at the end of the eschatological discourse complicates this
argument, and it is not all that easy to think of Luke in his
chaps. 12 and 17 deliberately using non-Markan sections of the
pre-synoptic tradition and leaving the Markan sections for his
chap. 21, since he knew he would need them there.

Chapter 5

THE DESOLATING SACRILEGE AND THE PRE-SYNOPTIC TRADITION
(MT 24:15-22, MK 13:14-20, LK 21:20-24)

In chapters 1-3 the material at the end of the
eschatological discourse (in Matthew, Mark and Luke) was
examined, and it was argued that all three evangelists drew from
a common pre-synoptic tradition of parables and exhortation. In
chapter 4 Lk 17:22-37 (and parallels) was looked at, and it was
suggested that the pre-synoptic tradition included this material
as well (though we did not work out all the details of this
suggestion). This chapter takes the argument a further step
backwards through the discourse and shows that the section
describing the desolating sacrilege or the desolation of
Jerusalem (Mt 24:15-20/Mk 13:14-18/Lk 21:20-24) was also in the
pre-synoptic tradition./1/

1.   PRELIMINARY OBSERVATIONS

1.1   The implications of the previous chapter

Our examination of the evidence of Luke 17 showed that the
pre-synoptic tradition contained the warnings of the false
prophets found in Mt 24:23-28, Mk 13:21-23 (cf. Lk 17:21,23),
and also the description of the great distress found in
Mt 24:21,22 and Mk 13:19,20, the Lukan equivalent of this being
Lk 17:22. Luke, it was suggested, locates these traditions in a
context that is not original and modifies them accordingly; but
both Matthew and Mark attach these traditions to the description
of the desolating sacrilege, and it is a reasonable presumption
that this may be the pre-synoptic context.

/1/ Much of the substance of this chapter appeared in my
article '"This generation will not pass..." A study of Jesus'
future expectation in Mark 13' in *Christ the Lord*, ed. H. H.
Rowdon (London: IVP, 1982) pp. 127-150.

1.2. The evidence of 2 Thessalonians 2

Paul's evidence in 2 Thessalonians 2 is significant, since
his description of the man of lawlessness is strongly
reminiscent of - and probably related to - the synoptic
description of the desolating sacrilege./1/ Note the following
points:

1.2.1. The context
Paul gives his teaching about the man of lawlessness to
prevent the Thessalonians being 'quickly shaken in mind or
excited, either by spirit or by word, or by letter purporting to
be from us, to the effect that the day of the Lord has come.
Let no one deceive you in any way ...'/2/ In the synoptic
eschatological discourse the description of the desolating
sacrilege is also preceded by a section warning people: '...lest
anyone deceive you. Many will come in my name saying that I am
(he) and will deceive many. When you hear of war and rumours of
wars, don't get excited. It must happen, but the end is not
yet'. (Mk 13:5-7) The exact meaning of the Markan phrase
'saying that I am' (λέγοντες ὅτι ἐγώ εἰμι) is debated by
scholars; but one, and perhaps the best, explanation of the
phrase (and of the equivalent in Matthew - λέγοντες· ἐγώ εἰμι ὁ
χριστός; Luke has λέγοντες· ἐγώ εἰμι, καὶ ὁ καιρὸς ἤγγικεν) is
that the reference is to deceivers who would claim to be Jesus
returned for his second coming (see discussion in chapter 8
below, pp.295-96 ; in any case it is evident that they are
people proclaiming the imminent or actual arrival of the end.
The problem warned of in the synoptics is thus very much the
same as that being faced by Paul in Thessalonica - a problem of
excessive excitement and of deception involving the idea of an
imminent second coming. It is interesting that the same
unusual word θροεῖσθαι is found in Matthew/Mark and in
2 Thessalonians; there is also a close parallel between Matthew/
Mark's βλέπετε μή τις ὑμᾶς πλανήσῃ and Paul's μή τις ὑμᾶς
ἐξαπατήσῃ, though the verbs are different and the idea is
obvious enough. It is widely recognized by commentators that
the function of the whole Markan apocalypse was to cool down
eschatological excitement, and this is also Paul's purpose in

---

/1/ I am assuming that 2 Thessalonians is genuinely Pauline,
though my overall case would not necessarily be undermined if
this assumption were mistaken. In this section I am drawing
extensively on my 'Paul and the Synoptic Apocalypse', 349-52.
/2/ For a useful discussion of the meaning of ἐνέστηκεν in
2 Thess 2:2 see Holman, *Eschatological Delay*, pp. 175-185.

2 Thessalonians. There are, of course, differences of emphasis:
in the synoptics the excitement seems caused by wars,
persecutions and other events; in 2 Thessalonians the immediate
cause seems to have been some sort of misunderstanding or
distortion of Paul's teaching (though this misunderstanding
might have been encouraged by the sort of things referred to in
the synoptics). But, despite these differences, the general
similarity remains.

1.2.2. A horrible event to precede the end

In countering the false notions, Paul and the synoptists
agree in describing one major horrible event which must precede
the end. Paul is explicit when he says that the end will not
come 'unless the rebellion comes first and the man of
lawlessness is revealed'; the synoptists are not quite so
explicit, but in Mark 13 at least the dynamics of the chapter
seems to be that vv 5-13 describe the period before the end
when excitement is out of place and endurance is the order of
the day; but then v 14 (ὅταν δὲ ἴδητε τὸ βδέλυγμα ....) marks
the beginning of the significant action.

Not only do Paul and the synoptists agree that one horrible
event must precede the end, but they also seem to agree that in
some sense the horrible event will lead to the coming (or a
coming) of Christ. Thus Paul refers to the Lord destroying the
lawless one 'by the appearing of his coming' (ἐπιφανείᾳ τῆς
παρουσίας), while the synoptics after describing the days of
the horrible event say: 'Immediately after the distress of
those days' (Matthew) or 'In those days after that distress'
(Mark) the heavenly bodies will be upset, and 'then the sign of
the Son of man will appear' (Matthew) 'and they will see the
Son of man coming' (Matthew/Mark). The exact chronological
relationship between the horrible event and the coming of the
Son is not made clear in either Paul or the synoptics; but
there at least seems to be a connexion.

1.2.3. The nature of the event

The nature of the horrible event is similar in Paul and
the synoptics. In Paul it is an evil blasphemous person; in
the synoptics the 'desolating sacrilege' need not be personal,
though Mark's use of the masculine ἑστηκότα suggests that he at
least saw it as much. It is in any case evidently something
horribly evil that is envisaged, and the Danielic background to
the synoptic phrase suggests that it is a blasphemous object or
person. The Danielic background is, of course, an important
point of contact between Paul's description of the man of

lawlessness and the synoptic desolating sacrilege: both draw on
Daniel's description of Antiochus Epiphanes and his blasphemous
actions to portray the future horrible event, Paul using the
description of Antiochus to portray the future man of
lawlessness and the synoptists borrowing the description of his
blasphemous altar to characterize the future sacrilege.

1.2.4. The place of the horrible event

Paul speaks of the man of lawlessness sitting in 'the
temple of God', and Matthew and Mark of the desolating sacrilege
standing 'in the holy place' (Matthew), 'where it ought not'
(Mark cryptically). The point of contact here is obvious
enough, whether we take the references by Paul and the
synoptists literally or somehow metaphorically./1/ The
agreement may be partly explicable via the Danielic background;
but Daniel does not speak of Antiochus as sitting in the
temple, so that Paul's description of the lawless one in terms
that fit the synoptic sacrilege better is of interest.

1.2.5. The accompanying deceptive signs and wonders

Having described the lawless one and having in fact
described his destruction, Paul says that his coming will be
with Satanic power and with 'pretended signs and wonders
(σημείοις καὶ τέρασιν ψεύδους) and with wicked deceit for those
who are to perish'. It is not said that he himself performs
these signs and wonders, though this could be supposed. Matthew
and Mark after their description of the desolating sacrilege and
of the awful suffering that will go with it (and after a
reference to the ending of those terrible days) go on to warn of
false prophets and false Christs arising, who 'will do signs and
wonders (σημεῖα καὶ τέρατα) to mislead, if possible, the elect'.
The exact chronological relationship of this deceptive assault
to the previously described events connected with the desolating
sacrilege is not clear in the synoptics, though the τότε of
Mt 24:23/Mk 13:21 can very plausibly be taken to mean that it is
an accompaniment of the events. But whatever the answer to that
and despite the differences between Paul and the synoptists

/1/ The synoptic 'holy place' or 'where it ought not' could be
either the city of Jerusalem or the temple; in the light of the
Danielic background the latter may be more likely. Burnett's
argument that Matthew should have been more explicit had he
intended the temple (Testament, 312-321) depends on the
assumption that Matthew has modified Mark, and is in any case
unpersuasive.

(e.g. Mk 13:21 has no parallel in 2 Thessalonians), the
coincidence in the positioning of a reference to deceivers
cannot easily be dismissed as accidental./1/

1.2.6. Conclusion
The different points of similarity between Paul's and the
synoptists' description of the horrible crisis to precede the
end are considerable and strongly suggest that their traditions
are in some way related. The agreement is much more in
substance than in wording. The most striking verbal agreements
are θροεῖσθαι and σημεῖα καὶ τέρατα; and of these the latter is
such a common phrase that it cannot be taken to prove a
literary connexion or a significant connexion at the Greek stage
of tradition. The former is more striking, and may suggest some
contact at the level of Greek tradition; but it is certainly
insufficient to prove that Paul and the synoptists are drawing
primarily or to a significant extent on a common Greek
tradition. Even though the verbal parallelism is slight,/2/
the substantial parallelism is remarkably extensive, and it
includes parallelism of structure as well as of ideas, since
Paul's teaching in 2 Thess 2:1-12 runs roughly parallel to much
of the first part of the eschatological discourse (from Mk 13:
5 to 13:22).

/1/ Note the probable and important parallel in Revelation 13,
where the description of the blasphemous beast is followed by a
description of another beast (identified in Rev 19:20 as the
ψευδοπροφήτης) performing signs to deceive men into believing
in the first beast. In Did. 16:4 the κοσμοπλάνος himself does
σημεῖα καὶ τέρατα.
/2/ D. Ford, The Abomination of Desolation in Biblical
Eschatology (Washington: University Press of America, 1979) 223,
notes that the terms βδέλυγμα and ἀνομία are sometimes
equivalent in the LXX, and also the terms ἐρήμωσις and ἀπώλεια.
Cf. also Burnett, Testament 327-33 on ἀνομία and βδέλυγμα in
Daniel and Matthew, and my discussion in TynB 31 (1980) 155-162.
It is possible that the Pauline phrases ὁ ἄνθρωπος τῆς ἀνομίας
and ὁ υἱὸς τῆς ἀπωλείας might both be linked with the synoptic
τὸ βδέλυγμα τῆς ἐρημώσεως.

It is hard to avoid the conclusion that Paul's traditions
and the synoptic traditions are related. If they are, then the
suggestion that the desolating sacrilege tradition was part of
the pre-synoptic eschatological discourse is obviously
plausible; certainly the tradition has primitive roots. Paul
does not in this case say explicitly that he is citing a 'word
of the Lord'; but neither does he say that when quoting the
thief-in-the-night tradition. In both cases, however, he
refers to the tradition in question as one already known to the
Thessalonians (1 Thess 5:2, 2 Thess 2:5). It is interesting that
in both passages Paul has not just a single echo of a synoptic
tradition, but a cluster of echoes: so in 2 Thessalonians 2
Paul has not simply the man of lawlessness, but also the
preceding warning of deceivers and the subsequent mention of
deceptive signs and wonders. The natural conclusion is that we
have a similar situation in both places with Paul drawing on a
pre-synoptic tradition that resembled our present synoptic
traditions. In this case the resemblance is particularly to
Matthew and Mark, who follow the description of the desolating
sacrilege with the warning of deceptive false prophets. This
conclusion will have to be explored further through a detailed
study of the relevant texts.

2. *PRE-SYNOPTIC TRADITION IN MT 24:15-20/Mk 13:14-18/Lk 21:20-
    23*

The texts are as follows:

Mt 24:15-20	Mt 13:14-18	Lk 21:20-23
ὅταν οὖν ἴδητε	ὅταν δὲ ἴδητε	ὅταν δὲ ἴδητε
τὸ βδέλυγμα τῆς	τὸ βδέλυγμα τῆς	κυκλουμένην ὑπὸ
ἐρημώσεως τὸ ῥηθὲν	ἐρημώσεως ἑστηκότα	στρατοπέδων
διὰ Δανιὴλ τοῦ	ὅπου οὐ δεῖ, ὁ	Ἰερουσαλήμ, τότε
προφήτου ἑστὸς ἐν	ἀναγινώσκων νοείτω,	γνῶτε ὅτι ἤγγικεν ἡ
τόπῳ ἁγίῳ, ὁ	τότε οἱ ἐν τῇ	ἐρήμωσις αὐτῆς. τότε
ἀναγινώσκων νοείτω,	Ἰουδαίᾳ φευγέτωσαν	οἱ ἐν τῇ Ἰουδαίᾳ
τότε οἱ ἐν τῇ	εἰς τὰ ὄρη. ὁ (δὲ)	φευγέτωσαν εἰς τὰ ὄρη,
Ἰουδαίᾳ	ἐπὶ τοῦ δώματος μὴ	καὶ οἱ ἐν μέσῳ αὐτῆς
φευγέτωσαν εἰς τὰ	καταβάτω μηδὲ	ἐκχωρείτωσαν, καὶ οἱ
ὄρη, ὁ ἐπὶ τοῦ	εἰσελθάτω ἄραι τι ἐκ	ἐν ταῖς χώραις μὴ
δώματος μὴ καταβάτω	τῆς οἰκίας αὐτοῦ,	εἰσερχέσθωσαν εἰς
ἄραι τὰ ἐκ τῆς	καὶ ὁ εἰς τὸν ἀγρὸν	αὐτήν, ὅτι ἡμέραι
οἰκίας αὐτοῦ, καὶ ὁ	μὴ ἐπιστρεφάτω	ἐκδικήσεως αὐταί
ἐν τῷ ἀγρῷ μὴ	εἰς τὰ ὀπίσω ἄραι τὸ	εἰσιν τοῦ πλησθῆναι
ἐπιστρεφάτω ὀπίσω	ἱμάτιον αὐτοῦ. οὐαὶ	πάντα τὰ γεγραμμένα.
ἄραι τὸ ἱμάτιον αὐτοῦ.	δὲ ταῖς ἐν γαστρὶ	οὐαὶ ταῖς ἐν γαστρὶ
οὐαὶ δὲ ταῖς ἐν	ἐχούσαις καὶ ταῖς	ἐχούσαις καὶ ταῖς

Mt 24:15-20	Mt 13:14-18	Lk 21:20-23
γαστρὶ ἐχούσαις καὶ	θηλαζούσαις ἐν	θηλαζούσαις ἐν
ταῖς θηλαζούσαις ἐν	ἐκείναις ταῖς	ἐκείναις ταῖς
ἐκείναις ταῖς	ἡμέραις. προσεύχεσθε	ἡμέραις·
ἡμέραις. προσεύχεσθε	δὲ ἵνα μὴ γένηται	
δὲ ἵνα μὴ γένηται ἡ	χειμῶνος·	
φυγὴ ὑμῶν χειμῶνος		
μηδὲ σαββάτῳ·		

A comparison of Lk 21:20-23 with the parallel passages in Matthew and Mark shows a curious range of agreements and disagreements.

1. They all start with the words ὅταν ἴδητε....

2. Matthew and Mark have as object τὸ βδέλυγμα τῆς ἐρημώσεως τὸ ῥηθὲν .. ἐστὸς ἐν τόπῳ ἁγίῳ/ἐστηκότα ὅπου οὐ δεῖ...., /1/ whereas Luke has κυκλουμένην ὑπὸ στρατοπέδων Ἱερουσαλήμ. This is a striking difference, but note (a) that Matthew and Mark agree with Luke that the event in question is something to do with Jerusalem (though they probably have in mind the temple in particular), and (b) that Luke has the word ἐρήμωσις in the next phrase.

3. Matthew and Mark continue with the slightly obscure ὁ ἀναγινώσκων νοείτω whereas Luke has τότε γνῶτε ὅτι ἤγγικεν ἡ ἐρήμωσις αὐτῆς.

4. All three evangelists then agree word for word in the next phrase: 'Then let those in Judea flee to the mountains'.

5. Matthew and Mark then continue with the saying (considered briefly above, pp. 160-65) about 'he who is on the house ....his cloak'. Luke had quite a close parallel to this in 17:31, but the wording of his equivalent saying here is quite different.

/1/ Beasley-Murray, *Jesus and the Future*, 255-58, favours the wording suggested by the Syriac texts of Matthew, i.e. ὅταν δὲ ἴδητε τὸ σημεῖον τοῦ βδελύγματος ....; but the textual support for the variant is slight. Against Beasley-Murray see Ford, *Abomination*, 143.

6. All three evangelists then agree again word for word in the
    next sentence 'Woe to those with child and to those giving
    suck in those days'.

    How is this rather complicated state of affairs with Luke
see-sawing between agreement and disagreement with Matthew/
Mark to be explained?

2.1. Lk 21:20-23 A blending of material from Mark and a Lukan special source?

    There would seem to be at least two possible explanations: one
possibility is that Luke is here drawing on a special tradition
distinct from the Matthew/Mark tradition, but that he has
inserted into that tradition a couple of phrases from Mark,
notably vv 21a and 23. It can be argued in favour of this
(a) that it explains the alternation between Markan/Matthean and
non-Markan/Matthean phraseology, (b) that with v 21a omitted the
sequence of thought is good; (c) in particular that this
explains the difficulty of αὐτῆς in Lk 21:21: this ought
strictly to refer back to Ἰουδαίᾳ in the previous clause (the
Markan clause); but it evidently really refers back to
Jerusalem, which was described in the preceding verse (the
supposedly non-Markan tradition). This suggestion has definite
attractions;/1/ but it is not a total solution to the problems.
Indeed it may be said only to push the problems back a stage,
since it moves us from the question of Luke and Matthew/Mark to
the question of the relationship of the pre-Lukan tradition to
the Matthew/Mark tradition. The traditions are clearly linked
and must be ultimately related, and yet they have diverged
considerably. We must suppose on this theory that the original
form of the saying got substantially modified, whether in the
Matthew/Mark or in the Lukan stream of tradition or in both -
hence the divergence of the traditions; Luke then tried to bring
the two traditions together (rather unsuccessfully, we may
feel!) by inserting phrases from the Markan tradition into the
non-Markan tradition.

2.2. Lk 21:20-23: divergences due to Lukan redaction

    An alternative explanation of the present texts is that
the differences between them are, for the most part at least,

_____

/1/ Cf. C. H. Dodd, *More New Testament Studies* (Manchester
University Press, 1968) 69-83; Marshall, *Luke*, 771.

due to Lukan redaction./1/ This explanation is simpler in that
we do not have to postulate two distinct and rather contrary
redactional stages - first pre-Lukan redaction (to explain the
divergences) and then Lukan redaction (to explain the Markan
elements within the Lukan tradition) - but only one. The
fluctuation between Markan and non-Markan elements in Lk 21:20-
24 is due, according to this explanation, to the fact that Luke
felt a need to change certain things in the Matthew/Mark
tradition and not others. More specifically (a) he alters the
obscure Matthew/Mark references to the 'desolating sacrilege
......let the reader understand' to a more easily intelligible
statement about the encirclement and desolation of Jerusalem.
(b) He alters the 'he that is on the house ....' saying to avoid
sounding repetitious, since he has already used this saying (out
of context) in 17:31./2/ He rephrases the saying in a way that
links it with his previous verse about Jerusalem - the αὐτῆς of
v 21 picking up the αὐτῆς of v 20. It is true that the αὐτῆς
of v 21b (meaning Jerusalem) is slightly awkward after the
'Ιουδαίᾳ of v 21a; but there is little to choose between the
view that this awkwardness was caused by Luke's inserting of his
v 21a (Markan material) into a context where it does not fit and
between the view that the awkwardness was caused by Luke
carrying on the same redactional train of thought before and
after v 21a./3/ (c) The only material in Lk 21:20-24 that is

/1/ So Geiger, *Endzeitreden*, 202,203; Zmijewski,
Eschatologiereden, 181-83. A common, but uncertain, view is
that Luke's alterations were adaptations of the tradition in the
light of events.
/2/ So Schmid, *Lukas*, 277, and Farmer, *Synoptic Problem*, 271,
who notes the same procedure in Lk 21:12-19.
/3/ F. Neirynck, 'Marc 13 Examen critique de l'interprétation
de R. Pesch', in J. Lambrecht, ed., *L'Apocalypse johannique et
L'Apocalyptique dans le Nouveau Testament* (Gembloux: Duculot,
1980), 384, notes that the thought of Jerusalem dominates this
section. He dissents from Zmijewski's suggestion that 'Ιουδαία
should be understood as a reference to Judaism rather than to
the locality of Judea (*Eschatologiereden* 211,212), a suggestion
that seems neither necessary nor likely. For a similar
suggestion on Mark see Pesch, *Naherwartungen*, 226. Against
this see J. Dupont, 'La ruine du temple et la fin des temps
dans le discours de Marc 13' in *Apocalypses et Théologie de
L'Espérance* ed. L. Monloubou (Paris: Cerf, 1977), 231.

not so obviously explicable as Lukan rewriting of the Matthew/
Mark tradition is his v 22 ὅτι ἡμέραι ἐκδικήσεως αὗταί εἰσιν
τοῦ πλησθῆναι πάντα τὰ γεγραμμένα. But it is possible that this
is Luke's equivalent of the Matthew/Mark ὁ ἀναγινώσκων νοείτω./1/
The meaning of this Matthew/Mark phrase is, of course,
disputed; but Matthew has just previously referred to τὸ ῥηθὲν
διὰ Δανιὴλ τοῦ προφητοῦ and it is probable that *his* call to the
reader to understand is a call to understand the OT allusion.
It seems quite likely that Mark also intended the phrase to be
taken this way - given the preceding allusion to Daniel and
Mark's consistent use of ἀναγινώσκειν elsewhere (2:25, 12:10
and 26; only in 12:26 is the OT book explicitly referred to)./2/
But, whatever Mark's intentions, it is entirely feasible
that Luke may have understood the phrase in this way and that
his v 22 is his equivalent of the Matthew/Mark phrase.

    The suggestion that the divergences between Luke and
Matthew/Mark are to be explained largely as due to Lukan
redaction may be confirmed by the observation that Luke's
divergences are notably Lukan in style and vocabulary./3/   Thus,
for example, in v 20 ἤγγικεν ἡ ἐρήμωσις αὐτῆς, ἐγγίζειν is a
favourite Lukan word, and the phrase even has two Lukan
parallels within Luke 21 (i.e. vv 8 and 28).   In v 21: μέσος
and χώρα (cf. ἐκχωρεῖν) are common Lukan terms.   In v 22:
ἐκδίκησις (and the verb ἐκδικεῖν) is not found in the synoptics
except in Luke; interestingly all the other four uses are in
Luke's eschatological parable of the unjust judge (18:3,5,7,8),
and there is one usage in Acts 7:24. πίμπλημι is common in
Luke-Acts, and πάντα τὰ γεγραμμένα is a Lukan phrase (18:31;
24:44; Acts 13:29).

/1/ See further discussion below on pp. 188,189.   For a
different explanation see Marshall, *Luke*, 773.
/2/ Cf. B. Rigaux, *Biblica* 40 (1959) 682; E. J. Prycke,
Redactional Style in the Marcan Gospel (Cambridge: UP, 1978)
56-58; Ford, *Abomination*, 20,21 & 170,171. Marshall's suggestion
that the phrase 'let the reader understand' is to be taken as
the main clause following the preceding ὅταν clause (*Luke*, 772),
rather than as in parentheses, has a lot to be said for it.
/3/ Cf. Zmijewski, *Eschatologiereden*, 184,185.

On the basis of this evidence, the balance of probability
seems to lie with the view that Luke's divergences from Matthew
and Mark in 21:20-23 are largely due to Luke's redaction.

2.3. Evidence of the pre-synoptic tradition

But although Lk 21:20-23 is largely explicable as Lukan
redaction of something like Mark, Luke may still give us some
clues, when it comes to comparing the Matthean and the Markan
traditions and to considering the possibility of a pre-synoptic
form of tradition.

2.3.1. Surrounding Jerusalem and setting up the sacrilege
The suggestion that Luke substituted his description of
Jerusalem being surrounded by armies for the reference to the
desolating sacrilege that we find in Matthew and Mark is
plausible, since it is easy to see why Luke might have wished
to avoid the obscure phraseology of Matthew and Mark. And yet,
if it was just a case of Luke trying to be clearer, we might
have expected him simply to have reworded the Matthew/Mark
tradition. Instead he substitutes a description of the siege
of the city of Jerusalem for the reference to the setting up of
the desolating sacrilege in the temple. How is this
substitution to be explained? Has there, as some have
suggested, been a significant shift of emphasis from a
religious event to a military event and from the temple to
Jerusalem?

It is doubtful if very much should be read into the change.
In the first place, the context of Luke's discourse, as of
Matthew's and Mark's, is a prediction of the destruction of the
temple (21:5-7), so that there is no doubt that the description
of Lk 21:20-24 includes that event. In the second place,
although there is nothing explicitly military described in the
Matthew/Mark tradition (something which enables critics to
argue for the unlikely view that the 'sacrilege' or
'abomination' is zealot defilement of the temple/1/), 'any

/1/ Against this view and on the 'desolating sacrilege'
generally see Ford, *Abomination*, 142-75. He comments that
שקוץ in its O.T. contexts ... is always associated with a
desecrating attack on Jerusalem and its temple', p. 67. It may
be argued that the call to flight in face of the 'desolating
sacrilege' and the known facts of the Jewish war fit better if

reader who understood' the Danielic background to the Matthew/
Mark passage would know that in Daniel the desolating sacrilege
was brought by a pagan invader attacking the city of
Jerusalem with armed forces: the place of the sanctuary was
'thrown down' (Dan 8:10,11) and trampled underfoot (8:13).
Anyone familiar with the story of the Maccabees would know that
Antiochus destroyed at least parts of the temple and intended
to destroy more (1 Macc 4:38, and cf. 1:22; 2:11,12; 3:45,51,58;
4:48). The very phrase 'desolating sacrilege' may be
interpreted (e.g. in the LXX of Daniel, and in 1 Maccabees) as
meaning 'a sacrilege that makes desolate', i.e. that lays
waste./1/ When then Matthew and Mark speak of the 'desolating
sacrilege', they are referring, albeit obliquely, to a
military attack, such as was implied by Jesus' prediction
before the discourse.'There will not be left here one stone
upon another, that will not be thrown down' (Mt 24:2, Mk 13:2,
cf. Lk 21:6). In connection with this prediction and the
desolating sacrilege passage, it is at least an interesting
coincidence that in the Hebrew of Dan 8:11 there is a reference
to the place of the sanctuary being 'overthrown' (שׁלך) and that
in the LXX this is translated: the sanctuary will be 'made
desolate' (ἐρημοῦν). The overthrow which Jesus predicted *is*
the desolation brought by the pagan invader.

If this argument is correct, then Luke's picture of
Jerusalem being surrounded by armies is *not* significantly
different from the picture implied by Matthew and Mark (and
certainly need not be seen as a vaticinium ex eventu/2/). The
pictures are complementary descriptions of two aspects of an
Antiochus-like event; this conclusion is reinforced by the

---

the sacrilege is taken to be zealot abominations than if it is
taken of the Roman invasion. But this is probably to
misunderstand the prophecy, taking it to be a detailed
description in advance (or ex eventu) of the events of AD 70,
whereas, if we may judge from the Danielic language used, it
was more probably intended as a general prediction of a second
Antiochus-type situation, i.e. a situation when a pagan
destroyer came, desecrated the sanctuary, and the faithful fled
to the hills.
/1/ Cf. Gaston, *No Stone on Another*, 24; Lambrecht, *Redaktion*,
151; Pesch, *Naherwartungen*, 143.
/2/ This has in any case been argued on the basis of the OT
background notably by C. H. Dodd in *More New Testament Studies*,
69-83.

evidence of Dan 11:31, where both pictures occur together in the
one verse *'Forces from him shall appear* and profane the temple
and fortress, and shall take away the continual burnt offering.
And *they shall set up the abomination that makes desolate'*.

To recognize that the three synoptic accounts are
complementary is important, but it is not the same as saying
that they are identical. It remains the case that Luke refers
to one aspect of the coming event (the arrival of hostile
armies) and that Matthew and Mark refer to a different aspect
(the profanation of the temple). And this difference calls for
explanation. It is possible that Luke, faced with the
obscurity of the phrase in Matthew and Mark, has simply drawn
on his knowledge of Daniel and/or his historical imagination
for something more straightforward. But in the light of the
previous discussion, it is also possible that the pre-synoptic
tradition was like Dan 11:31 and contained both the Lukan and
the Matthew/Mark phraseology, reading perhaps

> When you see Jerusalem surrounded by armies and the
> desolating sacrilege standing where it should not let the
> reader understand. Then let those in Judea....

This possibility would simply explain the Lukan text: he has
avoided the direct Danielic reference, but not imported any new
idea into the context. But Matthew and Mark, on this view,
have eliminated the reference to the armies around Jerusalem.
That they could have done this is by no means impossible, since
it is striking (on any view) that they echo the Danielic
description of Antiochus without bringing out explicitly the
thought of military invasion./1/ Also it is notable that
Matthew and especially Mark seem to be deliberately
obscure in this section ('where it ought not', 'let the reader
understand'), and it is possible that they are being
particularly cautious about the military/political dimensions of
the desolating sacrilege event.

/1/ Cf. Dupont, 'La ruine du temple', 235-37, who argues that Mark
deliberately downplays the idea of destruction, concentrating
rather on the religious desecration. This point should not be
over-emphasized: given the context of the discourse (Mk 13:1-4)
and the appeal to the reader to read between (or behind!) the
lines (13:14), it seems more likely that Mark has the military/
political aspect of things in his mind, but that he is trying
to keep that obscurely in the background, than that he is trying
to give a purely religious interpretation of the Danielic allusion.

There is then a possibility that Luke gives us a clue
concerning the pre-synoptic form through his opening phrase
referring to Jerusalem being surrounded by armies. But it is
only a possibility, and, unless other evidence is forthcoming,
it would be unwise to build on this suggestion.

2.3.2. The reference to prophecy

The case for seeing Lk 21:22 'for these are days of
vengeance, to fulfil all that is written' as a partial Lukan
equivalent of the Matthean and Markan reference to the
desolating sacrilege is plausible; in his v 20 Luke had omitted
the other synoptists' OT allusion because of its obscurity,
though he retained the call to 'know' (γνῶτε, cf. Matthew/
Mark's νοείτω) and the word ἐρήμωσις. So in v 22 he makes up
for his preceding omission by including a differently
formulated reference to the fulfilment of prophecy. This has
to be a reference to prophecy in general, not to a specific
text, and is formulated in distinctly Lukan terms./1/ But its
function is similar to that of the OT allusion in Matthew and
Mark in that it explains why flight is called for.

But how does this suggestion about Luke's v 22 help with
the quest for the pre-synoptic tradition? The answer is that
Luke may possibly shed light on a difference between Matthew
and Mark. In the saying about the desolating sacrilege Matthew
has a phrase not found in Mark - τὸ ῥηθὲν διὰ Δανιὴλ τοῦ
προφήτου. It is easy enough to explain that this is a Matthean
clarification of the brief and enigmatic Markan form, especially
as the expression τὸ ῥηθέν is distinctively Matthean./2/ However,
it is possible to argue that Luke's phrase τοῦ πλησθῆναι πάντα
τὰ γεγραμμένα is more likely derived from something like the
Matthean τὸ ῥηθὲν διὰ Δανιὴλ τοῦ προφήτου + ὁ ἀναγινώσκων
νοείτω than from the simpler Markan ὁ ἀναγινώσκων νοείτω,
which (as modern scholars' interpretations testify) is not even
an unambiguously clear reference to OT prophecy. This
suggestion might receive some support from a possible 'Q'

/1/ πίμπλημι is a distinctively Lukan word, though he does not
use it elsewhere of the fulfilment of prophecy. He repeatedly
uses the perfect of γράφειν in referring to OT fulfilment.
/2/ Cf. Gundry, Matthew, 481. Most of the uses are in Matthew's
formula citations: the two exceptions are Mt 22:31 and 24:15,
cf. also 3:3.

parallel, i.e. Mt 3:3/Lk 3:4, since Matthew there has ὁ ῥηθείς
διὰ 'Ησαίου τοῦ προφήτου and Luke has ὡς γέγραπται ἐν βίβλῳ
λόγων 'Ησαίου τοῦ προφήτου; the variation between ῥηθείς/
γέγραπται is parallel to that in Mt 24:15/Lk 21:22 ῥηθέν and
γεγραμμένα./1/ In the light of this and other evidence, it is
possible to speculate that Matthew's τὸ ῥηθὲν διὰ Δανιἡλ τοῦ
προφήτου may have been in the pre-synoptic tradition or that it
is a Matthean version of some equivalent phrase./2/ Luke
betrays his knowledge of the phrase in his πάντα τὰ γεγραμμένα;
Mark has omitted it, perhaps for brevity, or because of his
desire here for obscurity, cr because of his relative lack of
interest in the OT./3/

This suggestion is admittedly speculative, and again we
have at most a possible clue about the pre-synoptic tradition.

2.3.3. *The saying about 'the one on the housetop'*
We are on more promising ground with the saying about 'the
one on the housetop' (Mt 24:17,18; Mk 13:15,16). Matthew and
Mark have a number of small differences in this saying,
i.e. Mark has a second verb in the first clause μηδὲ εἰσελθάτω
which has no parallel in Matthew. Mark has a singular ἆραι τι
ἐκ τῆς οἰκίας and Matthew a plural ἆραι τὰ ἐκ τῆς οἰκίας./4/
Mark has εἰς τὸν ἀγρὸν and Matthew ἐν τῷ ἀγρῷ. Mark has εἰς τὰ
ὀπίσω for Matthew's simple ὀπίσω. Luke 21:21 is no help for
the explanation of these differences, since it is a Lukan

/1/ The argument on this is complicated by Mark's evidence in
Mk 1:2. For other possible parallels see Mt 22:24/Mk 13:19/
Lk 20:28, where Matthew has εἶπεν for Mark's and Luke's ἔγραψεν
and Mt 22:31/Mk 12:26/Lk 20:37, where Luke again eliminates a
reference to 'reading'.
/2/ E.g. ὡς γέγραπται ἐν τῷ βίβλῳ τοῦ Δανιἡλ τοῦ προφήτου.
/3/ Another possible example of such abbreviation might be
Mk 4:11,12, if this is correctly regarded as an abbreviation of
the longer Mt 13:13-15. See my discussion in *TynB* 23 (1972)
17-30; though note that I might now wish to argue in terms of
Markan use of a pre-synoptic tradition like Matthew, not for
Mark's direct dependence on Matthew. See also below on
pp. 342-46 for a further possible explanation of Luke's 21:22b.
/4/ Some texts have τι in Matthew; this is probably a scribal
improvement of the more original and better attested τά,
reflecting perhaps the influence of Mark. *Pace* A. Schlatter,
Der Evangelist Matthäus (Stuttgart: Calwer, 1959) 705.

paraphrase. However, it was suggested that Luke paraphrases
here because he has already used something like the Matthew/Mark
form of the saying in Lk 17:31. The saying in Lk 17:31 was, it
was argued (pp. 160-65 above) out of context in chap. 17; if it
was, then it seems quite probable that Luke knew it in, and
took it from, its present Matthew/Mark context. Lk 17:31 is
then the form to compare with Matthew/Mark in the search for the
most original wording. The texts are as follows:

Mt 24:17,18	Mk 13:15,16	Lk 17:31
ὁ ἐπὶ τοῦ δώματος μὴ καταβάτω ἆραι τὰ ἐκ τῆς οἰκίας αὐτοῦ, καὶ ὁ ἐν τῷ ἀγρῷ μὴ ἐπιστρεφάτω ὀπίσω ἆραι τὸ ἱμάτιον αὐτοῦ.	ὁ ἐπὶ τοῦ δώματος μὴ καταβάτω μηδὲ εἰσελθάτω ἆραι τι ἐκ τῆς οἰκίας αὐτοῦ, καὶ ὁ εἰς τὸν ἀγρὸν μὴ ἐπιστρεφάτω εἰς τὰ ὀπίσω ἆραι τὸ ἱμάτιον αὐτοῦ.	ἐν ἐκείνῃ τῇ ἡμέρᾳ ὃς ἔσται ἐπὶ τοῦ δώματος καὶ τὰ σκεύη αὐτοῦ ἐν τῇ οἰκίᾳ, μὴ καταβάτω ἆραι αὐτά, καὶ ὁ ἐν ἀγρῷ ὁμοίως μὴ ἐπιστρεφάτω εἰς τὰ ὀπίσω.

The comparison of these texts is interesting, since
Lk 17:31 turns out to have three agreements with Mt 24:17,18
against Mk 13:15-16./1/ (i) He agrees with Matthew in omitting
Mark's μηδὲ εἰσελθάτω. (ii) He agrees in having ἐν for εἰς.
These two agreements (especially the second) could be
coincidental. But (iii) he agrees with Matthew in having a
plural ἆραι αὐτά (Luke) ἆραι τά ... (Matthew) for Mark's ἆραι τι.
This last agreement may seem quite insignificant, especially in
view of the differences between Luke and Matthew, Luke having τὰ
σκεύη αὐτοῦ ἐν τῇ οἰκίᾳ ... αὐτά and Matthew τὰ ἐκ τῆς οἰκίας
αὐτοῦ. However, it should be observed that the agreement is not
only an agreement in number, but also in sense, and that,
despite the apparent differences, the Lukan form may be plausibly
explained as a modification of the Matthean form. Thus compare:

Matthew	and Luke
ὁ ἐπὶ τοῦ δώματος	ὃς ἔσται ἐπὶ τοῦ δώματος καὶ <u>τὰ σκεύη ἐν τῇ οἰκιᾳ</u>
μὴ καταβάτω	μὴ καταβάτω
ἆραι <u>τὰ ἐκ τῆς οἰκίας αὐτοῦ</u>	ἆραι αὐτά

/1/ The agreements are even greater, if the original Markan text
was καταβάτω εἰς τὴν οἰκίαν, (ed. G. D. Fee, *NovT* 22 (1980) 20)
and τι ἆραι not ἆραι τι.

A plausible explanation of this comparison is that Luke has
known the Matthean form of the saying and has moved the final
Matthean phrase before the verb μὴ καταβάτω for the sake of
improved sense. That he has done this is suggested by the
slight awkwardness of the hanging nominatival phrase καὶ τὰ
σκεύη αὐτοῦ ... ./1/ The results of this one Lukan change in
order are (1) that Luke has to have a ὃς ἔσται construction
instead of ὁ ἐπί ... (though this may also be partially
explained by the sequence of material in the pre-synoptic
tradition; see pp.164,165 above); (2) that Luke has to add
σκεύη (quite a common Lukan word); (3) that he has to have ἐν
τῇ οἰκίᾳ for ἐκ τῆς οἰκίας; (4) that he has αὐτά at the end of
the clause. The Lukan form is thus a simple alteration of the
Matthean form.

   The combination of agreements between Matthew and Luke
against Mark is unlikely to be coincidental;/2/ it shows that Luke
knew something like the Matthean form of the saying. That by itself
would not necessarily point to the existence of a pre-synoptic
form of the tradition known to all three evangelists. However,
a further relevant consideration is that in two out of the
three cases where Matthew and Luke agree against Mark the
Matthew/Luke common tradition is quite likely more original
than the Markan tradition. Thus (1) Mark's μηδὲ εἰσελθάτω,
which is not found in Matthew/Luke, is probably a Markan
addition clarifying the more succinct picture of Matthew./3/
(2) Mark's ἆραι τι has a distinctly Markan ring about it, and
may well be his replacement for the Matthew/Luke ἆραι τά ... .
/4/

   These last observations do not by themselves prove
anything. But they + the fact of Matthew's and Luke's
agreements are very satisfactorily explained on the pre-synoptic

---

/1/ Jeremias, *Sprache* 269, says that the anakolouthon is non-
Lukan and therefore pre-Lukan. But it may be that Luke was
forced into an untypical construction by his rearrangement.
/2/ *Pace* Zmijewski, *Eschatologiereden* 473-77, who explains
Luke's differences from Mark as Lukan redaction and who too
hastily dismisses the agreements with Matthew.
/3/ The function of this addition is rather similar to the
function of Luke's positioning of the phrase καὶ τὰ σκεύη αὐτοῦ
ἐν τῇ οἰκίᾳ.
/4/ Cf. Mark's use of τι in 4:22, 9:22, 11:13,25. Fee, *NovT* 22,
p. 20, recognizes that Mark could have changed Matthew's τά, as

discourse hypothesis. The only other really feasible
explanation that might work within this section is the
Griesbach hypothesis, i.e. that Matthew was used by Mark and
Luke; there is little in the Matthean form that seems secondary
to Mark and Luke,/1/ except perhaps that Mark's εἰς τὸν ἀγρόν
could be more original than the more usual ἐν τῷ ἀγρῷ of
Matthew and Luke. However, in view of the evidence already
accumulated for a pre-synoptic form of the tradition known to
all three evangelists, this must be the preferable explanation
here./2/

2.3.4. *Conclusions on the Lukan evidence*

Lk 21:20-23 is a Lukan paraphrase of something like Mt 24:
15-20/Mk 13:14-18. But he gives possible clues about the pre-
synoptic form (1) in his opening 'When you see Jerusalem
surrounded by armies' and (2) in his reference to the
fulfilment of Scripture (v 22), which may be linked with
Matthew's 'what was spoken through the prophet Daniel'. And (3) he
gives a probable clue to the pre-synoptic form of the house-top
saying through his 17:31: his evidence here confirms the whole
idea of a pre-synoptic form of the tradition, and suggests that
in this case Matthew has preserved the form best. The one
point regarding Luke that has not been discussed is his omission
altogether of the exhortation to prayer found in Mt 24:20/
Mk 13:18. It seems probable that this was in the pre-synoptic
tradition, and that Luke omitted it for some reason, perhaps
because it was not a relevant exhortation for his Gentile
readers - they were not involved in the crisis in Judea being
described./3/

---

did later copyists of Matthew; but he considers that Matthew
could have changed Mark - for reasons now unclear.
/1/ E.g. Matthew's ὀπίσω in his v 18 is probably more original
than Mark/Luke's εἰς τὰ ὀπίσω, which conforms to the LXX of
Gen 19:24.
/2/ There are other possible explanations, e.g. in terms of a
'Q' form of the house-top saying which Luke uses in chap. 17
and Matthew merges with the Markan form in 24:17. cf. Gundry,
Matthew, 483. But these possibilities are much more
complicated than the hypothesis of a pre-synoptic discourse
form.
/3/ For suggested explanations see Geiger, *Endzeitreden*, 205,
Zmijewski, *Eschatologiereden*, 186, Marshall, *Luke*, 773.

2.4. The evidence of Matthew and Mark

The logic of the preceding argument is that Matthew and
Mark have preserved the pre-synoptic form rather than Luke.
Their versions are quite similar, but there are a number of
differences. As has been seen Matthew's version of the house-
top saying has a strong claim to being more original, and his
reference to the prophecy of Daniel may also have been in the
pre-synoptic tradition. The other differences between Matthew
and Mark are these:

2.4.1. Matthew has τὸ βδέλυγμα τὸ ῥηθὲν ... ἑστὸς ἐν
τόπῳ ἁγίῳ where Mark has τὸ βδέλυγμα ἑστηκότα ὅπου οὐ δεῖ.
Mark's form of words here is the more difficult, both because
of the masculine ἑστηκότα with the neuter noun and because of
the obscurity of his ὅπου οὐ δεῖ. This might seem to point to
the greater originality of Mark's version. So might Paul's
evidence in 1 Thessalonians 2, since he there describes a
personal 'Antichrist' (cf. Mark's ἑστηκότα), not a blasphemous
object (cf. Matthew's ἑστός). Matthew could, then, be thought
to have clarified Mark's obscurity, but also to have
depersonalized Mark's form.

However, this argument is quite uncertain: (1) So far as
Matthew's explicit reference to the temple is concerned, this
has a parallel in Paul's description of the man of lawlessness
(2 Thess 2:3&4). Matthew's explicitness is not therefore a sign
that his way of putting things is late. Since Mark appears to
be trying to be deliberately obscure, it is quite as likely
that he avoided Matthew's directness as that Matthew has
translated Mark's obscurity into something clearer. (2) So far
as the grammatical oddity of the Markan βδέλυγμα ἑστηκότα is
concerned, it seems unlikely that such an oddity would have
survived unaltered in any extended process of transmission.
This means that, if Matthew and Luke were drawing on Mark, they
might have been expected to alter Mark's wording; but it also
means - and this is the significant point - that it is rather
unlikely that Mark's wording goes back to a stage of tradition
behind Mark, i.e. to the pre-synoptic tradition. It seems on
balance more likely that Mark created the form to express his
particular understanding of the desolating sacrilege than that
he received it in the tradition and that he left it unaltered.
And it may well be that the thought that lies behind Mark's
obscure ἑστηκότα also explains his obscure 'where it ought not':
Mark is being deliberately enigmatic in both places.

The upshot of these arguments must be that Matthew's form
of words has at least as good a claim to originality as Mark's,
and perhaps better. What then of the evidence of
2 Thessalonians 2, where Paul has the very personal man of
lawlessness, not the desolating sacrilege? It is possible that
this represents the most primitive form of the eschatological
discourse and that for some not very obvious reason the
synoptists have deliberately and completely depersonalized the
tradition (except for Mark's enigmatic participle). It is also
possible that the pre-synoptic tradition (like the book of
Daniel) made mention both of a personal Antiochus-like figure
and of the sacrilege that he perpetrated,/1/ and that Paul and
the synoptists have used it differently. Again the difficulty
is in explaining the almost total suppression of the personal
Antichrist motif from the synoptics. The third possibility is
that Paul's description of a personal Antichrist is a
development of something that is only implied in Matthew and
Mark - Paul brings the perpetrator of the sacrilege into
prominence. This development would be easily intelligible,
given the Danielic background of the desolating sacrilege idea.
It is also possible that Paul's thinking could have been
influenced by the emperor Caligula's threatened profanation of
the temple in AD 40; and/or that he could be 'depoliticizing'
the synoptic tradition (with its very specific reference to the
city of Jerusalem) and giving it a more 'religious'
interpretation./2/

If the third possibility - that Paul has personalized the
tradition - is correct, then Mark's ἑστηκοτα could be seen as
reflecting the same development of thought as we find in Paul
and so as secondary to the more impersonal Matthew./3/ But,
even if the personal Antichrist conception were considered more
primitive than the desolating sacrilege idea, it would still be
rather complicated to argue that Mark's ἑστηκότα is primitive

---

/1/ Ford, *Abomination*, 212, notes the oscillation between
masculine and neuter terms in 2 Thessalonians 2 and in
Revelation 13 and 17.
/2/ Cf. Ford, *Abomination*, Chapter 5, pp. 193-242.
/3/ In view of Paul's evidence, it is not necessary to think of
Mark's reinterpretation of the primitive tradition as reflecting
a post AD 70 situation - this being the suggestion of N. Walter,
ZNW 57 (1966) 43.

in its present context: if, for example, the pre-synoptic
tradition read 'When you see the man of lawlessness standing
where he ought not', Mark's ἐστηκότα would fit; but it would be
hard to explain why Mark substituted 'desolating sacrilege' for
'man of lawlessness', and yet left the masculine participle
unaltered. It is more likely that Mark has added the personal
dimension to the description of the sacrilege by making the
participle masculine.

2.4.2. The other difference between Matthew and Mark that
has not yet been discussed is that Matthew has προσεύχεσθε δὲ
ἵνα μὴ γένηται ἡ φυγὴ ὑμῶν χειμῶνος μηδὲ σαββάτῳ for Mark's
προσεύχεσθε δὲ ἵνα μὴ γενήται χειμῶνος./1/ Matthew could have
added both ἡ φυγὴ ὑμῶν and μηδὲ σαββάτῳ to Mark's account, for
the sake of clarity in the case of the first phrase /2/ and
because of his Jewish interests in the case of the second
phrase.

However, it may not be taken for granted that Matthew's
'nor on a sabbath' reflects the evangelist's known interest in
maintaining the Jewish law: he does not say that flight may not
be undertaken on the sabbath, but he implies that such flight
would be difficult or dangerous. Perhaps he has in mind the
spiritual danger to those involved; but it may be that he is
reflecting simply on the practical difficulties of travelling
on the sabbath (e.g. the lack of company, unavailability of
supplies, etc.)./3/ This would fit in with what precedes: it was
unusual and dangerous to travel in Palestine when expectant or
with young children (v 19) or in winter or on the sabbath
(v.20). If the phrase is more of a practical reflection on travel
in Palestine than a theological reflection about sabbath-
breaking, then the case for seeing it as a Matthean addition is
weakened.

In any case it is quite as likely that the Matthean form
of the saying with the double phrase 'in winter nor on a
sabbath' (which follows on well from the preceding two-clause
sayings of Mt 24:17-19, Mk 13:15-17) is the pre-synoptic form,
and that Mark has abbreviated it, leaving out 'not on a
sabbath', because of his Gentile readers.

/1/ A large number of Markan MSS include the phrase ἡ φυγὴ
ὑμῶν.
/2/ Cf. Fee, *NovT* 22 (1980) 21.
/3/ So Gundry, *Matthew*, 483 (who sees the phrase as Matthean).

In this particular verse, then, it is not possible to
reach a definite decision about the probable pre-synoptic form.

2.5. Conclusions on Mt 24:15-20/Mk 13:14-18/Lk 21:20-23

The really solid findings to emerge from the preceding
discussion of Mt 24:15-20 and parallels have been few; it has
often been a case of 'perhaps' or 'possibly'. But the
hypothesis of a pre-synoptic tradition received strong support
from the evidence of the 'house-top' saying, and in that saying
Matthew appeared to be closest to the pre-synoptic form.
Matthew may also reflect the pre-synoptic form in the verse
describing the desolating sacrilege, though Luke too may give
some clues about this. If Matthew is indeed closest to the
pre-synoptic form in his vv 15-18, it may be surmised that his
form of the exhortation to pray (his v 20) may also be close to
the pre-synoptic form.

3. PRE-SYNOPTIC TRADITION IN MT 24:21,22/MK 13:19,20/ LK 21:23,24

In the previous chapter it was argued that Lk 17:22, where
Luke speaks of the 'coming days' when people will long for the
coming of the Son of man, is a sort of Lukan equivalent of the
verses describing the great distress in Mt 24:21,22/Mk 13:19,
20. It is not perhaps surprising then that Luke does not
reproduce these Matthean/Markan verses in his chap. 21 (where
we might expect them). However at exactly the same point in
the eschatological discourse Luke has some verses of his own -
about 'great trouble' and about Jerusalem being conquered and
trampled underfoot.

Compare:

Mt 24:21,22	Mk 13:19,20	Lk 21:23,24
ἔσται γὰρ τότε θλῖψις μεγάλη, οἵα οὐ γέγομεν ἀπ' ἀρχῆς κόσμου ἕως τοῦ νῦν οὐδ' οὐ μὴ γένηται. 22. καὶ εἰ μὴ ἐκολοβώθησαν αἱ ἡμέραι ἐκεῖναι, οὐκ ἂν ἐσώθη πᾶσα σάρξ· διὰ δὲ τοὺς ἐκλεκτοὺς κολοβωθήσονται αἱ ἡμέραι ἐκεῖναι.	ἔσονται γὰρ αἱ ἡμέραι ἐκεῖναι θλῖψις, οἵα οὐ γέγονεν τοιαύτη ἀπ' ἀρχῆς κτίσεως ἣν ἔκτισεν ὁ θεὸς ἕως τοῦ νῦν καὶ οὐ μὴ γένηται. 20. καὶ εἰ μὴ ἐκολόβωσεν κύριος τὰς ἡμέρας, οὐκ ἂν ἐσώθη πᾶσα σάρξ· ἀλλὰ διὰ τοὺς ἐκλεκτοὺς οὓς ἐξελέξατο ἐκολόβωσεν τὰς ἡμέρας.	ἔσται γὰρ ἀνάγκη μεγάλη ἐπὶ τῆς γῆς καὶ ὀργὴ τῷ λαῷ τούτῳ, 24. καὶ πεσοῦνται στόματι μαχαίρης καὶ αἰχμαλωτισθήσονται εἰς τὰ ἔθνη πάντα, καὶ Ἰερουσαλὴμ ἔσται πατουμένη ὑπὸ ἐθνῶν, ἄχρι οὗ πληρωθῶσιν καιροὶ ἐθνῶν.

What is to be made of the divergence here between Matthew/
Mark and Luke?

3.1.   The case for seeing Lk 21:23,24 as Lukan redaction

The obvious explanation may seem to be that the Lukan form
is a Lukan redactional substitute for the Matthew/Mark form.
Luke has drawn on the Matthew/Mark form in chap. 17, and so,
just as he rewords the saying about the man on the roof-top
when he comes to use it a second time (see previous discussion
of 17:31 and 21:21 on pp.160-65,183), so he here puts a substitute
for the Matthew/Mark form of the distress saying. The Lukan
substitute saying is a specific and explicit saying about
military attack on Jerusalem, whereas the original Matthew/
Mark form was a vague one about widespread and awful distress;
this may be thought to reflect the same Lukan editorial
tendency as is found in the earlier verses (vv 20,21), as Luke
there has an explicit description of Jerusalem being surrounded
by armies in place of Matthew/Mark's more obscure reference to
the desolating sacrilege; he also relates the saying about 'the
person on the house-top' specifically to Jerusalem. It is a
common assumption that Luke has rewritten the apocalyptic
Matthew/Mark form in the light of the historical events of
AD 70, and this could help explain his changes throughout this
section.

This apparently plausible explanation of Luke's divergences
from the Matthew/Mark tradition in his vv 23,24 should not be
accepted uncritically. Not all the factors that may have led

to Luke's rewriting of his traditions in his vv 20-23a are
present in these later verses. Thus, if Luke in the earlier
verses felt compelled to avoid or paraphrase the obscure
Matthew/Mark phrase 'the desolating sacrilege', there is nothing
so obviously obscure in the Matthew/Mark form of the later
verses (though see below, pp.213,214, on the awkward tension in
the Matthew/Mark form). And if he felt compelled in the earlier
verses to paraphrase the saying about the person on the house-
top because he had used it before in his 17:31, it is not clear
that the same sort of consideration would have led to his
avoidance of the Matthew/Mark form of the saying about the
distress (Mt 24:21 / Mk 13:19 cf. Lk 21:23b): Luke's previous
use of this saying in 17:22 was very paraphrastic, and there
was thus no need for him to change the Matthew/Mark form here.
Another respect in which the situation in the earlier verses is
not analogous to the situation in the later verses is that,
whereas in the earlier verses Luke's content is much the same
as that found in Matthew/Mark, despite the variation in wording,
in the later verses Luke's content diverges substantially from
Matthew/Mark's. We should then have to argue that the factors
which led Luke to modify his traditions in vv 20-23a - to
rephrase and to make things explicit that were not explicit -
led him to much more radical and creative editing in vv 23b,24.
What is, however, true is that in the earlier and the later
verses the Lukan picture is that of a military invasion
including an attack on Jerusalem and that this is a different
emphasis from what we find in Matthew and Mark. It does seem
likely that a common factor lies behind this similar divergence
in the earlier and later verses. But it is not clear that the
factor was Luke's experience of AD 70; indeed it was considered
possible that Luke's reference to Jerusalem being surrounded by
armies in 21:20 could have come from the pre-synoptic tradition.
(See above, pp. 185-188.)

*3.2. The case for including Lk 21:23b,24 in the pre-synoptic
       tradition*

    This same possibility needs exploring so far as Lk 21:23b,
24 is concerned. Since all three evangelists were familiar with
a pre-synoptic form of the preceding verses (Mt 24:15-20 and
parallels) and of the following verses (Mt 24:23-27 and
parallels), it is likely that there was also a pre-synoptic
section in-between and it is at least sensible to see if this
explains the synoptic divergences here.

3.2.1. Matthew/Luke agreement against Mark

Matthew and Luke have a small agreement against Mark which may confirm that they were familiar with a pre-synoptic form of those verses. Compare:

Matthew's	ἔσται γὰρ τότε θλῖψις μεγάλη
Luke's	ἔσται γὰρ ἀνάγκη μεγάλη
with Mark's	ἔσονται γὰρ αἱ ἡμέραι ἐκεῖναι θλῖψις

Mark's wording here is awkward enough to have been changed by both Matthew and Luke, but their agreement in the sort of change they make may reflect common tradition./1/ The agreement could be accounted for by Lukan knowledge of Matthew or Matthean knowledge of Luke, but it could also be explained via a common pre-synoptic tradition.

Such a common pre-synoptic tradition could also be a partial explanation of Mark's rather difficult construction 'those days will be distress'. Mark's wording may be seen as a slightly half-hearted modification of a pre-synoptic form like that found in Matthew/Luke: Mark sounds as though he is going to say something like 'those days will be days of distress' - picking up the phrase 'those days' from the preceding v 17 and perhaps influenced by the LXX of Dan 12:1 ἐκείνη ἡ ἡμέρα θλίψεως, οἵα οὐκ ἐγενήθη - ; but then he does not quite carry this through, reverting to the pre-synoptic form in his θλῖψις and ending up with a cross between what he intended and the Matthew/Luke form./2/

3.2.2. Evidence in Paul for 21:23b being a primitive tradition

If Luke's agreement with Matthew suggests the possibility of pre-synoptic tradition in Lk 21:23a, Paul supplies evidence that may point to Luke's vv 23b,24 being primitive.

/1/ Beasley-Murray, *Jesus and the Future*, 78, notes Exod 11:6 κραυγὴ μέγαλη as a possible parallel to the form of words in Matthew and Luke.
/2/ Lambrecht, *Redaktion*, 161, calls the awkward expression typical of Mark. See also Zmijewski, *Eschatologiereden*, 201.

Compare:

Lk 21:23,24   ἔσται .. ὀργὴ τῷ λαῷ τούτῳ ... ἄχρι οὗ πληρωθῶσιν
               καιροὶ ἐθνῶν
Rom 11:25   πώρωσις ἀπὸ μέρους τῷ 'Ισραὴλ γέγονεν ἄχρι οὗ τὸ
               πλήρωμα τῶν ἐθνῶν εἰσέλθῃ
1 Thess 2:16   ἔφθασεν δὲ ἐπ' αὐτοὺς ἡ ὀργὴ εἰς τέλος

These verses (a) agree with each other in speaking of a
judgment on the Jews. (b) All three have a somewhat similar
structure: compare ὀργή/πώρωσις/ὀργή, ἔσται/γέγονεν/ἔφθασεν,
τῷ λαῷ τούτῳ/τῷ 'Ισραήλ/ἐπ' αὐτούς, ἄχρι ο /ἄχρι οὗ/εἰς τέλος.
(c) All three suggest that the judgment on the Jews is somehow
connected with opportunity for the Gentiles: Luke speaks of the
καιροὶ ἐθνῶν being fulfilled, Romans of the fulness of the
Gentiles coming in, and 1 Thessalonians explains that the
judgment comes on the Jews because of their opposition to
Gentile mission, the implication quite probably being that the
judgment will facilitate Gentile mission. (d) Luke and Romans
set a time limit on the judgment ἄχρι οὗ; and εἰς τέλος in
1 Thess 2:16 may also be taken to mean 'until the end', though it
is more usually translated 'at last', 'finally', or 'utterly'./1/
(e) Luke agrees with 1 Thessalonians in referring the
judgment specifically to the Jews of Palestine and in the use of
the word ὀργή. (f) Luke agrees with Romans in having a
similarly worded 'until' clause.

   Possible objections
   These points of similarity suggest that we probably have a
common tradition here. But it may be objected that some of the
similarities may be more apparent than real. For example, some
scholars take Luke's καιροὶ ἐθνῶν to refer not to times of
Gentile mission, but to the period of Gentile domination over
Jerusalem. It can be argued that this interpretation fits the
Lukan context best; and the phrase may be linked to the thought
of Dan 12:11, where the abomination stands for 'one thousand two
hundred and ninety days'./2/ However, it may well be that the

----

/1/ εἰς τέλος can have (or may include) the sense 'until the
end' in all but one of its NT occurrences: see Mt 10:22/24:13/
Mk 13:13 and Jn 13:1. But in each case there is possible
ambiguity, and for a different sense see Lk 18:5 and *T. Levi* 6:
11. See also below, pp. 283,284.
/2/ Cf. B. Rigaux, *L'Antéchrist et l'Opposition au Royaume
Messianique dans l'Ancien et le Nouveau Testament* (Gembloux:
Duculot, 1932) 211. Also Beasley-Murray, *Mark 82*; Dupont, 'La
ruine du temple', 240.

phrase has more positive connotations in line with Luke's use
of καιρός elsewhere and in line with his interest in the Gentile
mission. D. Bosch finds both negative and positive connotations
in the phrase: comparing Mt 23:37-38/Lk 13:34-35 and Lk 19:41-44
for the thought of the Jews forfeiting their καιρός, he suggests
that the καιροὶ ἐθνῶν in 21:24 are 'nicht nur eine Zeit, in der
die Heiden Gewalt über die heilige Stadt haben, sondern auch
als eine Zeit, in der sie die Träger des von Israel verworfenen
Heils sind'./1/ But even were the Lukan phrase intended purely
negatively, this would not disprove the argument for linking
Rom 11:25, 1 Thess 2:16 with the Lukan verse, since Paul could
have reinterpreted the phrase in a positive way.

Another possible objection to the linking of the Lukan and
Pauline traditions is that in Romans at least (and possibly in
1 Thessalonians) Paul is speaking of a spiritual judgment on
the Jews, whereas in Luke the ὀργή is physical judgment on
Jerusalem as is made clear by his vv 24a and b which come
between his reference to the ὀργή and his reference to the
'times of the Gentiles'. But this is not a great difficulty:
it is quite possible that originally the ὀργή was understood as
a primarily physical judgment on the Jews of Palestine, and
that in Romans Paul has reinterpreted this in a spiritualizing
way (hence πώρωσις for ὀργή); alternatively, and perhaps more
likely, Paul may have seen the πώρωσις as one aspect of the
ὀργή, that would also have a physical manifestation. So far as
1 Thess 2:16 is concerned, it is hard to know what Paul's
understanding of the ὀργή that 'has come upon them' (i.e. the
Jews of Palestine) is. In view of the probable echoes in this
passage of Mt 23:29-38 & par. (traditions that refer to
the destruction of Jerusalem in the synoptics), it is possible
that Paul was speaking here prophetically of the imminent
destruction of Jerusalem./2/ But it is also possible that he
is referring, as in Romans, to the spiritual hardening of the
Jews; in that case we may again have a case of Paul interpreting
the synoptic tradition in a particular way. This suggestion

/1/ *Die Heidenmission in der Zukunftsschau Jesu* (Zürich: Zwingli,
1959), 172-74. Cf. also J. Ernst, *Die Eschatologische
Gegenspieler in den Schriften des N.T.* (Regensburg: Pustet,
1967), 9. See also further discussion in chapter 7 below,
pp. 268-84.
/2/ See my 'Paul and the Synoptic Apocalypse', 361-63, for
further discussion of this and for references.

might fit in with the earlier observations about the
relationship of Paul's man of lawlessness and the synoptic
desolating sacrilege, since there too the synoptics have a more
military/political emphasis on destruction/desecration and Paul
a more religious emphasis.

It is indeed possible to link the ὀργή of 1 Thess 2:16
with the man of lawlessness of 2 Thessalonians.
1 Thessalonians 2 speaks of a judgment on the Jews of Palestine
and 2 Thessalonians 2 of the coming of an Antiochus-like figure
to 'the temple'. These could be quite unrelated events, but
they could have been connected (if not by Paul, then at least
in pre-Pauline tradition). In fact it could be that
2 Thessalonians 2 is in part at least a clarification of
1 Thessalonians 2: if the Thessalonians knew the tradition that
linked the judgment of the Jews with the coming of the Son of
man, then Paul's remark in 1 Thess 2:16 about the ὀργή 'having
come' on the Jews may have encouraged the Thessalonians to
think that the day of the Lord had come (2 Thess 2:2); Paul
then had to clarify the situation in 2 Thessalonians 2 and to
point out that the desecration of the temple by the lawless one
must precede the second coming. His remark then in
1 Thessalonians 2 about the 'wrath' having come on the Jews of
Palestine would either have been prophetic and a reference to
what was about to happen or may have been referring to the
'hardening' of the Jews which Paul saw as part of the 'wrath'
and as leading up to the desecration of the Jerusalem temple.

Perhaps the same 'hardening' of the Jews may be referred
to in 2 Thess 2:7, where Paul says that the 'mystery of
lawlessness' is already at work, although 'lawlessness' is not
the word we might expect of the Jews./1/ Paul could well have
seen the unbelief of the Jews as the 'mystery of lawlessness'
beginning to work and as the firstfruits of the 'wrath' of God
on the Jews; the coming of 'the man of lawlessness' and the
desecration of the temple would then be the culmination of that
'wrath'. This could also be the sense of 2 Thess 2:3 where
Paul says that the end will not come 'unless the apostasy comes
first and the man of lawlessness is revealed'; Paul may believe

_____

/1/ But see Mt 23:28 and Burnett, *Testament*, 255. It is
interesting that in Rom 11:25 the 'hardening' of Israel is
introduced as 'this mystery' (or as part of it) and that the
only other negative 'mystery' in Paul is the 'mystery of
lawlessness' in 2 Thess 2:7.

that the 'apostasy' has begun in the unbelief of the Jews.

These somewhat speculative reflections about Pauline
theology are interesting and could fit in with the suggestions
we are proposing. But the immediately important point is
simply that the difference between the physical ὀργή of
Lk 21:23,24 and the spiritual hardening of Rom 11:25 (and perhaps
1 Thess 2:16) is not a weighty argument against the linking of
those texts.

Conclusions
Various other considerations may strengthen the case for
linking Lk 21:23,24, Rom 11:25, 1 Thess 2:16, including our
earlier argument for linking Lk 21:34-36 with 1 Thessalonians 5
and Romans 13 (see above pp.109-117): if there are some common
traditions in the three books, it is not unlikely that there
are others. Also, quite apart from the last phrase of
1 Thess 4:16 that we have been considering, there is good reason for
thinking that Paul is drawing on traditional material in
1 Thess 2:14-16 - the strangeness of Paul's language here and the
links with Mt 23:29-36/Lk 11:47-50 suggest this (see further
below, pp. 346-48); if Paul was here drawing on tradition, he
could well have put together elements from different traditions.
When all these things are considered, the argument for saying
that Lk 21:23,24, Rom 11:25 and 1 Thess 2:16 reflect a common
tradition is plausible. It is not plausible to suggest that
Luke was dependent on Paul for the tradition, since he would
then have been involved in a rather extraordinary conflation of
different Pauline traditions. It is much more likely that there
was a common 'pre-synoptic' tradition known to Paul and Luke./1/

3.2.3. The Lukan tradition in the pre-synoptic discourse
To argue that Lk 21:23b,24 contains primitive tradition
that was also known to Paul is not to prove that these
traditional elements were ever part of the eschatological
discourse. Luke could have welded the traditions on to this
context as a substitute for what we have in Matthew and Mark.
However there are reasons that suggest that Luke has retained
the sayings in their pre-synoptic context.

/1/ Further arguments might be added for the traditional nature
of the Lukan verses. Marshall, for example, maintains that
ὀργή is not a Lukan word (*Luke*, 773).

General
(a) The tradition in question referring to judgment on the
Jews - the Jews of Palestine according to Luke and also
according to 1 Thess 2:16 - must have belonged in some context.
(b) It fits well into the eschatological discourse where Luke
has it. Not only do the Lukan tradition in question and the
Matthew/Mark desolating sacrilege tradition both have a common
Danielic background (e.g. Daniel 8 and 11); but it is also
arguable that something like Lk 21:23 is needed in the Matthew/
Mark context: Matthew and Mark lead us to expect some
description of the destruction of Jerusalem (cf. Mt 24:2,
Mk 13:2), but, when we apparently come to the crucial point,
they never actually give us what we expect - explicitly at least.
(c) It has already been argued that Luke was familiar with the
pre-synoptic form of the immediately preceding section of the
eschatological discourse (i.e. the description of the desolating
sacrilege, the saying about the man on the house-top, etc.); so
it is probable that he knew the pre-synoptic form of what
follows, and it is quite possible that he is using it in
Lk 21:23,24.

Paul's testimony
Paul's evidence is fourfold. (a) Paul has been seen to be
quite heavily dependent on the pre-synoptic, eschatological
discourse in 1 and 2 Thessalonians; so the suggestion that the
pre-Pauline tradition being considered may also have come from
that discourse makes good sense. (b) In particular Paul shows
himself in 2 Thessalonians 2 to have been familiar with the
context in which Luke places the saying about the wrath on
Jerusalem. We would thus expect him to know that saying, if
Luke has preserved the pre-synoptic context; 1 Thess 2:16 may be
evidence that he did. (He does not use it in 2 Thessalonians 2,
since he focuses here on the personal and religious side of the
desolating sacrilege not on the national dimension). (c) Paul
shows elsewhere that material that is only found in Luke 21, not
in Matthew and Mark, was part of the pre-synoptic tradition (see
the earlier discussion of 1 Thessalonians 5 and Lk 21:34-36 on
pp. 109-117 above); we must then be open to other 'L' elements
from the discourse being primitive, and the 'wrath' saying would
be such an element. (d) In 1 Thess 2:14-16 Paul appears to link
together the tradition about the 'wrath' on the Jews with other
material concerning the fall of Jerusalem, material which
Matthew (though not Luke) places just before the eschatological
discourse (Mt 23:31-36, cf. Lk 11:47-51). This Pauline
combination of traditions would be the more easily explicable
if the traditions were adjacent in the pre-synoptic tradition.

The evidence of Revelation
a. Revelation 13
It has been seen that the synoptic desolating sacrilege
and Paul's man of lawlessness are probably variant versions of
a common tradition: in both cases there is description of an
awful sacrilegious person/event and then of associated
deceptive signs and wonders; in both cases it is Jesus at his
parousia who brings salvation from this evil. The description
in Revelation 13 of the 'beast' must be another version of the
same tradition: the beast blasphemes God and his dwelling and
has worldwide authority, and he is accompanied by a second
beast who does great and deceptive signs. And just as in
2 Thess 2:8 the man of lawlessness is finally destroyed by the
Lord through 'the breath of his mouth', so in Revelation the
beasts are finally put down by the risen Christ from whose
mouth issues a sharp sword (Rev 19:15,20).

The interesting thing about Revelation 13 for the question
of Lk 21:23,24 is that after the opening description of the
blasphemous beast there is reference to the beast 'making war'
on the saints and 'conquering' them (Rev 13:7), and then there
is the saying 'If any one is to be taken captive, to captivity
he goes; if any one slays with the sword, with the sword must he
be slain' (13:10). This is a similar sequence of thought to
that found in Luke 21, where Luke's reference to the desolation
of Jerusalem (i.e. his equivalent of the desolating sacrilege
passage) is followed by the verses describing wrath on the Jews
and people 'falling by the sword' and being 'taken captive'
(21:24).

An agreement of this sort between Luke and Revelation might
prove nothing more than that the author of Revelation knew Luke.
However, the significant point is that Revelation 13 contains a
combination of motifs that are found separately in Matthew/Mark
and in Luke: the reference to war, captivity and slaying with
the sword is paralleled in the Lukan form of the eschatological
discourse; but the portrayal in Revelation 13 of the
blasphemous beast and then of the second beast doing deceptive
signs is much closer to the Matthew/Mark form of the discourse
than to the Lukan form: Luke, for example, does not have any
explicit reference to the 'desolating sacrilege' (cf. the 'beast'),
nor does he have the warning of false prophets doing deceptive
signs. So we have in Revelation 13 this combination of motifs:

Revelation	Matthew/Mark	Luke
The blasphemous beast	The desolating sacrilege	(Desolation of Jerusalem)
War/captivity/sword		Wrath/sword/ captivity
Other beast doing signs to deceive	False prophets doing signs to deceive	

This combination   could be an early example of the harmonizing
of gospel traditions; but it is probably simpler to suggest
that the Matthew/Mark traditions and the Lukan traditions
belonged together in the pre-synoptic tradition, and that
this tradition was known to the author of Revelation, who has
already been seen to have had some possible knowledge of the
pre-synoptic tradition (p. 56 above).

Against this hypothesis various objections may be raised:
(1) It is arguable that there is a considerable difference
between the Lukan description of anger on 'this people' (i.e. on
Jerusalem and Judea) and the description in Revelation of war
on 'the saints'. But this difference simply reflects an
interpretative shift (from the old Israel to the new Israel –
see further discussion below). (2) It may be pointed out that
the verse in Revelation about people going to captivity and
being slain by the sword seems to be an echo of Jer 15:2 and
perhaps of Mt 26:52 /1/ rather than of Luke 21. On this it
must be admitted that the verbal parallelism between Revelation
13 and Luke 21 is not very close; so, if the author of
Revelation is using the same tradition as Luke represents, he is
using it very freely, drawing in other material as well,
including Jer 15:2. But (a) this is not improbable in view of
the author's writing technique elsewhere; for example, his
portrayal of the Antichrist as a 'beast' is his distinctive
re-presentation of the tradition. (b) It may be significant
that, whereas Jer 15:2 refers to pestilence, sword, famine and
captivity, Rev 13:10 only refers to captivity and sword (as does
Lk 21:24a). (3) It is possible to argue that the agreements
of Luke and Revelation are due to the influence on both of the
book of Daniel (notably chaps. 8 and 11) and so to dismiss the
idea of a pre-synoptic tradition. However, although the
appearance of common Danielic features in Luke and Revelation
could be due to the respective authors' independent use of the

---

/1/   Cf. G. R. Beasley-Murray, *The Book of Revelation* (London:
Oliphants, 1974) 214.

OT, it is quite as likely that some or all of their agreements
reflect their use of a shared tradition including those features.

b. Revelation 11

Revelation 11 may be a similar case. There are a number
of distinct similarities to Lk 21:24 here: (i) in v 2 there is
the thought of Jerusalem and the outer court of the temple
being trampled over (πατήσουσιν) by the nations (ἔθνεσιν),
which is similar to Lk 21:24 Ἰερουσαλὴμ ἔσται πατουμένη ὑπὸ
ἐθνῶν (though it also has an OT background, e.g. Zech 12:3LXX).
(ii) In Revelation and in Luke the trampling is given a time-
limit (cf. also Dan 8:13,14). In Revelation it is said that the
trampling will last for 'forty two months'; and this is
immediately followed by reference to the 'two witnesses' who
will prophesy for '1260 days', which is also 42 months. It
is probable that the two witnesses of Revelation are the church
as the witnessing people of God;/1/ so we have in Revelation the
thought of a period of 42 months when Jerusalem is trampled upon
and the church carries on its witness. In Lk 21:24 the time-
limit for the trampling is less specific - 'until the times of
the Gentiles are fulfilled'. But if this phrase is understood
not just negatively, but also as including the idea of the
Gentile mission, then the parallelism of thought to the thought
in Revelation is unmistakable: in both there is promised a period
of trampling + witness. (iii) 42 months is also the period of
the beast's rule according to Rev 13:5, so that it is possible
that for the author of Revelation the period of the beast's
rule = the period of the trampling of Jerusalem = the period of
the church's witness. Certainly the 'beast' appears in
Revelation 11: he makes war on the two witnesses conquering and
killing them (v 7). It seems probable that this 'conquering' of
the beast is to be linked with his 'conquering' of the saints in
Rev 13:7. In any case we have another case of the beast being
involved in warfare against God's people, and perhaps therefore
another reflection of Lk 21:20-24 with its description of
Jerusalem being attacked (though in Revelation 11 the 'war'
comes after the period of witness, whereas in Luke it precedes
it). It may well be significant that in Revelation 11 the
bodies of the witnesses are left in the city 'where their Lord
was crucified' (v 8): the beast's attack is on God's people in
'Jerusalem', however Jerusalem is interpreted.

/1/ Cf. G. R. Beasley-Murray, *Revelation*, 176-84.

The three strands of evidence from Revelation 11 suggest
that the author of Revelation was familiar with the traditions
of Lk 21:20-24: he could have derived them directly from Luke;
but the motif of the beast, as has already been observed, is
more obviously reminiscent of the Matthew/Mark tradition than
of the Lukan tradition. Also the idea of the *temple* (or the
outer court of the temple) being trampled and defiled, which is
found in Revelation 11, is only implied in Luke; the author of
Revelation could have derived this thought from the OT (e.g.
Dan 8:13,14), but he would also have found the thought of the
temple being desecrated in Matthew and Mark. So we have again
in Revelation a combination of motifs attested in Matthew/Mark
and in Luke, and this combination could be a reflection of the
pre-synoptic tradition.

  c. Revelation 6
    That the author of Revelation was familiar with Lk 21:24c
'until the times of the Gentiles are fulfilled' may be
confirmed by the evidence of Rev 6:11: here in the middle of a
chapter that parallels the eschatological discourse in many
respects there is reference to the suffering saints who have
been killed for their 'testimony' and whose blood has been
shed. They ask ἕως πότε, and are told to wait ἔτι χρόνον
μικρόν, ἕως πληρωθῶσιν καὶ οἱ σύνδουλοι .... (vv 9-11).
πληροῦν is an infrequent word in Revelation (occurring
otherwise only in 3:2), and it is possible that we have here an
echo of Luke's ἄχρι οὗ πληρωθῶσιν καιροὶ ἐθνῶν, if this was
understood of the church's mission. The verbal link between
the texts by itself would not suggest this - Revelation speaks
of the number of martyrs, not Gentile converts, being
'fulfilled' - , but there is also the contextual link, the
phrase being preceded by reference to killing and being
followed by description of cosmic upheavals, a sequence of
ideas that parallels that found in Luke 21. Given the verbal
and the contextual link, it seems quite probable that the
author of Revelation is here picking up and using a phrase from
Luke 21.

    This suggestion is the more probable if the period
described in Revelation 6 when people are being killed for
their testimony and when they have to wait 'until the number of
their fellow servants is filled up' is correctly identified
with the period described in Revelation 13 when the beast
makes war on the saints and conquers them and when the saints
are called to endure, and also with the period described in

Revelation 11 when the outer courts of the temple are trampled
and when the church witnesses and is attacked and killed for
three and a half days. If chapters 6,11 and 13 of Revelation
are correctly associated in this way, then the case for linking
6:11 with Lk 21:24 is clearly strengthened, since Lk 21:24 has
probable connections with chapters 11 and 13 of Revelation.

It is possible that the thesis being proposed might help
to explain where the idea of the souls 'under the altar' of
Rev 6:9 comes from: in Revelation 11 and 13 there is not only
reference to God's people being attacked, but also mention of
the temple of God or the dwelling of God being blasphemed and
defiled; and it was suggested that this conjunction of ideas
could reflect a pre-synoptic tradition which included the
Matthew/Mark description of the desecration of the temple as
well as the Lukan description of an attack on God's people. If
the same pre-synoptic tradition lies behind Rev 6:11, then it is
possible that the 'altar' of Rev 6:9 reflects it: not that the
thought in Revelation resembles the synoptic passage at all
closely, but it could be that the synoptic desolating sacrilege
sparked off the train of thought that we find in Revelation.

d. The reinterpretation of tradition in Revelation
This last suggestion is evidently speculative. But the
suggestion that the author of Revelation was familiar with a
version of the eschatological discourse which included elements
attested separately in Matthew and Mark on the one hand and in
Luke on the other hand is plausible. If he was familiar with
a pre-synoptic tradition of this sort, including the sayings of
Lk 21:23,24, then he has reinterpreted it, so that the focus is
no longer on literal Jerusalem, but on the church. Thus in
Revelation 11 there is reference to the 'temple', the 'altar'
and the 'holy city', but the thought is of the church under
pressure, not of literal Jerusalem. Similarly in Rev 13:7 the
beast blasphemes God and his 'dwelling': God's dwelling is
defined as 'those who dwell in heaven', and the beast's attack
is on 'the saints'. Similarly in Revelation 6 the 'altar' is
no longer the literal altar in Jerusalem, and the slain who
wait for their number to be complete are again Christian
witnesses. There is a consistent pattern of interpretation
here: the original literal description of the attack on
Jerusalem and on the Jews has become descriptive of the
sufferings of the new Israel, i.e. Christians. Not that the
'Antichrist' has been made unhistorical and unpolitical: the
'beast' of Revelation seems to be portrayed in the colours of
the Roman state (e.g. in Revelation 13). But instead of

attacking Jerusalem and the Jews, the Roman 'beast' is now seen
as attacking the church. This reinterpretation of the synoptic
tradition is well explained if the usual Domitianic dating of
Revelation is accepted: the literal destruction of Jerusalem by
the Romans was past, and the author of Revelation, living in a
time when the church was under pressure, reinterprets the
eschatological discourse in the light of his situation. Perhaps
he sees the Roman threat to Christians as a continuation and
extension of what happened in AD 70; perhaps he simply uses the
language of the eschatological discourse in a new context./1/ The
synoptic eschatological discourse speaks, of course, not only
of the fall of Jerusalem, but in adjacent contexts of Christians
under pressure and being 'killed' (e.g. Mt 24:9, Mk 13:12,
Lk 21:16) and of the 'elect' being in distress (so Mt 24:22/Mk 13:20,
but not Luke); it is possible that the author of Revelation,
while making use of all the traditions, has allowed one theme
from the context (the theme of Christians suffering) to
override and reinterpret the other (the theme of the fall of
Jerusalem, which was not directly relevant post AD 70). So,
for example, Rev 6:9-11 may be seen as some sort of equivalent
of the whole of Mt 24:9-22/Mk 13:9-20/Lk 21:12-24.

     It would be possible and perhaps desirable to spend much
longer exploring the interpretation of Revelation. But even
though the preceding discussion has been dangerously cursory,
enough has probably been said to show that there is some reason,
though not proof, for thinking that the author of Revelation
may have known and used a form of the eschatological discourse
in which the Lukan sayings of 21:23,24 were present in the
context of the desolating sacrilege.

3.3. *The reconstruction of the pre-synoptic form of the*
       discourse

     A considerable amount of evidence has been accumulated
that points to Luke 21:23,24 being primitive tradition, and
there is some reason to believe that it belonged in the pre-
synoptic eschatological discourse. But that still leaves us
with the question of how the Lukan tradition is to be related
to the Matthew / Mark tradition. That indeed is the vital
question: the evidence from Paul and Revelation is not
unimportant; but it is only indirect evidence, and it is making
sense of the synoptic evidence that is decisive.

/1/ Perhaps he has been influenced by the Danielic background
to the discourse, since in Daniel it is the saints of God who
are attacked by Antiochus.

One possibility is that Luke's form of the tradition with
its description of the fall of Jerusalem is the pre-synoptic
tradition and that Matthew's and Mark's description of
'distress such as has never been' is a secondary modification
of it. Against this is (a) the preceding and following
sections in Matthew and Mark (the desolating sacrilege
tradition + the description of the false prophets) have been
shown already to have been part of the pre-synoptic tradition;
it is at least odd if the material in-between is secondary.
(b) Luke in his 17:22 appears to be using a pre-synoptic form
of the tradition that included a reference to the 'great
distress', even affecting the elect; this was argued above on
pp. 137-39. (c) The suggestion would leave us with the
difficult problem of explaining how Matthew's and Mark's form
of words came to be substituted for the Lukan form.

The alternative and preferable explanation is similar to
the explanation offered of the conclusion of the discourse,
i.e. that both the Matthew/Mark and the Lukan traditions were
in the pre-synoptic tradition. It is suggested that the pre-
synoptic form of the tradition was approximately as follows:

1. Warning of desolating sacrilege/armies
   around Jerusalem. Call to flee .....   so Mt/Mk/Lk

2. For there will be (great) ἀνάγκη on the
   land and wrath on this people ....

   Jerusalem will be trodden .... until
   the times of the Gentiles are fulfilled   so Lk

3. And in those days/then there will be
   (great) θλῖψις as has not been .. no
   human being would be saved ... but for
   the sake of the elect, he shortened
   the days.   so Mt/Mk

4. And then if anyone says to you, 'Lo,
   here is the Christ ...'; warning of
   false Christs and prophets.   so Mt/Mk

5. But in those days after that tribulation
   the sun will be darkened .. they will see
   the Son of man. (Or And there will be
   signs in sun and moon ... And they will
   see ...)   so Mt/Mk/Lk

There are some uncertainties in this reconstruction, and it is
not claimed that the details are all necessarily correct. For
example, it is not certain whether the adjective μεγάλη was
originally with the Lukan ἀνάγκη, in which case Matthew has
transferred it to θλῖψις, or whether it was originally with
θλῖψις, in which case Mark has omitted it and Luke has
transferred it to ἀνάγκη, or whether possibly it was with both
nouns./1/ A quite different possibility is that the
second section began simply 'For there will be wrath on this
people', and that Luke's ἀνάγκη μεγάλη ἐπὶ τῆς γῆς is taken
from the third section. But, although there is room for doubt
about some points of detail, the suggestion that the pre-
synoptic tradition was roughly as proposed makes a lot of sense.

3.3.1. Evidence of the reconstruction in Revelation
There is, of course, no gospel text that has the
description of the destruction of Jerusalem (Luke) followed by
the reference to a great and worldwide distress (Matthew/Mark).
If there was such a gospel text, there would be no problem! The
nearest we have to direct evidence for the combination of the
Matthean/Markan and the Lukan motifs may be the book of
Revelation. In Rev 13:7 it is said that the beast was given
(a) to wage war on and to conquer the saints, (b) to have
authority over 'every tribe, people, tongue and nation'; this
authority led to earth's inhabitants worshipping the beast,
except for those whose names were written in the book of life.

/1/ Whichever explanation is correct (but especially if μεγάλη
was with both nouns), it may seem that the proposed
reconstruction undercuts the earlier argument for the pre-
synoptic tradition on the basis of Matthew's and Luke's
agreement against Mark, since according to the reconstruction
Matthew and Luke have drawn some or all of their common non-
Markan phraseology from two different pre-synoptic sayings, not
from one. However, the argument is perhaps not wholly
invalidated; Matthew's and Luke's agreement to differ from Mark
is not coincidental, but is because Mark has diverged from the
pre-synoptic tradition; and although Matthew and Luke may both
have 'corrected' Mark on the basis of different pre-synoptic sayings from
the pre-synoptic discourse, those sayings were parallel and
adjacent, and so Matthew and Luke may be said at least to
testify indirectly to each other. In any case the argument for
the pre-synoptic tradition stands on other grounds.

If the 'saints' are Revelation's equivalent of Jerusalem and
the Jews (see discussion above, pp. 205-09), then we may have
here a parallel to the proposed pre-synoptic tradition that
describes first an attack on Jerusalem and then a distress
affecting all flesh, including the elect (cf. those written in
the book of life)./1/

But more important than this evidence from Revelation,
which is of uncertain weight, is the fact that the proposed
reconstruction accounts well for the present synoptic texts,
recognizing the primitiveness of the traditions in Matthew/Mark
and also in Luke.

   3.3.2.   Matthew/Mark explained from the proposed pre-
synoptic tradition
   One of the strongest arguments in favour of the proposed
reconstruction is that it helps explain the tension that there
is in the present Matthew/Mark version of this section.   The
tension is between the opening verses of the section (Mt 24:15-20/
Mk 13:14-18) and the closing verses (Mt 24:21,22/Mk 13:19,20):
the opening verses describe events in Jerusalem and Judea, and
Jesus' hearers are urged to flee.   We expect next to find a
description of the destruction of the temple and city; instead
we find in the closing verses a broad description of
unparalleled tribulation, which apparently involves the elect
and from which they could presumably not flee.   These verses may
be taken of the fall of Jerusalem and nothing more; but the
generality of the language and the references to 'all flesh' and
'the elect' suggest that we have unexpectedly stepped out of the
narrow Palestinian arena into something bigger affecting all of
humanity and all of the elect (though perhaps including the fall
of Jerusalem)./2/   Given this tension it is not surprising that

---

/1/ Revelation 13 does not have the exact order of the pre-
synoptic tradition, since it goes on next to refer to
'captivity' and 'sword', reverting to the earlier thought of
conquering and killing.   Revelation 11 also has a local focus on
Jerusalem (vv 2,8) and an international focus (e.g. v 9).   But,
although the implication may be that the beast has a national
and international role and clientele, it would be unwise to make
much of this evidence.
/2/ This interpretation of Mt 24:21,22 & par. is probably
reflected in Did. 16:15 τότε ἥξει ἡ κτίσις τῶν ἀνθρώπων εἰς τὴν
πύρωσιν τῆς δοκιμασίας.   A. Feuillet, RevBib 55 (1948) 496,497,
points out against this view that similar very strong language
is used in the OT of historical judgments and in Josephus of the

some scholars have taken the section to be describing the fall
of Jerusalem in AD 70, others have taken it of a future
antichrist, and others have argued that it is somehow
describing both.

The tension that gives rise to these differing hypotheses
is simply explained through the proposal about the form of the
pre-synoptic tradition. On this view the opening verses about
the desolating sacrilege were indeed followed by a description
of the destruction of Jerusalem (that being preserved in Luke);
but Matthew and Mark omitted this, going straight on to the
following broader section.

As well as this tension which is found in both Matthew and
Mark the comparatively minor difficulty of Mark's 'those days
will be tribulation' may be explained by the hypothesis
proposed. It has already been suggested that Mark's form of
words may be a half-hearted modification of the Matthew/Luke
(= pre-synoptic) form, Mark introducing the reference to 'those
days' (see p. 199 above). It may now be further suggested
that Mark's form of words is in fact a combination of the
wordings of sections 2 and 3 in the reconstruction, i.e. of
ἔσται γὰρ :.... (ἀνάγκη) and of καὶ ἐν ἐκείναις ταῖς ἡμέραις
.... The apparent, though slight, repetitiousness of Mark (with
'those days' in both v 17 and v 19) is the result of his
omission of intervening material; Matthew has avoided this by
substituting τότε in his v 21.

One obvious problem with the argument about the tension in
Matthew and Mark is that it entails Matthew and Mark producing
a more difficult text on the basis of a simpler text. But
their difficult text does need some explaining, and it is not
hard to suggest how and why they changed the underlying
tradition.

So far as the 'how' is concerned, Matthew/Mark have simply
jumped from one prediction in the postulated original to a

---

events of AD 70. This point may be allowed; but there is still
a shift of emphasis between Mt 24:20 and 21 from the specific,
local and historical to the general, universal and
eschatological. (See my discussion of the interpretation of
the discourse in '"This generation will not pass"' especially
pp. 130-32.)

second similarly constructed prediction – from ἔσται ἀνάγκη to
ἔσται θλῖψις.

As for the 'why' of the alteration, it could have been
accidental. But that seems a rather unsatisfactory
explanation. If it was deliberate compression, it could
simply have been for the sake of brevity; but a much more
likely explanation is suggested when one notes their earlier
cryptic language when referring to the 'desolating sacrilege'
'let the reader understand'. Given the opening of the chapter
and the prediction there of the destruction of the temple,
there is little doubt that this is what Matthew and Mark are
now coming on to describe; but for some reason they use quite
obscure language at this crucial point. This could be normal
apocalyptic obscurity; but it could also be because of the
sensitivity of the subject in a particular historical
situation./1/ It seems quite likely that the factors that led
to this obscurity also led to the omission of the direct
description of the destruction of Jerusalem which was in the
postulated source tradition.

It is not difficult then to suggest how and why Matthew/
Mark abbreviated the postulated underlying text. And
positively in favour of the hypothesis is its ability to
explain the tensions in the Matthew/Mark text./2/

3.3.3. Luke explained from the pre-synoptic tradition
    If Luke knew the pre-synoptic tradition, he retained the
saying about the destruction of Jerusalem, but omitted the
Matthew/Mark saying about the great tribulation (καὶ ... ἔσται/
ἔσονται θλῖψις) and the following warning of false prophets,

/1/ V. Taylor, *The Gospel according to St. Mark* (London:
Macmillan, 1952), 512, postulates a tense situation of
persecution. Cf. also J. Jeremias, *Eucharistic Words of Jesus*
(London: SCM, 1966), 131. Lambrecht, *Redaktion* 154, dismisses
such an idea as pure speculation; but in the light of our
proposals the idea may carry more weight.
/2/ A possible complication with this argument is that on the
hypothesis being proposed both Matthew and Mark will have known
the pre-synoptic tradition, and both of them have made the same
striking omission. But this is not extraordinary if Matthew
knew Mark as well as the pre-synoptic tradition, or if Mark
knew Matthew.

moving straight into a description of the heavenly signs (καὶ
ἔσονται σημεῖα). It is interesting that his description of the
heavenly signs has the same construction as the Matthew/Mark
saying about the great tribulation which he has omitted (καὶ
ἔσται/ἔσονται + nom.). It is possible to explain either that
Luke has taken over the construction of what he has omitted and
used it in the description of the heavenly signs, or that he
had a source containing the phrase καὶ ἔσονται σημεῖα, in
which case the jump from καὶ ἔσται/ἔσονται θλῖψις to καὶ ἔσονται
σημεῖα would have been very simple.(See further below, pp.306-11.

But if the mechanics of Luke's editing are explicable, what
was his motivation? His retention of the saying about the
destruction of Jerusalem is no problem and simply shows that he
did not share the inhibitions that led Matthew and Mark to
suppress the description of the siege of Jerusalem. This same
lack of inhibition is also reflected in his immediately
preceding reference to the 'armies surrounding Jerusalem'
(21:20). The suggestion was made earlier that this Lukan phrase
may have been in the pre-synoptic tradition and have been
omitted by Matthew and Mark; this suggestion about 21:20 would
obviously fit in with what is now being suggested about 21:23,
24.

As for Luke's omission of the Matthew/Mark saying about
the great tribulation and the false prophets, this must be
explained on any view involving Matthean/Markan priority. One
suggestion that has been made is that Luke wished to keep quite
distinct the fall of Jerusalem and the events of the end-time;
this might explain why in this context Luke retains the
reference to the historical crisis in Judea but drops the
description of the world-wide, eschatological distress. But,
although some such explanation could be correct it is not very
obvious that Luke's omission does have the effect of separating
the historical and the eschatological: in fact it may almost
have the opposite effect since it brings the description of the
fall of Jerusalem (21:20,24) into immediate proximity with the
description of the parousia (21:25-28), and, whereas Matthew
and Mark indicate that the parousia comes 'after the distress'
(Mt 24:29, Mk 13:24), Luke does not very clearly separate the
time of the fall of Jerusalem from the time of the parousia,
except through the phrase 'until the times of the Gentiles are
fulfilled'.

A simpler explanation of Luke's omission is suggested by
our earlier analysis of Lk 17:22,23, since it was argued that

these Lukan verses were based on Mt 24:21-26/Mk 13:19-22. Luke
then had already used the Matthew/Mark saying about the great
tribulation and the following warning of false prophets; his
omission, then, of those traditions in his chapter 21 is
explicable in terms of his desire to avoid repetition, and is
of a piece with his omission in chap. 21 of almost all the
other sections from the eschatological discourse that he had
already used ahead of context in chaps. 12 and 17. (His
21:12-15 is an exception to this rule, since he does here repeat
previously used tradition, cf. 12:11,12; but even here he
reexpresses the tradition to avoid repetitiousness.)

4. CONCLUSION

The conclusion of our discussion of Mt 24:21,22/Mk 13:19,20/
Lk 21:23,24 is that a pre-synoptic form of tradition lies
behind this material, and that it probably included both the
Lukan description of Jerusalem being trampled underfoot etc.
and the Matthew/Mark description of a period of unparalleled
distress. This conclusion agrees with our argument about the
preceding verses (Mt 24:15-20/Mk 13:14-18/Lk 21:20-22), since
there too we argued for all three evangelists having known and
used a pre-synoptic tradition.

The whole section will have been approximately as follows
in the pre-synoptic tradition:/1/

When you see Jerusalem surrounded by armies and the
desolating sacrilege, which was spoken of by Daniel the
prophet, standing in the holy place, let the reader
understand.

Then let those in Judea flee into the mountains. Let
him who is on the house not go down to get the things from
his house, and let him who is in the field not return back
to get his garment. Woe to those with child and to those
giving suck in those days. Pray that your flight may not
be in winter, nor on the sabbath.

For there will be great distress on the land and
anger for this people, and they will fall by the mouth of
the sword and they will be taken as prisoners into all
the nations, and Jerusalem will be trodden down by
Gentiles until the times of the Gentiles are fulfilled.

/1/ For a further somewhat speculative suggestion regarding
this section, see below pp. 346-49.

And there will be great tribulation then, such as has not been from the beginning of the world until now, nor will be./1/ And if those days had not been shortened, all flesh would not have been saved. But for the sake of the elect those days will be shortened.

And then if anyone says to you ....

This conclusion fits in well with the conclusion of earlier chapters, notably chapter 3, where it was shown that the uniquely Lukan section of 21:34-36 was in the pre-synoptic tradition, though it was omitted (almost entirely) by Matthew and Mark. As with the pre-synoptic conclusion to the discourse, it was found that Paul knew the pre-synoptic traditions in question, as did the author of Revelation. Both Paul and the author of Revelation have used the traditions in a quite distinctive way: Paul retains the idea of the Jews suffering judgment, but appears to downplay the political/military side of the judgment and to portray a spiritual judgment and a religious antichrist - was he perhaps influenced by some of the same factors that make Matthew and Mark inexplicit on this point? The author of Revelation retains more of the political/ military imagery, but uses it of the new people of God, the church. The important thing, however, for the thesis of this book is not how they use the traditions, but the fact that they do use the traditions; and it is significant that they both use the desolating sacrilege traditions in a context which suggests that they probably knew those traditions not as isolated logia, but in connection with other parts of the eschatological discourse./2/ We are thus well on the way to establishing the existence of a pre-synoptic form of the whole discourse.

/1/ It is not of great importance to decide between the Matthean 'from the beginning of the world' and the Markan 'from the beginning of creation, which he created'. But there is probably a case for seeing the rather redundant Markan 'which he created' as his work, also the 'whom he chose' in the next verse ('the elect whom he chose'). Cf. V. Taylor, *Mark*, 50-52, on Mark's pleonasms; also Lambrecht, *Redaktion*, 162,163 and 166. /2/ 2 Thessalonians 2 appears to echo the warnings of Mt 24:4/ Mk 13:5/Lk 21:8 and of Mt 24:23-26/Mk 13:21-23, as well as the desolating sacrilege passage. Revelation 6 echoes much of the eschatological discourse, and Revelation 13 echoes the desolating sacrilege passage and the following warnings of false prophets.

Chapter 6

THE SAYINGS ABOUT APPEARING BEFORE THE AUTHORITIES AND THE
MISSION DISCOURSE: MT 10:17-20, MK 13:9-11, LK 12:11,12,
LK 21:12-15

The preceding chapters have shown that there was a pre-
synoptic form of the whole of the second half of the
eschatological discourse - from the description of the
desolating sacrilege onwards.   In this and the next chapter we
turn to the immediately preceding section that describes the
suffering and persecution that the disciples will face
(Mt 24:9-14, Mk 13:9-13, Lk 21:12-19). The quest for the pre-
synoptic tradition is more complicated than in the sections already
considered, because Matthew at this point diverges quite sharply
from Mark and Luke.   The question then is: if there was a pre-
synoptic form of the tradition, has Matthew retained it?   Or
have Mark and Luke done so?   And, in either case, how is their
divergence to be explained?   The usual explanation is that
Matthew used the Markan traditions ahead of context in his chap.
10, and so had to substitute something else in his chap. 24.
However, there are good reasons for questioning that
explanation, and this chapter will show that the sayings about
the appearance of the disciples before the authorities (Mt 10:
17-20, Mk 13:9-11, Lk 12:11,12 and 21:12-15) are correctly
located by Matthew in the context of a mission discourse and
that Mark has relocated them in the eschatological discourse.
This finding will then pave the way for discussion in the next
chapter of the relevant section of the eschatological discourse.
This chapter will inevitably be a study as much of the mission
discourse(s) as of the eschatological discourse.

1.   *EVIDENCE FOR A NON-MARKAN VERSION OF THE TRADITION ABOUT
     APPEARING BEFORE THE AUTHORITIES*

It is commonly thought that Mt 10:17-22 is material taken
by Matthew from the Markan eschatological discourse.   However,
a close comparison of the four relevant synoptic texts puts

this view in doubt. /1/   Compare:

Mt 10:17-19	Mk 13:9-11	Lk 21:12-15	Lk 12:11-12
προσέχετε δὲ ἀπὸ	βλέπετε δὲ ὑμεῖς	πρὸ δὲ τούτων	ὅταν δὲ εἰσφέρωσιν
τῶν ἀνθρώπων·	ἑαυτούς·	πάντων ἐπιβαλοῦσιν	ὑμᾶς ἐπὶ τὰς
παραδώσουσιν γὰρ	παραδώσουσιν ὑμᾶς	ἐφ' ὑμᾶς τὰς	συναγωγὰς καὶ τὰς
ὑμᾶς εἰς	εἰς συνέδρια καὶ	χεῖρας αὐτῶν καὶ	ἀρχὰς καὶ τὰς
συνέδρια, καὶ ἐν	εἰς συναγωγὰς·	διώξουσιν,	ἐξουσίας, μὴ
ταῖς συναγωγαῖς	δαρήσεσθε καὶ ἐπὶ	παραδιδόντες εἰς	μεριμνήσητε πῶς ἢ
αὐτῶν	ἡγεμόνων καὶ	τὰς συναγωγὰς καὶ	τί εἴπητε· 12. τὸ
μαστιγώσουσιν	βασιλέων	φυλακάς,	γὰρ ἅγιον πνεῦμα
ὑμᾶς· 18. καὶ ἐπὶ	σταθήσεσθε ἕνεκεν	ἀπαγομένους ἐπὶ	διδάξει ὑμᾶς ἐν
ἡγεμόνας δὲ καὶ	ἐμοῦ, εἰς μαρτύριον	βασιλεῖς καὶ	αὐτῇ τῇ ὥρᾳ ἃ δεῖ
βασιλεῖς	αὐτοῖς. 10. καὶ εἰς	ἡγεμόνας ἕνεκεν	εἰπεῖν.
ἀχθήσεσθε ἕνεκεν	πάντα τὰ ἔθνη πρῶτον	τοῦ ὀνόματός μου·	
ἐμοῦ, εἰς	δεῖ κηρυχθῆναι τὸ	13. ἀποβήσεται	
μαρτύριον αὐτοῖς	εὐαγγέλιον. 11. καὶ	ὑμῖν εἰς μαρτύριον.	
καὶ τοῖς ἔθνεσιν.	ὅταν ἄγωσιν ὑμᾶς	14. θέτε οὖν ἐν	
19. ὅταν δὲ	παραδιδόντες, μὴ	ταῖς καρδίαις ὑμῶν	
παραδῶσιν ὑμᾶς, μὴ	προμεριμνᾶτε τί	μὴ προμελετᾶν	
μεριμνήσητε πῶς ἢ	λαλήσητε, ἀλλ' ὃ	ἀπολογηθῆναι·	
τί λαλήσητε·	ἐὰν δοθῇ ὑμῖν ἐν	15. ἐγὼ γὰρ δώσω	
δοθήσεται γὰρ ὑμῖν	ἐκείνῃ τῇ ὥρᾳ,	ὑμῖν στόμα καὶ	
ἐν ἐκείνῃ τῇ ὥρᾳ	τοῦτο λαλεῖτε.	σοφίαν, ᾗ οὐ	
τί λαλήσητε.		δυνήσονται	
		ἀντιστῆναι ἢ	
		ἀντειπεῖν ἅπαντες	
		οἱ ἀντικείμενοι	
		ὑμῖν.	

/1/ A non-Markan tradition has been recognized by various
scholars, including Lambrecht, *Biblica* 47 (1966) 321-60; also
Redaktion, 115-120; H. Schürmann, *Traditionsgeschichtliche
Untersuchungen zu den synoptischen Evangelien* (Düsseldorf,
Patmos 1968) 137-155; L. Gaston, *No Stone*, 17,18.   My argument
agrees with these authors' arguments at various points, and
readers are referred to their works for further discussion.

It is immediately obvious that Mt 10:17-22 and Mk 13:9-13 are
very similar to each other. It is less obvious, but very
significant, that Mt 10:17-22 has agreements with both the Lukan
passages against Mark.

1.1. Agreements of Mt 10:17-22 and Lk 12:11,12.

The agreements between Matthew 10 and Luke 12 against Mark
are (i) both have ὅταν δέ for Mark's καὶ ὅταν;/1/ (ii) both
have the command μὴ μεριμνήσητε πῶς ἢ τί/2/ for Mark's μὴ
προμεριμνᾶτε τί.... . (iii) Immediately following that clause,
Mark continues with another command ἀλλ' ὃ ἐὰν δοθῇ ὑμῖν ἐν
ἐκείνῃ τῇ ὥρᾳ τοῦτο λαλεῖτε, whereas Matthew and Luke have
instead a similarly constructed promise:

Matthew: δοθήσεται γὰρ ὑμῖν   ἐν ἐκείνῃ τῇ ὥρᾳ   τί λαλήσητε

Luke: τὸ γὰρ ἅγιον   ἐν αὐτῇ τῇ ὥρᾳ   ἃ δεῖ εἰπεῖν
          πνεῦμα διδάξει ὑμᾶς

The similarity is the more striking, when it is noted that
Matthew's δοθήσεται is circumlocution for the divine name -
compare Luke's reference to the Holy Spirit-, and when it is
realised that εἰπεῖν in Lk 12:11 and 12:12 is his equivalent of
λαλεῖν in the Matthean/Markan traditions. (See pp.226,234 below.)

These two agreements are sufficient to suggest that the
Matthew 10 and Luke 12 traditions are somehow related
independently of Mark, and this may be confirmed by the fact
that both Matthew and Luke place the tradition in question in
somewhat similar contexts: thus Luke has the saying about
persecution almost immediately after the exhortation to
fearless confession (Lk 12:2-9), and Matthew has the saying
shortly before that exhortation (Mt 10:26-33). This agreement
to place the persecution saying in the proximity of the 'Q'
exhortation to fearless confession could be coincidental,
especially as the order of the sections is different in Matthew

---

/1/ This and other points are noted by A. Fuchs, *Sprachliche
Untersuchungen zu Matthäus und Lukas* (Rome: Biblical Institute,
1971), 173,174.
/2/ There is some textual variation at this point; but most
scholars agree that the text of Matthew and Luke should read
πῶς ἢ τί.

and Luke. But, given the agreements in wording, it seems more likely that the agreement in context is significant.

1.2. Agreements of Mt 10:17-22 and Lk 21:12-15

The suggestion of a non-Markan link between Matthew 10 and Luke may be confirmed by the evidence of Lk 21:12-15. These Lukan verses have three agreements with Mt 10:17-22: (i) They both refer to the disciples being 'brought before' (ἄγειν/ ἀπάγειν + ἐπί + accusative) kings and rulers, whereas Mark speaks of them 'standing before' (ἵσταναι + ἐπί + genitive)./1/ (ii) After the injunction not to be worried, they both have a promise (Matthew 'it will be granted to you..', Luke 'I will give you...'), not a promise + command as Mark has ('What is given, this speak'). (iii) They both omit Mk 13:10, the saying about the preaching of the gospel to the Gentiles. This need not indicate knowledge of a non-Markan tradition, since the Markan verse looks out of place in its Markan position, so that Mark's followers might have been expected to improve his version. Furthermore, it can be argued that Matthew and Luke show knowledge of the Markan verse in Mt 10:18 (καὶ τοῖς ἔθνεσιν), 24:14, Lk 21:24. However, the very fact of the awkwardness of the verse in Mark's context points to a pre-Markan tradition lacking it; and it is quite possible that Matthew's and Luke's common divergence from Mark reflects such a tradition.

This last argument about Matthew's and Luke's omission of Mk 13:10 carries little weight, certainly seen in isolation from the preceding arguments. But the three points about Mt 10:17-22 and Lk 21:12-15 together reinforce the case for Matthew and Luke having a common non-Markan tradition./2/

/1/ Luke's fondness for compound verbs simply explains his ἀπάγειν for Matthew's ἄγειν. Mark has ἄγειν in his v 11. See further discussion of this below, pp. 223-25.
/2/ Fuchs, *Sprachliche*, 173,174, notes the Matthew-Luke agreements and concludes that Matthew and Luke both used a revision of Mark. This hypothesis is questionable on general grounds: what was the nature of the postulated revision and how did it disappear? It is also complicated by, among other things, the fact that Luke and Matthew agree not only in the minor changes, but also in including Mt 10:26-33/Lk 12:2-9 in nearby contexts. Fuchs does not adequately explore the option of explaining the Matthew-Luke agreements as due to the influence of a non-Markan tradition.

2. THE ORIGINAL NON-MARKAN WORDING

If the case for Matthew and Luke having a common non-Markan tradition is accepted, is it possible to decide anything about the original non-Markan wording? The majority opinion among those scholars who have recognized the existence of a non-Markan tradition common to Matthew and Luke seems to be that Luke's short form of words in Lk 12:11,12 is the more primitive form, which Matthew has expanded, perhaps under the influence of Mk 13:9-13./1/

There are, however, good reasons for questioning this view and for thinking that Lk 12:11-12 is a compression of a fuller form, such as we have in Mt 10:17-20 (cf. Mk 13:9-13).

2.1. Evidence from Lk 21:12

We have already noted the agreement between Lk 21:12 and Mt 10:17,18 in the use of the word ἄγειν rather than ἱστάναι (as in Mark). A close examination of this agreement suggests that the non-Markan version did not begin with a ὅταν clause (such as is found in Lk 12:11). The relevant texts are as follows:

Mt 10:17,18	Mk 13:9	Lk 21:12
παραδώσουσιν γὰρ ὑμᾶς εἰς συνέδρια, καὶ ἐν ταῖς συναγωγαῖς αὐτῶν μαστιγώσουσιν ὑμᾶς· καὶ ἐπὶ ἡγεμόνας δὲ καὶ βασιλεῖς ἀχθήσεσθε ἕνεκεν ἐμοῦ.	παραδώσουσιν ὑμᾶς εἰς συνέδρια καὶ εἰς συναγωγὰς· δαρήσεσθε καὶ ἐπὶ ἡγεμόνων καὶ βασιλέων σταθήσεσθε ἕνεκεν ἐμοῦ.	ἐπιβαλοῦσιν ἐφ' ὑμᾶς τὰς χεῖρας αὐτῶν καὶ διώξουσιν, παραδιδόντες εἰς τὰς συναγωγὰς καὶ φυλακάς, ἀπαγομένους ἐπὶ βασιλεῖς καὶ ἡγεμόνας ἕνεκεν τοῦ ὀνόματός μου.

Matthew's and Luke's agreement in the use of ἄγειν to describe the disciples' appearance before kings and governors could be coincidental, Matthew and Luke both happening to use here the verb that Mark uses a moment later (in v 11). But, quite apart from the other evidence which indicated Matthean and Lukan knowledge of a non-Markan tradition, there is also the oddity of

/1/ So Schürmann and Lambrecht, though the latter does not invoke the influence of Mark.

the Lukan construction in v 12 to be explained: having spoken
generally of the persecution in language unparalleled in
Matthew and Mark (in his v 12a), Luke then appends the two
participial clauses παραδιδόντες...... ἀπαγομένους, the latter
of which is a most awkward accusative. I. H. Marshall not
surprisingly is perplexed as to why Luke did not use the much
simpler Markan form./1/

    There is, however, a relatively simple explanation ready
to hand: it is that Luke began v 12 independently of the Markan
or Matthean traditions (perhaps following a source of his own,
or perhaps just rendering freely) - ἐπιβαλοῦσιν ... καὶ
διώξουσιν; but then, having gone his own way for a moment, he
returns to the Matthew/Mark tradition and incorporates what he
has omitted from them by means of participial constructions -
παραδιδόντες... ἀπαγομένους./2/ The incorporation of the
Markan/Matthean tradition worked well with the active, but less
well with the passive of ἄγειν/ἀπάγειν.

    If this is the probable explanation of Luke's difficulty
here, this reinforces the view that he knew the Matthean form
of words (ἀχθήσεσθε), not the Markan form (σταθήσεσθε). That
he should have produced the awkward ἀπαγομένους on the basis of
a form like Matthew's is easy enough to understand; that he
should have produced it on the basis of Mark's quite different
verb is hardly credible. Mark does, of course, have the verb
ἄγειν in his v 11; but this does not substantially strengthen
the case for Luke having used Mark. On the contrary it is
arguable that in his v 11 Mark probably betrays his knowledge
of the Matthean version, his ὅταν ἄγωσιν ὑμᾶς παραδιδόντες
(with its main verb and almost redundant participle) being well
explained if Mark knew the Matthean tradition and if he has
brought together here the verb that he previously omitted, i.e.
ἄγειν, and the verb that is here in the Matthean tradition,
i.e. παραδίδοναι.

    Even without the preceding arguments and without the

/1/ *Luke*, 767.
/2/ He leaves out altogether the reference to beatings in the
synagogues, perhaps because of his Gentile readership; he
refers instead to the more general φυλακάς (a common term in
Acts).

evidence of Mt 10:19/Lk 12:11 we might have suspected that one of Mark's verbs was an addition to the tradition. Our first inclination might have been to suppose that ὅταν ἄγωσιν ὑμᾶς was the original tradition, and that παραδιδόντες was Mark's addition resuming the train of thought begun in v 9 and interrupted by v 10./1/ However ὅταν ἄγωσιν ὑμᾶς does not make very good sense by itself without the following παραδιδόντες and seems unlikely to have been the original form of words. On the other hand, the simple suggestion that ἄγωσιν was Mark's addition to tradition also has problems: the verb occurs only three times in Mark's gospel and is only used transitively on this occasion, and in any case it is not obvious why Mark should have bothered to introduce the verb at all. These points are, however, all accounted for on our hypothesis: the non-Markan ἄγωσιν is indeed taken from the tradition, but it belonged originally in the saying of v 9. Having omitted it there, Mark brings it back here in v 11 instead of the more original παραδῶσιν, which he turns into a participle.

This argument confirms the hypothesis of a common non-Markan tradition attested in both Matthew and Luke, and it suggests that the tradition was something like Mt 10:17-19, not just like 10:19. Luke has thus compressed the tradition in his 12:11-12.

/1/ Cf. J. Dupont, 'La Persécution comme Situation Missionnaire (Marc 13,9-11)' in *Die Kirche des Anfangs* für H. Schürmann, ed. R. Schnackenburg et al. (Freiburg: Herder, 1978) 110-11, who finds parallels to this participial usage in 4:31, 7:3,19, 11:25, and who cites M.-E. Boismard, *Synopse des Quatre Évangiles en Français*, II (Paris: Cerf, 1972), 363, on the rarity of ἄγειν in Mark. Luke's ὅταν δὲ εἰσφέρωσιν in 12:11 might be cited as supporting the originality of ὅταν ἄγωσιν. But εἰσφέρειν (probably a Lukan term, *pace* Jeremias, *Sprache*, 214) could have been Luke's rendering of an original παραδίδοναι. More probably Luke's choice of verb reflects the fact that his 12:11 may be seen as a paraphrase of all the traditions attested in Mt 10:17-19a which included a reference to the disciples being 'brought' before rulers (Mt 10:18), not just of Mt 10:19a (see further below). Less probably Luke could have been influenced here by Mark's secondary wording.

2.2. Evidence from Lk 12:11-12

The evidence of Lk 12:11-12 points in the same direction.
Note the following points:

2.2.1.
Lk 12:11, ὅταν δὲ εἰσφέρωσιν ὑμᾶς ἐπὶ τὰς συναγωγὰς καὶ
τὰς ἀρχὰς καὶ τὰς ἐξουσίας μὴ μεριμνήσητε..., is slightly abrupt
(though not at all impossible) in the context of chap. 12.
This abruptness is explained if Luke has compressed a fuller
tradition, which described the persecution before recommending
a response.

2.2.2.
Lk 12:11 is simply explained as a compression of Mt 10:17-
19: εἰσφέρειν, a word used elsewhere by Luke, is a simple
replacement for παραδιδόναι (and/or ἄγειν); his reference to
being brought to συναγωγὰς .. ἀρχὰς .. ἐξουσίας replaces the
description of trouble with the Jewish συνέδρια and συναγωγαί
on the one hand and the ἡγεμόνες and βασιλεῖς on the other./1/
For his Gentile readership he keeps only the one reference to
the Jewish synagogues and he does not refer to 'beatings in the
synagogue' (compare 21:12, where συνέδρια is replaced by
φυλακάς and again the 'beating' disappears); and he uses the
common phrase 'principalities and powers', probably as a
replacement for the reference to 'governors and kings' and
meaning Gentile powers.

Then he follows the non-Markan tradition in μὴ μεριμνήσητε
πῶς ἢ τί (so Matthew; different Mark); but he completes the
phrase with his own verb ἀπολογήσησθε, a term used much more
frequently by Luke than any other NT writer and also used by
him in the parallel 21:14 (μὴ προμελετᾶν ἀπολογηθῆναι). He
then adds ἢ τί εἴπητε: this superfluous additional phrase is
probably to be explained as his equivalent of the Matthean/
Markan (ἢ) λαλήσητε. Having diverged from the tradition
momentarily in the use of the verb ἀπολογεῖσθαι, he here
incorporates the tradition's form of words alongside his own./2/
This suggestion is confirmed by the following verse, Lk 12:12,
where again εἰπεῖν is Luke's equivalent of Matthew/Mark's
λαλεῖν./3/

/1/ On these Lukan terms cf. Dupont, 'La Persécution', 107,108.
/2/ Cf. Dupont, 'La Persécution', 108.
/3/ On this see also below, pp. 234-36. And cf. Lambrecht,

2.2.3.

A good reason can be given for Luke's elimination of the opening wording of the tradition: the context in which Luke places it in chap. 12 is not a context describing the disciples' mission (or eschatological events), but is one of exhortation to fearless confession and of encouragement. It is therefore intelligible that, when incorporating this tradition, Luke reduces the description, but retains the exhortation and promise. More specifically, it may well have been the thought of the Holy Spirit in the immediately preceding saying (12:10b) that led Luke to include vv 11,12 with their reference to the Spirit at this particular point; if it was - and the fact that τὸ ἅγιον πνεῦμα in that word order occurs in Luke only in 12:10b and 12:12 would seem to suggest this connection of thought/1/ - then it is understandable that he abbreviates the description leading up to that reference.

2.2.4.

It has been argued that Lk 12:11 is an abbreviation of the Matthean form of the opening of the persecution logia. What about Lk 12:12 and the ending of the sayings? It was noted that Lk 12:12 'For the Holy Spirit will teach you ... what you ought to say' is similar to Matthew's 10:19 'For it will be given you ... what you should speak', both in being a simple promise (not promise-cum-command, as in Mark) and in the end wording ἃ δεῖ εἰπεῖν which is close to Matthew's τί λαλήσητε (εἰπεῖν also being used for λαλεῖν in the previous verse). But Matthew goes on with 10:20 'For it is not you that speak, but the Spirit of your Father that speaks in you'. It is possible that Mt 10:20

Redaktion, 118. Whether εἰπεῖν was Luke's replacement for the original λαλεῖν or whether his εἰπεῖν is the more original term, as Dupont suggests with some plausibility ('La Persécution', 108, cf. also L. Hartman, *Testimonium Linguae* (Lund: Gleerup, 1963) 74),is debatable, and does not affect our argument very significantly.

/1/ Cf. Dupont, 'La Persécution', 103. There are other examples of this word order in Acts. As for why Luke has this order here, could it simply have been that he wished to avoid adding yet one more article to the phrase in 12:10 τῷ εἰς τὸ... πνεῦμα βλασφημήσαντι (as he would have done if he had had τὸ πνεῦμα τὸ ἅγιον)? Then v 12 could have been assimilated to that form. But see Dupont, pp. 108,109.

is Matthew's addition to a briefer non-Markan form: he could
have been influenced by the Markan form to add a γάρ clause
(v 20) to explain a γάρ clause (v 19). On the other hand,
(a) Matthew's Semitic use of the passive for the divine name in
v 19, δοθήσεται, seems more likely to be original than Luke's
explicit τὸ ἅγιον πνεῦμα διδάξει ὑμᾶς.

Admittedly it might be argued that Matthew has been
influenced by Mark's δοθῇ; however, if the Markan and non-
Markan traditions are related, then Mark's evidence could just
as well be seen as supporting Matthew's δόθησεται. More
significant is the evidence of Lk 21:15: Luke here agrees with
Matthew and with Luke 12:12 in having a promise of help for the
persecuted disciple; but, whereas in 12:12 it was a promise of
the Holy Spirit's teaching, in 21:15 it is a promise that 'I
will give you...'. This variation in Lk 12:12 and 21:15 is
particularly well explained if Luke knew the Matthean δόθησεται:
in the two places he paraphrases the passive differently,
referring once to the Spirit and the next time to Jesus./1/
The situation will thus have been like this:

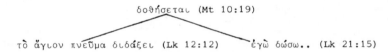

δοθήσεται (Mt 10:19)

τὸ ἅγιον πνεῦμα διδάξει (Lk 12:12)   ἐγὼ δώσω.. (Lk 21:15)

(b) Although Luke could have added the reference to the Holy
Spirit in 12:12 on his own initiative (or under the influence
of Mark), it seems likely that the tradition he is drawing on
in 12:11,12 had a reference to the Spirit such as is found in
Matthew's v 20, since this helps explain Luke's positioning of
these verses (following v 10). (c) If Luke did place these
verses here because of the Holy Spirit link, this would help to
explain not only his abbreviation of the opening section (as
was argued above), but also his contraction of the ending: he

---

/1/ Against this, so far as Lk 12:12 is concerned, might be
Dupont's claim that there are several rather unLukan features
in the verse, e.g. εἰπεῖν, τὸ ἅγιον πνεῦμα, the formulation of
the idea of the Holy Spirit teaching, and the use of δεῖ in the
sense found here ('La Persécution', 108,109). On these points:
(1) We agree that εἰπεῖν could have been in Luke's tradition.
(2) On τὸ ἅγιον πνεῦμα see the preceding note. (3) It is
possible that in paraphrasing the tradition about the Holy
Spirit he was influenced by a different tradition (cf. Jn 14:
26). (4) δεῖ is frequent in Luke-Acts, and the sense, for

compresses the fuller Matthean form of the tradition in order
to get quickly to the point. These three observations make it
probable that the non-Markan tradition of the persecution
sayings was more like Mt 10:17-20 than Lk 12:11,12 at the end
as well as at the beginning.

2.3. Conclusion on the non-Markan wording

The preceding arguments about the original non-Markan
wording suggest that this wording is best preserved in
Mt 10:17-20 (rather than in the Lukan passage). The non-Markan form
turns out to have been quite similar to the Markan form of
Mk 13:9-11, containing the opening warning ('they will hand you
over....'; Mt 10:17, Mk 13:9) and probably the closing promise
of the Holy Spirit's help (Mt 10:20, Mk 13:11b).

3. THE RELATIONSHIP OF THE MARKAN AND NON-MARKAN TRADITIONS: PRELIMINARY OBSERVATIONS

It has been seen that Matthew and Luke knew a non-Markan
version of the sayings about appearing before the authorities
and that that version was quite similar to Mk 13:9-11. The
observation of that similarity does not of itself resolve the
question of the relationship of the Markan and non-Markan
traditions. However, in the course of the preceding discussion
some evidence did emerge to suggest that Mk 13:9-11 is, in
certain respects at least, a modification of the non-Markan
tradition reflected in Mt 10:17-20. This would mean that the
two traditions do have a common origin and that the relationship
is not a simple one of Markan priority.

The evidence was: (a) Mark's ὅταν ἄγωσιν ὑμᾶς παραδιδόντες
(13:11) is probably a Markan replacement for the simpler ὅταν
παραδῶσιν ὑμᾶς which Matthew retains (24:19). Mark brings the
verb ἄγειν in here, having omitted it earlier (13:9) and having
replaced it there with the verb ἱστάναι. (b) His 13:10 is
probably a Markan interpolation in the context; if it is, then
the pre-Markan tradition was like the non-Markan tradition in
this respect.

Further arguments may be adduced for considering the
Markan tradition to be a modification of something like the
Matthean wording: (c) The opening of Mk 13:9 βλέπετε δὲ ὑμεῖς

---

example, in the preceding and following uses of the word in Luke
(11:42, 13:14) is not very different from what we have here.

ἑαυτοὺς may be Mark's substitute for the more original
προσέχετε δὲ ἀπὸ τῶν ἀνθρώπων of Mt 10:17. There are several
other places where Mark has βλέπετε and where Matthew and/or
Luke have προσέχετε (Mk 12:38/Lk 20:46, Mt 16:6/Mk 8:15/Lk 12:1,
Mk 13:33/Lk 21:34 - as discussed already on p.120 above).
It is possible that on all these various occasions Matthew and
Luke both independently alter the Markan usage in the same
way./1/ But it is probably simpler to suppose that Mark who
never uses προσέχειν and for whom βλέπειν is a key word in this
chapter (chap. 13), is responsible for the change here./2/ A
comparison with the other uses of προσέχετε in Matthew and Luke
suggests that the original form of words here may in fact have
been προσέχετε (ὑμεῖς) ἑαυτοῖς ἀπὸ τῶν ἀνθρώπων. Matthew has
retained προσέχετε and ἀπὸ τῶν ἀνθρώπων, but in line with his
usage elsewhere has omitted ἑαυτοῖς (cf. 7:15, 16:6,11,12).
Mark has replaced προσέχετε with βλέπετε, but has retained the
ἑαυτοὺς, producing a form of expression that is unparalleled in
the gospels (but cf. Phil 3:2, 2 Jn 8). It may possibly have
been this change that led on to his omission of ἀπὸ τῶν
ἀνθρώπων: would βλέπετε.. ἑαυτοὺς ἀπό... have been a natural
expression? This omission leaves the verse that follows without
any expressed subject (παραδώσουσιν, etc.)./3/

/1/ Matthew and Luke never use βλέπετε exactly as Mark uses it
in 8:15, 12:38, 13:9. But they do have a similar hortatory use
in Mt 24:4, Lk 8:18, 21:8, Acts 13:40; and at least in Lk 21:34
Luke could have used the Markan word.
/2/ Cf. Lambrecht, Redaktion, 119.
/3/ If Dupont, 'La Persécution', 101, is correct in suggesting
that Matthew's specific reference to 'men' (in 'beware of men')
reflects his immediately preceding verse, 10:16, which speaks
of 'sheep' and 'wolves', this could be supposed to favour the
view that it is a Matthean addition to the tradition. But it is
not certain that Dupont's explanation is correct (see Matthew's
later references to 'men', e.g. in 10:32,33). Even if it is,
it could be that Matthew has retained the saying in its
original context (see further discussion below), and that
Mark's alteration of context was a factor encouraging his
omission of Matthew's now superfluous ἀπὸ τῶν ἀνθρώπων, as well
perhaps as his addition of the emphatic ὑμεῖς.
     If the suggestion about the original wording of the
προσέχετε clause is correct, then Jeremias's view, Sprache, 211,
that προσέχετε ἑαυτοῖς is a distinctively Lukan usage is put in
doubt. It could well have been in the pre-synoptic tradition
here and also in 12:1, 21:34. It is notable that in 20:46 Luke

(d) It is possible to argue that Mark's 'Holy Spirit' is more usual and less original than Matthew's 'Spirit of your Father'/1/ and, (e), that Mark's ἀλλ' ὅ ἐάν... construction is Markan phraseology and a modification of the simpler future construction found in Matthew./2/

The evidence mentioned above is not all of equal weight. But it does point towards the conclusion that the non-Markan tradition known to Matthew and Luke was more likely Mark's source than a modification of Mark. It may well be another case of a pre-synoptic tradition known to all three evangelists./3/

4. THE TRADITIONS IN THE CONTEXT OF MATTHEW 10

This tentative conclusion is confirmed strikingly by further evidence from Matthew 10, which shows (a) that Matthew is using a form of tradition in his chap. 10 which had the sayings in the context of a mission discourse (not in the eschatological discourse), and (b) that this form of the tradition lies behind not only Matthew 10, but also the Markan and Lukan texts. In other words, the evidence points to a pre-synoptic mission discourse known to all three evangelists and including the sayings about the disciples appearing before the authorities.

One small piece of evidence already noted that points to the sayings belonging in the mission discourse is the agreement of Matthew 10 and Luke 12 in having the sayings adjacent to the call to fearless proclamation (Mt 10:26-33/Lk 12:2-9), unless this section is supposed to have been in the eschatological discourse. But the key to the argument is the difficult verse Mt 10:23, because it seems probable that this belonged in Matthew's tradition with Mt 10:17-20. This has been argued by

---

does not add ἑαυτοῖς to προσέχετε, as Jeremias might expect.
/1/ *Beasley-Murray, Mark,* 46. But see Dupont, 'La Persécution', 106.
/2/ Lambrecht, *Redaktion,* 132. P. Gaechter, *Das Matthäus Evangelium* (Innsbruck: Tyrolia, 1963) 331, argues that πῶς ἤ in the Matthew-Luke tradition is an addition since the phrase is not picked up in the clause that follows. But this is hardly a cogent argument.
/3/ It could be a case of Matthean priority; but Mark is probably more original than Matthew at least in his use of the passive δαρήσεσθε (10:17). See pp. 234,236-39 below.

Schürmann and others,/1/ and the case can be strengthened by
various considerations.

The evidence is this:

4.1. *Links between the tradition and Mt 10:23*

4.1.1. *Formal parallelism of 10:19,20 and 10:23*
There is obvious formal parallelism between 10:19,20 and
10:23:

ὅταν δὲ παραδῶσιν ὑμᾶς/μὴ μεριμνήσητε/γάρ clause; the Holy
                                          Spirit will aid you

ὅταν δὲ διώκωσιν ὑμᾶς/φεύγετε   /γάρ clause; the Son of
                                          man will come.

A different tense is used in the two places, but Mark
interestingly has present tenses in the first case ὅταν ἄγωσιν
... μὴ προμεριμνᾶτε. He may well be more original than Matthew
in this respect (cf. Lk 12:11 ὅταν εἰσφέρωσιν). Perhaps Matthew
put an aorist παραδῶσιν for an original παραδίδωσιν having the
moment of the trial in mind, whereas he uses the present
διώκωσιν suggesting a general policy - 'whenever'. In any case
the difference in tense does not alter the fact that the
relevant clauses are structurally parallel.

4.1.2. *Awkwardness of 10:23*
The formal parallelism could, of course, be Matthew's work.
But in two respects 10:23 is slightly awkward, and this
awkwardness may more simply be explained if Matthew is working
redactionally with sources than if he is creating material from
scratch: (i) 10:23 seems something of an afterthought in its
present position following the climactic 'he who endures to the
end shall be saved' (10:22). Although Matthew could himself be
responsible for the afterthought - the sequence of ideas is not
intolerable - it is perhaps easier to speculate that he is here
reverting to his source after two interpolated verses (vv 21,
22)./1/ (ii) The parallelism between 10:23 and the earlier
verses is imperfect, since the ὅταν παραδῶσιν clause picks up
the preceding παραδώσουσιν..., whereas the ὅταν διώκωσιν

/1/ Cf. E. Schweizer, *Matthew*, 242, who wonders if 10:19,20 and
10:23 originally belonged together or whether Matthew has
assimilated the saying behind 10:23 to the form of the earlier
sayings. Note that we shall come back to the question of the

introduces a new thought, slightly abruptly, and there is no
preceding διώξουσιν.... The earlier v 14 does contain a
similar thought, but it does not have the word διώκειν, and it
is too far back to provide a natural lead into v 23. If
Matthew were deliberately creating v 23's ὅταν διώκωσιν as a
parallel to ὅταν παραδῶσιν, we might expect him to do a more
thorough job; the imperfection of the parallelism is, however,
simply explained if v 23 is regarded as a fragment of the
tradition that he used in vv 17-20 and to which he now reverts.

4.1.3. A lost διώξουσιν clause

The logic of the immediately preceding argument may
suggest that Mt 10:23 comes from the same tradition as Mt 10:
19,20. But, if ὅταν διώκωσιν is parallel to ὅταν παραδῶσιν and
if ὅταν παραδῶσιν picks up the preceding παραδώσουσιν, would we
not expect ὅταν διώκωσιν to be preceded by a διώξουσιν?
Otherwise the parallelism on which the argument depends is at
best partial with ὅταν παραδῶσιν having obvious backward
reference and ὅταν διώκωσιν having no such obvious backward
reference.

Compare   παραδώσουσιν ὑμᾶς

               ὅταν παραδῶσιν ὑμᾶς   ὅταν διώκωσιν ὑμᾶς

The complete absence of the expected διώξουσιν clause in
Mt 10:17-22, Lk 12:11,12 (and in Mark 13) might appear to tell
against the hypothesis being proposed. However there is other
evidence to consider.

a. Evidence from Luke 21

The parallel passage in Luke 21 has precisely the verb
that we have postulated, διώξουσιν, in precisely the right
position.

Thus Lk 21:12 reads: ἐπιβαλοῦσιν ἐφ' ὑμᾶς τὰς χεῖρας αὐτῶν
                       καὶ διώξουσιν,
                       παραδιδόντες εἰς τὰς συναγωγὰς καὶ
                       φυλακάς, ἀπαγομένους ἐπὶ βασιλεῖς καὶ
                       ἡγεμόνας....

intervening verses, Mt 10:21,22; they seem not to belong in
this context within the mission discourse.

Since we have already noted the influence of the non-Markan
tradition on Lk 21:12 (see p. 222 above), the fact that we
find the postulated καὶ διώξουσιν here is clearly important
evidence supporting the hypothesis. It is true that Lk 21:12a,
including καὶ διώξουσιν, could simply be Luke's free rewording
of Mark;/1/ but since we have had reason to postulate a
διώξουσιν in the tradition at this point, it would seem
perverse to deny that Luke was probably influenced by it.

This suggestion may in fact enable us to explain more
precisely what Luke was doing in 21:12. If we tentatively
suppose that the tradition was something like this:

A. παραδώσουσιν ὑμᾶς εἰς συνέδρια, καὶ εἰς συναγωγὰς δαρήσεσθε

B. καὶ διώξουσιν ὑμᾶς (?ἐν ταῖς πόλεσιν), καὶ ἐπὶ ἡγεμόνας...
    ἀχθήσεσθε

then in Lk 21:12 Luke has summarised clause A, especially the
reference to beating in the synagogues, with a Septuagintal
phrase suggesting physical violence ἐπιβαλοῦσιν ἐφ' ὑμᾶς τὰς
χεῖρας αὐτῶν (cf. Gen 22:12, Exod 7:4, 2 Sam 18:12, Isa 5:25);
he then reproduces clause B almost unchanged καὶ διώξουσιν.
But having thereby omitted various elements from the tradition,
he adds the participial clauses that pick up exactly what he
has omitted from clauses A and B παραδιδόντες ... ἀπαγομένους.
/2/ It may be objected that, if Luke wanted to do the sort of
thing that we have suggested, he could have done it more
felicitously; but that is not a substantial objection, since on
any view Luke could have been more felicitous. Our explanation
does, however, offer a simple explanation of Luke's procedure,
and supports the hypothesis of a lost διώξουσιν.

/1/ Cf. Zmijewski, *Eschatologiereden*, 150-157, arguing that
Luke uses here terminology found also in the book of Acts.
/2/ For other examples of Luke operating in some tension
between, on the one hand, a desire to reexpress the tradition
in his own way and, on the other hand, a feeling of constraint
to stay close to the tradition, see 12:11, where ἀπολογήσησθε
is probably Lukan and (ἢ) τί εἴπητε tradition (see above,
p. 226). The same tension is also evident in 21:14,15 (see
below, pp.235,236).

Further evidence suggesting that this may have been Luke's
procedure in this section is to be found in Lk 21:15. It has
been argued by some scholars that Lk 21:15 must be primitive,
since Luke would not have removed the reference to the Holy
Spirit that is found in the synoptic parallels./1/ However, it
has already been seen that the pre-synoptic form was probably
similar to what we have in Mt 10:19,20, and that Luke's δώσω
ὑμῖν is not in fact Luke's equivalent of the Matthew/Mark
reference to the Spirit, but is in the first instance at least
his equivalent of the third person passive δοθήσεται. Luke
paraphrases that Semitism with 'I will give... '. Luke probably
continues to paraphrase in what follows, since, as A. Fuchs has
shown, the vocabulary in what follows is very Lukan;/2/ and it
is in the phrase σοφίαν, ᾗ οὐ δυνήσονται ἀντιστῆναι that we
probably find Luke's hint of the work of the Spirit. This is
suggested by Acts 6:10 where we find very similar phraseology
οὐκ ἴσχυον ἀντιστῆναι τῇ σοφίᾳ καὶ τῷ πνεύματι ᾧ ἐλάλει, and
where 'wisdom' and Spirit are closely linked, if not identified.
In the light of this verse, it seems probable that his reference
in 21:15 to irresistible wisdom is Luke's implicit reference to
the Spirit - his paraphrase of that part of the pre-synoptic
tradition.

But - and this is the interesting point for an
understanding of Luke's editorial procedure - Luke adds to that
phrase the words στόμα καὶ (σοφίαν ᾗ οὐ δυνήσονται ἀντιστῆναι)
ἢ ἀντειπεῖν. These words have no equivalent in the Acts
verse, but the effect of them is to bring the thought of the
phrase into line with the pre-synoptic tradition, which Luke is
paraphrasing here, since that focussed on *speaking* (Lk 12:11,
12 εἰπεῖν). It seems then that Luke paraphrases the tradition
freely using phraseology of his own, but he feels constrained
by the tradition and so ensures that he keeps in line with the
sense (and even to some extent with the wording) of the
tradition. This is exactly what was suggested with regard to
12:11,12, where he adds ἢ τί εἴπητε to his own word ἀπολογήσησθε
for the same reason. It is also what we have suggested in
connection with 21:12, where the διώξουσιν is part of Luke's

/1/ E.g. C. K. Barrett, *The Holy Spirit and the Gospel
Tradition* (London: SPCK, 1947) 131-32, cf. Gaston, *No Stone*,
21.
/2/ *Sprachliche Untersuchungen*, 175-189.

tradition. There is a consistent pattern in Luke's editing,/1/ and our suggestions about Lk 21:12 are confirmed.

   b. Other evidence of the lost διώξουσιν clause
   The hypothesis may also receive some rather uncertain support from (i) Mt 23:34. In a passage addressed to the Jewish leaders Jesus speaks of the church's mission in terms distinctly reminiscent of Matthew 10. Compare ἰδοὺ ἐγὼ ἀποστέλλω ... ἐξ αὐτῶν μαστιγώσετε ἐν ταῖς συναγωγαῖς ὑμῶν καὶ διώξετε ἀπὸ πόλεως εἰς πόλιν (23:34) with ἰδοὺ ἐγὼ ἀποστέλλω ... ἐν ταῖς συναγωγαῖς αὐτῶν μαστιγώσουσιν ... ὅταν διώκωσιν ὑμᾶς ἐν τῇ πόλει (10:16-23). The link between the two passages has often been observed, and it has been explained that Matthew in chap.23 elaborates the 'Q' traditions that he is reproducing with phraseology drawn from his earlier mission discourse. This general explanation, which would help explain the differences between Matthew 23 and the apparently parallel Luke 11, would probably work even better on the basis of the proposed pre-synoptic text, since this would have had διώξουσιν (maybe even some such wording as διώξουσιν ὑμᾶς ἀπὸ πόλεως εἰς πόλιν) not just ὅταν διώκωσιν, and it would have had this phrase close to the sentence about beatings in the synagogues. The parallelism of the two passages would thus have been the more obvious, and the temptation to assimilation the greater. It might be noted in favour of this that Luke has exactly the sort of parallelism we are suggesting: the phrase καὶ διώξουσιν occurs only twice in his gospel - in 21:12 (as we have seen) and in 11:49 , his equivalent of Mt 23:34. On the other hand, it should be said that Matthew's reference to 'beating in the synagogues' in 23:34 could be original, not assimilation to Matthew 10; Luke could have omitted the phrase; compare his rephrasing of the similar phrase in 21:12. In this case the parallelism between Mt 10:17 and Mt 23:34 would be the more striking, and, although the argument about the assimilation of the sayings would be weakened, Mt 23:34 could still be used as indirect testimony to the proposed wording of Mt 10:17, being an echo of the earlier verse./2/

/1/ καὶ μὴ μετεωρίζεσθε in Lk 12:29 may similarly have been added by Luke to his preceding μὴ ζητεῖτε in order to bring the sense of the saying into line with μὴ μεριμνήσητε of the tradition (cf. Mt 6:31). Cf. R. A. Guelich, *The Sermon on the Mount* (Waco: Word, 1982) 343.
/2/ There could still have been some assimilation of the

(ii) Further possible support for the διώξουσιν hypothesis may come from Jn 15:20: in the course of a part of John that has numerous contacts with Mt 10:17-25/1/ one particular similarity is between Mt 10:24,25 οὐκ ἔστιν μαθητῆς ὑπὲρ τὸν διδάσκαλον οὐδὲ δοῦλος ὑπὲρ τὸν κύριον αὐτοῦ ... εἰ τὸν οἰκοδεσπέτην βεεζεβοὺλ ἐπεκάλεσαν, πόσῳ μᾶλλον τοὺς οἰκιακοὺς αὐτοῦ and Jn 15:20 οὐκ ἔστιν δοῦλος μείζων τοῦ κυρίου αὐτοῦ. εἰ ἐμὲ ἐδίωξαν, καὶ ὑμᾶς διώξουσιν (cf. also Jn 13:16)./2/ This Johannine διώξουσιν is not in the precise context we are postulating for it, but it is not impossible that the Johannine wording has been affected by the pre-synoptic wording.

(iii) In *Did.* 16:4 we read αὐξανούσης γὰρ τῆς ἀνομίας μισήσουσιν ἀλλήλους καὶ διώξουσι καὶ παραδώσουσι καὶ τότε φανήσεται .... It is a debated question as to whether the Didache's tradition is independent to any degree of the synoptics. In this passage the Didache could be dependent to a large extent on Mt 24:10-12; but the phrase καὶ διώξουσι(ν) is notably absent from Mt 24:10, and it could be that the Didache here betrays knowledge of the postulated pre-synoptic version (of Mt 10:17-22), which had παραδώσουσιν and διώξουσιν in

---

sayings: e.g. Matthew's μαστιγώσουσιν (10:17) for Mark's δαρήσεσθε (13:9) could be a case of assimilation in the opposite direction. See further below, pp. 238,239.

/1/ Cf. H. F. D. Sparks, *JTS* 3 (1952) 58-61; R. E. Brown, *The Gospel according to John*, XII-XXI (London: Chapman, 1971) 693-95

/2/ Jn 15:20 is an explicit echo of 13:16 ('Do you remember the word?'), and it is interesting that Jn 13:16 is a double saying like Mt 10:24: 'A slave is not greater than his master, nor an apostle than the one who sent him'. (Note the use of οὐδέ as in Mt 10:24.) It is also interesting that the saying about the slave and master in both Jn 13:16 and 15:20 is followed by a saying to the effect that he who receives Jesus receives the one who sent him (so Jn 13:20 positively, 15:21,23 negatively); this same thought is found - perhaps significantly - in Mt 10:40 (positively) and Lk 10:16 (positively and negatively). John could be thought thus indirectly to testify to a pre-synoptic form that combined the sayings of Mt 10:40 and Lk 10:16. Cf. also my discussion in *JSNT* 14 (1982) 113-118, especially p. 116.

parallel./1/

Against these three last points in favour of the lost
διώξουσιν, it may be reasonably objected that the occurrence of
similar sayings, and even more of similar phrases, in different
contexts does not necessarily prove any connection between the
traditions; we would expect Jesus himself to have repeated
sayings when speaking on similar themes. However, even though
this point must be given full weight, the case for the lost
διώξουσιν seems strong enough even without the last three
arguments; and, given that conclusion, it is not unreasonable
to bring in these three weaker points as possible, though
uncertain, additional evidence.

c. *A possible objection to the* διώξουσιν *hypothesis*
Against the hypothesis being proposed, it may be argued
that, if there was indeed a pre-synoptic form of the tradition
known to all three evangelists that included a διώξουσιν
clause, then it is unlikely that Matthew and Mark would both
have omitted it. However, it is not in fact very difficult to
see why Mark, having reproduced the original παραδώσουσιν..
δαρήσεσθε, might have wished to continue with the second person
passive form καὶ... σταθήσεσθε rather than returning to the
active καὶ διώξουσιν. Furthermore, it will later be argued that
Mark placed this material in the context of the eschatological
discourse precisely because of the occurrence of the word
παραδώσουσιν in the pre-synoptic form of the eschatological
discourse and in this section of the mission discourse (see
pp. 261,262 below); if this is correct, he might well have omitted
the thematically less relevant διώξουσιν. So far as Matthew is
concerned, it is not difficult to see that after his two third
person plurals παραδώσουσιν ... καὶ ... μαστιγώσουσιν (the
second being probably his alteration of the more original
Markan form) Matthew might have felt καὶ διώξουσιν to have been
stylistically cumbersome (and in any case redundant, so far as
sense is concerned), and so might have jumped on to καὶ
ἀχθήσεσθε. These considerations might explain why either
Matthew or Mark altered the pre-synoptic tradition; and, if,
despite their independent knowledge of the pre-synoptic

/1/ Cf. R. Glover, *NTS* 5 (1958-9) 23, who claims that on other
occasions where the Didache appears to add to Matthew Luke shows
that Matthew has omitted material retained by the Didache.
Our argument about διώξουσιν could strengthen his view.

tradition, Matthew and Mark were not wholly independent of each
other, as we shall suggest, their agreement in this alteration
is not very remarkable.

4.1.4. Conclusion on Mt 10.23 and the tradition about appearing before the authorities

The conclusion of all these arguments is that the case for
the pre-synoptic διώξουσιν is good, and so therefore is the case
for believing that Mt 10:23 belonged in the pre-synoptic
tradition with the sayings about the disciples appearing before
the authorities. Each of the evangelists retains some original
elements from this pre-synoptic tradition: for example, Matthew
has 10:23, Luke retains the διώξουσιν, and Mark probably
reflects the pre-synoptic tradition in the present tense of the
ὅταν clause (ὅταν ἄγωσιν... παραδιδόντες cf. Lk 12:11) and in
the passive of the verb of beating, δαρήσεσθε (contrast
Matthew's μαστιγώσουσιν/1/), this being parallel to the
preceding ἀχθήσεσθε.

4.2. Links between the persecution tradition, Mt 10:23 and earlier parts of Matthew 10

To suggest that Mt 10:23 belongs with the tradition about
the disciples being persecuted and appearing before the
authorities may appear to conflict with the fact that 10:23b
with its specific reference to 'the cities of Israel' is
reminiscent of 10:5,6, where we find the command not to go to
the Gentiles or to a Samaritan city, but 'to the lost sheep of
the house of Israel'. It might therefore be argued that 10:23
belongs with that distinctively 'M' tradition rather than with
the tradition of 10:17-20, which is also attested in Luke and
which seems to have a more international focus./2/

/1/ As observed already, Matthew could conceivably have been
influenced in his use of the active here by the saying in 23:34.
Dupont, 'La Persécution', 106, sees Matthew's 'their synagogues'
as secondary.
/2/ Cf. 10:18 καὶ τοῖς ἔθνεσιν, and note generally the
impression that in 10:17-22 we are dealing with something bigger
than the limited Palestinian mission.

Dupont offers one possible solution to this when he argues
that vv 23a and 23b did not originally belong together and that
it is 23b which belongs with vv 5,6; in favour of this he
argues among other things that τελεῖν in 23b makes better sense
in a mission context than in a context talking about persecution
and flight./1/ This last argument for splitting the verse is
not very convincing: we may agree that τελεῖν is more
appropriate of completing a mission than of running out of
hiding places (despite A. Feuillet),/2/ but in the total
context of Matthew 10 the fleeing disciples are both running
for their lives and also running with the gospel message; so
τελεῖν may convey the thought of 'completing' the task within a
persecution context. Against Dupont Feuillet argues plausibly
that v 23b goes well with 23a;/3/ even if it is possible that
23a once existed without a sequel like 23b or that Matthew has
substituted 23b for another saying, such radical verse-
splitting is undesirable when the verse coheres well together.
Feuillet's explanation of the situation is that 10:23, while
reflecting a similar sort of perspective on the Jewish mission
as vv 5,6, does not actually belong with those verses, but
belongs to a later stage of Jesus' ministry (nearer its
completion).

There is, however, a simpler explanation of things than
either Dupont or Feuillet offers, but which combines some of the
insights of them both; it is that 10:23a and 23b belong with
each other *and* with the earlier particularist sections of
Matthew 10. In other words, it is suggested that not only did
10:23 belong in the pre-synoptic tradition with the sayings
about appearing before the authorities (10:17-19), but so too
did the injunction about going only to the 'lost sheep of the
house of Israel' (10:5,6). What are the arguments for and
against this view-point?

4.2.1.
It enables us to do justice to the arguments, discussed
already, for linking 10:23a with 10:17-19, 10:23b with 10:5,6
and 10:23a with 10:23b.

/1/ *NovT* 2 (1958) 228-44. Bosch, *Heidenmission*, 156,157, also
divides 10:23a and 23b.
/2/ *CBQ* 23 (1961) 185,186.
/3/ Cf. also E. Bammel, *Studia Theologica* 15 (1961) 80,81.

4.2.2.

It is an economical hypothesis having the virtue of
simplicity. The usual opinion of scholars is that the early
part of Matthew 10 is a mixture of (a) Markan material, (b) 'Q'
material, i.e. that which is paralleled in Luke 10, the sending
of the seventy, and (c) 'M' material, i.e. the particularist
verses 5 and 6 (and perhaps 23). We might add (d) that 10:17-19
would normally be regarded as a quite separate and distinct
Markan or 'Q' tradition. Our hypothesis ascribes all the last
three categories of material to one tradition - a mission
discourse evidently -, and involves Matthew in a relatively
simple editorial process. (See further discussion below on the
relationship of the Markan and non-Markan traditions.)

4.2.3.

It helps explain the different positioning of the 'Q'
saying 'Behold I send you out as lambs in the midst of wolves'
in Lk 10:3 (at the very beginning of the discourse to the
seventy) and in Mt 10:16 (later in the discourse). Various
explanations of this difference may be possible; but if the
pre-synoptic tradition had the saying about not going among
Gentiles and Samaritans at the beginning of the discourse, as
does Matthew, then a very simple explanation of the divergence
is immediately evident: Luke, probably writing for Gentiles,
did not wish the opening command to 'go'/1/ to include an
apparently unfriendly reference to Gentiles and Samaritans; so
he leaves out that reference, substituting for it the saying
about sending them out as lambs among wolves - a saying found
later in the same discourse in Matthew and probably also in the
pre-synoptic tradition. In favour of this suggestion is not
only (i) that it neatly explains the difference discussed; but
also (ii) that the warning about lambs among wolves seems to
fit better later on in the mission discourse (as in Matthew)
rather than right at the beginning (as in Luke); and (iii) we
saw some admittedly uncertain evidence for the pre-synoptic
form of 10:16-23 being associated with Mt 23:34 (p. 236
above), and one of the points of contact between the two
passages was the phrase ἰδοὺ ἀποστέλλω ..., found in 10:17 and
23:34. This could favour the suggestion that Matthew has
preserved the pre-synoptic location of the saying in question.

/1/ Compare Luke's ὑπάγετε and Matthew's πορεύεσθε.

4.2.4.
The idea of one discourse lying behind at least the non-Markan sections of Mt 10:1-16 (including vv 5,6) and behind 10:17-23 may appear to be contradicted by Luke's evidence. But his omission of the prohibition on mission to Gentiles and Samaritans is easily explained, as we have seen. His separation of the discourse to the seventy (chap. 10) and the persecution logia (chap. 12) is rather more of a puzzle; but it is only a serious problem if Luke's central section is thought to be chronologically arranged and/or if it is supposed that Luke will have felt bound to follow the order of the pre-synoptic tradition. But neither assumption may be taken for granted. If, for example, the pre-synoptic tract was an oral tradition, the order of which was not felt rigidly binding by Luke, then we might expect to find Luke sometimes departing from the pre-synoptic order, while still showing knowledge of it and returning to it from time to time. It seems quite likely that something like this has happened in this part of Luke. Thus after 10:12 Luke gets distracted from the order of the mission discourse and inserts some topically related material (vv 13-15); then he rounds off the mission discourse with the concluding saying of 10:16, which has an interesting parallel in Mt 10:40 (Luke: 'He who hears you hears me, and he who rejects you rejects me, and he who rejects me rejects him who sent me.' Matthew: 'He who receives you receives me, and he who receives me receives him who sent me.') And then he takes up other material from the mission discourse in subsequent contexts, e.g. in 12:11,12, where the immediate explanation of the positioning of the saying is thematic, witness and the Spirit being the theme of 12:10 and 12:11,12. This sort of editorial procedure is exactly the sort of thing we have observed in considering other parts of the Lukan travel narrative.

4.2.5.
Another possible objection to viewing Mt 10:1-16 (at least the non-Markan sections) and 10:17-23 as part of the same pre-synoptic discourse is that 10:1-16 may seem to be describing the first Galilean mission and the later verses - with references to 'kings' and 'Gentiles' (v 18) - may appear to be portraying a more global mission. However, it has already been argued that 10:17-19, including the references to 'kings' and 'Gentiles', belong with 10:23, which suggests that we are still thinking in this section of a Palestinian mission (unless 'cities of Israel' is taken in a broader sense). In any case

it is only necessary to recall Jesus' own experience to see that
appearances before 'kings' and 'Gentiles' do not necessarily
mean removal from the Palestinian arena./1/ To say that is not
to deny that the pre-synoptic mission discourse may well have
had wider relevance than just for the first Galilean mission,
but it is to deny that the second half of the discourse fits
inappropriately with the first half.

4.2.6.

The conclusion of the preceding arguments is that the link
between Mt 10:23 and the earlier 10:5,6 does not disprove the
suggestion that 10:23 should be linked with 10:17-20. On the
contrary, it seems that 10:17-20 belonged with 10:5,6 and 10:23
in the pre-synoptic mission discourse.

4.3. Excursus: *The relationship of the different mission traditions*

It is not essential for the point being made to explore
the pre-synoptic mission discourse in greater detail. But for
the sake of completeness it may be useful very briefly to
suggest how the findings discussed above fit in with a broader
view of the mission discourse traditions.

4.3.1. *The two source hypothesis reviewed*

The usual view is that there are two synoptic mission
discourse forms, the Markan and the 'Q' forms. Matthew has
merged the two traditions in his chap. 10, Mark by definition
has the Markan form, and Luke has the Markan discourse in his
chap. 9 and the 'Q' discourse in his chap. 10. This
explanation is, at least as described, an oversimplification.
It is, in particular, an oversimplification to call Lk 9:1-5
the Markan discourse, since Luke has a string of significant
agreements with Matthew and against Mark in this section:

Compare:

/1/ Cf. Schlatter, *Matthäus*, 338,339.

Mt 10:1-9	with Mk 6:7,8	and Lk 9:1-3
καὶ προσκαλεσάμενος τοὺς δώδεκα μαθητὰς αὐτοῦ	καὶ προσκαλεῖται τοὺς δώδεκα, καὶ ἤρξατο αὐτοὺς ἀποστέλλειν δύο δύο,	συγκαλεσάμενος δὲ τοὺς δώδεκα
ἔδωκεν αὐτοῖς ἐξουσίαν πνευμάτων ἀκαθάρτων ὥστε ἐκβάλλειν αὐτά, καὶ θεραπεύειν πᾶσαν νόσον καὶ πᾶσαν μαλακίαν.	καὶ ἐδίδου αὐτοῖς ἐξουσίαν τῶν πνευμάτων τῶν ἀκαθάρτων	ἔδωκεν αὐτοῖς δύναμιν καὶ ἐξουσίαν ἐπὶ πάντα τὰ δαιμόνια καὶ νόσους θεραπεύειν.

2-4 Names of twelve

5,6 τούτους τοὺς δώδεκα ἀπέστειλεν ὁ Ἰησοῦς παραγγείλας αὐτοῖς λέγων· εἰς ὁδὸν ἐθνῶν μὴ ..... Ἰσραήλ.	8 καὶ παρήγγειλεν αὐτοῖς ἵνα	2 καὶ ἀπέστειλεν αὐτοὺς
7 πορευόμενοι δὲ κηρύσσετε λέγοντες ὅτι ἤγγικεν ἡ βασιλεία τῶν οὐρανῶν.		κηρύσσειν τὴν βασιλείαν τοῦ θεοῦ καὶ ἰᾶσθαι
8 ἀσθενοῦντας θεραπεύετε.....		3. καὶ εἶπεν προς αὐτοὺς·
9 μὴ κτήσησθε χρύσον.....	μηδὲν αἴρωσιν εἰς ὁδόν ...	μηδὲν αἴρετε εἰς τὴν ὁδόν ....

The agreements between Matthew and Luke against Mark in these verses hardly need to be spelled out. But note (1) Matthew and Luke have a participle προσκαλεσάμενος/συγκαλεσάμενος + an aorist ἔδωκεν for Mark's προσκαλεῖται + an imperfect ἐδίδου, and within the same sentence they omit Mark's καὶ ἤρξατο αὐτοὺς ἀποστέλλειν δύο δύο. (2) Mark speaks of Jesus giving them authority over unclean spirits; but Matthew adds 'and to heal every disease and every infirmity' (θεραπεύειν πᾶσαν νόσον...) and Luke speaks of authority over all demons (πάντα τὰ δαιμόνια) and 'to heal diseases' (νόσους θεραπεύειν). Matthew and Luke have the same additional thought and the same wording.
(3) Matthew, after listing the names of the twelve, says that Jesus 'sent' them (ἀπέστειλεν) and Luke similarly has the verb

ἀπέστειλεν. Matthew then has the saying about not going to the Samaritans or Gentiles, which occurs in neither Mark nor Luke. But then Matthew has the instruction that they are (1) to preach saying that the 'kingdom of heaven has come near', (2) to 'heal the sick'. This has no parallel here in Mark, but it has a close parallel in Luke's next words '(he sent them) to proclaim the kingdom of God and to heal'.

This range of agreements between Matthew and Luke both in additions to and omissions from Mark must mean that Matthew and Luke are related other than via Mark in these verses (or at least not only via Mark). In the verses that follow, the situation is slightly different: Luke here seems much closer to Mark, adding nothing and omitting little (compare Mk 6:8-11/ Lk 9:3-5); but there are a few verbal agreements with Matthew - e.g. Luke agrees with Matthew in the use of direct rather than indirect speech, in excluding the carrying of 'a staff' and in speaking of κονιορτόν on the feet, whereas Mark speaks of χοῦν.

What is to be made of this evidence and also of the agreements between Matthew 10 and Luke 10 (the sending of the seventy)? The conventional explanation in terms of Mark and Q is not impossible: but (a) in view of our earlier arguments, the 'Q' mission discourse must have included not only the material common to Matthew 10 and Luke 10, but also the 'M' sayings about not going to the Gentiles etc. and the persecution sayings about appearing before the authorities. The discourse to the seventy in Luke 10 is not therefore the complete 'Q' discourse, but is a substantial extract from it. (b) The discourse in Luke 9 cannot simply be explained as Luke's version of the Markan discourse, since it has substantial agreements with Matthew 10 against Mark: we would probably have to say that Luke, while following Mark here, has been heavily influenced by the 'Q' form. In other words, not only would Matthew 10 be deemed a mixture of the Markan and 'Q' traditions, but so also to a lesser extent would Luke 9. This at least complicates the picture, since it is not obvious why Luke should have assimilated the traditions in Luke 9. (c) There is in any case the question as to how the Markan and 'Q' traditions relate: are they two versions of the same discourse, or what?

An attractive possible answer to that question might be that the Markan discourse was a discourse to the twelve and the 'Q' discourse was, as Luke 10 suggests, a discourse to the seventy. It may be suggested that the particularist 'M'

material of Matthew 10, which we must include in the 'Q'
discourse, would fit very well into the Lukan context: after
the trouble with the Samaritan villages recorded in Lk 9:52,
Jesus' command to 'Go nowhere among the Gentiles, and enter no
town of the Samaritans' would make a lot of sense - more sense
than in the context of a local mission within Galilee./1/ The
warning about being 'pursued from city to city' (Mt 10:23) would
fit in well after the trouble in the Samaritan villages and in
the context of Lk 10:1 'he sent them on ahead of him, two by
two, into every town and place where he himself was about to
come'. The promise too of Mt 10:23 'You will not have gone
through all the towns of Israel, *before the Son of man comes*'
(ἔρχεται) would make sense, albeit mundane sense, after Lk 10:1
with its reference to 'every town and place where he himself
was about to come' (ἔρχεσθαι)./2/

An explanation on these lines is possible, and the
relationship of the Markan and the 'Q' discourse would be that
they are similar, but distinct, traditions. However, a more
likely explanation is that there was only one pre-synoptic
mission discourse, which lies behind the so-called Markan and
'Q' traditions, and that this is preserved most fully in
Matthew 10.

4.3.2. The pre-synoptic mission discourse

This suggestion can most easily be explained by setting
out a tentative reconstruction of the proposed pre-synoptic
mission discourse. It may have included the following elements:

	Matthew	Mark	Luke 9	Luke 10
1. (Saying about harvest being ripe & labourers few)	9:37,38	-	-	10:2

/1/ Cf. Schürmann, *Traditionsgeschichtliche Untersuchungen*,
144-145.
/2/ Cf. Dupont, *NovT* 2, pp. 233,234; *contra* Feuillet, *CBQ* 23,
p.188, Schürmann, *Traditionsgeschichliche Untersuchungen*, 152. On
the other hand, the similarity of ideas in Mt 10:17-23 and Mt
23:34-36 could be thought to favour the view that Mt 10:23 may
be referring to the fall of Jerusalem.

2. And calling the twelve, Mt 10:1   Mk 6:7   Lk 9:1   -
    he gave them authority
    over unclean spirits to
    cast them out and to
    heal diseases

3. And he sent them out   10:5a   6:7   9:2a   -
    two by two.

4. And he instructed them,   10:5b,6   -   -   (10:3 =
    Do not go into the way   no.16)
    of the Gentiles ..but
    ..to the lost sheep of
    the house of Israel.

5. Proclaim saying that   10:7,8   -   9:2   -
    the kingdom has come
    near. Heal.. Freely
    you received, freely
    give.

6. Do not take for the   10:9,10a   6:8,9   9:3   10:4a
    journey (prohibited
    items)

7. For the labourer is   10:10b   -   -   (10:7b)
    worthy of his hire.

8. But into whatever   10:11a   -   -   (10:8)
    city (or village) you
    enter (seek out one
    who is worthy and) eat
    what is set before you.

9. Do not greet anyone   -   -   -   10:4b
    on the way.

10. But when you enter a   10:12   -   -   10:5,6
    house, say 'Peace....'
    .. If not, it will
    return to you.

11. Into whatever house you   (10:11b)   6:10   9:4   10:7a
    enter, stay there until
    you go out.

12. Eat and drink what they   -   -   -   10:7b
    provide for you.

13. And do not go from   -   -   -   10:7d
    house to house.

14. Whatever city receives Mt -   Mk -   Lk -   10:8a,9
    you, heal its sick &
    say, 'The kingdom has
    come near you'

15. But whatever place   10:14   6:11   9:5 10:10,11
    does not receive you,
    going out from that
    city, shake off the
    dust....etc.

16. Truly, I tell you, it   10:15   -   -   10:12
    will be more tolerable
    for Sodom....

17. Behold, I send you out   10:16   -   -   (10:3)
    as lambs.......

Etc.

The proposed reconstruction has a coherent structure: section 4 describes the mission field, and section 5 the missionary task. The following sections deal with the journey: sections 5,6 and 7 all address the question of preparations and provisions. Sections 8 and 9 discuss greetings, and lead into sections 10-12, which deal with the receiving of hospitality. The following sections move on to the questions of response, persecution, etc.

Each of our synoptic accounts may be derived relatively simply from this proposed pre-synoptic form.

·a. *Matthew* reproduces much of the tradition, but he omits some of sections 8-12, e.g. the prohibition of greetings on the way and the instructions about eating food provided, and this leads to some dislocation and rearrangement.

To look at Matthew in more detail: he has sections 1-6 in the pre-synoptic order, except that before section 3, which refers to Jesus sending out his disciples (ἀποστέλλειν), he inserts a list of the names of the 'apostles' (10:2-4). When he comes to section 6, Matthew speaks of the labourer being worthy of his 'food', whereas the pre-synoptic tradition probably had the word 'hire'. /1/ Matthew's choice of word probably

_____

/1/ Luke retains the more original μίσθος and has the saying close to the sayings about eating (and drinking) what is provided (10:7,8). Paul probably alludes to the saying in question in 1 Cor 9:14, and he goes on to speak shortly afterwards of his μίσθος (9:17,18, cf. 1 Tim 5:18). It may not be accidental that

indicates that he knows that this statement was followed in the
pre-synoptic tradition by a saying concerning eating whatever is
provided (pre-synoptic section 8). But, although (or perhaps
because) he has alluded to that saying, Matthew does not proceed
to reproduce it, except for the opening words. Instead he
produces a conflation of material from sections 8, 10 and 11 in
his 10:11-13. In doing so Matthew omits both of the pre-synoptic
sayings about accepting food (cf. sections 8b and 12), and also
the prohibition of greetings en route (section 9), though he
shows his knowledge of this tradition in his ἀσπάσασθε in 10:12.
Matthew omits sections 13 and 14, but rejoins the pre-synoptic
tradition with section 15.

   b. *Mark* quite typically abbreviates the pre-synoptic
tradition. He opens with a conflation of sections 2 and 3,
putting the reference to 'sending' the twelve before, not after,
the giving of authority (6:7). Then he only gives brief extracts
from the discourse, drawing on pre-synoptic sections 6, 9 and 11.
He puts some of the material into indirect speech (6:8,9); this
then compels him to add καὶ ἔλεγεν αὐτοῖς, a phrase unparalleled
in Matthew or Luke, when he reverts to direct speech in 6:10. His
use of imperfects in this section (ἐδίδου... παρήγγειλεν... καὶ
ἔλεγεν αὐτοῖς) may be an indication of his consciousness that he
is not reproducing the tradition as he found it; he is
consciously summarizing and extracting./1/

   c. *Luke* in chapter 9 follows the Markan outline, but in
9:1,2 he draws very extensively on the pre-synoptic tradition
(sections 2-5), omitting the saying about going only to the lost
sheep of the house of Israel, but in other respects agreeing
remarkably with Matthew. In vv 3-5 he returns to the Markan
outline, adhering rather closely to it, but occasionally
modifying Mark in the light of the pre-synoptic tradition.

   In chapter 10 Luke follows the order of the pre-synoptic
tradition for the most part: his major changes result (a) from
his avoidance of the saying about going only to Israel, (b) from
his jumping over and then coming back to sections 7 and 8.

Paul also has a possible echo of pre-synoptic section 7, 'eat
what is set before you', in 1 Cor 10:27

/1/ The imperfect καὶ ἔλεγεν in 12:35,38 might be comparable.
Cf. H.G.Jameson, *The Origin of the Synoptic Gospels* (Oxford:
Blackwells, 1922) 120, for the suggestion that καὶ ἔλεγεν in Mark
marks a departure from an original Matthew. Also, for the view
that the imperfect ἔλεγεν reflects consciousness of a loose
historical context see M.Zerwick, *Untersuchungen zum Markus-
Stil* (Rome: Pontifical Biblical Institute, 1937) 60-62.

To explain Luke 10 in more detail: Luke attaches the pre-synoptic discourse to his description of the sending out of the 70 (10:1), using the rather loose link ἔλεγεν δέ... . A result of his relocation of the discourse is that section 1 ('The harvest is plentiful ... pray the Lord to send out ...') comes after the description of the sending of the 70, where it fits less appropriately than in Matthew and in the postulated pre-synoptic tradition where it precedes the sending of the disciples. Luke then avoids the saying about going to the lost sheep of Israel, not simply omitting it this time, but substituting for it the 'go' saying from later in the discourse, 'Go, I send you out as sheep among wolves' (i.e. pre-synoptic section 16). Perhaps as a consequence of introducing this pessimistic saying, he omits as inappropriate here the command to 'preach and heal' (pre-synoptic section 5), and he proceeds straight into pre-synoptic section 6, the prohibition of provisions. He then jumps over sections 7 and 8 (on the labourer and on eating what is given), going straight on to the next prohibition, 'Do not greet anyone on the way' (pre-synoptic section 9). He then reproduces sections 9-15, modifying them slightly and now incorporating the two sayings that he had omitted (sections 7 and 8, the second of which is slightly awkwardly placed in Luke /1/). When he comes to pre-synoptic section 16, the saying about lambs and wolves, he omits it, having already used it in his v 3; having to break off at this point, he introduces sayings from a different context (his vv 13-15/Mt 11:20-24), but he then comes back to the conclusion of the pre-synoptic discourse in 10:16, cf. Mt 10:40.

One small additional piece of evidence that might support the view that Luke knew that the discourse to the twelve and the discourse to the 70 were originally one may be Lk 22:35,36, where Jesus addresses the twelve but echoes the discourse to the 70, 'When I sent you out without purse and bag and sandals...' (cf. 10:4), though this is hardly a decisive argument, since Luke could have understood that the twelve were with the seventy when Jesus gave the instructions of Lk 10:2-16./2/

  d. *Conclusions* The preceding explanation of the history

/1/ The phrase about eating what is provided in Lk 10:8 seems redundant after the preceding similar statement in 10:7. I am indebted to Mr S. McKnight for alerting me to this and others points discussed in this and earlier chapters.
/2/ Some of the twelve are present in the immediately preceding 9:52-54, and it seems likely that the 'messengers' of 9:52 were all or some of the twelve.

of the mission discourse traditions in terms of an underlying
pre-synoptic form may well be mistaken in certain respects. But
the broad outline of the solution proposed is probably correct,
accounting well for the synoptic data. The solution fits in well
well with our conclusions about the pre-synoptic tradition
elsewhere and about the relationship of the synoptic gospels
to it: Matthew, as elsewhere, retains the form of the mission
discourse best; Mark abbreviates it; Luke sits most lightly to
original contexts. That last point, however, might perhaps be
qualified in this case: although it is possible that in Luke's
chap. 10 the evangelist has attached the pre-synoptic discourse
to a secondary context (the sending of the seventy), it is also
possible that in this case Luke may have preserved at least
traces of the pre-synoptic context and that the discourse
could have been in the context of a major journey of Jesus and
of trouble with a Samaritan village. As was observed above
(pp.245,246), this would make good sense of the command to go
only to Israel and of other features of the discourse./1/

      This, however, is not a point of great moment so far as
the analysis of the mission traditions is concerned. It has in
any case only been possible in this excursus to outline a
proposed explanation of the traditions, not to explore the
matter in detail, nor to consider all the other possible
explanations. So far as the sayings about appearing before the
authorities are concerned, the proposed explanation would fit
in excellently with the earlier arguments for seeing those
sayings as part of the mission discourse; but those arguments
stand, whether or not the proposal is correct in all respects.

· 5.   THE MARKAN/LUKAN LOCATION OF THE TRADITIONS IN MARK 13/
       LUKE 21

      The corollary of the preceding arguments is that Mark's
and Luke's positioning of the sayings about appearing before
the authorities in the eschatological discourse is secondary.
Against this it might be argued that the Fourth Evangelist uses
the traditions (or at least very similar traditions) in his
farewell discourses (see above, p. 237), so that he may be seen

_____
/1/ Is it possibly significant that in Mt 11:1 immediately
after the discourse Matthew has the rather vague 'when Jesus
finished instructing the twelve' instead of his more usual 'when
Jesus finished all these sayings' (so, approximately, Mt 7:28,
13:53, 19:1, 26:1)? Does Matthew thus hint that he knows that
the discourse he has in chap.10 (or part of it, e.g. 10:42)
comes from a different historical context?

as supporting Mark's location of the sayings; also the Didache, if it does indeed echo the sayings about appearing before the authorities in 16:4, has the echo in a context that unmistakably resembles the eschatological discourse.

But neither of these observations weighs heavily against the hypothesis being suggested. The question of the ordering of materials in the fourth gospel is a complex and controversial one, and it would be unwise to build much on the assumption that the author has adhered to a chronological order. There is, of course, no mission discourse in John outside the farewell discourses, and it seems entirely intelligible that the author of the gospel might have incorporated material from the mission discourse in his farewell discourses. So far as the Didache is concerned, the appearance of the phrase καὶ διώξουσιν in 16:4 is simply explicable in terms of assimilation of similar traditions. It is also not impossible that the authors of John's gospel and of the Didache might, either or both, have known and been influenced by Mark 13/Luke 21.

As for Mark and Luke themselves, there is no great difficulty in explaining their relocation of the sayings. It is quite possible that, having omitted the sayings in question in his abbreviated mission discourse, Mark might have decided after all to include them in a later and quite appropriate context. This will be seen to be the more plausible when further consideration is given to the original form of this part of the eschatological discourse. It will be argued that Matthew most nearly retains the original form, and that it began with a reference to people 'handing you over'. If this is correct, then it is easy to see how and why Mark might here have introduced the verses from the mission discourse, which also spoke of men 'handing you over'.

Luke's positioning of the sayings in his chap. 21 is to be explained as reflecting Markan influence. He follows the Markan tradition, but (a) he betrays his knowledge of the pre-synoptic form in numerous ways, as we have seen. And (b) he modifies the wording of the tradition quite considerably, partly perhaps to avoid word-for-word repetition of Lk 12:11-12.

It is then not difficult to explain Mark's and Luke's location of the sayings about appearing before the authorities, although we have anticipated the argument of the next chapter to some extent. The view, then, that those sayings belonged in the pre-synoptic mission discourse, not in the pre-synoptic eschatological discourse may be considered very probable.

Chapter 7

THE PRE-SYNOPTIC ESCHATOLOGICAL DISCOURSE AND THE WARNING OF
COMING SUFFERINGS: MT 24:9-14, MK 13:9-13, LK 21:12-15

The previous chapter concluded that the sayings about
appearing before the authorities were not part of the pre-
synoptic eschatological discourse. But that conclusion leaves
almost as many questions unanswered as it answers so far as the
relevant section of the discourse goes. For example, there has
been no discussion of the other sayings found in this section
of the discourse in both Matthew and Mark (i.e. Mt 24:9b,13,14;
Mk 13:10,12,13), nor of the relationship of the distinctively
Matthean traditions (24:9a,11,12) to those found in Mark, nor of
Lk 21:18. We have not even established whether there was any
section of warning about coming sufferings in the pre-synoptic
eschatological discourse, let alone anything about the wording
of such a tradition if it existed. These questions must now be
addressed.

It seems reasonable to start, at least, from Matthew's
version of the material (Mt 24:9-14). Since he has the sayings
from the mission discourse in their original context and since
he certainly preserves other parts of the pre-synoptic
eschatological discourse, it is possible that he has preserved
the pre-synoptic tradition here. The more usual opinion is
that Matthew, having used the sayings about appearing before
the authorities in his chap. 10, substitutes something else for
these sayings when he comes to his chap. 24. This could be the
case, even granted our argument about Matthew 10: if Matthew was
familiar with the non-Markan tradition of the mission discourse
and also the Markan version of the eschatological discourse,
his 24:9-14 could still be regarded as a Matthean substitute
for the Markan material. It is arguable that Mt 24:9-14 is a
Matthean composition made up of elements taken from the Markan
eschatological discourse: compare Mt 24:10b with Mk 13:12,13
and Mt 24:11 with Mk 13:22, and note what may be regarded as
Matthean vocabulary in this section, e.g. σκανδαλίζειν and
ἀνομία. There are, however, a number of things that are not
taken account of in this apparently simple explanation and that
point in a different direction.

1. THREE OBSERVATIONS ABOUT THE MATTHEAN TEXTS

1.1. The overlap between Mt 24:9-13 and Mt 10:17-22/Mk 13:9-13

Any idea that Matthew in 24:9-14 is trying to avoid
repeating what he has said before is complicated by the fact
that he does repeat some of what he has said before exactly.
A comparison of 24:9-14 with 10:17-22/Mk 13:9-13 shows that
Matthew avoids repeating the material about the disciples
appearing before the authorities (10:17-20/Mk 13:9-11), but he
does repeat (at times almost word for word) what follows (i.e.
10:21-22/Mk 13:12,13). Thus compare:

Mt 10:17-22 (cf. Mk 13:9-11)	Mt 24:9-13
17-20 προσέχετε... παραδώσουσιν γὰρ ὑμᾶς εἰς συνέδρια	(9 παραδώσουσιν ὑμᾶς εἰς θλῖψιν)
21 παραδώσει δὲ ἀδελφὸς ἀδελφὸν εἰς θάνατον ... καὶ θανατώσουσιν αὐτούς	9 παραδώσουσιν ὑμᾶς εἰς θλῖψιν καὶ ἀποκτενοῦσιν ὑμᾶς
22 καὶ ἔσεσθε μισούμενοι ὑπὸ πάντων διὰ τὸ ὄνομά μου	καὶ ἔσεσθε μισούμενοι ὑπὸ πάντων τῶν ἐθνῶν διὰ τὸ ὄνομά μου
	10-12 καὶ τότε σκανδαλισθήσονται πολλοί .... φυγήσεται ἡ ἀγάπη τῶν πολλῶν
ὁ δὲ ὑπομείνας εἰς τέλος, οὗτος σωθήσεται.	13 ὁ δὲ ὑπομείνας εἰς τέλος, οὗτος σωθήσεται

It is seen that Mt 24:9a is similar in sense to 10:21; 24:9b
and 13 are almost identical to Mt 10:22, even though what is
together in one verse in 10:22 (and Mk 13:13) is split up in
Mt 24:9b and 13.

This evidence is rather difficult to explain on a simple
view of Markan priority; for, if Matthew is trying not to
repeat what he has already used in his chap. 10, he is very
half-hearted about it. A different explanation may be
suggested by the fact that the sayings which Matthew omits in
24:9-13 are precisely those which we previously assigned to the

mission discourse: this suggests the possibility that Matthew
did not include those sayings in his chap. 24, because he knew
that they did *not* belong here in the pre-synoptic tradition,
whereas he included the other sayings because he knew that they
did belong here.

But what would this mean for those other sayings, i.e.
10:21,22/24:9,13? If these sayings belonged in the
eschatological discourse, did they also belong in the mission
discourse? Or were they not an original part of the mission
discourse? The probable answer to these questions is that Mt
10:21,22 are an intrusion in the context of the mission
discourse.

1.2. Mt 10:21,22 an intrusion in the mission discourse

The reasons for regarding Mt 10:21,22 to be an insertion in
Matthew 10 emerged in the previous chapter, since it was argued
there that 10:23 comes as a slightly awkward afterthought
following the climactic 'he who endures to the end shall be
saved'(10:22) and that 10:23 originally went together with the
traditions of 10:17-20 (see pp.232,233 above). The almost
inevitable implication of this argument is that vv 21,22 are to
be seen as an insertion in the context. This conclusion may be
supported by the observation that vv 21,22 present a grimmer
picture than the surrounding verses in the mission discourse./1/
This is not a decisive argument; there are comparably grim
warnings later in the mission discourse (Mt 10:28-36). But
still within the immediate context (i.e. Mt 10:17-25) vv 21,22
stand out: the thought is not just of the disciples being
harassed and persecuted by their opponents, but of inter-
familial treachery and murder and of universal hatred. The
blackness of the picture in these verses and the word about
'enduring to the end' probably fit better into the eschatological
discourse than in this relatively encouraging section of the
mission discourse./2/ The surmise then that Matthew repeats
these sayings from chap. 10 (but not those about the disciples
appearing before the authorities) in the eschatological

/1/ Cf. Zmijewski, *Eschatologiereden*, 147,148.
/2/ The exact meaning of the phrase εἰς τέλος is, of course,
disputed; but it may at least be said that it has a feeling of
some finality about it.

discourse because he knew that they belonged in that context
receives support, though there are still unanswered questions,
for example about why Matthew has them at all in his chap. 10,
to which we shall return.

1.3. Mt 24:10-12 an intrusive chiastic tradition

The verses in Mt 24:9-14 that have no close parallel in
either Mt 10:17-22 or Mk 13:9-13 are vv 10-12. They read as
follows:

καὶ τότε σκανδαλισθήσονται πολλοὶ καὶ ἀλλήλους παραδώσουσιν
καὶ μισήσουσιν ἀλλήλους· 11 καὶ πολλοὶ ψευδοπροφῆται
ἐγερθήσονται καὶ πλανήσουσιν πολλούς· 12 καὶ διὰ τὸ
πληθυνθῆναι τὴν ἀνομίαν ψυγήσεται ἡ ἀγάπη τῶν πολλῶν.

Various points are notable about these verses.

1.3.1.
The verses are not just a Matthean rewording of the Mark 13/
Matthew 10 traditions, since several of the ideas contained in
these verses have no parallel in Mk 13:9-13/Mt 10:17-22, for
example the ideas of apostasy and false prophecy.

1.3.2.
It cannot very plausibly be explained that Matthew
composed the sayings to avoid being repetitious, since, if
anything they increase his repetitiousness, increasing the
number of references to 'handing over', 'hatred' and 'false
prophecy' within Matthew 24.

1.3.3.
Although there may be some Matthean stylistic features in
vv 10-12, e.g. the words σκανδαλίζειν and ἀνομία (though these
cannot be seen as exclusively Matthean terms), some of the
vocabulary is quite untypical of Matthew, e.g. ἀλλήλους used
twice in v 10 is used only once elsewhere in Matthew (25:32),
and πληθύνειν, ψύχειν, οἱ πολλοί (used as here with the definite
article) and ἀγάπη are found only here in Matthew. This could
suggest a non-Matthean origin for the verses, as could the
strongly paratactic style of the verses with καί introducing
each of the six clauses. Although Matthew could use parataxis,
he is much less fond of καί than Mark, as source critics have
often observed, and he regularly uses δέ where Mark has καί.
The only comparable passage stylistically within Matthew's
gospel is Mt 27:51-53, another eschatological tradition which

may well be non-Matthean./1/

1.3.4.

A much more significant point is that Mt 24:10-12 are a
unit of tradition with a well-defined structure. The structure
is as follows:

A.   καὶ τότε σκανδαλισθήσονται πολλοὶ
  B.   καὶ ἀλλήλους παραδώσουσιν
  B.   καὶ μισήσουσιν ἀλλήλους.
  C.   καὶ πολλοὶ ψευδοπροφῆται ἐγερθήσονται
  C.   καὶ πλανήσουσιν πολλούς.
A.   καὶ διὰ τὸ πληθυνθῆναι τὴν ἀνομίαν ψυγήσεται ἡ
    ἀγάπη τῶν πολλῶν.

The observation of this chiastic structure makes it clear that
we have here no collection of sayings carelessly strung
together; it is rather a carefully structured section on the
subject of a great apostasy.

1.3.5.

It has already been observed that Mt 24:10-12 split up the
sayings about being 'hated by all' (v 9) and about 'enduring
to the end' (v 13), which are together in Matthew 10 and Mark
13. This, together with the previous observation about the
chiastic structure of Mt 24:10-12, strongly suggest that these
verses are a distinct unit of tradition that Matthew has
inserted into this context. It seems unlikely that they are
Matthean redaction, not only because of the stylistic points
noted above, but also because it would seem odd for Matthew to
have created such a carefully structured small unity in the
middle of this section of the discourse; it is much easier to
imagine him slipping in a tradition that he had received and
which was obviously relevant to the context./2/

/1/ Cf. J. Jeremias, *New Testament Theology*, vol 1 (London:
SCM, 1971) 309,310, though see my cautions on his argument in
TynB 24(1973)45,46. For a contrary view see D. Senior, *The
Passion Narrative according to St Matthew* (Leuven: Leuven UP,
1975) 311-18.
/2/ It is just possible that the verses could have been a
tradition composed by Matthew on some other occasion and now
incorporated into the gospel. But this is a relatively
unlikely hypothesis.

1.3.6.
Before leaving Mt 24:10-12, it is worth noting that these
verses may mirror both the content and even the structure of the
central section of the eschatological discourse, at least if the
first and last clauses are understood against a Danielic
background. I have argued elsewhere that Dan 12:4, which is
translated in the LXX ἕως καιροῦ συντελείας ἕως ἂν ἀπομανῶσιν
οἱ πολλοὶ καὶ πλησθῇ ἡ γῆ ἀδίκιας, may well have been understood
to refer to a time when 'many will apostasize and evil will
multiply',/1/ and that this may lie behind the first and last
clauses of Mt 24:10-12 (σκανδαλισθήσονται πολλοὶ ... διὰ τὸ
πληθυνθῆναι τὴν ἀνομίαν...). But, even if that precise
connection is dubious, the picture in Mt 24:10a and 12 is still
of a time of great apostasy and evil, such as is associated in
the book of Daniel with the reign of Antiochus and with the
setting up of the desolating sacrilege. If such Danielic ideas
lie behind 24:10a and 12, then the following interesting
comparison can be made between the central section of the
eschatological discourse and Mt 24:10-12:

```
        Compare 24:9-28 .....        ..... 24:10-12
                (cf  Mk 13:12-23)


                                     B1. Apostasy (v 10a)
        A.  Handing over/hatred      A.  Handing over/hatred
            (vv 9-14)                    (v 10b)
        B.  Sacrilegious apostasy
            (vv 15-22)
        C.  False prophecy           C.  False prophecy (v 11)
            (vv 23-28)

                                     B2. Apostasy (v 12)
```

It turns out that 24:10-12 may be seen as a very succinct
summary of what is described at length in the central section of
the eschatological discourse./2/

/1/ See *TynB* 31 (1980) 155-162 for a more extended discussion
of Mt 24:10-12. Also on the Daniel link see McNeile, *Matthew*,
347, and Hartman, *Prophecy*, 169-72.
/2/ It would hardly be possible to argue the opposite, i.e. to
see the sayings of Mt 24:10-12 as the basis of the
eschatological discourse.

If the verses are such a summary, then various things
would follow: it would confirm that the verses are probably not
Matthean redaction, since it seems unlikely that Matthew would
create a summary of this section of the eschatological discourse
and then insert it in the eschatological discourse. It would
mean that in 24:10-12 we have a pre-Matthean and probably non-
Matthean witness to the form of the central section of the
discourse./1/ This could have all sorts of implications for
the analysis of the history of the traditions in this section:
for example, it could be significant on the one hand that
vv 10-12 do not speak of a personal Antichrist (contrast Paul)
and on the other hand that v 12 does speak of 'lawlessness'
(compare Paul's 'man of *lawlessness*'). Perhaps the suggestion
that ἀνομία is some sort of equivalent of βδέλυγμα would receive
support./2/ It could also have significant implications for the
interpretation of the eschatological discourse, since it could
indicate that the whole central section was taken to refer to
one complex of events.

However, it is not necessary to explore all these possible
implications here. The significant thing for the immediate
argument is that this suggestion about the relationship of
Mt 24:10-12 to the eschatological discourse would strengthen the
already weighty case for seeing 24:10-12 as an intrusion in its
context in Matthew 24.

2. THE PRE-SYNOPTIC 'HANDING OVER' SAYINGS IDENTIFIED

If the evidence from Matthew, which we have just examined,
is a guide, then the pre-synoptic tradition of this section of
the eschatological discourse will not have included Mt 24:10-12,
these being an insertion in the context; but it may well have
included Mt 24:9 and 13. This would explain why Matthew
repeats this material from Matthew 10, and would fit in with
the observation that Mt 10:21,22 seem to be an insertion in the
context of the mission discourse.

/1/ Note that if Mt 24:10-12 is drawing on Dan 12:4, the general
sense, but not the wording, of the LXX is reproduced. The
Matthean verses could well reflect an independent translation
of the Hebrew.
/2/ For this possibility see above, p. 179.

But the equation is not quite as simple as we may have suggested, since Mt 24:9a, παραδώσουσιν ὑμᾶς εἰς θλῖψιν καὶ ἀποκτενοῦσιν ὑμᾶς is similar, but not identical, to Mt 10:21/ Mk 13:12 παραδώσει ἀδελφὸς ἀδελφὸν εἰς θάνατον καὶ πατὴρ τέκνον, καὶ ἐπαναστήσονται τέκνα ἐπὶ γονεῖς καὶ θανατώσουσιν αὐτούς. Are we then to suppose that the pre-synoptic tradition contained the form of the saying found in Mt 24:9a, or that found in Mt 10:21, or both? How does the hypothesis of a pre-synoptic tradition account for this evidence?

There are at least three possibilities: one is that Mt 24:9a is the original form, which has been expanded in the Mt 10:21/ Mk 13:12 tradition, perhaps under the influence of Mic 7:6 and/ or of the sayings of Jesus recorded in Mt 10:34-36 (about the sword and family divisions)./1/ A second possibility is that the Mt 10:21/Mk 13:12 form is original (perhaps with an introductory τότε), and that Matthew in 24:9a has modified it./2/ But it is not obvious why Matthew should have modified this and not the following material.

The third and best possibility is that in the pre-synoptic tradition both forms were found, and that the original sequence was:

τότε παραδώσουσιν ὑμᾶς εἰς θλῖψιν
καὶ ἀποκτενοῦσιν ὑμᾶς.   (Mt 24:9)

παραδώσει (γὰρ) ἀδελφὸς ἀδελφὸν
εἰς θάνατον καὶ πατὴρ τέκνον,
καὶ ἐπαναστήσονται τέκνα ἐπὶ γονεῖς
καὶ θανατώσουσιν αὐτούς.   (Mt 10:21/Mk 13:12)

+ the sayings on hatred and endurance

/1/ Cf. Lambrecht, *Redaktion*, 137, on the possible connections. If Mt 24:10-12 is a primitive paraphrase of the relevant section of the eschatological discourse (see above p. 258), then ἀλλήλους παραδώσουσιν (24:10) could be seen as equivalent of the phrase παραδώσει ἀδελφὸς ἀδελφόν, and this could tell against the view that Mt 10:21/Mk 13:12 is an expansion of Mt 24:9a.
/2/ Zmijewski, *Eschatologiereden*, 147, notes that Mk 13:8 would lead well into Mk 13:12.

This proposal makes good sense of each of the gospels.

2.1. Matthew's evidence

The proposal involves Matthew in a simple editorial
process. We do not have to suppose that Matthew (or a pre-
Matthean editor) changed the original pre-synoptic wording,
either in 10:21 or in 24:9. He simply used the one pre-
synoptic saying in one context, and the other in the other.

The suggestion that the pre-synoptic eschatological
discourse had two handing-over sayings (a) παραδώσουσιν....
(b) παραδώσει.... may help to explain Matthew's insertion of
Mt 10:21,22 into the mission discourse (something that
needs explanation). What Matthew does is to reproduce the
παραδώσουσιν saying that belonged in the mission discourse
(Mt 10:17-20); this then takes his mind over to the similar
παραδώσουσιν saying in the eschatological discourse and leads
him to include the explanatory παραδώσει saying from that
context in the mission discourse./1/

Matthew's omission of the saying of 10:21 in his chap. 24
is presumably connected with his earlier use of it in chap. 10.
He may have wished to avoid *unnecessary* repetition, and the
saying of 10:21, being only explanatory, could be omitted
without great loss in chap. 24. It is possible that Matthew
inserted his vv 10-12 as some sort of compensation for the
omission: the phrase ἀλλήλους παραδώσουσιν in v 10 may be seen
as an equivalent of the omitted verse (see above p. 260), but
is differently expressed and thus less glaringly repetitious.
(In any case if vv 10-12 are correctly seen as a brief
paraphrase of the central section of the eschatological
discourse, then they may be seen as testimony to the presence
of Mt 10:21/Mk 13:12 in the pre-Matthean tradition.)

2.2. Mark's evidence

The converse of the argument about Matthew's location of
his 10:21,22 in the mission discourse may be applied to
Mk 13:9-13, since the proposal that the pre-synoptic
eschatological discourse had two 'handing-over'sayings -
(a) παραδώσουσιν.... (b) παραδώσει... makes it easy to

/1/ But see further discussion of the relation of Matthew and
Mark in this respect below, p. 179.

understand how Mark came to insert the παραδώσουσιν material
from the mission discourse into the eschatological discourse at
this particular point (his 13:9-11). He simply substituted the
more substantial παραδώσουσιν saying(s) from the mission
discourse, which he had not previously used, for the
eschatological discourse's παραδώσουσιν saying./1/ He then
continued with the eschatological discourse's παραδώσει saying.

     This proposal, as has been mentioned already (p. 238
above), helps to explain Mark's omission of the pre-synoptic
διώξουσιν clause from the sayings about appearing before the
authorities: it was the thought of 'handing over' that was
dominant in the eschatological discourse and that led Mark to
include the sayings from the mission discourse at this point;
the thought of 'persecution' (διώξουσιν) was a different thought
and understandably got left out in the new Markan context.

2.3. Luke's evidence

     Luke follows Mark in inserting the 'handing over' material
from the mission discourse in his 21:12-15. But his v 16 may
be seen - interestingly - as a combination of the two 'handing
over' sayings that were in the pre-synoptic eschatological
discourse (i.e. of Mt 24:9 and Mt 10:21/Mk 13:12):

     παραδοθήσεσθε δὲ καὶ ὑπὸ γονέων καὶ ἀδελφῶν καὶ συγγενῶν
     καὶ φίλων, καὶ θανατώσουσιν ἐξ ὑμῶν.

Note that Luke agrees with Matthew 24:9 in having (a) only two
clauses, one referring to handing over, the second to killing,
whereas Mt 10:21/Mk 13:12 has the additional ἐπαναστήσονται
clause, (b) in having a second person (the subject of a passive
in Luke 'You will be handed over', the object of an active in
Matthew 'They will hand you over'). But Luke agrees in other
respects in his 21:16 with Mt 10:21/Mk 13:12 - thus the
reference to relatives and the use of the verb θανατοῦν.
Lk 21:16 could be based only on Mk 13:12, and the similarities
to Mt 24:9 could be coincidental. But the distinctive form of
Luke's saying is particularly well explained from the proposed
pre-synoptic tradition with its two 'handing-over' sayings./2/

/1/ B. C. Butler, *The Originality of St Matthew* (Cambridge: CUP,
1951) 81, explains Mark's substitution of the one saying for the
other in terms of his pastoral interest in the subject of
persecution; see, e.g., Mk 10:30.
/2/ Luke's ἐξ ὑμῶν may be a reflection of the rather similar
saying of Lk 11:48/Mt 23:34, which Matthew has in a nearby
context.

2.4. Interdependence between Matthew and Mark

The proposal that the pre-synoptic tradition of the
eschatological discourse included the saying of Mt 24:9a and the
sayings of Mt 10:21,22/Mk 13:12,13 makes very good sense of the
relevant passages in Matthew, Mark and Luke, and dovetails with
our earlier observations about the mission discourse.

One final observation may be added to complete this part of
the argument: the implication of the proposal that has been made
is that, on the one hand, Mark has material from the mission
discourse in his eschatological discourse, and, on the other
hand, that Matthew has material from the eschatological
discourse in his mission discourse. Such double cross-
fertilization of the traditions could sound unlikely, but is not
really hard to imagine in view of what has been said and in view
of the similarity of the two traditions./1/ What is, however,
more surprising, if Matthew and Mark made their respective
insertions independently, is that they end up with an identical
conjunction of originally separate material in Mt 10:20 + 21 and
Mk 13:11 + 12. It is not impossible that Matthew and Mark could
have reached this result independently; but, especially when this
this evidence is taken together with the earlier observation
that they both omit the pre-synoptic διώξουσιν, it seems more
likely that there is some interdependence.

If there is such interdependence, it seems slightly simpler
to think of Matthew being dependent on Mark than vice versa.
Thus it may be slightly easier to see why Mark might have
inserted the material from the mission discourse into the
eschatological discourse (without prompting from Matthew) than
to see why Matthew should have inserted material from the
eschatological discourse into the mission discourse (without
prompting from Mark): Mark, when coming to the eschatological
discourse simply substituted one fuller παραδώσουσιν saying
(which he had earlier omitted) for another παραδώσουσιν saying,
and there was no dislocation in the sequence of thought; Matthew,
on the other hand, had less obvious reason for inserting the
παραδώσει saying into his chap. 10, especially as he was going to
use the saying(s) later anyway. Also, it may be slightly easier
to explain Mark's omission of the pre-synoptic διώξουσιν clause
than Matthew's: Mark, as has been seen, may have omitted it in

---

/1/ For another possible example of the cross-fertilizing of
these traditions see Did. 16:4 and our earlier comment on
διώξουσι there, pp. 237,238 above.

his chap. 13, because he is retaining the emphasis on 'handing-over' of the pre-synoptic eschatological discourse. (See above p. 262.)

For both these reasons it is probably easier to see Matthew as dependent on Mark rather than the opposite: Matthew, we may suppose, when he came in the mission discourse to the sayings about appearing before the authorities, was influenced by his knowledge of Mark, and following Mark he omitted the pre-synoptic διώξουσιν clause and then inserted into the context the sayings of 10:21,22, before reverting to the pre-synoptic sequence in 10:23. This suggestion may be confirmed by the observation that in 10:21,22 Matthew comes very much closer to Mark's wording than in what precedes, perhaps because here he is reproducing Mark rather than the pre-synoptic tradition. This could explain the small difference between Mt 10:20 'You will be hated by all...', which is the Markan form of the saying, and Mt 24:9 'You will be hated by all the nations', which may be the pre-synoptic (and more Jewish) form of the saying./1/

2.5. Conclusion on the 'handing over' sayings

Whether or not the suggestion that Matthew was influenced by Mark is correct, the acknowledgement of some possible interdependence between Matthew and Mark helps to account for an agreement between them that might otherwise seem surprising on the hypothesis being proposed. We conclude that the pre-synoptic tradition contained (a) the Matthean saying about handing over

---

/1/ To appeal to Matthean use of Mark could be seen as a retreat from our consistent explanation of Matthew in terms cf the pre-synoptic tradition rather than from Mark, and it might be argued that, if Matthew is influenced by Mark in 10:21,22, he might well have been similarly influenced in 10:17-20, as indeed the two-source hypothesis suggests. However, on this point note: (a) although it is possible that some of the agreements between Mt 10:17-20 and Mk 13:9-11 are due to Markan influence on Matthew (and not at all to the influence of pre-synoptic tradition), we have seen good reasons for believing that Matthew was heavily dependent on the pre-synoptic tradition in both 10:17-20 and 24:9-13. (b) There is no a priori improbability in the idea that the evangelists were heavily dependent on pre-synoptic tradition as well as interdependent.

to tribulation and death (24:9a cf. Lk 21:16), (b) the Matthew/
Mark saying about brother handing over brother (Mt 10:21/Mk 13:12
cf. Lk 21:16), (c) the sayings about universal hatred and
the call to endure to the end (Mt 10:22, 24:9b and 13, Mk 13:13,
Lk 21:17-19). We shall look further at these last sayings
(about hatred and endurance), but the ability of the hypothesis
proposed to explain the different 'handing-over' traditions in
the different gospels tells strongly in favour of the proposal.

3. THE PRE-SYNOPTIC SAYINGS ABOUT HATRED AND ENDURANCE

It has already been argued that the saying about universal
hatred (Mt 10:22a/24:9b/Mk 13:13a/Lk 21:17) and the saying
about enduring to the end (Mt 10:22b/24:13/Mk 13:13b/Lk 21:19)
were part of the pre-synoptic eschatological discourse. This
followed from the observation that they seemed to be an
intrusion in Matthew 10, and also explains why Matthew repeats
the sayings in his chap. 24.

If they were part of the pre-synoptic tradition, then the
only question that need be considered is the probable wording
of that tradition. The answer to that question is relatively
simple, since Matthew and Mark, who both had access to the pre-
synoptic form of this part of the eschatological discourse,
agree almost word for word. It seems very probable that they
both reflect the pre-synoptic form.

3.1. 'All the nations' in Mt 24:9

Their only divergence is, as has been noted, that Matthew
in 24:9 speaks of being hated by all the nations, whereas
Mark (and Luke and Matthew in 10:22) speak of being hated by
all. Various scholars have regarded Matthew as responsible for
this alteration, including recently S. Brown,[1] who argues
that Matthew has rewritten the tradition in the light of the

/1/ *JSNT* 4 (1979) 2-27, esp. p. 8. Brown's argument depends,
among other things, on his assumption that Matthew has
redactionally eliminated the references to persecution of
Christians by Jews found in Mk 13:9; we have argued that Mark
inserted this here not that Matthew eliminated it. With regard
to Brown's view that the Matthean coming of the Son of man (Mt
24:29-31) is descriptive of the fall of Jerusalem not a
reference to the parousia, see my discussion of a similar

Jewish war and who sees the sufferings described in this section
of the discourse as the sufferings that Jewish Christians
endured along with the Jews at the hands of the Romans. This
hypothesis is improbable: the discourse is addressed
specifically to the disciples, who have been very clearly
distinguished by Matthew from the Jews in the previous chapter
(chap. 23), and the sufferings being described here are 'for my
name's sake'; given this, the sufferings can hardly be the
sufferings that Christian Jews shared with Jews in the Jewish
war. In any case 'all the nations' is not a very natural
designation of the Roman armies, and it is much more likely that
the thought is of suffering in the course of worldwide mission
(cf. Mt 24:14, 25:31-46). There are no doubt simpler ways of
explaining Matthew's 'nations' compatible with the view that it
is a Matthean addition; it could simply be a case of Matthew's
desire for a little variation after 10:22.

However, it is equally possible, in view of our earlier
arguments, to regard the wording of Mt 24:9 as the original
pre-synoptic wording and to suppose that Mark, followed by Luke
(and Matthew in his 10:22, where he may well be dependent on
Mark), has dropped a reference to Gentiles that has a slightly
Jewish-Christian ring about it./1/ It is possible that in the
pre-synoptic tradition there was a progression from the thought
of Jewish and local persecution (Mt 10:21 'brother will hand
over brother') to the thought of international and Gentile
opposition (Mt 10:22 'you will be hated by all the nations'):
Matthew has preserved this sequence of thought; Mark and Luke
have obscured it slightly by the omission of 'the nations' in
the ·second saying, though their insertion of the sayings about
appearing before synagogues and sanhedrins before the sayings
about 'brother handing over brother' might reflect
consciousness of the pre-synoptic sense of that saying./2/

---

interpretation of Mark in '"This generation will not pass... "',
pp. 138-142. For another explanation of Matthew's 'nations' see
W. G. Thompson, *JBL* 93 (1974) 251-55, who again builds on a
comparison with Mark.

/1/ Cf. J. Ernst, *Die Eschatologische Gegenspieler*, 7.
/2/ But the picture is then complicated by the 'kings and
governors' of Mk 13:9, Lk 21:12.

3.2. Lk 21:18,19

If Matthew and Mark have preserved the pre-synoptic tradition in the sayings about hatred and endurance, then Luke must be thought secondary in his vv 18,19, which read καὶ θρὶξ ἐκ τῆς κεφαλῆς ὑμῶν οὐ μὴ ἀπόληται· 19. ἐν τῇ ὑπομονῇ ὑμῶν κτήσασθε τὰς ψυχὰς ὑμῶν. This supposition may be confirmed by the evidence of Acts 27:34, where we have a closely parallel saying to Lk 21:18: οὐδενὸς γὰρ ὑμῶν θρὶξ ἀπὸ τῆς κεφαλῆς ἀπολεῖται. Although this could be a reminiscence or quotation of the saying of Lk 21:18, it is quite probably a case of common Lukan phraseology in the two places./1/ It may also be confirmed by the observation that the words ὑπομονή and κτᾶσθαι in Lk 21:19 are probably Lukan (cf. 8:15, 18:12, Acts 1:18, 8:20, 22:28).

But, although both the verses in question could be Lukan redaction, it must be admitted that, whereas Lk 21:19 looks very much like a Lukan paraphrase of the Matthew/Mark saying, 21:18 is a rather mysterious interloper in the context. Why did Luke introduce this saying here, breaking the sequence between the hatred saying and the endurance saying?

One possible explanation is that the verse is a Lukan echo of, or cross-reference to, the sayings found in the mission discourse in Mt 10:28-31/Lk 12:4-7, including the saying about the hairs of the head being numbered./2/ That Luke's mind goes over to that material may not be surprising in view of the immediately preceding extract from the mission discourse (21:12-15). And yet this is a relatively complex explanation in that it involves Luke in (a) following Mark in the use in this context of material from the mission discourse, (b) picking up a saying from the mission discourse that is not used here by Mark, (c) modifying that saying quite radically, (d) placing it in a position that is slightly separated from the other verses taken from the mission discourse.

A preferable explanation is that Luke's v 18, 'Not a hair of your head will perish' is a very free paraphrase of the Matthew/Mark promise 'He who endures to the end will be saved'.

/1/ Marshall, Luke, 769, suggests that the saying sounds proverbial.
/2/ Cf. Geiger, Endzeitreden, 191.

This is suggested by the evidence of Acts 27 where the phrase
'Not a hair of the head of any of you will perish' is a
hyperbolic equivalent of the immediately preceding phrase 'your
salvation' (ὑμετέρας σωτηρίας) and where the context has
several references to being 'saved' (σῴζειν 27:20,31, cf. 27:
43)./1/ Luke, then, in 21:18 gives us a very free paraphrase
in the second person of the pre-synoptic promise about the one
who endures being saved. What then of v 19? It seems
probable that Luke realises that his v 18 is an almost
unrecognizably free paraphrase of the pre-synoptic tradition
and that it did not even mention the need for endurance. So he
adds v 19, which brings us much closer to the tradition. We
have then in vv 18 and 19 very much the same sort of editing as
in the earlier 21:12-15: Luke paraphrases quite freely, but is
conscious of the constraint of the tradition and so includes a
more literal rendering of the tradition. Whether Luke was also
influenced in his editing of vv 18,19 by theological
considerations, e.g. by a desire to portray the sufferings in
question as 'ordinary' rather than eschatological sufferings,
is doubtful, but not impossible./2/

3.3. Conclusion on the hatred/endurance sayings

The conclusion of the preceding discussion is that the
pre-synoptic sayings about hatred and endurance were as we have
them in Matthew and Mark, with Matthew's 'hated *by all the
nations*' being slightly preferable to Mark's 'hated by all'. Luke
follows Mark in his 21:17 and paraphrases freely in his vv 18,
19.

*4. THE SAYING ABOUT PREACHING TO THE GENTILES   MT 24:14/
MK 13:10*

The saying about the preaching to the Gentiles (Mt 24:14/
Mk 13:10) has been left out in the discussion of the pre-
synoptic tradition of the eschatological discourse, but a good

/1/ Note that in Acts 27 it is 'souls' that are saved - 27:10,
22,37 - and compare Lk 21:19.
/2/ Some such explanation might possibly explain why he
paraphrases the pre-synoptic saying about 'enduring' but not
the preceding saying about being 'hated'.

case can be made out for considering it a part of that
tradition.

4.1. Part of the pre-synoptic eschatological discourse

The relevant points are as follows:

4.1.1.
Since the saying is found in roughly the same context in
both Matthew and Mark, it is probable that either the one
evangelist has been influenced by the other, or that they both
knew it in this context in the pre-synoptic tradition.

4.1.2.
It has been argued that Matthew in this section of the
discourse is not dependent on Mark, or at least not wholly
dependent on Mark. Indeed, except for the inserted vv 10-12
(which are not Markan) he has followed the order and form of
the pre-synoptic tradition in vv 9-13. Given this evidence, it
is at least plausible to suggest that Matthew found v 14 in the
same pre-synoptic tradition.

4.1.3.
It may be added to this that the other sayings that
Matthew and Mark have in common in this section (i.e. the
hatred saying of Mt 24:9/Mk 13:13a and the endurance saying of
Mt 24:13/Mk 13:13b) have been seen to belong to the pre-
synoptic tradition of the eschatological discourse.

4.1.4.
We agree with most scholars that Mk 13:10 is an
interpolation in its Markan context./1/ This conclusion is
suggested (a) by the evidence of Mark itself, since v 10
interrupts the flow of thought between vv 9-11, and also (b)
by our earlier arguments concerning the original form and
context of the sayings of Mk 13:9,11,12, since the saying of
Mk 13:10 would hardly fit in the discourse about the
disciples' mission to Israel from which Mk 13:9,11,12 were
seen to be derived. This conclusion has two possibly
significant implications: (i) it means that, if the saying was

---

/1/ Against this see Beasley-Murray, *Jesus and the Future*, 252
-55, who makes an interesting, but relatively complicated
suggestion about a pre-synoptic form of Mk 13:9,10, and Bosch,
Heidenmission, 154, whose failure to see that Lk 12:11 combines
ideas from Mk 13:9 and 11 leads him to argue that Lk 12:11

in the pre-synoptic tradition, Matthew is a more likely guide
to its original position than Mark. This fits in with what has
already been suggested about Matthew in this section following
the order and form of the pre-synoptic tradition. (ii) It
lends some indirect support to the view that the pre-synoptic
tradition contained this saying: we could indeed suppose that
Mark created the saying of 13:10 or that he took it from some
unknown context and placed it in 13:10; Matthew then could
have followed Mark, except that he moved the saying to his
24:14. However, this possibility is relatively complicated: not
only does it involve Mark creating one context for the saying
and Matthew another; but, more seriously, it is not very easy
to imagine Mark creating such an awkwardly-fitting saying out
of the blue without some provocation, or even to imagine him
importing the saying from a quite different context and placing
it here./1/ It is considerably simpler to suggest that Matthew
has retained the saying in its original pre-synoptic context;
Mark then is the only one who has made an alteration, and he
has not created something or imported something from far; he
has just moved the saying forward a little (for reasons that
will be considered below).

An alternative explanation is offered by J. Lambrecht, who
argues that Mk 13:10 was created by Mark out of an underlying
form of 13:9 that read ἕνεκεν ἐμοῦ καὶ τοῦ εὐαγγελίου εἰς
μαρτύριον αὐτοῖς καὶ τοῖς ἔθνεσιν./2/ This argument for an
original 13:9 including the words καὶ τοῦ εὐαγγελίου is
ingenious, but unpersuasive. If anything, the evidence of Mk
8:35 & par. and Mk 10:29 & par., two places where Mark has ἕνεκεν
ἐμοῦ καὶ τοῦ εὐαγγελίου and Matthew and Luke do not have the
words καὶ τοῦ εὐαγγελίου, suggests that καὶ τοῦ εὐαγγελίου is
Markan redaction (not part of Mark's source). Perhaps the
addition of 13:10 could be seen as reflecting the same Markan
editorial tendency as his addition of καὶ τοῦ εὐαγγελίου in

---

shows that Mk 13:11 was originally separate from Mk 13:9.
/1/ It is not easy to imagine a saying like Mk 13:10 or even
like Mt 24:14 floating free of any context.
/2/ *Redaktion*, 124, cf. *Biblica* 47 (1966) 328, also J. P. Brown,
JBL 80 (1961) 33.

8:35 and 10:29./1/ But against any idea that Mark created the
saying, including Lambrecht's suggestion, is the difficulty of
explaining why in this case Mark created a saying that fits
uneasily in the context. It is simpler to suppose that he
found the saying in the pre-synoptic context, and moved it to
his 13:10 for some reason.

4.1.5.
Various observations about Mk 13:10 fit in with the
hypothesis that it is based on something like Mt 24:14. For
example, L. Gaston argues with some force that Mk 13:10 is
rather obscure as it stands - what does πρῶτον mean in the
Markan context? - but that it must mean what Mt 24:14 expresses
more clearly./2/ Matthew could, of course, be thought to have
improved the more difficult reading, but that leaves the
difficulty of the Markan verse unexplained. The difficulty is,
however, explicable as the result of Mark's adaptation of
something like the Matthean form for the new context: Mark, it
may be suggested, brought the phrase 'to all the nations' to
the start of the saying in order to link up with the preceding
description of appearing before kings and governors, and he
also abbreviated the whole saying, as is understandable in an
interpolated aside. This explains the relative obscurity of
his saying.

It has also been argued by some that Mk 13:10 is
distinctly Markan in style./3/ This too would be explained on
the hypothesis that the verse is Mark's adaptation of the saying
to the new context. However this argument is of doubtful
weight, since there is little in 13:10, except for the
absolute τὸ εὐαγγέλιον, that can be confidently designated as
distinctively Markan.

4.1.6
If the earlier argument about Mt 10:21-22 being an
extract from the eschatological discourse is correct and if the
saying about enduring to the end (10:22, 24:13) was followed in

---

/1/ Cf. J. Gnilka, *Das Evangelium nach Markus* 2 (Zürich:
Benziger, 1979) 189. See further below pp. 274,275.
/2/ *No Stone*, 20.
/3/ Lambrecht, *Redaktion*, 127-130; Pryke, *Redactional
Style* 53,54.

the eschatological discourse by the saying on preaching to
Gentiles (24:14), this helps explain why Matthew reverted to the
mission discourse tradition in his 10:23. He could not have the
reference to Gentile evangelization in the mission discourse
which was all about a mission exclusively directed to the 'lost
sheep of the house of Israel', and so he naturally jumps back
in 10:23 to the verse referring to the cities of Judea.

Other commentators have postulated a link between Mt 10:23
and the saying about the evangelization of the Gentiles,/1/ some
seeing Mk 13:10/Mt 24:14 as a modification of the apparently
narrow-minded 10:23. Our suggestion involves a less direct link,
which does not involve any radical rewriting of the traditions.

4.2. *Luke's omission of the saying*

The preceding six arguments add up to a strong case for
considering Mk 13:10/Mt 24:14 to have been part of the pre-
synoptic eschatological discourse. A possible difficulty with
the suggestion may seem to be Luke's omission of the saying.

But this is hardly a serious objection to the suggestion,
since Luke's omission of the saying has to be explained just as
much on the two-source hypothesis as on the hypothesis we have
proposed. Perhaps the omission may seem the more surprising if
Luke knew the saying both in the pre-synoptic tradition and also
in Mark: on the other hand, if the pre-synoptic tradition had
the saying in the Matthean position not the Markan position,
then the divergence in Luke's two sources over the location of
the saying could have contributed to his omission of the saying;
Luke could have omitted Mk 13:10 because he knew that the saying
did not belong at this point in the pre-synoptic tradition, and
he could have omitted the saying in its pre-synoptic position
under the influence of Mark. If that suggestion sounds
improbably subtle, it could more simply be that Luke omitted
Mk 13:10 because of its awkwardness in the context and that he did
not bother to put it back in its pre-synoptic position.

Other explanations have been proposed: perhaps as
plausible as any is the explanation of the omission in terms of
the sequence of thought within the Lukan form of the discourse./2/
In this section (Lk 21:12-19) Luke is describing sufferings

/1/ Cf. Lambrecht, *Redaktion*, 331,337.
/2/ Cf. J. Dupont, 'Les épreuves des chrétiens avant la fin du

'before' the end (cf. 21:12), and the saying about the end following the evangelization of the Gentiles may not have seemed to fit in well at this point. Luke's omission of 'to the end' from the saying about endurance (21:19/Mt 24:13/Mk 13:13) could reflect the same thing: Luke, it may be supposed, has in mind here the ordinary sufferings of the church (in line with the original sense of the sayings taken from the mission discourse) rather than the tribulation of the end-time. This explanation is possible, but the evidence in its favour is not very strong. Less plausible is the suggestion that Luke deliberately keeps references to the Gentile mission until after the resurrection and that Lk 24:47, 'that repentance and forgiveness of sins should be preached in his name to all nations', is Luke's equivalent of Mk 13:10./1/ Against this is (a) the evidence of Lk 21:24, if the phrase 'the times of the Gentiles' is correctly interpreted as referring to Gentile mission (see pp. 200, 201 above), and (b) the observation that the idea of the disciples being sent out in mission is a well-attested feature of the resurrection narratives, not something specially Lukan./2/ This makes it unlikely that Mk 13:10 is the source of Lk 24:47, though the wording of the Lukan resurrection tradition could possibly have been influenced by the Markan saying.

These particular explanations of Luke's omission of the saying of Mk 13:10 may not carry much conviction. The explanation may have been more mundane - see our earlier remarks about Luke working with two divergent traditions - or Luke may have been influenced by a number of factors./3/ In any case his

---

monde Lk 21,5-19' in *Trente-troisième dimanche ordinaire* (Assemblées du Seigneur, 2nd ser., 64. Paris, 1969) 83-86.

/1/ Cf. Dupont, 'La ruine du temple', 240.
/2/ Cf. Mt 28:19,20; Jn 20:21. Also see my discussion in *TynB* 24 (1973) 36-41 and I. H. Marshall, *TynB* 24, pp. 91-94.
/3/ For other explanations of Luke's omission see Zmijewski, *Eschatologiereden*, 162; Marshall, *Luke*, 768. A contributory factor could be Luke's apparent lack of partiality to the word εὐαγγέλιον. The suggestion that Luke omitted the saying because he considered the Gentile mission to be complete is quite unlikely (*contra* E. Grässer, *Das Problem der Parusieverzögerung* [Berlin: de Gruyter, 1977³] 160 and Schmid, *Lukas* 306,307).

omission is no greater difficulty for the pre-synoptic
hypothesis being proposed than for the two-source hypothesis,
and it is not a serious difficulty for either hypothesis.

4.3. The Markan location of the saying

The arguments already marshalled for regarding the saying
concerning the preaching to the Gentiles as part of the pre-
synoptic tradition pointed to Matthew having preserved the
original context of the tradition and to Mark having moved it
forward a few verses. But why did Mark move the saying from
its pre-synoptic position to its less comfortable context in
Mk 13:10?

The immediate and obvious answer to that question is that
the thought of witness for Christ's sake to 'leaders and
kings' in Mk 13:9 brought the saying about the 'gospel being
preached to all nations' to the evangelist's mind, and so he
inserted it as an aside in 13:10. It is not surprising that
that saying should have come to his mind, since, although Mark
is at this point inserting some sayings from the mission
discourse into the eschatological discourse, he still has the
relevant section of the eschatological discourse very much in
mind. He has, as it were, raided the mission discourse for a
fuller 'handing over' saying, but his train of thought is still
controlled by the eschatological discourse (hence his omission
of the διώξουσιν clause, see pp. 238,262 above, and his
reversion to the eschatological discourse in 13:12). It is
therefore not surprising that the saying about the evangelism
of the Gentiles came to Mark's mind, when he reproduced the
saying about witnessing to 'leaders and kings'. Mark therefore
inserts his 13:10, blending together the two traditions he is
using.

Mark's editing here is thus readily explained, and it is
perhaps all the more explicable if there was a Markan tendency
to amplify the phrase ἕνεκεν ἐμοῦ with the additional words
καὶ τοῦ εὐαγγελίου (8:35, 10:29. See above, pp.270,271). In this
case he amplifies the phrase ἕνεκεν ἐμοῦ of 13:9 not with the
usual words, but, because it is ready to hand, with the pre-
synoptic saying of 13:10. Mark's failure to amplify in his
usual way and his insertion of 13:10 are thus both explained.

Mark's editorial addition is particularly well-explained
if the pre-synoptic form of the saying about appearing before
rulers and kings was as in Mt 10:18 εἰς μαρτύριον αὐτοῖς καὶ

τοῖς ἔθνεσιν. It is easy to see that, if he had found this
perhaps slightly enigmatic phrase in his tradition, Mark might
have substituted for it the saying about witness to the
Gentiles, i.e. Mt 24:14/Mk 13:10.

4.3.1. Excursus 1: The wording of the 'witness' clause

The problem about the last suggestion is that it is
uncertain whether the pre-synoptic tradition did include the
words καὶ τοῖς ἔθνεσιν. G. D. Kilpatrick has argued for a
punctuation of Mark that would lend weight to the view that it
did: the relevant clause would read σταθήσεσθε ἕνεκεν ἐμοῦ εἰς
μαρτύριον αὐτοῖς καὶ εἰς τὰ πάντα τὰ ἔθνη./1/ This punctuation
would bring Mark into line with Mt 10:18, at least so far as the
phrase about witness is concerned. But Kilpatrick's view has
been criticized forcefully by several scholars;/2/ and, even
though their criticisms have been directed more effectively at
his punctuation of earlier parts of Mk 13:9 than at his
suggestion that αὐτοῖς καὶ εἰς πάντα τὰ ἔθνη be taken as one
phrase, that suggestion can only be regarded as an uncertain
possibility./3/

If Kilpatrick's punctuation of the Markan witness clause is
rejected, Matthew's καὶ τοῖς ἔθνεσιν may well be seen as
Matthew's addition to the simpler and more original Markan εἰς
μαρτύριον αὐτοῖς (cf. Luke's εἰς μαρτύριον) and not as part of
the pre-synoptic tradition. Matthew may have added the phrase
under the influence of Mk 13:10.

/1/ See 'The Gentile Mission in Mark and Mark 13:9-11' in
Studies in the Gospels, ed. D. E. Nineham (Oxford: Blackwells,
1955) 145-158 and *JTS* 9 (1958) 81-86.
/2/ E.g. A. Farrer, *JTS* 7 (1956) 75-79; Beasley-Murray,
Commentary, 42-45; Lambrecht, *Redaktion*, 134,135, Pryke,
Redactional Style, 54.
/3/ In favour of the view see Chapman, *Matthew Mark and Luke*,
79,80, and Gaston, *No Stone*, 19. If their punctuation of
Mk 13:9,10 is accepted, our suggestion about what Mark has done works
perfectly well. But in appending the saying about Gentile
evangelization Mark understandably omits the phrase 'to the
Gentiles' to avoid repetition. He does, however, understand the
preaching of the gospel to be Gentile mission (hence his
inclusion of the tradition in question here) not preaching
to Jews, *contra* Kilpatrick, 'The Gentile Mission', 155.

Against this it can be argued: (a) If our earlier
argument about Mt 10:17-20 being based on the pre-synoptic
tradition is correct, the idea that Matthew added καὶ τοῖς
ἔθνεσιν here under Markan influence seems unlikely. However,
we also argued for some Markan influence on this section of
Matthew, i.e. in the omission of the διώξουσιν clause and in
the addition of Mt 10:20,21; so it is possible that the phrase
in question is also inspired by Mark. (b) Matthew's chap. 10
is explicitly about mission to the Jews (10:5,6), and the
saying about preaching to the Gentiles would have been out of
place. It is thus quite intelligible that Matthew should have
omitted Mk 13:10 in his chap. 10 (especially as he knew the
verse's proper context). What is less intelligible is the idea
that, while omitting the Markan verse, which would have been
incongruous here, he deliberately retained from the omitted
verse the phrase καὶ τοῖς ἔθνεσιν. It would be an example of
remarkably ingenious editing, since, as Matthew uses it, the
phrase is not incongruous in his chap. 10: the thought in
Matthew is not of Gentile mission as such (contrast Mk 13:10),
but of Jewish mission that led to appearance and witness before
Gentile authorities. It is possible to see a progression of
thought from the thought of confronting Jewish authorities
(10:17) to the thought of facing Gentile authorities (10:18).
Matthew could have derived the phrase from Mark and have
integrated it into the new context in the way we have suggested;
but it is simpler to suppose that the phrase was in the pre-
synoptic tradition. (c) Mark's omission of the phrase καὶ τοῖς
ἔθνεσιν in his 13:9 is no proof that it was not in the pre-
synoptic tradition of the witness saying, since *ex hypothesi* he
has incorporated the phrase into Mk 13:10 (or he has hung the
saying on to the phrase). Indeed so far as Mark is concerned
the opposite point has already been suggested, i.e. that the
existence of the phrase in the pre-synoptic tradition helps to
explain Mark's placing of Mk 13:10 here. (d) Luke's omission
of the phrase proves little, and could be explained in various
ways. For example, he could be reflecting his Markan source in
this omission; or he could have considered the phrase redundant.
But note that Luke also omits Mark's αὐτοῖς, probably because
he has reexpressed the whole phrase in such a way that αὐτοῖς
is redundant (ἀποβήσεται ὑμῖν εἰς μαρτύριον); καὶ τοῖς ἔθνεσιν
would naturally have dropped out in the same process.

The conclusion of this discussion is that καὶ τοῖς ἔθνεσιν
may well have been part of the pre-synoptic tradition; but the
argument is fairly finely balanced, and in any case Mark's
insertion of 13:10 is explicable whichever view is correct.

Before leaving the question of the pre-synoptic wording of the 'witness' saying it may be noted that some scholars have argued that the earliest form of the saying of Mk 13:9 lacked not only καὶ τοῖς ἔθνεσιν but also εἰς μαρτύριον αὐτοῖς./1/ Even this view would not undermine the general position for which we have argued, but the view is probably to be rejected: (a) the absence of the phrase from Lk 12:11 proves nothing at all, since it is a highly compressed form of the sayings involved (see previous discussion, pp. 223-229). (b) The comparison of Mt 10:14, Mk 6:11, Lk 9:5, 10:11 does not prove anything decisive. If Mark's εἰς μαρτύριον αὐτοῖς in 6:11/Lk 9:5 is an explanatory addition to the tradition there, Mark could in fact have been influenced in this addition by the saying of Mk 13:9, since, according to the view for which we have argued, this saying belonged in the mission discourse not far from the saying of Mk 6:11. (c) The unanimity of Matthew, Mark and Luke in including the phrase in a verse where each has been seen to have been drawing on the pre-synoptic tradition (Mt 10:18/Mk 13:9/Lk 21:12,13) suggests that it was in that tradition; contrast their divergences in Mt 10:14, Mk 6:11, Lk 9:5, 10:11.

4.3.2. Excursus 2: the meaning of the μαρτύριον *phrase*
The view that Mark inserted his 13:10 to pick up the theme of 'witness' from the preceding verse could seem to be complicated by the arguments of those who understand the 'witness' of Mk 13:9 to mean testimony *for* the disciples and *against* the authorities rather than as witness *to* the Gentile rulers./2/ A negative interpretation of the phrase εἰς μαρτύριον αὐτοῖς is probable in Mk 6:11/Lk 9:5, 'Shake the dust off your feet *for a testimony to them*', and such an interpretation is also possible in Mk 13:9 & par. In that case Mark's saying about Gentile evangelization might be judged out of place in 13:10.

One way out of this might be to suggest that Mk 13:10 itself does not refer to Gentile evangelization, but to proclamation of the vindication of the gospel on the last day./3/

/1/ Cf. V. Taylor, *Mark*, 507; Gaechter, *Matthäus*, 331; Dupont, 'La Persécution', 109,110.
/2/ E.g. Kilpatrick, 'The Gentile Mission', 155. See also Lambrecht, *Biblica*, 47, 330, arguing for this meaning in Q, and L. Hartman, *Testimonium Linguae*, 62-74, on Luke.
/3/ Cf. J. Jeremias, *Jesus' Promise to the Nations* (London: SCM, 1958) 22,23, for the suggestion that this was the original meaning.

But it is improbable that the phrase 'proclaiming the gospel' was ever intended to be taken in this unusual way in this saying, and certainly Matthew's and Mark's use of the phrase excludes this interpretation so far as they are concerned.

More substantially it can be argued that μαρτύριον often has the positive sense of explaining the gospel (e.g. Acts 4:33, 1 Cor 1:6, 2 Thess 1:10, 2 Tim 1:8); and even in a context like Mk 6:11 the testimony of shaking off the dust may have been primarily a warning of judgment, but also a parting appeal to the people. Certainly in the context of Mk 13:9,11 & par. there is no reason to suppose that the testimony of the disciples is a purely negative one. More probably the thought is that they will be a testimony to the gospel both in their persons and (to judge from 13:11) especially in what they say. Whether this testimony is a blessing or curse to those who hear will depend on their response: αὐτοῖς may be taken neutrally, not as meaning 'to their advantage' or 'to their disadvantage'. If this is the correct understanding of the saying,/1/ then the thought is not at all far-removed from that of Mk 13:10, since the preaching of the gospel too leads to salvation or judgment.

But, even if this interpretation of the phrase εἰς μαρτύριον αὐτοῖς were not accepted as the original meaning, for the purposes of our argument it is only necessary to say that Mark may have understood the phrase in the sort of way suggested, and his insertion of 13:10 at this point would strongly suggest this.

4.4. The pre-synoptic wording of the saying about preaching to the Gentiles

The preceding arguments have shown that the saying about the Gentile mission was part of the pre-synoptic eschatological discourse and that Matthew has preserved its original location. Mark has moved it and Luke omitted it - both for explicable reasons. The only question remaining concerns the pre-synoptic wording.

/1/ Cf. Beasley-Murray, *Commentary*, 40,41; Bosch, *Heidenmission*, 160,161. The alternative view is perhaps more plausible in Luke than in Matthew or Mark; but for Luke too the μαρτύριον probably refers to the 'apology' for the gospel that the disciples make (cf. Lk 21:14 ἀπολογεῖσθαι).

Compare:

Mt 24:14   Mk 13:10

καὶ κηρυχθήσεται τοῦτο τὸ   καὶ εἰς πάντα τὰ ἔθνη πρῶτον
εὐαγγέλιον τῆς βασιλείας ἐν   δεῖ κηρυχθῆναι τὸ εὐαγγέλιον
ὅλῃ τῇ οἰκουμένῃ εἰς μαρτύριον
πᾶσιν τοῖς ἔθνεσιν, καὶ τότε
ἥξει τὸ τέλος

Note the following points from this comparison: (a) The two
halves of the saying are reversed in the two gospels:

Matthew's opening .... καὶ κηρυχθήσεται τοῦτο τὸ
corresponds to   εὐαγγέλιον τῆς βασιλείας
Mark's ending .... δεῖ κηρυχθῆναι τὸ εὐαγγέλιον

Matthew's ending .... εἰς μαρτύριον πᾶσιν τοῖς
corresponds to   ἔθνεσιν καὶ τότε ἥξει τὸ τέλος
Mark's opening .... εἰς πάντα τὰ ἔθνη πρῶτον.

(b) Both Matthew and Mark speak of the gospel being preached
εἰς the nations, but Matthew has εἰς μαρτύριον πᾶσιν... and
Mark more simply εἰς πάντα.... (c) Mark's πρῶτον δεῖ is
comparable in position and implied sense to Matthew's καὶ τότε
ἥξει τὸ τέλος.

How are these points to be explained? (a) The reversal of
the two halves of the saying is, as has been suggested already,
probably due to Mark's insertion of the saying into the context
of Mk 13:9-11. Mark brings the phrase καὶ εἰς πάντα τὰ ἔθνη to
the front of 13:10 in order to link up with the preceding
saying. This makes especially good sense if the preceding pre-
synoptic saying ended with καὶ τοῖς ἔθνεσιν, as does Mt 10:18:
Mark then replaces that ending with his fuller 13:10 - compare
his replacement of Mt 24:9a with his 13:9,11 - but under the
influence of that ending he brings 'to the nations' of 13:10 to
the front of the saying. It is not so easy to explain the
reverse process: Matthew would have been under no compulsion to
reverse the Markan order.

(b) Mark's εἰς πάντα τὰ ἔθνη is also explicable as the
result of his insertion of the saying into a new context. If
the pre-synoptic tradition was, as in Matthew, εἰς μαρτύριον
πᾶσιν τοῖς ἔθνεσιν, then it is even clearer than it was before

how and why Mark came to locate that saying in the context of
Mk 13:10, because the preceding saying ends εἰς μαρτύριον
αὐτοῖς (καὶ τοῖς ἔθνεσιν). But in appending the saying to this
context Mark does not wish to repeat the linking phrases: so he
(i) drops the καὶ τοῖς ἔθνεσιν from the end of 13:9 in favour
of the comparable phrase in 13:10 (see discussion above), but
(ii) he does the opposite with εἰς μαρτύριον αὐτοῖς, retaining
it in 13:9, but dropping the comparable phrase in 13:10. Only
he keeps the preposition εἰς and so ends up with εἰς πάντα τὰ
ἔθνη for Matthew's dative construction (cf. Mk 1:39). It is
not so easy to explain the reverse process: perhaps Matthew
might have changed Mark's εἰς to a dative, though Matthew seems
to like ἐν with κηρύσσειν, and ἐν ὅλῃ τῇ οἰκουμένῃ may be his
expression and phraseology. (Compare 26:13, where he has
κηρύσσειν with ἐν ὅλῳ τῷ κόσμῳ for Mk 14:9 εἰς ὅλον τὸν κόσμον.)
It is less obvious to see why Matthew should have introduced
εἰς μαρτύριον in 24:14, but it could be that Matthew, though
drawing on a pre-synoptic tradition, was also influenced by
Mk 13:9 and 10 and that he put together the two Markan phrases
εἰς μαρτύριον αὐτοῖς + εἰς πάντα τὰ ἔθνη.

    (c) Mark's πρῶτον (δεῖ) is equivalent in sense to
Matthew's καὶ τότε ἥξει τὸ τέλος, and Matthew could be supposed
to have spelled out the meaning of Mark. But the relative
obscurity of Mark's phrase is then unexplained, and it is much
more probable that Mark, having inserted Mk 13:10 into that
context, has compressed the Matthean phrase, using terminology
that occurred before in his gospel (9:11 cf. Mt 17:10).

    The conclusion of this argument is that the pre-synoptic
wording was very much as we have it in Matthew with the
possible exception of his ἐν ὅλῃ τῇ οἰκουμένῃ, which could be
his addition to the saying (perhaps as an assimilation to the
saying of 26:13, especially if the pre-synoptic form of that
saying had the word οἰκουμένη rather than κόσμος). This is
what we might expect, given our earlier conclusion that
Matthew has retained the original location of the saying and
that Mark has inserted it into a new context. Our study of the
wording of the saying tends to confirm some of our earlier
conclusions, for example, suggesting that the pre-synoptic
wording of the 'witness' saying included the words καὶ τοῖς
ἔθνεσιν.

5. CONCLUSIONS: THE PRE-SYNOPTIC TRADITION, INTER-SYNOPTIC RELATIONSHIPS AND PAUL

5.1. The pre-synoptic tradition

The conclusion of this chapter is that the pre-synoptic tradition was approximately as follows:

Then they will hand you over to tribulation and they will kill you	Mt 24:9/ /(Lk 21:16)
(For) brother will hand over brother to death and father child, and children will rise against parents and will kill them.	Mt 10:21/Mk 13:12/(Lk 21:16)
And you will be hated by all (the nations), because of my name.	Mt $\frac{24:9}{10:22}$/Mk 13:13/Lk 21:17
But he who endures to the end will be saved.	Mt $\frac{24:13}{10:22}$/Mk 13:13/Lk 21:19
And this gospel of the kingdom will be preached (in all the world) for a testimony to all the nations, and then the end will come.	Mt 24:14/Mk 13:10/

5.2. The use of the tradition in the three gospels

Matthew has preserved the tradition quite accurately, except that he omits the saying about brother handing over brother to death, and he adds in the chiastic group of sayings (his 24:10-12). Mark has substituted the 'handing over' section from the mission discourse for the first 'handing over' saying from the eschatological discourse, and he has interpolated into that mission discourse material the saying about preaching to the Gentiles, a saying which should come later in the eschatological discourse. Luke words his section (21:12-19) quite differently from Matthew and Mark. He agrees with Mark in having the 'handing over' section from the mission discourse here; but he does not interpolate the saying about Gentile mission, and in other ways too he shows knowledge of

the pre-synoptic tradition both of the mission discourse and
also of the eschatological discourse.

5.3. The inter-synoptic relationships

All three evangelists show independent knowledge of the
pre-synoptic tradition, however their traditions may be
related to each other. The fact that Luke and Mark both put
the material from the mission discourse at the same point in
the eschatological discourse most probably indicates a
relationship between those two gospels. Since Luke has already
used the tradition in question in his chap. 12, it seems more
likely that he is influenced by Mark - hence his repetition -
than that the opposite is the case. Furthermore, the moving
of the material from the mission discourse to the
eschatological discourse is more intelligible given the Markan
wording of 13:9 (παραδώσουσιν....) than the Lukan wording
(21:12). If Luke was responsible for the move, as the Griesbach
hypothesis would presumably suggest, then Mark followed Luke's
order, but reverted to the pre-synoptic (or the Matthean) form
of words; this is less simple than the supposition that Mark
made the move and that Luke followed Mark's order, but
modified his wording. So far as the relationship of Matthew
and Mark is concerned, we saw some evidence in the previous
chapter to suggest that Matthew was familiar with Mark 13 and
influenced by it in his chap. 10. But in Matthew 24 there is
little or no evidence to suggest any influence of Mark on
Matthew.

5.4. Paul's knowledge of the pre-synoptic tradition?

In the light of Paul's evident knowledge of other parts of
the pre-synoptic eschatological discourse it seems quite
probable that he will also have been familiar with the part
relating to the disciples' sufferings. Certainly in 1 and
2 Thessalonians there is a strong stress on the sufferings
(θλῖψις/θλίβεσθαι) that are the lot of the believer. It was
something that Paul had taught the Thessalonians about
(1 Thess 3:3,4), something to which they should react with
endurance (ὑπομονή) and faith, and something that will lead
those who do endure to reward in the kingdom of God at the
parousia (2 Thess 1:4-7). This seems very much the same teaching
as occurs in the eschatological discourse, and it may well be
that Paul is drawing on the discourse for these ideas, as elsewhere
in his writings (e.g. Rom 5:3 ἡ θλῖψις ὑπομονὴν κατεργάζεται and

12:12 τῇ θλίψει ὑπομένοντες)./1/

The other theme from this section that is, of course, very
important in Paul is the preaching of the gospel to the
Gentiles. Paul only uses those actual words in Gal 2:2 (cf.
Col 1:23, 1 Thess 2:9); but it is clear that for Paul the
preaching to the Gentiles was of the utmost importance and of
eschatological moment./2/ This theological idea could have
come to Paul by direct revelation. But it would also make a
lot of sense if Paul knew the saying of Mt 24:14/Mk 13:10,
which explicitly connects the preaching of the gospel to the
nations with the coming of the end.

We have earlier seen reason to link Rom 11:25 and
1 Thess 2:16 with Lk 21:24 'until the times of the Gentiles are
fulfilled'. But it may be that the earlier saying from the
eschatological discourse should also be brought in: certainly
if Mt 24:14/Mk 13:10 preceded the Lukan verse in the
eschatological discourse, as has been argued, the Lukan verse
must have been understood in the light of the earlier verse –
and hence of the Gentile mission. And it is probably that much
easier to derive Paul's thought from the two synoptic texts
than only from the relatively inexplicit Lk 21:24.

In 1 Thess 2:16 in particular there are several possible
links with the relevant section of the pre-synoptic
eschatological tradition: Paul speaks of the Jews 'preventing
us speaking to the Gentiles (τοῖς ἔθνεσιν) that they may be
saved' (σωθῶσιν). It is possible that we have here ideas
derived from the traditions of Mt 24:13,14, which speak of the
steadfast person being 'saved' (σωθήσεται) and then of the
gospel being preached to 'all the nations' (τοῖς ἔθνεσιν).
Then Paul speaks of the wrath coming on the Jews εἰς τέλος, a
phrase without any exact parallel in the Pauline corpus, but

/1/ Also in Rom 12:11,12 the phrases τῷ κυρίῳ δουλεύοντες.....
τῇ προσευχῇ προσκαρτεροῦντες both could have roots in the
eschatological discourse. Note too the references to ἀνάγκη and
θλίψις both in 1 Thess 3:7 and 1 Cor 7:26-29.
/2/ See, for example, Romans 11. Conversely opposition to the
Gentile mission is seen as the climactic sin of the Jews in
1 Thess 2:9.

with an exact parallel in Mt 24:13 & par. It does seem quite
possible that in writing 1 Thess 2:16 Paul is drawing ideas from
various parts of the eschatological discourse, including the
sayings of Mt 24:13,14 (which have the word τέλος twice), and
making his own synthesis./1/ We may have the same sort of
situation in Rom 11:25,26: if Paul is echoing the phraseology of
Lk 21:24 and Mt 24:14/Mk 13:10 in his ἄχρι οὗ τὸ πλήρωμα τῶν ἐθνῶν
εἰσέλθῃ, it is just possible that his following καὶ οὕτως πᾶς
'Ισραὴλ σωθήσεται may also be picking up some of the phraseology
of Mt 24:13 (σωθήσεται) and of Mt 24:14 (καὶ τότε ἥξει τὸ τέλος).
But the links are rather tenuous.

It is possible to speculate further and to suggest that,
if Paul knew Mt 24:14 & par., this probably lends support to the
view that the 'restraining force/restrainer' of 2 Thess 2:6,7 is,
or involves, the preaching/preacher of the gospel./2/ Note
also how in Revelation 11 the two witnesses prophesy for a set
period, after which the beast appears, or reappears, only to be
destroyed by Christ at his return./3/ But such speculations,
though not without plausibility, are unimportant for our
immediate purpose, and may be a distraction from more solid
arguments.

We conclude that in 1 and 2 Thessalonians (and elsewhere)
Paul may well reflect his acquaintance with the section of the
pre-synoptic eschatological discourse that we have been
considering; but the evidence is not so clear as by itself to
demand this explanation. The argument is only possible
confirmation of a thesis already established on other grounds.

/1/ The argument may support the view that εἰς τέλος in
1 Thess 2:16 should be interpreted to mean 'until the end' - as
this seems the probable meaning of the phrase in the context
of the pre-synoptic eschatological discourse, where it preceded
the saying of Mt 24:14.
/2/ For a useful discussion of the 'restrainer', see Holman,
Eschatological Delay, 203-28. He concludes that God is the one
who 'restrains' as he works out his plans (including for
evangelization). Cf. also Ford, *Abomination*, 211-25.
/3/ Revelation also has two calls for endurance both in
connection with the 'beast' (13:10 and 14:12), which could be
echoes of the pre-synoptic saying about enduring to the end.
Cf. also 2 Tim 2:12.

5.5. *Final observations*

The conclusions reached in this chapter about the section
of the eschatological discourse describing the coming
sufferings fit in well with the findings of previous chapters.
The pre-synoptic eschatological discourse included this section,
and it was known in this form to all three evangelists and
probably also to Paul./1/

/1/ The chapter also has interesting implications for the
interpreting of the structure of the eschatological discourse,
suggesting that the section describing the sufferings of the
disciples (Mt 24:9-14, cf. Mk 13:9-13, Lk 21:12-19) should be
taken with the following section that describes the desolation
of Jerusalem: the two sections are describing the same period
from different angles. Matthew in any case suggests this
interpretation by linking his 24:15-28 with the preceding verses
by οὖν. It may also be suggested (a) by the overlap of ideas in the
two sections, (b) by Mt 24:10-12, if these verses are correctly
seen as a summary of the relevant sections of the discourse
(see pp.258,259 above), (c) by the book of Revelation, where the
time of the beast is also the time of persecution, witness and
endurance (see pp.205-213 above, also Rev 13:10, 14:12), (d) by
the merging of ideas from the different sections in *Did*. 16:3-5.

Chapter 8

OTHER PARTS OF THE ESCHATOLOGICAL DISCOURSE

The hypothesis of a pre-synoptic form of the eschatological discourse has been established with a high degree of probability in the preceding seven chapters. This chapter does not claim to add many new arguments of substance to support the thesis; but it examines in order the sections of the discourse that have not yet been discussed, and considers how they fit in with the thesis. In view of the preceding discussion it is reasonable to approach the remaining material with the expectation that, at least where they are in broad agreement, the evangelists are probably reproducing the pre-synoptic tradition.

The ground to be covered will be:
1. The opening of the discourse (Mt 24:1-3 & par.).
2. The warnings against premature excitement (Mt 24:4-8 & par.).
3. The description of the coming of the Son of man (Mt 24:29-31 & par.)
4. The parable of the fig tree and the sayings about the timing of the end (Mt 24:32-36 & par.).

To cover so much ground in one chapter means a more superficial discussion than in the previous chapters; no attempt will be made to give a comprehensive discussion of all the questions arising in these sections, but a few remarks will be made about relevant points.

1.   THE INTRODUCTION TO THE DISCOURSE (MT   24:1-3/MK 13:1-4/LK 21:5-7)

The relevant texts are as follows:

Mt 24:1-3	Mk 13:1-4	Lk 21:5-7

καὶ ἐξελθὼν ὁ Ἰησοῦς
ἀπὸ τοῦ ἱεροῦ
ἐπορεύετο, καὶ
προσῆλθον οἱ μαθηταὶ
αὐτοῦ ἐπιδεῖξαι αὐτῷ
τὰς οἰκοδομὰς τοῦ
ἱεροῦ. 2. ὁ δὲ
ἀποκριθεὶς εἶπεν
αὐτοῖς· οὐ βλέπετε
ταῦτα πάντα; ἀμὴν
λέγω ὑμῖν, οὐ μὴ
ἀφεθῇ ὧδε λίθος ἐπὶ
λίθον ὃς οὐ
καταλυθήσεται.
3. καθημένου δὲ αὐτοῦ
ἐπὶ τοῦ ὄρους τῶν
ἐλαιῶν προσῆλθον
αὐτῷ οἱ μαθηταὶ κατ'
ἰδίαν λέγοντες· εἰπὲ
ἡμῖν, πότε ταῦτα
ἔσται, καὶ τί τὸ
σημεῖον τῆς σῆς
παρουσίας καὶ
συντελείας τοῦ αἰῶνος;

καὶ ἐκπορευομένου αὐτοῦ
ἐκ τοῦ ἱεροῦ λέγει αὐτῷ
εἷς τῶν μαθητῶν αὐτοῦ·
διδάσκαλε, ἴδε ποταποὶ
λίθοι καὶ ποταπαὶ
οἰκοδομαί. 2. καὶ ὁ
Ἰησοῦς εἶπεν αὐτῷ·
βλέπεις ταύτας τὰς
μεγάλας οἰκοδομάς; οὐ
μὴ ἀφεθῇ ὧδε λίθος ἐπὶ
λίθον ὃς οὐ μὴ
καταλυθῇ. 3. καὶ
καθημένου αὐτοῦ εἰς τὸ
ὄρος τῶν ἐλαιῶν
κατέναντι τοῦ ἱεροῦ,
ἐπηρώτα αὐτὸν κατ'
ἰδίαν Πέτρος καὶ
Ἰάκωβος καὶ Ἰωάννης
καὶ Ἀνδρέας· 4. εἰπὸν
ἡμῖν, πότε ταῦτα
ἔσται, καὶ τι τὸ
σημεῖον ὅταν μέλλῃ
ταῦτα συντελεῖσθαι
πάντα;

καί τινων
λεγόντων περὶ τοῦ
ἱεροῦ, ὅτι
λίθοις καλοῖς καὶ
ἀναθήμασιν
κεκόσμηται,
εἶπεν· 6. ταῦτα
ἃ θεωρεῖτε,
ἐλεύσονται
ἡμέραι ἐν αἷς
οὐκ ἀφεθήσεται
λίθος ἐπὶ λίθῳ
ὃς οὐ
καταλυθήσεται.
7. ἐπηρώτησαν
δὲ αὐτὸν
λέγοντες·
διδάσκαλε, πότε
οὖν ταῦτα ἔσται;
καὶ τί τὸ
σημεῖον ὅταν
μέλλῃ ταῦτα
γίνεσθαι;

1.1. Agreements of Matthew and Luke against Mark

There are a number of very small agreements of Matthew and
Luke against Mark in the introductory verses that precede the
eschatological discourse.

(a) Mark has 'one' of the disciples making the remark about the
beauty of the temple; and Jesus replies to him βλέπεις....
Matthew and Luke ascribe the remark to a group (the 'disciples'
in Matthew, 'some' in Luke), and Jesus replies accordingly οὐ
βλέπετε (Mt), θεωρεῖτε (Lk).   (b) Mark has the remark in vivid
direct speech.   Matthew and Luke both have indirect speech,
though quite different wording. (c) Jesus' reply in Mark is
βλέπεις ταύτας τὰς μεγάλας οἰκοδομάς; Matthew and Luke both lose
the reference to the buildings: οὐ βλέπετε ταῦτα πάντα (Mt) ταῦτα
ἃ θεωρεῖτε (Lk).   (d) Mark has (λίθον) ὃς οὐ μὴ καταλυθῇ, Matthew

and Luke have ὃς οὐ καταλυθήσεται. (e) Mark has the next question
addressed to Jesus by Peter and James and John and Andrew, and
one singular verb is used ἐπηρώτα. Matthew and Luke fail to
name the questioners, and have a plural main verb (Matthew:
προσῆλθον, Luke: ἐπηρώτησαν) + a participial λέγοντες. Perhaps
the evidence of Lk 17:22 may be added in: if Luke is here
drawing on the eschatological discourse, he has it addressed
πρὸς τοὺς μαθητάς; this agrees with Mt 24:3,4 since it is οἱ
μαθηταί who ask the question and receive the eschatological
discourse in reply. (f) Mark introduces the discourse proper
with ἤρξατο λέγειν αὐτοῖς; Matthew and Luke with εἶπεν (αὐτοῖς).

It would be unwise to base any argument for a pre-synoptic
tradition just on these agreements of Matthew and Luke with
each other, since they are very minor, and Matthew's and Luke's
respective agreements with Mark are much more considerable.
However, given on other grounds that there was probably a pre-
synoptic form of the tradition known to Matthew and Luke, some
or all of their agreements could well reflect the influence of
that form.

1.2.   Suggestions about the pre-synoptic form

1.2.1.   The first question: Mt 24:2/Mk 13:2/Lk 21:6
The hypothesis of a pre-synoptic form could explain the
situation in Mt 24:2 and parallels: the pre-synoptic tradition
could have been something like Matthew, perhaps βλέπετε
ταῦτα; ἀμὴν λέγω ὑμῖν, οὐ μὴ ἀφεθῇ..... Matthew is quite close
to this, though he adds πάντα to ταῦτα (cf. also 24:33 & par.).
Luke also keeps quite close, but typically avoids ἀμὴν λέγω
ὑμῖν. Mark, however, has had a single questioner in what
precedes and has added the direct speech ἴδε, ποταπαὶ λίθοι
καὶ ποταπαὶ οἰκοδομαί. So he follows this up with βλέπεις
ταύτας τὰς μεγάλας οἰκοδομάς; οὐ μὴ ἀφεθῇ...., omitting ἀμὴν
λέγω ὑμῖν, perhaps because he has changed over to a singular
(and ἀμὴν λέγω σοι would not be quite right) and because his
revised version reads well without the phrase.

1.2.2.   The second question: Mt 24:3/Mk 13:4/Lk 21:7
Another point at which the hypothesis of a pre-synoptic
tradition may help is in Mt 24:3 & par. Here, if anything, Luke
may be suspected of being most original with his simple
διδάσκαλε, πότε οὖν ταῦτα ἔσται, καὶ τί τὸ σημεῖον ὅταν μέλλῃ
ταῦτα γίνεσθαι;.

In favour of this: (1) it is not very easy to explain the
Lukan phrasing as Lukan redaction of Mark. It would be
untypical for Luke to introduce the address διδάσκαλε into a
saying which, according to Matthew and Mark at least, was
addressed to Jesus by the disciples. It is possible that Luke
means to alter the Matthew/Mark tradition in this respect, and
to have the eschatological discourse addressed to the general
public, not to the disciples. But this seems improbable (see
below pp. 291,292). As for Luke's ταῦτα γίνεσθαι, it is not easy to
see why Luke should have substituted this for Mark's ταῦτα
συντελεῖσθαι πάντα. Dupont considers that Luke has deliberately
narrowed the question because he wants to keep apart the
question of the destruction of Jerusalem and the question of the
end./1/ But, if that was Luke's intention, he is curiously
unsuccessful: he goes from the question straight into discussion
of the expectation of the second coming (vv 8,9), and later in
the discourse he does not have a very clear demarcation between
the historical and the eschatological events (e.g. 21:25 and
21:31,32).

(2) Luke's use of γίνεσθαι in the question is picked up in
what seems (within the structure of the whole discourse) to be
the direct answer, i.e. Lk 21:31,32 & par.: ὅταν ἴδητε ταῦτα
γινόμενα, γινώσκετε ὅτι ἐγγύς ἐστιν ἡ βασιλεία τοῦ θεοῦ. ἀμὴν
λέγω ὑμῖν ὅτι οὐ μὴ παρέλθῃ ἡ γενεὰ αὕτη ἕως ἂν πάντα γένηται.
Perhaps Luke could be supposed to have reworded the question to
fit the answer; but then we might have expected more
assimilation of the two sayings, e.g. with ταῦτα πάντα in both
places as in Mark.

(3) It is intelligible that Mark might have broadened
Luke's simple ταῦτα γίνεσθαι to his ταῦτα συντελεῖσθαι πάντα in
order to make the scope of the question correspond more
obviously to the scope of Jesus' answer and under the influence
of Dan 12:6,7 LXX συντελεσθήσεται πάντα ταῦτα. Mark's hanging
πάντα would be explicable thus.

(4) Matthew may then be thought to have made what is
implicit in Mark explicit, hence his τῆς σῆς παρουσίας καὶ
συντελείας τοῦ αἰῶνος.

/1/ 'La ruine du temple', 241.

1.2.3. The setting

Matthew and Mark agree (a) in having Jesus deliver the
eschatological discourse after he had 'gone out of the temple'
and (b) in regarding the discourse as addressed to the disciples.
Luke makes neither of these points clear.

It is possible to argue that Luke is secondary to Matthew/
Mark in both respects. One explanation that has been favoured
by some is that Luke quite deliberately altered the Markan
opening, because he wished to portray the discourse as public
proclamation within the temple rather than as private
instruction of the disciples outside the temple. In favour of
this it is noted that the form of address used by Jesus'
questioners in Lk 21:7, the vocative διδάσκαλε, is used
elsewhere in Luke only by people other than the disciples./1/
This particular explanation, however, is not compelling: (a) If
Luke had wished to specify that the discourse was delivered in
the temple, he could have made this much clearer than he does in
his 21:5, 'as some spoke of the temple... ' (compare the more
vivid Mk 13:1,2). (b) In 17:22 Luke makes it clear that the
disciples were the addressees in the eschatological discourse.
It is true that he might still have portrayed things differently
in chap. 21; but (c) in view of the content of the chapter, e.g.
vv 12-19,28, it is hard to suppose that Luke had a different
audience in mind. (d) So far as διδάσκαλε is concerned, this
usage here could reflect the influence of the pre-synoptic
tradition, or of Mark 13:1. But too much should not in any case
be made of it: Mark too ascribes the form of address usually to
non-disciples, but he has two exceptions (4:38, 13:1). There is
no reason why Luke should not have had an exception too; he has
no deep-seated aversion to using the noun of Jesus (cf. 22:11
and 6:40).

Although that particular explanation of Luke's redaction of
Matthew/Mark is less than cogent, there may be other possible
explanations. Luke's omission of Jesus' exit from the temple
could simply reflect a Lukan dislike of too many stage
directions. It is notable that he omits the other Markan
references to Jesus leaving Jerusalem during this period of
ministry (Mk 11:11,19), though he knows that Jesus did come and
go (cf. Lk 19:47, 21:37). His failure to mention the disciples
at least in connection with the saying about the beauty of the
temple (Mt 24:1/Mk 13:1/Lk 21:5) could reflect some Lukan
reserve towards the temple and towards temple buildings.

/1/ Cf. Dupont, 'La ruine du temple', 238.

Compare his omission of Mk 14:57-60, where Jesus is accused of
promising to destroy and rebuild the temple, also Acts 7:48,
17:24.

However, although Luke can be explained on the basis of
Matthew/Mark, it is by no means impossible that his 21:5
preserves certain features of the pre-synoptic tradition.   It is
possible that the Matthew/Mark reference to Jesus leaving the
temple is an added connection, or that it did not originally
lead straight into the dialogue that follows it.   (See n. 1
on p. 350 below.)   It is also possible that specific mention of
the disciples as the questioners in Mt 24:1/Mk 13:1 is an
addition to the pre-synoptic tradition.   Even Matthew and Mark
imply that this first question and Jesus' reply about 'stone
not being left on stone' were said in public, since they go on
to refer to Jesus being asked a further question by the
disciples 'in private' (Mt 24:3/Mk 13:3).   We have the familiar
pattern of a public pronouncement of Jesus being followed by
private explanation given only to the disciples (cf. Mt 13:10/
Mk 4:10/Lk 8:9,/1/ Mt 15:12,15/Mk 7:17, Mk 10:10).

1.2.4.   The tradition reconstructed
On the basis of the preceding arguments it is not possible
to reconstruct the pre-synoptic form of the discourse
introduction with any confidence.   But perhaps it was roughly as
follows.

> (And Jesus came out of the temple; and his disciples came
> to him and) showed him the buildings of the temple.   And he
> said to them: Do you see these things? Truly I tell you
> one stone will not be left on another that will not be
> pulled down. (And he sat down on the Mount of Olives.) And
> his disciples came to him/asked him, saying: Teacher, tell
> us when these things will be, and what will be the sign
> when these things are going to happen?

1.3.   Additional note: some implications for interpretation

Although the preceding reconstruction of the pre-synoptic
text was only tentative, it may be observed that the arguments
put forward have - potentially at least - significant

/1/ In this case only Mark specifies that the explanation was
given exclusively and privately to the disciples, though Matthew
and Luke assume that the disciples are being addressed.

implications for various scholarly theories.

For example, it has commonly been suggested that the saying
of Jesus about the destruction of the temple may be related to
the similar sayings found elsewhere in the gospels, e.g.
Mt 23:38, Mk 14:58, Lk 19:44, Jn 2:19. /1/ This possibility is not
excluded by the supposition that the saying was in the pre-
synoptic context of the eschatological discourse (see the
discussion of Lk 19:44 below pp.346-50). But at least the idea
that Mark was responsible for taking the saying from a different
context and locating it here is ruled out. The temptation to
identify all sorts of similar sayings without good reason must
in any case be resisted.

The proposals about the pre-synoptic text would also tell
against the view of R. Hummel that Matthew's οὐ βλέπετε ταῦτα
πάντα in 24:2 picks up the ταῦτα πάντα of 23:36 and means 'Do
you not understand what I have been saying about the coming
judgment on Jerusalem and the temple?',/2/ since ταῦτα in the
pre-synoptic tradition would refer back to the temple buildings
(as Mark rightly saw) not to the preceding discourse. But that
view of Mt 24:2 is implausible in any case: βλέπειν is not used
in Matthew as an equivalent of συνιέναι, but almost always
retains the idea of 'seeing'; where it is used metaphorically
(e.g. 13:13,14, which is in any case a citation from the LXX),
the thought of eyes being involved is close at hand. In its
context the οὐ βλέπετε ταῦτα πάντα of Mt 24:2 must be connected
with the immediately preceding description of the disciples
'showing' Jesus the temple buildings. There is no problem about
the gender change: for a very similar ταῦτα following a feminine
noun (also in the context of 'showing') see Mt 4:8,9: δείκνυσιν
.. πάσας τὰς βασιλείας ... ταῦτά σοι πάντα δώσω . (cf. also
19:18-20).

F. W. Burnett builds on the view that the ταῦτα πάντα of
Mt 24:2 should be linked with the same phrase in 23:36, and his
whole thesis concerning Matthew 24 depends heavily on the
opinion that Mt 24:3 is the beginning of a quite new section.

/1/ See, for example, Lambrecht, *Redaktion*, 75-79; Pesch,
Naherwartungen, 86-93; Dupont, *Biblica* 52, pp. 301-20.
/2/ *Die Auseinandersetzung zwischen Kirche und Judentum im
Matthäusevangelium* (München: Kaiser, 1963) 85,86. He has been
followed by other scholars.

He sees vv 1,2 as referring to the destruction of Jerusalem, and
vv 3ff. as a referring exclusively to the parousia. /1/ Quite
apart from the questions we have already expressed about linking
the ταῦτα πάντα of 24:2 too closely with the same phrase six
verses before, there are other objections to his tnesis:
notably, it is unnatural to split 24:1-2 from 24:3ff, and the
ταῦτα of v 3 from the ταῦτα of v 2. We have already suggested
that we have here an example of a public statement being
followed by private elucidation to the disciples, and Burnett's
argument that the ταῦτα of v 3 is explained epexegetically in
καὶ τί τὸ σημεῖον τῆς σῆς παρουσιάς ..... seems entirely
improbable. Remarkably Burnett fails even to mention Mt 24:34/
Mk 13:30/Lk 21:32, though this verse with its reference to
πάντα ταῦτα together with the following Mt 24:36 & par. has often
been linked to the opening of the discourse and could show that
Matthew in his discourse has been speaking both of an imminent
historical crisis in Judea and of the parousia. There is in any
case a strong prima facie case for such a dual focus in all
three synoptic versions of the eschatological discourse.

2. *WARNING AGAINST PREMATURE EXCITEMENT: THE BEGINNING OF THE*
    WOES (MT 24:4-8/MK 13:5-8/LK 21:8-11)

     The relevant texts are as follows:

Mt 24:4-8   Mk 13:5-8   Lk 21:8-11

καὶ ἀποκριθεὶς ὁ   ὁ δὲ 'Ιησοῦς ἤρξατο   ὁ δὲ εἶπεν· βλέπετε
'Ιησοῦς εἶπεν αὐτοῖς·   λέγειν αὐτοῖς·   μὴ πλανηθῆτε· πολλοὶ
βλέπετε μή τις ὑμᾶς   βλέπετε μή τις ὑμᾶς   γὰρ ἐλεύσονται ἐπὶ τῷ
πλανήσῃ. 5. πολλοὶ γὰρ   πλανήσῃ. 6. πολλοὶ   ὀνόματί μου λέγοντες·
ἐλεύσονται ἐπὶ τῷ   ἐλεύσονται ἐπὶ τῷ   ἐγώ εἰμι, καὶ ὁ καιρὸς
ὀνόματί μου λέγοντες·   ὀνόματί μου   ἤγγικεν· μὴ πορευθῆτε
ἐγώ εἰμι ὁ χριστός, καὶ λέγοντες ὅτι ἐγώ   ὀπίσω αὐτῶν. 9. ὅταν
πολλοὺς πλανήσουσιν.   εἰμι καὶ πολλοὺς   δὲ ἀκούσητε πολέμους
6. μελλήσετε δὲ   πλανήσουσιν.   καὶ ἀκαταστασίας, μὴ
ἀκούειν πολέμους καὶ   7. ὅταν δὲ ἀκουσήτε   πτοηθῆτε· δεῖ γὰρ
ἀκοὰς πολέμων· ὁρᾶτε   πολέμους καὶ ἀκοὰς   ταῦτα γενέσθαι πρῶτον,
μὴ θροεῖσθε· δεῖ γὰρ   πολέμων, μὴ   ἀλλ' οὐκ εὐθέως τὸ
γενέσθαι, ἀλλ' οὔπω   θροεῖσθε· δεῖ   τέλος. 10. τότε ἔλεγεν
ἐστιν τὸ τέλος.   γενέσθαι, ἀλλ' οὔπω   αὐτοῖς ἐγερθήσεται
7. ἐγερθήσεται γὰρ   τὸ τέλος.   ἔθνος ἐπ' ἔθνος καὶ
ἔθνος ἐπὶ ἔθνος καὶ   8. ἐγερθήσεται γὰρ   βασιλεία ἐπὶ
βασιλεία ἐπὶ   ἔθνος ἐπ'ἔθνος καὶ   βασιλείαν, 11. σεισμοί

/1/ Burnett, *Testament*, 117-208.

Mt 24:4-8	Mk 13:5-8	Lk 21:8-11

βασιλείαν, καὶ
ἔσονται λιμοὶ καὶ
σεισμοὶ κατὰ
τόπους· 8. πάντα
δὲ ταῦτα ἀρχὴ
ὠδίνων.

βασιλεία ἐπὶ βασιλείαν.
ἔσονται σεισμοὶ κατὰ
τόπους, ἔσονται λιμοί·
ἀρχὴ ὠδίνων ταῦτα.

τε μεγάλοι καὶ κατὰ
τόπους λιμοὶ καὶ
λοιμοὶ ἔσονται,
φόβητρά τε καὶ ἀπ'
οὐρανοῦ σημεῖα
μεγάλα ἔσται.

There is a considerable measure of agreement between the
three synoptic gospels in this opening section of the discourse.
But there are a few observations worth making in connection
with the hypothesis of a pre-synoptic discourse.

2.1. The evidence of 2 Thessalonians 2

As has already been observed (pp.176,177 above) there is
similar phraseology in 2 Thessalonians 2 and in this section of
the discourse, especially as it is worded in Matthew and Mark.

Compare 2 Thess 2:2,3   and Matthew/Mark

εἰς τὸ μὴ ταχέως
σαλευθῆναι ὑμᾶς ἀπὸ
τοῦ νοὸς μήδε
θροεῖσθαι ....
ὡς ὅτι ἐνέστηκεν ἡ
ἡμέρα τοῦ κυρίου
μὴ τις ὑμᾶς
ἐξαπατήσῃ

βλέπετε
μή τις ὑμᾶς πλανήσῃ.
πολλοὶ (γὰρ) ἐλεύσονται
ἐπὶ τῷ ὀνόματί μου
λέγοντες ὅτι ἐγώ εἰμι
(ὁ χριστός)
.... μὴ θροεῖσθε.

Given the evidence already amassed for Paul's familiarity with
the pre-synoptic eschatological discourse, the similarity here
between Paul and the synoptists in idea, expression (e.g.
θροεῖσθαι occurs only once in the NT apart from these parallels)
and context (leading up to a description of the desolating
sacrilege/man of lawlessness) can hardly be accidental, and it
seems very probable that once again Paul is drawing on the pre-
synoptic eschatological discourse. His evidence suggests that
Matthew and Mark have preserved the pre-synoptic wording
better than Luke, and it probably lends support to the view
that the many who say 'I am he' (Mark; 'I am the Christ',
Matthew; 'I am he and the moment has come near', Luke) are, or
were in the pre-synoptic tradition, people who claim to be
Christians ('in my name' - so all three synoptists) and who

prematurely announce Jesus' parousia. There is in any case
reason for adopting that interpretation of Mark's phrase./1/
Paul has no equivalent of the synoptic description of 'wars' and
'rumours of wars' (Mt 24:6-8 & par.), but this evidence cannot
plausibly be used to show that this material was absent from the
eschatological discourse. Not only would the material in
question have been irrelevant to Paul's concerns in
2 Thessalonians 2, but we have already noted that Paul focuses
on the religious rather than the political side of things in
that chapter (see above p. 218).

2.2. *The evidence of Revelation 6*

It has been noted already that Revelation 6 is roughly
parallel in contents to the eschatological discourse. This
observation may throw light on the opening section of the
eschatological discourse. The woes of Revelation 6 are as
follows:

1. Conquering

2. People killing each other with the sword

3. Famine

4. Pestilential death

/1/ So Lambrecht, *Redaktion*, 95-100, who argues that the
combination of the phrases ἐπι τῷ ὀνόματί μου and λέγοντες ὅτι
ἐγώ εἰμι demands this interpretation. So also, hesitantly,
V. Taylor, *Mark*, 504. Hartman, *Prophecy*, 159-62, argues that
the phrase is a claim to divinity, linking it with the
blasphemous claims of pagan kings in the OT, cf. Isa 47:8,10,
Zeph 2:15 and the Antiochus figure of Daniel 7-11. But he has
to explain that in the synoptics the blasphemous claim originally
associated with the desolating sacrilege has got separated from
it, and that Matthew, Luke and Paul (in 2 Thess 2:2) have
altered the original sense. None of this is necessary if the
controversial phrase is interpreted in the context of the
parousia expectation (being a dominant theme in the
eschatological discourse) rather than in the light of the
supposed OT background.

5. The dead under the altar waiting until the number of
    their brothers is completed

6. Earthquake and heavenly signs.

The sequence of ideas here is similar to what is found in the
eschatological discourse (though the earthquake comes at the
end in Revelation and earlier in the synoptics), and the first
four woes correspond to the opening section of the discourse.
The possible relevance of this in the quest for the pre-synoptic
tradition is that Revelation agrees with Luke in referring to
pestilence, something not mentioned in Matthew and Mark. On the
other hand Revelation disagrees with Luke in what follows, since
after the reference to pestilence and famine Luke refers to
'fearful things and great signs from heaven', whereas Revelation
refers to the 'slain' under the altar.

    This evidence may be quite insignificant, and it would be
unwise to make much of the very common combination of ideas -
'famine and pestilence'. But in view of the already
accumulated evidence that suggests that the author of
Revelation may have been familiar with the pre-synoptic
eschatological discourse, it may not be entirely speculative to
suggest that he may have known a tradition, which (a) included
the Lukan reference to 'pestilence', (b) did not include at this
point the Lukan references to 'fearful things and great signs',
but instead (c) went straight from the description of
earthquakes, famines, etc. into a description of the sufferings
of the saints (cf. Mt 24:9) and of the events associated with
the desolating sacrilege. (Cf. our previous discussion of
Rev 6:9-11 and Lk 21:20-24 & par. on pp. 208,209 above.)

2.3. Textual variants in Mt 24:7b, Mk 13:8b, Lk 21:11.

    The exact relationship between the three synoptic gospels
in the listing of the woes is difficult to determine. Compare:

Mt: ἔσονται λιμοὶ (καὶ λοιμοὶ) καὶ σεισμοὶ κατὰ τόπους

Mk: ἔσονται σεισμοὶ κατὰ τόπους, ἔσονται λιμοί (καὶ ταραχαί)

Lk: σεισμοί τε μεγάλοι καὶ κατὰ τόπους λιμοὶ καὶ λοιμοὶ ἔσονται,
     φόβητρά τε καὶ ἀπ' οὐρανοῦ σημεῖα μεγάλα ἔσται

The textual situation in these texts is complicated. A
large number of manuscripts add καὶ λοιμοί to Matthew's λιμοί.
This may be explained as assimilation to Luke, or simply as the
result of the association of two similar ideas; but the phrase
could be original./1/ A more serious possibility is that
Mark's text should read λιμοὶ καὶ ταραχαί; the large majority
of texts include ταραχαί, though some important manuscripts
omit it (including B and D). It is not very easy to see how or
why scribes should have added καὶ ταραχαί. One suggestion is
that it was added for the sake of improved rhythm and/or that
scribes were influenced by the following word ἀρχή./2/ The
suggestion is possible, though not very persuasive: rhythmic
considerations hardly demand the addition of anything to λιμοί,
and the derivation of ταραχαί from ἀρχή is not very obvious;
a scribe looking for another noun might more naturally have
added καὶ λοιμοί, harmonizing with Luke (cf. the textual
tradition of Matthew). On the other hand, it is possible that
an original ταραχαί dropped out of Mark by accidental
homoioteleuton (ταραχαί/ἀρχή).

Two observations may strengthen the case for retaining
ταραχαί in Mark. (a) It is interesting to observe the number
of verbs and nouns in the three gospels at this point:

Matthew   A   ἔσονται λιμοί (καὶ λοιμοί) καὶ σεισμοί...

Mark   A   ἔσονται σεισμοί ....
          B   ἔσονται λιμοί (καὶ ταραχαί)

Luke   A   σεισμοί ..... λιμοὶ καὶ λοιμοὶ ἔσονται
          B   φόβητρα ... καὶ .. σημεῖα ... ἔσται

Mark and Luke agree in having two clauses. Matthew and Luke
(and perhaps Mark in clause B) agree in having two or more
nouns in each clause. This may prove nothing at all, but it
could be that Luke reflects the original form (even if not the
wording) of the saying in having two verbs each with two (or
more) nouns, and that Matthew and Mark have simplified the
original form in different ways. If correct, this could tell
in favour of καὶ ταραχαί in Mark.

/1/ So Beasley-Murray, *Commentary*, 36,37.
/2/ Cf. Beasley-Murray, *Commentary*, 36.

(b) It has not often been noted that the Markan variant
reading καὶ ταραχαί might be connected with Luke's φόβητρά τε
καὶ...σημεῖα.. ταραχή suggests something disturbing
(literally or metaphorically), and so is not far removed in
sense from the Lukan idea. If Luke knew a Markan λιμοὶ καὶ
ταραχαί, this might explain why he added his slightly
unexpected φόβητρά τε καὶ... σημεῖα at this point after his
λιμοί καὶ λοιμοί.

Given these two observations, it seems a good possibility
that καὶ ταραχαί was in Mark. And we may go further, and
suggest that the pre-synoptic text might have been a chiastic
ἔσονται σεισμοὶ κατὰ τόπους καὶ λιμοί, ἔσονται λοιμοί καὶ
ταραχαί. It is not difficult to see how each of our synoptic
texts could have evolved from this: Matthew and Mark make some
omissions and rearrangements (for reasons that are admittedly
unclear). Luke follows the pre-synoptic form, but links λιμοί
with λοιμοί (or λοιμοί with λιμοί - according to some texts) -
a common pairing; this leaves him with ταραχαί, which he rende
renders with φοβητρά and pairs with σημεῖα (probably under the
influence of the later part of the discourse; see discussion
below, pp. 301-04).

Such an explanation of our present texts is speculative,
and no more than a possibility.

2.4. The Lukan peculiarities

In addition to his λοιμοί, which we have discussed, Luke
differs from Matthew and Mark in two respects in this opening
section of the discourse. First he has the inserted τότε
ἔλεγεν αὐτοῖς in his v 10; then he has his φόβητρά τε καὶ ἀπ'
οὐρανοῦ σημεῖα μεγάλα ἔσται in v 11.

2.4.1. Luke's τότε ἔλεγεν αὐτοῖς
Luke's distinctive τότε ἔλεγεν αὐτοῖς is a slightly
mysterious feature in the Lukan discourse, if Luke is thought
to have been dependent at this point on Mark or something like
Mark and Matthew. Why did he insert the phrase between the
warning of Mk 13:7 and the explanatory γάρ clause of Mk 13:8?

Dupont explains that Luke inserted τότε ἔλεγεν in order to
distinguish sharply between the period before the end (vv 8,9)
and the period of the end (vv 10,11)./1/ But (a) it is not

/1/ 'Les épreuves', 81.

obvious that vv 10,11 describe a quite different period (the
end-time) from vv 8,9 (the period before the end). Luke may have
inserted his τότε ἔλεγεν αὐτοῖς between the two sets of verses,
but it is still hard to distinguish the 'wars and rebellions'
of v 9 from the 'nation rising up against nation and kingdom
against kingdom' of v 10. Despite the absence of Matthew/Mark's
γάρ, Luke's v 10 (like Matthew's and Mark's equivalent verses)
seems to be description explaining and following up what has
already been alluded to in the exhortation in v 9. It seems
probable that vv 8,9 as well as vv 10,11 describe for Luke the
eschatological birthpangs - if anything, Luke's v 9b suggests
this more than Mark's v 7b - , but vv 8,9 describe only the
beginning of those pangs (to use the phrase of Matthew/Mark) and
vv 10,11 their beginning and ending (cf. the heavenly signs).
(b) It is rather mysterious that, on Dupont's hypothesis, Luke
took Mark's v 7 of the events before the end and Mark's v 8 of
the eschatological events though the one verse is explanatory
of the other in Mark. (c) Had Luke really wished to avoid
confusing the period before the end, he would have done better
to have interpreted Mark's v 8 as well as his v 7 of the events
before the end and not to have introduced his complicating
reference to 'heavenly signs' in his v 11b. He could then have
presented the whole section from vv 8-19 as events before the
end.

        Dupont's explanation of Luke's τότε ἔλεγεν αὐτοῖς is,
therefore, not convincing. But it may still be possible to
regard the phrase as Luke's addition to the tradition. There
is a rather similar Lukan phrase that is not paralleled in
Matthew or Mark in Lk 21:29 - καὶ εἶπεν παραβολὴν αὐτοῖς (cf.
also 5:36, 6:39) - and both of these additional Lukan phrases
may be seen as the evangelist's editorial devices, perhaps
simply designed to maintain narrative interest or more probably
intended to divide the discourse up into (a) an opening section
of exhortation (vv 8,9) (b) a central section of description
of future events (vv 10-28), and (c) a closing section of
conclusion and application (vv 29-end)./1/

        Some such explanation may be correct. However, the
alternative possibility is that the Lukan structure is actually
the pre-synoptic structure and that the Lukan phrase in question
derives from the pre-synoptic tradition. It may be argued that
the phrase δεῖ γενέσθαι, ἀλλ' οὔπω τὸ τέλος (Mt 24:6/Mk 13:7,

---

/1/ Cf. Zmijewski's suggestion, *Eschatologiereden*, 265.

cf. Lk 21:9) is a natural conclusion to the opening section of the
discourse; compare Mt 24:14, καὶ τότε ἥξει τὸ τέλος, which is,
according to our earlier arguments (pp. 268-75), the conclusion
of a later section. But in Matthew and Mark the phrase has lost
- or almost lost - this function in the structure of the
discourse, because the following sentence, ἐγερθήσεται
γὰρ ἔθνος ἐπ' ἔθνος ...., seems to be a continuation
of the preceding thought. The δεῖ γενέσθαι ... τέλος
thus appears after all not to be a conclusion, but more
of an incidental comment. This observation could explain why
Luke altered the Matthew/Mark tradition, but then the situation
in Matthew/Mark would be unexplained. That situation is,
however, explained if Matthew and Mark have eliminated the
Lukan phrase (or a pre-synoptic equivalent). By doing so they
have obscured the structure of the discourse.

It may in any case be thought easier to envisage Matthew/
Mark eliminating the superfluous phrase and joining the sayings
concerned with a γάρ than to envisage Luke separating the
sayings with the phrase in question./1/ We have seen other
examples of Luke retaining and Matthew/Mark eliminating such
phrases (e.g. Lk 12:41, 17:37; see pp. 57-62 and 167-170 above),
and we have seen reason to believe that Luke is influenced by the
pre-synoptic tradition in this part of his gospel, hence his
λοιμοί. There is then at least a possibility that this
Lukanism is derived from the pre-synoptic tradition.

2.4.2. Luke's φόβητρά τε καὶ ... σημεῖα
When considering Luke's additional reference to φόβητρά τε
καὶ ἀπ' οὐρανοῦ σημεῖα μεγάλα ... (21:11), two points must be
considered: (a) Immediately after this Lukan sentence, Luke has
another phrase unparalleled in Matthew/Mark πρὸ τούτων πάντων
This introduces the description of future persecutions. The
impression given through this phrase is that Luke, after
referring to terrors and heavenly signs, now goes into reverse
and considers things that must come first. (b) The description
of v 11 of φόβητρά τε καὶ ἀπ' οὐρανοῦ σημεῖα (ἔσται) is
distinctly reminiscent of the later description in v 25 of the

---

/1/ T. Schramm, *Der Markus-Stoff bei Lukas* (Cambridge: CUP,
1971), 175, claims that, had Luke been responsible for the
phrase, we would expect εἶπεν not ἔλεγεν, and he maintains that
Luke's tendency was to unify not to break up discourses (cf.
Luke 8). This is an uncertain argument: ἔλεγεν is frequent in
Luke, and the evidence of Luke 8 hardly demonstrates an
invariable Lukan tendency of the sort suggested by Schramm.

'signs in sun, moon and stars' (ἔσονται σημεῖα) and of events
that cause men to faint from fear (φόβου)./1/

When these two points are put together, the probable
explanation must be that Luke runs ahead in 21:11 from the
thought of earthquakes, famines and pestilence on to the thought
of the fearful signs that herald the end. But then he has to
check himself in 21:12 (πρὸ τούτων πάντων), and before he
describes the end he describes the persecutions and all that
must take place first./2/ As to why Luke in 21:11 telescopes
into one list the disasters before the end + the disasters of
the end, this could simply have been a case of his mind
jumping from one list to another slightly similar list. But,
if the suggestions made in the last section about the Markan
text and the pre-synoptic tradition were correct, then the word
ταραχαί could have taken Luke's mind over to the later
description of the heavenly signs and shakings that evoke
fear./3/

/1/ If Matthew's σημεῖον ... ἐν οὐρανῷ (Mt 24:30) is to be
connected with the σημεῖα of Lk 21:25, the connections become
the stronger. See later discussion of this on pp. 304-21.
/2/ Dupont is on stronger ground when he suggests that Luke
wishes to distinguish vv 12ff. (as historical events) from
vv 9,10,11 (as eschatological events), than when he makes the same
distinction with regard to vv 8,9 and 10,11 (which we discussed
above), cf. 'Les épreuves', 83-86. Luke's addition in v 11 of
φόβητρα ... σημεῖα could be seen as his attempt to make clear
that vv 10,11 have been describing the eschatological programme
of events, and his πρὸ τούτων πάντων as an attempt to show that
vv 12ff. are describing something quite different. Luke's
awareness that vv 12ff. derived from the mission discourse
could have encouraged him to differentiate this material from
the surrounding eschatological material. However, if Luke
wished to distinguish vv 12ff. as historical rather than
eschatological events, he does not make it very clear where he
reverts to the eschatological, whether at v 16, v 20 or v 25.
It is probably simpler to see Luke's πρὸ τούτων πάντων as his
announcement that, having jumped forward in the eschatological
story through his mention of the heavenly signs, he is now
jumping back to an earlier point in the same story.
/3/ If φόβητρα is a Lukan equivalent of ταραχαί, then σημεῖα
was perhaps added to balance the phrase. For the ταράσσειν
root used of eschatological shaking see Is 24:19,21,23, where
the earth is shaken and the heavenly bodies are affected.

It has been argued by others that the 'signs' of Lk 21:11 are disasters that precede the end, and that they are not the same signs as are referred to in Lk 21:25 and that happen actually at the end./1/ One argument used is that Luke's omission in the earlier context of the Matthew/Mark phrase 'these things are the beginning of pangs' (Matthew πάντα δὲ ταῦτα ἀρχὴ ὠδίνων, Mark ἀρχὴ ὠδίνων ταῦτα) shows that Luke is trying to distinguish the 'signs' of his 21:12 from the really eschatological signs of 21:25. But this argument may in fact be reversed: Luke may well have omitted the phrase 'these are the beginning of pangs', because the 'terrors and signs from heaven' which he describes in v 11 are not the 'beginning' of the pangs, but are the signs that actually accompany the end. Luke has jumped ahead beyond the 'beginning of pangs' to the end itself; and so, far from saying, as Matthew does, πάντα ταῦτα ἀρχὴ ὠδίνων, he has to say πρὸ τούτων πάντων.

It may in fact be that the Lukan phrase is a reflection of the Matthean form of the saying about the 'birth pangs', hence the two evangelists' agreement in speaking of πάντα ταῦτα (Luke: τούτων πάντων) at precisely the same point in the eschatological discourse. The way Matthew and Luke use the words is, of course, different; but, since our proposals about Luke's editing of the previous verse would also explain how Luke derived his πρὸ τούτων πάντων from Matthew's πάντα ταῦτα ἀρχὴ ὠδίνων, the suggestion that they are related is attractive.

2.4.3. Conclusions
On the basis of the preceding discussion it may tentatively be concluded that Luke's τότε ἔλεγεν αὐτοῖς may quite possibly be pre-synoptic tradition, but that his φόβητρά τε καὶ ἀπ' οὐρανοῦ σημεῖα μεγάλα are Lukan in origin. Luke may indirectly testify to a pre-synoptic ταραχαί and an original πάντα ταῦτα ἀρχὴ ὠδίνων.

2.5. Reconstruction
Various of the suggestions made above concerning the pre-synoptic form of the opening of the eschatological discourse have been speculative, and few of them have been compelling. But the evidence, such as it is, points to a reconstruction approximately as follows:

/1/ Cf. Zmijewski, *Eschatologiereden*, 124.

(And he/Jesus said)

See that no one leads you astray.
For many will come in my name saying (that) I am (the
Christ),/1/ and will lead many astray./2/
But when you hear of wars and rumours of wars, do not be
disturbed. (For) it must happen (first),/3/ but the
end is not yet. (Then he said to them) Nation will rise
against nation, and kingdom against kingdom.
There will be earthquakes in various places and famines,
there will be plagues and disturbances.
But all these things are the beginning of pangs.

*3. THE COMING OF THE SON OF MAN   MT 24:29-31/MK 13:24-27/
LK 21:25-28*

This important and central section of the discourse has
already been worked around to a considerable extent (e.g. in
chapter 4 above), and it is clear that it was in the pre-
synoptic tradition. But what was the pre-synoptic form?

3.1. Paul's evidence

The eschatological traditions that Paul transmitted to the
Thessalonians must have included description of the Second
coming, and it is possible from 1 and 2 Thessalonians to piece
together the Pauline picture of the event. This

/1/ It is probably simplest to see Matthew's 'I am the Christ'
and Luke's 'I am, and the time has come near' as expansions and
clarifications of the Markan phrase, the Lukan 'the time has
come near' being a parody of Jesus' own preaching by those
claiming to be Jesus (Mk 1:15,16. So J. Sheriff in his study
of Matthew 24).
/2/ The idea that the warnings against false prophets are a
doublet of the later verses about false prophecy (Mt 24:23-25/
Mk 13:21-23) is to be rejected on various counts: not only are
the two sections different in content, but Paul in
2 Thessalonians 2 indirectly attests both (see pp. 178,179 above.)
Both sections were, we have suggested, in the pre-synoptic
tradition.
/3/ Just possibly Luke's πρῶτον could be original, being echoed
in Mk 13:10. But the dependence may well be in the opposite
direction.

picture coincides in various respects with that given in the
section of the eschatological discourse being considered, and,
in view of Paul's knowledge of other parts of the discourse, it
seems quite probable that he is dependent on the discourse for
his picture. In any case Paul shows that the ideas in question
go back to a relatively primitive stage in Christian tradition.
The ideas common to Paul and the synoptic eschatological
discourse are these:

(1) Paul and the synoptists agree that Jesus will 'come'
(2 Thess 1:10, Mt 24:30 & par. cf. 1 Cor 16:22).

(2) The coming will be a 'heavenly' event - 'from heaven'
in Paul (2 Thess 1:7), 'in heaven' implied or stated in the
synoptics (Mt 24:30,31, Mk 13:26,27, Lk 21:27,28).

(3) It will be 'with the clouds' (1 Thess 4:17, Mt 24:30 &
par.). Although Jesus' coming is described by Paul as a
'descent' from heaven, neither he nor the synoptists refer to
Jesus arriving at the earth. Paul speaks of believers being
snatched up to meet the Lord in the air, and it seems probable
that this is the implied picture in the synoptics. (It is
explicit in Mt 24:40,41/Lk 17:34,35, if the 'taking' here is
correctly taken positively as describing salvation, as it
probably should be, following from Mt 24:31.)

(4) The coming will involve angels. So 2 Thess 1:7 and
perhaps 1 Thess 3:13, where the ambiguous ἅγιοι may be angels,
as in Zech 14:5/1/ (contrast Pauline usage elsewhere including
2 Thess 1:10). Also, 1 Thess 4:16 speaks of the archangel's
voice. Compare Mt 24:31/Mk 13:27, where the angels are sent out
to gather the elect.

(5) It will be a glorious and mighty coming. So
2 Thess 1:7-10, Mt 24:30 & par./2/

/1/ Cf. Best, *Thessalonians*, 152,153.
/2/ Orchard (*Biblica* 19, p. 32) suggests that Paul's somewhat
unusual phrase in 2 Thess 1:7 μετ' ἀγγέλων δυνάμεως αὐτοῦ echoes
the synoptic μετὰ δυνάμεως καὶ δόξης πολλῆς καὶ ἀποστελεῖ τοὺς
ἀγγέλους αὐτοῦ (Matt 24:30,31); Best (*Thessalonians* 258) and B.
Rigaux (*Epitres aux Thessaloniciens* [Paris: Gabalda, 1956] 627)
explain it as meaning - angels which belong to his power.

(6) It will be a coming to gather the elect to be with the Lord. So 1 Thess 4:14-17 (note v 14 ἄξει σὺν αὐτῷ), 2 Thess 1: 10, 2:1 (ἡμῶν ἐπισυναγωγῆς ἐπ' αὐτόν. Compare Mt 24:31/Mk 13:27 and note the use of the verb ἐπισυνάγειν.)

(7) It will be accompanied by a trumpet blast. So 1 Thess 4:16 ἐν σάλπιγγι θεοῦ and Mt 24:31 μετὰ σάλπιγγος μεγάλης (cf. 1 Cor 15:52)./1/

(8) It is a coming of judgment on the wicked. So 2 Thess 1:7-10. This is not explicit in Mark 13 (though compare 8:38). It is suggested by Mt 24:30 and Lk 21:25,26. (Cf. also Mt 24:37-51, 25:1-46).

On the basis of this evidence it may be concluded that a good number of the features of the synoptic description of the second coming are primitive and therefore could well have been in the pre-synoptic tradition. About half of the features are found in all three synoptic gospels. But the 'angels gathering together' are only in Matthew and Mark; the 'trumpet' is only found in Matthew; the theme of judgment is hinted at more in Matthew and Luke than in Mark.

3.2. Signs in heaven

The Pauline evidence does not get us very far. The synoptic evidence itself must be decisive. The opening of the section of the discourse being considered is quite different in Matthew and Mark on the one hand and in Luke on the other. Compare:

/1/ Burnett, *Testament*, 346, rules out a connection between the Pauline and the Matthean trumpets on the grounds that Matthew does not have with it the Pauline ideas of resurrection, transformation etc. But this is unpersuasive reasoning: Paul may well have known and developed something like the Matthean tradition.

Mt 24:29-30	Mk 13:24-26	Lk 21:25-27
εὐθέως δὲ μετὰ τὴν θλίψιν τῶν ἡμερῶν ἐκείνων ὁ ἥλιος σκοτισθήσεται, καὶ ἡ σελήνη οὐ δώσει τὸ φέγγος αὐτῆς, καὶ οἱ ἀστέρες πεσοῦνται ἀπὸ τοῦ οὐρανοῦ, καὶ αἱ δυνάμεις τῶν οὐρανῶν σαλευθήσονται. 30. καὶ τότε φανήσεται τὸ σημεῖον τοῦ υἱοῦ τοῦ ἀνθρώπου ἐν οὐρανῷ, καὶ τότε κόψονται πᾶσαι αἱ φυλαὶ τῆς γῆς καὶ ὄψονται τὸν υἱὸν τοῦ ἀνθρώπου ἐρχόμενον ἐπὶ τῶν νεφελῶν τοῦ οὐρανοῦ μετὰ δυνάμεως καὶ δόξης πολλῆς.	ἀλλὰ ἐν ἐκείναις ταῖς ἡμέραις μετὰ τὴν θλῖψιν ἐκείνην ὁ ἥλιος σκοτισθήσεται, καὶ ἡ σελήνη οὐ δώσει τὸ φέγγος αὐτῆς, 25. καὶ οἱ ἀστέρες ἔσονται ἐκ τοῦ οὐρανοῦ πίπτοντες, καὶ αἱ δυνάμεις αἱ ἐν τοῖς οὐρανοῖς σαλευθήσονται. 26. καὶ τότε ὄψονται τὸν υἱὸν τοῦ ἀνθρώπου ἐρχόμενον ἐν νεφέλαις μετὰ δυνάμεως πολλῆς καὶ δόξης.	καὶ ἔσονται σημεῖα ἐν ἡλίῳ καὶ σελήνῃ καὶ ἄστροις, καὶ ἐπὶ τῆς γῆς συνοχὴ ἐθνῶν ἐν ἀπορίᾳ ἤχους θαλάσσης καὶ σάλου, 26. ἀποψυχόντων ἀνθρώπων ἀπὸ φόβου καὶ προσδοκίας τῶν ἐπερχομένων τῇ οἰκουμένῃ· αἱ γὰρ δυνάμεις τῶν οὐρανῶν σαλευθήσονται. 27. καὶ τότε ὄψονται τὸν υἱὸν τοῦ ἀνθρώπου ἐρχόμενον ἐν νεφέλῃ μετὰ δυνάμεως καὶ δόξης πολλῆς.

It may at first sight seem probable that Luke has here modified
the more original form of words found in Matthew and Mark:
Luke has omitted the preceding Matthew/Mark reference to
the great θλῖψις (see earlier discussion pp.137-139), and so
here he has to modify the Matthew/Mark μετὰ τὴν θλῖψιν;/1/ he
also abbreviates and streamlines the references to the heavenly
signs (using the construction ἔσονται (γάρ) of the omitted
section). However, the picture is complicated by the fact that
he does not simply abbreviate; on the contrary he adds two
substantial sentences about events and reactions on earth,
which have no close parallel in Matthew or Mark. These
additions echo various OT passages, notably Ps 64(65) 8 LXX, and

---

/1/ It has been argued that Luke intends to loosen the link
between the historical fall of Jerusalem and the end. But (a)
his καί in v 25 does not mark a very clear break with what
precedes. (b) In vv 29-36 'these things' may (e.g. in v 36)
include the fall of Jerusalem and are closely associated with
the end.

Luke may be supposed to have created them redactionally. But
there are reasons, apart from the consideration that this
sort of redactional creation is not typical of Luke in this
chapter, for putting a question mark against this conclusion.

3.2.1. The 'signs' of Lk 21:11

Luke's reference here to 'signs' and fearful things was
anticipated by Luke in his v 11 (see previous discussion). Luke
in v 11 seemed to be drawing on this later section, not only on
its general meaning, but also on the words: compare φόβητρα ...
σημεῖα ... ἔσται with ἔσονται σημεῖα ... φόβου. It is possible
that, although in v 11 Luke uses ideas that come from later in
the discourse, the words that he uses are his own and that,
when he comes to the later section, he picks up his own words
that he has used. But this is less simple than to suppose that
he knew a tradition with this phraseology.

3.2.2. Similarity of Matthew and Luke

In support of this may be Matthew's evidence, since a
little further on in this same section he has the following:
(φανήσεται) τὸ σημεῖον τοῦ υἱοῦ τοῦ ἀνθρώπου ἐν οὐρανῷ./1/ This
rather mysterious phrase is not identical to Luke's; but it is
striking to compare this with Lk 21:11 ἀπ' οὐρανοῦ σημεῖα
(ἔσται) and Lk 21:25 (ἔσονται) σημεῖα ἐν ἡλίῳ. When the two
Lukan passages are taken together (as we suggested they should be,
pp. 301-03), Luke is seen to be closely parallel to the Matthean
wording, having σημεῖον + ἐν + an anarthrous οὐρανός (contrast
οὐρανός with the article in Mk 13:25 & par.)./2/ After their
respective references to the heavenly sign(s) both Matthew and
Luke have a balancing reference to distress on earth. Matthew
refers to the wailing of the tribes 'of the earth' (τῆς γῆς),
and Luke to ἐπὶ τῆς γῆς συνοχὴ ἐθνῶν (and then to men fainting
with fear). In addition to this curiously similar material,
Matthew and Luke have two more straightforward verbal
agreements against Mark in the saying about the Son of man's
coming: they both have (a) αἱ δυνάμεις τῶν οὐρανῶν for Mark's
αἱ δυνάμεις αἱ ἐν τοῖς οὐρανοῖς, (b) μετὰ δυνάμεως καὶ δόξης
πολλῆς for Mark's μετὰ δυνάμεως πολλῆς καὶ δόξης. These two
last agreements of Matthew and Luke are very minute, and,
although it is striking that in what precedes they both add to
Mark a reference to heavenly sign(s), their similarity there is
not very great. So it would be unwise to claim too much for

/1/ But note that the majority of MSS read ἐν τῷ οὐρανῷ.
/2/ Cf. also Did. 16:6.

this evidence by itself. But, given on other grounds the
hypothesis of a pre-synoptic form of tradition, it seems not
unreasonable to seek to explain Matthew's and Luke's convergence
in terms of that hypothesis and to suspect that Luke's σημεῖα
may be tradition not Lukan redaction.

3.2.3. Old Testament texts

The Matthew/Mark description of the sun being darkened,
the moon not giving her light, the stars falling from heaven
and the powers of heaven being shaken echoes several OT
passages. Thus Isa 13:10 reads οἱ γὰρ ἀστέρες τοῦ οὐρανοῦ καὶ
..... πᾶς ὁ κόσμος τοῦ οὐρανοῦ τὸ φῶς οὐ δώσουσιν, καὶ
σκοτισθήσεται τοῦ ἡλίου ἀνατέλλοντος, καὶ ἡ σελήνη οὐ δώσει τὸ
φῶς αὐτῆς. The word σκοτισθήσεται used with reference to the
sun resembles the Matthew/Mark description, and the description
of the moon not giving its light is very close to that in
Matthew/Mark. On the other hand, the order in Isaiah 13 -
stars, sun, moon - is different from that in the synoptics; and
the picture in Isaiah 13 is of the sun being dark when it rises,
not, as apparently in Matthew/Mark, of the sun being turned dark.
More Isaianic background is to be found in Isa 34:4, which
reads καὶ τακήσονται πᾶσαι αἱ δυνάμεις τῶν οὐρανῶν ... καὶ
πάντα τὰ ἄστρα πεσεῖται;/1/ this resembles the last two clauses
in Matthew/Mark, though the order is reversed.

The other OT passages that most resemble the synoptic
material are in Joel. First there is Joel 2:10 (= 3:15,LXX 4:15)
ὁ ἥλιος καὶ ἡ σελήνη συσκοτάσουσιν, καὶ τὰ ἄστρα δύσουσιν τὸ
φέγγος αὐτῶν. Note that we have here (a) the same order as
Matthew/Mark - sun/moon/stars, (b) the same first thought of
the sun becoming dark, (c) the word φέγγος, that is applied in
Matthew/Mark to the moon, but in Joel to the stars. Secondly
there is Joel 2:30 (LXX 3:4) ὁ ἥλιος μεταστραφήσεται εἰς σκότος
(and the moon to blood). Here we have the same thought about the
sun as is found in Matthew/Mark, though the following thought
about the moon is different./2/

/1/ This hexaplaric reading is not found in the LXX, but is
based on the MT.
/2/ On the Joel echoes cf. Lambrecht, Redaktion, 177-79,
Hartman, Prophecy, 232. But see also Dupont, 'La ruine du
temple', 249.

It is not easy to draw conclusions from such a mass of evidence. The Matthew/Mark text is a patchwork of OT allusions, and to try to say which of the OT texts was the primary influence may be a precarious exercise. However, there is something to be said for the view that the Joel passages were the primary influence, and that the other OT allusions were then drawn in. The Joel passages have (a) the idea of the sun turning dark (Joel 2:30, 2:10), though the actual word σκοτισθήσεται is found in Isa 13:10; (b) the correct order sun-moon (Joel 2:30), sun-moon-stars (Joel 2:10, 3:15); (c) the idea of the moon turning dark and the word φέγγος (Joel 2:10, but not 2:30), though the influence of Isa 13:10 is unmistakable in the moon saying. Certainly in the passage in Revelation 6 about the heavenly signs, which is no doubt related to our synoptic passage, the influence of Joel 2:30 is unmistakable, since here 'the sun became black as sackcloth, the full moon became like blood, and the stars of the sky fell' (6:12,13). It seems probable that the synoptic form of the saying has here been assimilated to the Joel wording, not that the Revelation wording is original; but the evidence shows that the author of Revelation in his mind connected the relevant tradition with Joel.

The relevance of this to Luke's σημεῖα is that Joel 2:10 reads δώσω τέρατα ἐν τῷ οὐρανῷ καὶ ἐπὶ τῆς γῆς ... ὁ ἥλιος μεταστραφήσεται εἰς σκότος. The word τέρατα is close in sense to the word σημεῖα, and indeed in the Acts quotation of the Joel passage (Acts 2:19) we find the two words used together: τέρατα ἐν τῷ οὐρανῷ καὶ σημεῖα ἐπὶ τῆς γῆς. This means that the Lukan reference to 'signs in heaven' as well as the Matthew/Mark description of the sun being darkened may be linked to Joel 2:10. A possible explanation for this might be that Luke recognized the Joel 2:10 echo in the Matthew/Mark form of the tradition, and so brought into his version a different echo of the same Joel passage. But a simpler possibility probably is that both the Lukan and the Matthew/Markan forms belonged together in the pre-synoptic tradition in some such way as:

    ἔσονται σημεῖα ἐν οὐρανῷ
    ὁ ἥλιος σκοτισθήσεται .....

this being a parallel sequence of thought to Joel 2:10

    τέρατα ἐν τῷ οὐρανῷ ...
    ὁ ἥλιος μεταστραφήσεται εἰς σκότος.

Both the Matthew/Mark and the Lukan forms of tradition are
explicable on the basis of such a pre-synoptic form; in both
cases there has been some abbreviation of the original.

This possibility would be no more than a possibility, were
it not for our earlier observations about Luke's σημεῖα (pp. 308,
309); but in the light of these observations, the suggestion has
some plausibility.

3.3. Distress on earth: Lk 21:25b,26

If the Lukan 'signs' were part of the pre-synoptic
tradition, the following Lukan phrases - 'on the earth distress
of nations in perplexity at the roaring of the sea and the
waves, men fainting with fear and with foreboding of what is
coming on the world' - must also have a claim to be regarded as
pre-synoptic tradition. Note that Matthew too has a saying
about international distress after the reference to a heavenly
sign - 'And all the tribes of the earth will mourn'./1/

3.3.1. Evidence from Revelation 6

Support for the view that the Lukan material may come from
pre-synoptic tradition may come from Revelation 6, a chapter
where the influence of the pre-synoptic tradition has already
been detected. In Revelation 6 after the description of the
signs in the heavens,/2/ there is description of disasters on
earth and of people reacting in fear: 'Every mountain and
island was removed from its place. Then the kings ... and
everyone ... hid in the caves and among the rocks of the
mountains, calling to the mountains and rocks, "Fall on us and
hide us from the face of him who is seated on the throne, and
from the wrath of the Lamb; for the great day of their wrath has
come, and who can stand before it?"' (6:14b-16). The ideas
expressed here, though not the wording, are distinctly
reminiscent of Lk 21:25,26, where people are terrified at the
roaring of the sea (compare the removal of the islands in
Revelation) and at what is about to happen. So it may be that
the author of Revelation indirectly attests the Lukan form of
the discourse.

/1/ Given the context, τῆς γῆς in Mt 24:30 is most naturally
taken to mean 'of the earth' (cf. Rev 1:7), not 'of the land'.
/2/ Compare Rev 6:12-14 sun ... moon ... stars ... heaven with
the synoptic sun ... moon ... stars ... powers of the heavens.

3.3.2. The saying of Rev 6:16 and Lk 23:30

A complicating factor, however, is the observation that, although it has some similarity to Lk 21:25,26, Rev 6:16 has even closer links with a later Lukan verse, viz. 23:30 'Then they will begin to say to the mountains "Fall on us", and to the hills "Cover us"'. The common saying derives from Hos 10:8, and the two NT uses of this OT text could be quite independent. However, it is at least striking that both Luke and Revelation have the verb order 'fall on us ... hide/cover us', whereas the MT and part of the LXX tradition of Hos 10:8 have the verbs in the reverse order. This at least must alert us to the possibility that the two NT uses of the OT verse are somehow related.

One possibility is that the author of Revelation was dependent on our Luke and brought together the two Lukan texts. Another real possibility is that the author of Revelation reflects the pre-synoptic form of the eschatological discourse and that this had the two Lukan texts together.

This possibility may sound far-fetched. But (1) it is quite possible that Lk 23:29,30 are Lukan interpolations in their present context and that both verses have been extracted from the eschatological discourse. (See pp. 347-49 below). (2) In 2 Thess 1:9 Paul may give an indirect hint that he was familiar with the Hosea saying about the 'mountains – hills' being used in connection with the description of the parousia. The hint is only indirect, because the verse actually quoted by Paul is Isa 2:10,11 LXX: εἰσέλθετε εἰς τὰς πέτρας καὶ κρύπτεσθε εἰς τὴν γῆν ἀπὸ τοῦ προσώπου τοῦ φόβου κυρίου καὶ ἀπὸ τῆς δόξης τῆς ἰσχύος αὐτου; compare 2 Thess 1:9 ὄλεθρον αἰώνιον ἀπὸ προσώπου τοῦ κυρίου καὶ ἀπὸ τῆς δόξης τῆς ἰσχύος αὐτοῦ. But the Isaianic text in question contains, quite evidently, a very similar thought to Hos 10:8 - both referring to hiding underground. It seems quite possible that Paul was led to think of the Isaiah passage by the presence in the pre-synoptic eschatological discourse of the Hosea citation, or that the eschatological discourse itself echoed the two OT verses. Certainly in Rev 6:15-17 both OT passages appear to be in mind.

3.3.3. Further light from Revelation 6

At the risk of appearing irresponsibly speculative the argument may be pressed one stage further and it may be suggested that several of the elements found in Revelation 6 and not found in the synoptic eschatological discourse may in fact have been part of the pre-synoptic discourse and that they would

cohere well together. For example, the relevant section of the
discourse could have included (after the description of the
signs in heaven):

(a) καὶ ἐπὶ τῆς γῆς ἔσται σεισμὸς μέγας.
A 'big earthquake' is mentioned in Rev 6:12, also in 11:13 (cf.
v 19) and 16:18. It is a recurrent feature in the author's
eschatological expectation, and it may have come from his
tradition of the eschatological discourse (though earthquakes
are common ingredients in Jewish apocalyptic). Note that in
16:18 the 'great earthquake' is described as 'such as has not been
since man was on the earth': this phraseology echoes Dan 12:1
and, perhaps significantly, is found in the eschatological
discourse describing the (**great**) tribulation in Mt 24:21/Mk 13:19.
The author of Revelation could have been influenced by this
verse. Note also that Luke does have a reference to 'great
earthquakes' (σεισμοὶ μεγάλοι) in 21:11, whereas Matthew and
Mark there do not have the word 'great'. Luke's addition of the
adjective would be explicable if the pre-synoptic tradition had
a reference later in the discourse to 'a great earthquake': Luke
has, as it were, conflated the earthquakes that are preliminary
to the end and the great earthquake of the end. This could help
explain why Luke has the reference to 'fearful things and
heavenly signs' in v 11: the thought of 'earthquakes' has taken
his train of thought forwards to the end-events.

(b) καὶ πᾶν ὄρος καὶ νῆσος ἐκ τῶν τόπων αὐτῶν κινηθήσονται.
Both Revelation 6 and 16 have the reference to the 'great
earthquake' followed shortly afterwards by a description of the
moving or removing of mountains and islands (6:14, 16:20). The
thought has no obvious OT or Jewish background,/1/ and its
occurrence twice in Revelation could again point to a tradition
taken from the eschatological discourse. Note that the saying
would not only follow on well from a preceding reference to a
great 'earthquake', but it would also lead on well into the
saying of Lk 21:25b about people's consternation over the
roaring of sea and waves.

(c) The substance of Lk 21:25b,26a could then have followed,
though it seems probable that Luke has paraphrased to some
extent, eliminating original parataxis.

/1/ So R. H. Charles, *A Critical and Exegetical Commentary on
the Revelation of St John* (Edinburgh: T. & T. Clark, 1920) 181.

(d) τότε ἄρξονται λέγειν τοῖς ὄρεσιν πέσατε ἐφ' ἡμᾶς καὶ τοῖς βουνοῖς καλύψατε ἡμᾶς ..... .
This wording is found in Lk 23:30 with a partial parallel in Rev 6:16.

3.3.4. Conclusion

The conclusion of the preceding discussion is that Luke's description of distress on earth may well have been taken from the pre-synoptic eschatological discourse. The evidence of Revelation 6 lends some support to this view, and it at least suggests the possibility that other material not found in the synoptic eschatological discourse (including Lk 23:30 and perhaps some other material found in Revelation 6) may have been in the pre-synoptic discourse. A similar suggestion was made earlier with regard to the saying of Mt 19:28 & par. (pp.128-34 above). But it is important to recognize that this is only an interesting possibility, not a firm or important conclusion.

3.4. The mourning of the tribes in Mt 24:30

It has been observed that Matthew, like Luke, has some material of his own in this section that is not found in either Mark or Luke (though Luke's material is slightly similar). Matthew first has a description of 'the sign of the Son of man' appearing in the heaven; we shall consider this shortly. He then has a reference to all the tribes of the earth mourning.

3.4.1. The evidence of Rev 1:7

Matthew's reference to the tribes mourning is a free quotation from Zech 12:10-14: καὶ ἐπιβλέψονται πρός με ἀνθ' ὧν κατωρχήσαντο καὶ κόψονται ἐπ' αὐτὸν ..... πᾶσαι αἱ φυλαί. The Matthean form of words, like the Lukan material just considered, has a parallel in Revelation, and the parallel is quite a close one. Thus Matthew has τότε φανήσεται τὸ σημεῖον τοῦ υἱοῦ τοῦ ἀνθρώπου ἐν οὐρανῷ, καὶ τότε κόψονται πᾶσαι αἱ φυλαὶ τῆς γῆς καὶ ὄψονται τὸν υἱὸν τοῦ ἀνθρώπου ἐρχόμενον ἐπὶ τῶν νεφελῶν τοῦ οὐρανοῦ ... and Rev 1:7 reads: ἰδοὺ ἔρχεται μετὰ τῶν νεφελῶν, καὶ ὄψεται αὐτὸν πᾶς ὀφθαλμὸς καὶ οὕτινες αὐτὸν ἐξεκέντησαν, καὶ κόψονται ἐπ' αὐτὸν πᾶσαι αἱ φυλαὶ τῆς γῆς. It seems very likely that the Matthean and Revelation traditions are related. This is suggested particularly (a) by their agreement in the wording and form of the last clause κόψονται (ἐπ' αὐτὸν) πᾶσαι αἱ φυλαὶ τῆς γῆς, which is a contraction and modification of the wording of Zech 12:10-14 LXX, (b) by the fact that both Matthew and Revelation combine the Zechariah citation with a citation of Daniel 7 about the Son of man's coming in th

clouds (although the order of the citations is opposite: Matthew
- mourning/seeing/coming in clouds, Revelation - coming/seeing/
mourning). This agreement of Matthew and Revelation would be
simply explained if the author of Revelation knew Matthew (and
modified Matthew's wording in line with the underlying OT
citation); but the author of Revelation quite probably knew the
pre-synoptic tradition, and could be drawing from it./1/

3.4.2. 'They will see'

Whatever the relationship of the Matthean and the
Revelation traditions, it is notable that in both traditions
'seeing the Son of man' and 'mourning' are linked (though in
Matthew the sequence of thought is complicated, since there is
first the appearing of the sign of the Son of man, then the
mourning, presumably provoked by the sign's appearance, and then
the seeing of the Son of man coming). It is clear that the
reference to 'seeing' in Rev 1:7 is to be linked to the
ἐπιβλέψονται of Zech 12:10 (hence the coordinate subject οἵτινες
αὐτὸν ἐξεκέντησαν in Rev 1:7), and it seems probable that the
same is true of Matthew's ὄψονται.

However, the ὄψονται is also found in Mk 13:26/Lk 21:27,
where there is no reference to the tribes mourning. In the
context of Mark and Luke the ὄψονται may be explained from
Daniel, since the seer in Dan 7:13 says ἐθεώρουν ἐν ὁράματι ...
καὶ ἰδοὺ ἐπὶ τῶν νεφελῶν τοῦ οὐρανοῦ ὡς υἱὸς ἀνθρώπου ἤρχετο./1/
If the Markan ὄψονται is correctly explained from Dan 7:13, then
it may perhaps be argued that the word brought Zech 12:10 to
Matthew's mind, and so led to his insertion of the Zechariah
quotation. But against this it may be argued that the ἐθεώρουν
of Daniel 7 is not very likely to have brought to mind the quite
different ἐπιβλέψονται of Zechariah 12, and in any case that we
might expect Matthew to have put the 'mourning' clause after the
'seeing' clause, not the other way round, if it was the
'seeing' that brought Zech 12:10 to Matthew's mind, since the
order in Zech 12:10 is 'seeing-mourning'.

/1/ Beasley-Murray, *Commentary*, 92, suggests that the phrase in
Matthew could be a scribal gloss taken from Rev 1:7. But the
textual support for its omission is minimal; and the argument we
are developing supports the originality of the phrase.
/2/ So Dupont, 'La ruine du temple', 252. He does not note the
possible Zechariah link.

An alternative and quite different suggestion is that Mark/
Luke's ὄψονται, as well as Matthew's, is to be linked with
Zech 12:10, and that Matthew's description of 'all the tribes
mourning' is probably a part of the pre-synoptic tradition
known to all three evangelists./1/ In favour of this are the
following points:

(a) Formally Zech 12:10 with its ἐπιβλέψονται πρός με is closer
to the synoptic ὄψονται than is Dan 7:13 ἐθεώρουν ... καὶ ἰδού.
The similarity is that much greater given the form of the
Zechariah citation found in Jn 19:37 ὄψονται εἰς ὃν ἐξεκέντησαν
and in Rev 1:7 καὶ ὄψεται αὐτόν ... . The use of ὄψονται/ὄψεται
for the LXX's ἐπιβλέψονται may well reflect a play on words with
κόψονται from Zech 12:10c./2/

(b) The suggestion (about the reference to the tribes mourning
being in the pre-synoptic tradition) would help explain why
there is any reference at all here in Mark/Luke to people
'seeing' the Son of man. The sense would have been perfectly
good without a reference to people 'seeing' and with a simple
description of the Son of man coming; so why does this emphasis
come in? If the Matthean reference to the tribes 'mourning'
(being an allusion to Zech 12:10c) was in the pre-synoptic
tradition, then we have an explanation as to how and why the
reference to 'seeing' comes in (from Zech 12:10b)./3/

(c) The suggestion means that we have a subject (πᾶσαι αἱ φυλαὶ
τῆς γῆς) for the otherwise impersonal ὄψονται./4/

(d) If the pre-synoptic tradition included the Matthean κόψονται
clause, it is not difficult to see why and how Mark and Luke

/1/ On the Zech 12:10 link see N. Perrin, *Rediscovering the
Teaching of Jesus* (London: SCM, 1967, 180-85); Marshall, *Luke*,
775,776.
/2/ Cf. Perrin, *Rediscovering*, 182.
/3/ We can also understand why the ἐπιβλέψονται of the LXX got
changed to ὄψονται - under the influence of the now immediately
preceding κόψονται.
/4/ Pesch, *Naherwartungen*, 167, claims that the use of the
impersonal third person is untypical for Mark, except of coming,
bringing or sending to Jesus.

might have omitted it - as a slightly obscure OT allusion./1/

The argument for explaining ὄψονται on the basis of Zech 12:10 is attractive, but not inescapable. Some have argued that the word was included in order to emphasize the visibility of the parousia and to counter the notions of the false prophets who say 'Behold here ... there' (cf. Mk 13:21 & par.)/2/ More simply it may be urged that the thought of people *seeing* the coming Son of man is an obvious one, which hardly needs subtle explanation. This point may appear to be confirmed by the observation that the idea of seeing the Son of man coming is found not only in the eschatological discourse, but also in Mt 16:28, Mt 26:64/Mk 14:62 and Ethiopic Enoch 62./3/ This may seem to show that we are dealing with an obvious and/or common idea, which does not need to be explained via Zech 12:10. However, this last point may not be quite as weighty as it looks: on the one hand, it is possible to argue that Zech 12:10 lies behind the 'seeing' of Mt 26:64/Mk 14:62, as well as behind the eschatological discourse; but this would hardly apply to Mt 16:28. On the other hand, it is possible to argue that both Mt 16:28 and Mt 26:64/Mk 14:62 may be dependent on the saying from the eschatological discourse for the reference to 'seeing the Son of man', since (i) the phrase is absent from the Markan and Lukan parallels to Mt 16:28, and Matthew may have altered the original 'see the kingdom' under the influence of the phrase from the eschatological discourse. (ii) The phrase is also absent from the Lukan equivalent of Mt 26:64/Mk 14:62,/4/ and it is possible

---

/1/ Our proposal could lend weight to the opinion of Pesch (*Naherwartungen*, 168) that the 'seeing' of Mk 13:26 is something threatening, suggesting judgment. On the other hand, while that idea may have been present in the pre-synoptic tradition, Mark's postulated omission of the saying about the tribes mourning could suggest that he is interested in the positive saving side of the parousia (cf. Dupont, 'La ruine du temple', 251-53, and Zmijewski, *Eschatologiereden*, 238, citing Mk 16:7).
/2/ Cf. Lambrecht, *Redaktion*, 180. But perhaps in this case we would expect an emphasis on everyone seeing the event.
/3/ Cf. Gnilka, *Markus*, 201.
/4/ Cf. Holman, *Eschatological Delay*, 318.

that Matthew and Mark have modified the more original Lukan form
under the influence of the eschatological discourse. But in any
case this saying could be considered an echo of the earlier
discourse.

The conclusion must be that the ὄψονται in the
eschatological discourse need not be explained on the basis of
Zech 12:10, but could well be so explained./1/ The case, then,
for the inclusion in the pre-synoptic tradition of the Matthean
citation of the OT verse is not proven, but not implausible.

3.5 The sign of the Son of man: Mt 24:30

3.5.1. Problems of interpretation
The Matthean 'sign of the Son of man' is one of the most
enigmatic features of his version of the eschatological
discourse. Scholars are unclear as to what the sign is intended
to be, as to where the idea comes from, and as to how it fits
into the Matthean chapter. Many opt for the view that the sign
is the coming Son of man himself./2/ But a (perhaps not
insuperable) problem with that is that the coming of the Son of
man is described two sentences later ('They will see the Son of
man coming ...'), and so other scholars (and the ancient
commentators who identified the sign with the cross) prefer the
view that the sign is some premonitory sign in the sky./3/ Some
scholars have explained the sign from the OT, since there are a
number of OT references to a 'standard' being raised - in
connection with the gathering of the people (e.g. Isa 11:12) and
in connection with the blowing of the trumpet (e.g. Isa 18:3,

---

/1/ Cf. E. Schweizer, *Matthew*, 457. Perrin, *Rediscovering*,
180-85, recognizes the significance of Zech 12:10 for the
'seeing' motif. He suggests that the testimonium with its
reference to 'piercing' was originally used of the crucifixion
(as in Jn 19:37) and then subsequently of the parousia. But it
is quite as likely that the testimonium with its reference to
remorse after the piercing was understood from the beginning to
refer to a post-crucifixion event, i.e. as a prophecy of the
parousia.
/2/ E.g. S. Brown, *JSNT* 4, p. 13.
/3/ E.g. K. Rengstorf, *TWNT* VII, 236-38.

Jer 4:21, 51:27)./1/

    This certainly has attractions, given the occurrence of
all those themes in the Matthean context, although the 'sign'
is not very closely connected with the trumpet or the gathering
in Matthew. Some scholars have linked the Matthean 'sign' with
the disciples' question of Mt 24:3 'What is the sign of your
parousia?'; but it is that question which seems to be left so
obscure in v 30! More plausibly others have seen the 'sign of
the Son of man' as a counterpart to the 'great signs' of the
false Christs and false prophets of Mt 24:24: in that earlier
passage the false prophets with their signs and deceptive
claims are contrasted with the Son of man whose coming is like
lightning that goes from the East and shines (φαίνεται) to
the West. It seems quite probable that the thought of this
passage is being picked up in v 30 with its description of the
sign of the Son of man that appears (φανήσεται) in heaven.

    3.5.2. The question of origin
    However, the significant point for our discussion is the
question of the origin of the saying, not the question of its
meaning within Matthew (though the two questions may not be
unrelated). It is possible to see the saying as wholly
Matthean and, for example, to suggest that Matthew has added it
(and the saying about all the tribes mourning) in order to
bring out the fact that the Son of man's coming will be utterly
visible to all./2/ But, although this may perhaps be one
effect of the addition, it must be said that Matthew has chosen
a remarkably obscure or complicated way of making the point.
It is true that, if his vv 26,27 are regarded as Matthew's
addition to the discourse, then his v 30 could be seen as a
similar addition. But vv 26,27 make the point quite clearly
(contrast v 30), and in any case we have argued that vv 26,27
were part of the pre-synoptic tradition.

    A number of other considerations favour the view that the
saying is pre-Matthean and that it goes back to the pre-synoptic
tradition. The fact that the saying is rather difficult to
interpret might suggest this;/3/ at least its omission by Mark

---

/1/ Cf. Beasley-Murray, *Commentary*, 92,93; E. Schweizer,
Matthew, 455,456.
/2/ Cf. Gundry, *Matthew*, 488.
/3/ Cf. Butler, *Originality of St Matthew*, 78.

and Luke would occasion no surprise. If the saying is picking up the theme of vv 24-27, albeit rather obscurely, this could favour a pre-synoptic origin, since the earlier verses were deemed part of the pre-synoptic tradition. If there is anything in the suggestion that the Matthean 'sign' and 'trumpet' have common OT background, then, as the 'trumpet' was probably part of the pre-synoptic tradition, the 'sign' may also have belonged there. In any case the earlier conclusion about the pre-synoptic origin of the Matthean trumpet must at least make us open to the possibility that other distinctively Matthean elements (including both the saying about the 'sign' and the saying about the tribes mourning) may also be traditional.

The further point that we have already noted about Matthew's sign and to which we must now return is that the phrase in question is somewhat similar to the Lukan description of heavenly 'signs' (Luke 21:25, cf. 21:11 and the discussion on pp. 308,309 above). It was suggested that Matthew and Luke in some way support each other by adding to Mark their respective references to heavenly signs. But how do they support each other? It was proposed that Luke knew a tradition that opened 'There will be signs in heaven. The sun will be darkened... '. It is possible that Matthew's 'sign of the Son of man' is somehow derived from this. But it is not obvious how Matthew got his obscure wording out of Luke's simpler wording, nor why he altered the position of the sayings. This, however, does not mean necessarily that there is nothing in the argument about the similarity of Matthew and Luke. It seems possible that the explanation here, as elsewhere, is that the respective Lukan and Matthean traditions both go back to the pre-synoptic tradition and that they complement each other.

3.6. A proposed pre-synoptic form

The pre-synoptic form could, we suggest, have been something like this:

1. And (after the distress of those days) there will be signs in heaven.

2. The sun will be darkened, the moon will not give her light; the stars will fall from heaven, and the powers of the heavens will be shaken.

3. And on earth there will be a great earthquake. And
    every mountain and island will be moved from their
    places. There will be confusion of nations in
    perplexity at the roaring of the sea and the waves.
    Men will faint with fear and anticipation at the things
    coming on the earth.
    They will (begin to) say to the mountains 'Fall on us'
    and to the hills 'Cover us'./1/

4. And then will appear the sign of the Son of man in
    heaven.
    And then all the tribes of the earth will mourn.
    And they will see the Son of man coming on the clouds
    (of heaven) with power and great glory.

Perhaps the most attractive thing about this reconstruction
is that it helps to explain the Matthean 'sign of the Son of man'
(even if it does not solve the question of its meaning). It is
not very clear how the phrase fits into the canonical gospel of
Matthew; but in the proposed pre-synoptic tradition the phrase
picks up the preceding 'There will be signs in heaven', and
there is an intelligible sequence of thought with a description
of general 'signs of heaven' + disasters on earth leading on to
the particular 'sign of the Son of man in heaven'. This sign
should most probably be understood in the light of the preceding
saying of Mt 24:27, but the phraseology used is more an echo of
the immediately preceding 'There will be signs in heaven' than
of the 'signs' of the false prophets of 24:24.

The proposed reconstruction means that the similar Matthean
and Lukan traditions are not the same; but they are
complementary to each other. And Matthew and Luke indirectly
testify to each other.

*3.6.1. The relationship of the pre-synoptic and synoptic
traditions*
It is not difficult to see how our present synoptic texts
could have evolved from the pre-synoptic form proposed. Each
of the evangelists has abbreviated the tradition. Mark has done
so most radically, omitting all reference to the distress on
earth, and going directly from the description of the heavenly

---

/1/ The reconstruction of this section is very tentative. See
earlier discussion, pp. 307-14 .

Jesus' eschatological discourse

signs, which he abbreviates slightly, to the description of the
heavenly coming of the Son of man. Matthew follows Mark to
begin with, but then includes the sayings about the sign of the
Son of man and about the mourning of the tribes. Luke appears
relatively independent: he abbreviates the opening description
of the heavenly signs but in a quite different way from Matthew
and Mark; he then reproduces the pre-synoptic description of
terrestrial distress (his 25b,26a), probably in an abbreviated
and edited form. Then like Mark he omits the sayings about the
sign of the Son of man and the mourning of the tribes. One
uncertainty on this hypothesis is why Luke has his 'for the
powers of the heavens shall be shaken' after, not before, the
description of the earthly distress. It is possible that he has
preserved the original order; but it seems more likely that his
compression of the description of the heavenly signs led to his
omission of the phrase at the earlier point and that he
reintroduces it here, perhaps under the influence of the saying
about the 'sign of the Son of man in heaven', but more probably
under the influence of Mark, whose sequence he resumes here.

3.6.2. Supporting evidence from Did. 16:6

To cite the Didache as evidence in favour of this
reconstruction is to cite a distinctly uncertain witness. But
we have seen earlier some evidence suggesting that the Didache
does occasionally reflect pre-synoptic forms of tradition. The
text in question is Did. 16:6 καὶ τότε φανήσεται τὰ σημεῖα τῆς
ἀληθείας· πρῶτον σημεῖον ἐκπετάσεως ἐν οὐρανῷ, εἶτα σημεῖον
φωνῆς σάλπιγγος καὶ τὸ τρίτον ἀνάστασις νεκρῶν. The interesting
thing about this is that immediately before the description of
the Lord's coming the Didache has a reference first generally
to 'signs' (σημεῖα) and then to three particular signs, the
first of which is a σημεῖον ἐκπετάσεως ἐν οὐρανῷ. This may be
seen as some sort of parallel to the proposed pre-synoptic
tradition with its σημεῖα and σημεῖον ... ἐν οὐρανῷ, especially
as the first sign in the Didache may be regarded as an
equivalent of Matthew's 'sign of the Son of man'./1/

There are clearly major differences between the Didache
and the reconstructed pre-synoptic text, not least in that the
Didache describes three separate signs. Also the plural 'signs
of truth' in the Didache are not celestial upheavals: they are a
contrast to the previously described 'signs' of the 'world

/1/ Cf. E. Stommel, *Römische Quartalschrift* 48 (1953) 28-30.

deceiver' (16:4), and they are explained in the immediately
following enumeration of the three signs. In the context of the
Didache all the signs, not only the first, might be designated
'signs of the Son of man'./1/ But, although there are these
differences, it is possible that the Didache is a reflection of
- and a development of - the proposed pre-synoptic tradition./2/

3.6.3. Conclusion

The proposed reconstruction of the pre-synoptic tradition
is tentative, and hardly a strong probability./3/ But, even if
some of the details are incorrect, the view that there was some
such pre-synoptic form of tradition would account for a lot of
the evidence explored in the preceding pages. It seems, then,
not improbable that the pre-synoptic tradition included the
Matthean sayings about the sign of the Son of man and about the
mourning of the tribes, and also the Lukan material about the
'signs in heaven' and the distress on earth.

3.7. The gathering of the elect: Mt 24:31/Mk 13:27/Lk 21:28

The three synoptists differ in a number of ways in their
description of the gathering of the elect. Compare

Mt 24:31	Mk 13:27	Lk 21:28
καὶ ἀποστελεῖ τοὺς ἀγγέλους αὐτοῦ μετὰ σάλπιγγος μεγάλης, καὶ ἐπισυνάξουσιν τοὺς ἐκλεκτοὺς αὐτοῦ ἐκ τῶν τεσσάρων ἀνέμων ἀπ' ἄκρων οὐρανῶν ἕως [τῶν] ἄκρων αὐτῶν.	καὶ τότε ἀποστελεῖ τοὺς ἀγγέλους καὶ ἐπισυνάξει τοὺς ἐκλεκτοὺς [αὐτοῦ] ἐκ τῶν τεσσάρων ἀνέμων ἀπ' ἄκρου γῆς ἕως ἄκρου οὐρανοῦ.	ἀρχομένων δὲ τούτων γίνεσθαι ἀνακύψατε καὶ ἐπάρατε τὰς κεφαλὰς ὑμῶν, διότι ἐγγίζει ἡ ἀπολύτρωσις ὑμῶν.

/1/ But if Stommel and also Rengstorf, TDNT VII, 261, are correct
in interpreting the σημεῖον ἐκπετάσεως in terms of the cross,
this was uniquely a sign of the Son of man.
/2/ Note the use of the verb φαίνεσθαι in Did. 16:6 and in
Mt 24:30.
/3/ The possibility that some of the distinctive material in the
different gospels, which has been assigned to the pre-synoptic
tradition, might in fact be redactional (being drawn by the
evangelist concerned from the OT) cannot be excluded.

3.7.1. Paul's evidence

Paul's evidence may throw some light on these differences: his use of the noun ἐπισυναγωγή (2 Thess 2:1) may reflect his familiarity with the Matthew/Mark tradition, and he shows that the association of the 'trumpet' with the parousia goes back a long way in Christian tradition (1 Thess 4:16).

3.7.2. The ending of Mt 24:31/Mk 13:27

The difference in the wording of the final phrase in Mt 24:31 and Mk 13:27 is variously explicable. Mark's ἀπ' ἄκρου γῆς ἕως ἄκρου οὐρανοῦ may be seen as a combination of two different phrases attested in the LXX of Deut 13:7,8 and 30:4; and Matthew's ἀπ' ἄκρων οὐρανῶν ἕως ἄκρων αὐτῶν may be seen as a simplification of the slightly odd Markan combination. On the other hand, Matthew's could be the more original form of wording: his is not a particularly easy phrase to interpret, and Mark may as it were, have wished to bring the gathering of the elect more down to earth — hence his curious combination of phrases. It is just possible that Luke in his 17:24 reflects knowledge of the Matthean form of the saying (see pp.150,151 above)./1/ And his 21:28, if it is a Lukan equivalent of the Matthew/Mark saying has a distinctly 'heavenly' orientation, which could fit with the view that Luke knew the Matthean form of the saying. It would be hazardous, however, to build anything on this Lukan evidence.

3.7.3. Lk 21:28

That brings us to Lk 21:28. Luke does not have the Matthew/Mark description of the gathering of the elect by the angels, but has instead 'When these things begin to happen look up and lift your heads, because your redemption is drawing near.' There are two possible explanations of this Lukan divergence.

One is that the Lukan saying may be seen as a Lukan substitute for the Matthew/Mark verse. In favour of this it can be argued (a) that there are reasons why Luke might have wished to alter the Matthew/Mark form. For example, he is not partial to the term 'elect' and he usually associates angels with God, not Jesus./2/

/1/ But the relationship could be the other way round.
/2/ Cf. Geiger, *Endzeitreden*, 220,221; Zmijewski, *Eschatologiereden*, 231.

(b) The vocabulary and form of expression is Lukan (e.g. ἐγγίζειν)./1/
(c) The Lukan verse conveys something of the same idea as the Matthew/Mark verse, i.e. the idea of salvation coming down from heaven.

These arguments, however, are hardly cogent: if there is anything in the first argument about Luke's aversion to the ideas expressed in the Matthew/Mark saying, this is not a positive argument in favour of seeing Lk 21:28 as a modification of the Matthew/Mark saying. It could just as well be argued that both the Matthew/Mark saying and Lk 21:28 were in the pre-synoptic tradition, and that Luke omitted the Matthew/Mark saying for the sort of reason suggested. So far as the Lukan vocabulary is concerned, it is always dangerous to argue that the presence of an evangelist's style proves much: it could be a case of Luke reexpressing a tradition in his own idiom,/2/ and at least one key term ἀπολύτρωσις is unparalleled in Luke/Acts. The third argument is equally inconclusive: the Lukan verse may convey something slightly similar to the Matthew/Mark saying, but it is not very similar. Indeed the verse in some ways resembles more the parable of the fig tree that follows in each of the gospels. We might then have to argue that the verse is a Lukan transitional formula combining the thought of the saying about the gathering of the elect and the thought of the following parable.

An alternative possibility is that the Lukan saying is a pre-synoptic transitional saying. This explanation would fit in with what we have found elsewhere with regard to Lukan material in the eschatological discourse, and it is possible that Paul may be echoing the saying in Rom 13:11, a passage where we have already detected possible echoes of the eschatological discourse (see pp.116-118 above).

/1/ Cf. Marshall, *Luke*, 777. Zmijewski, *Eschatologiereden*, 231, notes the links with the account of the ascension in Acts 1, and wonders (implausibly) if this verse is Luke's equivalent of the Matthew/Mark saying about the 'beginning of woes'.
/2/ Such reexpression may have happened more when Luke is drawing on the pre-synoptic tradition (if this was memorized oral tradition) than when he is drawing on Mark.

Compare Luke's   and Romans

ἀνακύψατε καὶ   ὥρα ἤδη
ἐπάρατε τὰς κεφαλὰς ὑμῶν   ὑμᾶς ἐξ ὕπνου ἐγερθῆναι.
διότι ἐγγίζει   νῦν γὰρ ἐγγύτερον
ἡ ἀπολύτρωσις ὑμῶν   ἡμῶν ἡ σωτηρία .... ./1/

The difficulty with this explanation may seem to be that we
have to explain two omissions, i.e. Luke's omission of the
Matthew/Mark saying and Matthew's and Mark's omission of the
Lukan saying. But this is hardly a great difficulty: Luke's
omission has in any case to be explained; and we have already
seen evidence to show that Mark is abbreviating the tradition,
so that he (followed by Matthew) could well have considered the
Lukan saying to be superfluous. The omission of the Lukan
saying leaves a slightly abrupt transition from Mt 24:31/Mk 13:27
to Mt 24:32/Mk 13:28: this slight abruptness is explicable
on the hypothesis being considered.

3.7.4. Conclusions

We may tentatively conclude that the pre-synoptic tradition
contained something very like Mt 24:31 (though there is some
uncertainty about the wording of the final clause), and that
this may have been followed by a form of Lk 21:28.

4.   THE PARABLE OF THE FIG TREE AND THE SAYINGS ABOUT THE TIME OF THE END (MT 24:32-36/MK 13:28-32/LK 21:29-33)

4.1.   The parable of the fig tree

The texts are:

/1/ See also Jas 5:8 for another possible echo of the Lukan
verse, followed by a reference to the judge being 'at the
doors'. Does James know the pre-synoptic tradition with the
Lukan verse followed by the saying of Mt 24:33/Mk 13:29? Compare
also 1 Pet 4:7 with Lk 21:28 and 34-36. Cf. P. H. Davids, *The
Epistle of James* (Exeter: Paternoster, 1982) 184,185.

Mt 24:32,33	Mk 13:28,29	Lk 21:29-31
ἀπὸ δὲ τῆς συκῆς μάθετε τὴν παραβολήν· ὅταν ἤδη ὁ κλάδος αὐτῆς γένηται ἀπαλὸς καὶ τὰ φύλλα ἐκφύῃ, γινώσκετε ὅτι ἐγγὺς τὸ θέρος· 33. οὕτως καὶ ὑμεῖς ὅταν ἴδητε πάντα ταῦτα, γινώσκετε ὅτι ἐγγύς ἐστιν ἐπὶ θύραις.	ἀπὸ δὲ τῆς συκῆς μάθετε τὴν παραβολήν· ὅταν ἤδη ὁ κλάδος αὐτῆς ἀπαλὸς γένηται καὶ ἐκφύῃ τὰ φύλλα, γινώσκετε ὅτι ἐγγὺς τὸ θέρος ἐστίν· 29. οὕτως καὶ ὑμεῖς, ὅταν ἴδητε ταῦτα γινόμενα, γινώσκετε ὅτι ἐγγύς ἐστιν ἐπὶ θύραις.	καὶ εἶπεν παραβολὴν αὐτοῖς· ἴδετε τὴν συκῆν καὶ πάντα τὰ δένδρα· 30. ὅταν προβάλωσιν ἤδη, βλέποντες ἀφ' ἑαυτῶν γινώσκετε ὅτι ἤδη ἐγγὺς τὸ θέρος ἐστίν· 31. οὕτως καὶ ὑμεῖς ὅταν ἴδητε ταῦτα γινόμενα, γινώσκετε ὅτι ἐγγύς ἐστιν ἡ βασιλεία τοῦ θεοῦ.

4.1.1. Its place in the discourse

All three evangelists agree in the inclusion of the parable of the fig tree after the description of the parousia, and there is no good reason to doubt that it was part of the pre-synoptic tradition. The argument that 'these things' in the application of the parable ('When you see *these things* happening', so Mk 13:29) cannot refer to the immediately preceding description of the parousia and that therefore the parable is misplaced is entirely unpersuasive:/1/ the discourse has described (a) the events that will lead up to the parousia and then (b) the parousia itself, and the natural way to take the parable in its context is as relating (a) and (b). There is no problem with this. If the saying of Lk 21:28 is correctly regarded as a pre-synoptic transitional verse, leading from the description of the parousia to the parable of the fig tree, this may help clarify the matter even further: the thought in Lk 21:28 is of a sequence of events leading up to redemption,/2/ the beginning of which is an indication that redemption is near. Given that context, the 'these things' of the parable of the fig tree must also be seen as the events leading up to the parousia.

/1/ For this view see, e.g., Gaston, *No Stone*, 35; E. Schweizer, *The Good News according to Mark* (London: SPCK, 1971) 278. Against it see Dupont, *RB* 75, p. 538.
/2/ The exact force of 'these things' in Lk 21:28 is not easy to determine. Does he mean the celestial and terrestrial signs 'of vv 25,26', or the whole sequence of events described in the discourse? See further discussion below on pp. 333,334.

4.1.2. The synoptic differences
Matthew's and Mark's versions of the parable are almost
identical, though Matthew has πάντα ταῦτα for Mark's (and
Luke's) ταῦτα and may be secondary in this respect. Compare his
ταῦτα πάντα in 24:2 for Luke's ταῦτα.

Luke's version differs from the Matthew/Mark version in
several respects: (a) For Matthew/Mark's 'From the fig tree
learn the parable' he has 'And he told a parable. See the fig
...'. (b) He adds to 'the fig' the words 'and all the trees'.
(c) For 'As soon as its branch becomes tender and it produces
leaves' he has 'As soon as they put forth (leaves), seeing...'.
(d) For 'He is near at the doors' he has 'The kingdom of God is
near'. Most of these variations may be seen as Lukan: he may be
supposed to have broadened the parable by referring to other
trees than just the fig tree and then to have varied the wording
about the coming of the leaves. He may also have replaced the
slightly enigmatic 'He (or it) is at the doors'/1/ with a
characteristically Lukan reference to the 'kingdom'
(cf. Lk 9:27, 17:20, 19:11, 22:16,18 etc.)./2/

It is less obvious that Luke's introductory 'And he told a
parable... ' is Lukan. It is certainly possible that he
considered the phraseology of Matthew/Mark rather odd (ἀπὸ δὲ
τῆς συκῆς μάθετε τὴν παραβολήν), and that he therefore
substituted his more straightforward phraseology. However, with
the earlier rather similar case, where Luke has an introductory
phrase that is absent in Matthew/Mark (Lk 21:10 & par.), we saw
that Luke's phrase could have derived from the pre-synoptic
tradition (pp. 300, 301 above), and the same could be true here.
In favour of this it may be argued that it could help to explain
the oddity of the Matthew/Mark phrase 'learn the parable'.
Having eliminated the Lukan introductory phrase in order to
avoid breaking up the discourse, Matthew and Mark had still
somehow to effect a transition into the parable, and they did
this by incorporating the introduction into the opening of the
parable and producing the otherwise unparalleled phrase 'learn
the parable'./3/ As with the earlier case (Lk 21:10 & par.) it is

---

/1/ Cf. Jas 5:9 for a possible echo of this.
/2/ Cf. Dupont, *RB* 75 (1978) pp. 534,535.
/3/ Various scholars, e.g. Gnilka, *Markus*, 203, have seen Mk 13:28a
as the evangelist's transitional introduction to the parable.

arguable that the resulting sequence in Matthew/Mark is slightly
uncomfortable: we jump straight from the description of the
parousia into the parable without warning. Luke's version is
more comfortable with his 21:28 rounding off the description of
the parousia, and 21:29 being the start of a new section.
Although Luke could be supposed to have imposed this scheme on
to the material, it is at least as likely that he reflects the
pre-synoptic tradition in this respect and that Matthew and Mark
have obscured the original structure, here and in Mt 24:7/
Mk 13:8/Lk 21:10.

We tentatively conclude that Luke is more original in this
respect, though less original in the wording of the parable./1/

4.2. The sayings about 'this generation' and Jesus' words

The texts are:

Mt 24:34,35	Mk 13:30,31	Lk 21:32,33
ἀμὴν λέγω ὑμῖν ὅτι	ἀμὴν λέγω ὑμῖν ὅτι	ἀμὴν λέγω ὑμῖν ὅτι οὐ
οὐ μὴ παρέλθῃ ἡ	οὐ μὴ παρέλθῃ ἡ	μὴ παρέλθῃ ἡ γενεὰ
γενεὰ αὕτη ἕως ἂν	γενεὰ αὕτη μέχρις	αὕτη ἕως ἂν πάντα
πάντα ταῦτα γένηται.	οὗ ταῦτα πάντα	γένηται. 33.ὁ οὐρανὸς
35.ὁ οὐρανὸς καὶ ἡ γῆ	γένηται. 31 ὁ οὐρανὸς	καὶ ἡ γῆ
παρελεύσεται, οἱ δὲ	καὶ ἡ γῆ	παρελεύσονται, οἱ δὲ
λόγοι μου	παρελεύσονται, οἱ	λόγοι μου οὐ μὴ
οὐ μὴ παρέλθωσιν.	δὲ λόγοι μου οὐ	παρελεύσονται.
	παρελεύσονται.	

/1/ The suggestion of Beasley-Murray, *Commentary*, 96, that the
parable originally read γινώσκεται ὅτι ἐγγὺς τὸ θέρος ἐστιν
(rather than γινώσκετε), though having some manuscript support,
is hardly necessitated by the following οὕτως καὶ ὑμεῖς... .
That phrase may be understood as contrasting 'you' the disciples
with a more general 'you' (in the preceding parable), or it may
be that the ὑμεῖς is not intended emphatically at all (cf. also
the καὶ ὑμεῖς in Mt 24:44/Lk 12:40). On a quite different
point: Beasley-Murray is correct to question the view that the
parable was originally about recognizing the signs of the
kingdom within Jesus' ministry (pp. 94-96). There is no reason
why the parable should not always have been about the future and
the signs of the end.

In the sayings following the parable of the fig tree all three synoptic gospels are almost identical. Matthew and Luke agree against Mark in having ἕως ἂν πάντα (ταῦτα Mt) γένηται for Mark's μέχρις οὗ ταῦτα πάντα γένηται, and they have οὐ μὴ παρέλθωσιν (Mt)/παρελεύσονται (Lk) for Mark's simple negative οὐ παρελεύσονται. In both cases the agreements could be reflections of the pre-synoptic form of the tradition, which may well have had the Lukan form of the phrase ἕως ἂν πάντα γένηται, ταῦτα having been added in Matthew/Mark under the influence of the preceding saying (Mt 24:33/Mk 13:29/Lk 21:31) and/or under the influence of the opening of the discourse (cf. Mt 24:3/Mk 13:4/ Lk 21:7)./1/

4.3.   'Of that day or hour knows no one ... '

    The texts are:

Mt 24:36   Mk 13:32

περὶ δὲ τῆς ἡμέρας ἐκείνης   περὶ δὲ τῆς ἡμέρας ἐκείνης ἢ τῆς
καὶ ὥρας οὐδεὶς οἶδεν, οὐδὲ   ὥρας οὐδεὶς οἶδεν, οὐδὲ οἱ
οἱ ἄγγελοι τῶν οὐρανῶν οὐδὲ   ἄγγελοι ἐν οὐρανῷ οὐδὲ ὁ υἱός,
ὁ υἱός, εἰ μὴ ὁ πατὴρ μόνος.   εἰ μὴ ὁ πατήρ.

    The final saying of the section, 'But of that day and/or hour knows no one... ', is found similarly worded in Matthew and Mark, but is absent from Luke. That the saying was in the pre-synoptic discourse was suggested by the arguments of chapters 1-3 (above), since it was seen that the saying belonged with and led into the closing section of the discourse./2/ As for why Luke omits it, this has to be explained as much on the Markan hypothesis as on the pre-synoptic hypothesis.

/1/ Note that some manuscripts of Mark read ἕως and πάντα ταῦτα; this can be explained as assimilation to the Matthew/Luke tradition. Lambrecht, *Redaktion*, 209, suggests that Mark's use of μέχρις may be due to the influence of the LXX.
    The similarity of the sayings in Mt 24:34,35 & par. to certain other synoptic sayings, e.g. Mt 23:36, Mk 9:1, Mt 5:18/ Lk 16:17, has led to speculation that the sayings are redactional creations based on some of the other traditions; so Lambrecht, *Redaktion*, 209,210 and 224,225, and Pesch, *Naherwartungen*, 182-88. But, while there may have been some assimilation of the similar traditions, there is no good reason to deny the primitive origin of these sayings (cf. Marshall, *Luke,* 780)./2/ Cf. Lambrecht, *Redaktion,* 228 for the connection.

One suggestion is that Luke has put his version of the saying in Acts 1:7, οὐχ ὑμῶν ἐστιν γνῶναι χρόνους ἢ καιροὺς οὓς ὁ πατὴρ ἔθετο ἐν τῇ ἰδίᾳ ἐξουσίᾳ./1/ This idea is not impossible: the sayings are broadly similar, and the substitution of the phrases 'times and seasons' for 'day and hour' is easy enough to understand, given the changed context. The substitution may in fact be paralleled in 1 Thess 5:1, if this is correctly seen as an echo of Mt 24:36/Mk 13:32 (see above pp. 123, 124)./2/ On the other hand, it must be said that the sayings of Mt 24:36/Mk 13:32 and of Acts 1:7 are nowhere near identical in sense, and that there is no very strong reason for identifying them. Furthermore, even if Acts 1:7 is a version of Mt 24:36/Mk 13:32, it is not obvious that this explains Luke's omission of the Matthew/Mark saying from his chap. 21. It seems rather improbable that Luke would have omitted it in his chap. 21 *because* he intended to use it in the book of Acts, though it is possible that, having omitted it in Luke 21 for some reason, he may have then decided to make use of it in Acts 1.

How then is Luke's omission to be explained? It is perhaps simplest to suggest that Luke, having used much of the closing section of the discourse in his chaps. 12 and 17, including the material immediately following the saying about 'that day .. hour', omitted that material when he came to the relevant point in his chap. 21 and also omitted with it the verse that introduced it, i.e. the saying of Mt 24:36/Mk 13:32. There may have seemed little point in preserving that saying if Luke was not going to include the parabolic material that went with it (the material retained by Matthew and partially by Mark). Luke may have considered that the thought of the absent verse had already been expressed in his chap. 17,/3/ for example in 17:20

/1/ Cf., for example, Dupont, 'La portée christologique de l'évangélisation des nations d'après Luc 24:47', in *Neues Testament und Kirche*, ed. J. Gnilka (Freiburg: Herder, 1974), 132. /2/ It might be possible to argue that Paul in 1 Thess 5:1 has been influenced by the wording of Acts 1:7, whether or not he identified that saying with the saying of Mt 24:36/Mk 13:32. But the influence could be the other way round. However, the phraseology is common enough (so Hartman, *Prophecy Interpreted*, 192), so that there need be no relationship. It is not in any case likely that 'times ... seasons' could have been the more original wording of the saying of Mt 24:36/Mk 13:32: the 'day ...hour' motif is characteristic of the pre-synoptic discourse ending. (See pp. 106,107 above.) /3/ Cf. Zmijewski, *Eschatologiereden*, 285.

itself, 'the kingdom of God does not come with observation'.

4.4. Conclusions

We suppose then that the pre-synoptic tradition was quite similar to the present Matthew/Mark wording, approximately as follows:

> And he told them a parable: see the fig. When its branch becomes tender and puts out leaves, you know that the summer is near. So you, when you see these things happening, know that he is near at the doors.
> Truly I tell you that this generation will surely not pass away until all (these) things happen. Heaven and earth will pass away, but my words will surely not pass away.
> But of that day and (or) hour knows no one, not even the angels in heaven nor the Son, except the Father.

5. CONCLUDING REMARKS

The preceding chapter has looked at four different sections of the eschatological discourse, and has made suggestions - some quite speculative, others more probable - about the history of the traditions. By way of general conclusion it is only necessary to say that the hypothesis of a pre-synoptic tradition known to all the evangelists and used by them in different ways is possible and sometimes illuminating in each of the passages examined.

6. ADDITIONAL NOTE ON THE INTERPRETATION OF THE SAYING ABOUT 'THIS GENERATION'

For discussion of the interpretation of Mk 13:30 see my '"This generation will not pass...."', where it is argued that the structure of the Markan discourse favours the view that the events to occur 'in this generation' are the things that must precede the end, culminating in the fall of Jerusalem, but not including the parousia, which is discussed in the following saying of Mk 13:32.

The tentative proposals made above concerning the pre-synoptic form of the same tradition could appear to point to a different interpretation of this tradition, since it is arguably more difficult to take the pre-synoptic (= Lukan) 'all things' of events other than the parousia. However, note that (1) 'all these things' of Lk 21:36 are probably the tribulations preceding the end (from which the saints may escape) not the inescapable parousia, so that 'all things' in Lk 21:32 (and in the pre-synoptic tradition) may be taken similarly. (On the notion of the great tribulation see R. Bauckham, *JTS* 25 (1974) 27-40.) (2) The pre-synoptic tradition may well have had the saying about 'this generation' of Mt 23:36/Lk 11:51 immediately preceding the eschatological discourse. (See the discussion of the context of the discourse in chapter 9 below.) This saying is quite explicitly referring to the fall of Jerusalem, not to the parousia, and may point to this interpretation of the later saying about 'this generation'. (3) The pre-synoptic tradition, like the Matthean and Markan traditions, has the statement about what will happen in 'this generation' followed by a contrasting statement concerning 'that day or hour'. 'That day or hour' is an unmistakable reference to the parousia, and it is a reasonable, though not certain, inference that the preceding statement refers to something else. (4) The pre-synoptic tradition continues with a number of parables in which the thought of waiting a long time for the parousia is prominent (e.g. the parables of the watchman, the virgins, the talents). These parables would perhaps be in some tension with the earlier statement about 'this generation', if this is interpreted of the parousia. These four observations add up to suggest that the pre-synoptic saying about 'this generation not passing away' refers to the events before the end.

An alternative possibility is to argue that γενεά does not refer to Jesus' generation, but has a broader significance. (So on Luke: E. E. Ellis, *The Gospel of Luke* (London: Nelson,

1966) 246,247; Marshall, *Luke*, 780; Zmijewski,
Eschatologiereden, 276-83; Geiger, *Endzeitreden*, 233-37. Also
on Mark, E. Lövestam in Lambrecht, ed., *L'Apocalypse*, 403,404).
It is doubtful, however, if this view can be accepted either
for Luke or the pre-synoptic tradition, given the context of
the disciples' question at the beginning of the discourse
(Mt 24:3 & par.) and the more immediate context of discussion
about times (i.e. Mt 24:32-33 and 36 & par.).

Other possibilities are that the saying means that the
whole eschatological drama will begin within a generation, but
not necessarily that it will be completed. Perhaps preferable
is the suggestion that, despite the verbal links, there is a
major break in the sequence of thought between the parable of
the fig tree and the saying about everything happening in a
generation which is introduced by the emphatic 'Truly I say to
you...'. The parable encourages alertness to the signs of the
end; but then the next verses turn more directly to the
question of 'When?', with the first saying, 'This generation
will not pass until all things happen', answering the disciples'
question about the fall of Jerusalem and the following saying,
'But of that day and hour no one knows', speaking about the
parousia. (For a different approach, making some of the same
points, see J. Dupont, 'La ruine du temple', 213-218.) None of
the proposed solutions is without difficulty and it is not
possible to do justice to the issues here.

Chapter 9

THE CONTEXT OF THE DISCOURSE

In the previous chapters we have examined the traditions found in the three synoptic versions of the eschatological discourse. In this chapter we turn our attention briefly to the context of the discourse and consider whether there was a pre-synoptic context and, if so, what it was. This is not only a matter of obvious interest, but it may also throw some light on the discourse itself and so contribute directly to the thesis being presented.

1. THE SAYINGS AGAINST THE SCRIBES AND PHARISEES

All three evangelists agree in placing the discourse after denunciation of the scribes (and Pharisees) by Jesus. But Matthew has a much more extensive section of denunciation including the 'woes' on the scribes and Pharisees, which Luke has elsewhere in his chap. 11 (if their traditions are the same). Instead of the woes Mark and Luke have before the eschatological discourse the story of the widow's mite, a tradition not recorded at all in Matthew. How are the relationships between the synoptic accounts to be explained here?

The obvious explanation may at first sight appear to be that Matthew has imported the 'woes' into this context. However, at least two things raise a question mark against this view: (a) Our findings in earlier chapters about Luke's redactional technique within his central section have shown that Luke regularly has traditions from the eschatological discourse out of their original context. There must be a suspicion that this is the case with the woes of Luke 11. (b) This suspicion may be strengthened when it is observed that the woes of Luke 11 include a saying (11:43 - about first seats in the synagogues and greetings in the market places) that has a parallel in Mt 23:5-7/Mk 12:38,39/Lk 20:46. This observation may prove nothing, but could suggest that the woes of Luke 11 have something to do with the later context.

That this is indeed the case may be shown through a brief consideration of the relevant synoptic texts./1/

1.1. A preliminary statement

It is suggested that the pre-synoptic form of the discourse against the scribes and Pharisees consisted (a) of some warnings about the scribes addressed to the disciples, (b) of the story of the widow's mite, (c) of a series of woes against the scribes and Pharisees. Matthew, it is suggested, has reproduced the tradition most fully, making some omissions (e.g. of the story of the widow's mite) and some additions. Mark, followed by Luke in Luke 20, has reproduced some at least of the warnings against the scribes, including one that is unparalleled in the usually accepted text of Matthew (i.e. Mk 12:40/Lk 20:47), but he may have omitted for his Gentile readership the most Jewish material (e.g. Mt 23:2-3) and he has omitted all the woes against the scribes and Pharisees, these being strongly Jewish and not of pressing relevance to his readers. Luke in 11:37-54 may be supposed to have drawn on the pre-synoptic tradition in question, appending it to and combining it with a different 'scribes and Pharisees' tradition. More precisely it seems that Lk 11:37-41 is to be linked with the tradition of Mk 7:1-23, a passage which Luke does not have in the Markan context./2/ Luke appears to have combined the tradition of that discussion with the scribes and Pharisees over hand-washing with the pre-synoptic tradition that included the woes on the scribes and Pharisees.

It is clearly necessary to justify this sweeping proposal, and this will be done briefly in what follows.

/1/ It is not possible here to interact with all the secondary literature. For further discussion of these traditions and bibliography, see Marshall, *Luke*, 490-508, and D. E. Garland, *The Intention of Matthew 23* (Leiden: Brill, 1979) pp. 9-33 and *passim*. I am grateful to Miss M. R. Diffenderfer for her comments on this chapter and on the issues discussed in it.
/2/ This possibility is mentioned but prematurely dismissed by Marshall, *Luke*, 491. For a somewhat similar suggestion see Chapman, *Matthew, Mark and Luke*, 250-52.

*1.2. Lk 11:37-41 a conflation of the traditions of Mark 7 and
Matthew 23*

The first point to establish is the proposal about Luke 11.

1.2.1. Links between Luke 11 and Mark 7
The resemblance of the sayings against the Pharisees and
scribes in Lk 11:37-54 to the comparable sayings in Matthew 23
is unmistakable. And Lk 11:39-41 ('You Pharisees cleanse the
outside of the cup...') has an evident parallel in Mt 23:25,26.
However, the opening verses of the Lukan section, 11:37-41, also
have interesting similarities to the traditions of Mk 7:1-23:

(a) In both passages there is debate with a Pharisee/
Pharisees and Sadducees over the question of hand-washing before
meals - in the one case about Jesus' practice, in the other case
about the disciples.   (b) In both contexts and nowhere else in
the NT the βαπτίζειν root is used of the ritual washing of
hands or vessels./1/   (c) There is discussion in both places
about the washing of 'cups' (ποτήριον), though this is also
found in Mt 23:25,26.   (d) There is, in both texts, discussion
of the 'inside' (ἔσωθεν) and the 'outside' (ἔξωθεν).   This
contrast is also in Mt 23:25, but in Luke (more than in Matthew)
the thought seems to move over from the thought of the inside
and outside of cups towards the thought of Mark 7 about the
inside and outside of people (cf. Mk 7:15-21).   (e) In both
passages the question of giving money is found: in Mark 7 it is
the korban question, in Luke 11 simply an injunction to 'give
alms'.   (f) In both there is the similarly expressed thought of
'all things' being cleansed or clean, cf. Mk 7:19, Lk 11:41.
This range of agreements between Luke 11 and Mark 7 might not
seem significant were it not for the further points to be made.

1.2.2. Differences between Luke 11 and Matthew 23
It is precisely those things that Lk 11:39-41 has in common
with Mark 7 that differentiate the Lukan form of the saying
about the inside and outside of the cup from the Matthean saying
of Mt 23:25,26. Although all the Lukan woes differ from the
Matthean woes in wording, there is nothing comparable to the
substantial difference between the thought of Lk 11:40,41,
ἄφρονες, οὐχ ὁ ποιήσας τὸ ἔξωθεν καὶ τὸ ἔσωθεν ἐποίησεν; πλὴν τὰ
ἐνόντα δότε ἐλεημοσύνην, καὶ ἰδοὺ πάντα καθαρὰ ὑμῖν ἐστιν, and
the thought of Mt 23:26, φαρισαῖε τυφλέ, καθάρισον πρῶτον τὸ

/1/ Even if ῥαντίσωνται not βαπτίσωνται is read in Mk 7:4, the
word βαπτισμούς occurs later in the verse.

ἐντὸς τοῦ ποτηρίου ἵνα γένηται καὶ τὸ ἐκτὸς αὐτοῦ καθαρόν. The other differences are all or almost all explicable as insignificant verbal variation or clarification; this difference is much more substantial, but is explicable if Luke has here conflated two sayings, as has been suggested.

1.2.3. Lack of logical sequence in Luke 11

As it stands, the saying of Jesus in Lk 11:40 about the inside and outside of a cup does not seem to follow on very obviously from the preceding context (i.e. Lk 11:37,38) where the question is about the washing of hands. This lack of logical sequence is explicable by the suggestion that Luke has conflated together the original answer and the cup saying.

1.2.4. Conclusion on Lk 11:37-41

These three observations together add up to suggest that Luke has here brought together two traditions that had much in common - both traditions concerning (the scribes and) the Pharisees, both referring to 'washings' and to the 'inside' and 'outside'. This conflation of traditions is very much in line with what was observed earlier of Luke's procedure in Lk 17:20-22 and especially in his parable of the pounds, if this is correctly seen as a conflation of the parable of the pretender to the throne with the parable of the talents.

1.3. A suggested reconstruction of the pre-synoptic woes

The argument that Luke combined the woes with other traditions in his chap. 11 does not by itself take us to the conclusion (outlined in section 1.1 above) that Matthew has retained the pre-synoptic arrangement in his chap. 23. It is necessary to go on and to consider the woes in Matthew and Luke, and then to consider the warnings against the scribes that precede the woes in Matthew and that are paralleled in Mark 12 and Luke 20.

So far as the woes are concerned, there is some plausibility in the view that Luke reflects the pre-synoptic form of the tradition in having some woes directed at the Pharisees and some at the scribes, rather than having them all directed at both groups as Matthew does. Quite apart from the Lukan evidence, it is arguable that a distinction may be drawn between the three woes of Mt 23:13-22 (shutting kingdom, making proselytes, teaching oaths), which all have to do with those who mislead and are blind guides to others and which would presumably be especially appropriate for the scribes, and the

three woes of Mt 23:23-28 (tithing, cups, whitewashed tombs),
which all have to do with hypocrisy and false appearances and
which would be especially appropriate for the Pharisees - note
the reference in v 26 to 'blind Pharisee' (with no reference to
the scribes) - ; the seventh woe (about building the tombs of
the prophets) does not go obviously with either group. It may
be accidental that Matthew has three woes that fit the
Pharisees especially well and three that fit the scribes, and
that Luke has three woes for each group. But it is at least
possible that they both reflect the form of the pre-synoptic
tradition in this respect, though they have varied the
ingredients that they have put into that form.

Can such a possible pre-synoptic form be suggested, from
which our present gospel texts may have been derived? It is
suggested that the pre-synoptic tradition may have been
approximately as follows:

1. Woe against the Pharisees for hypocritical tithing
2.   "   "   "   "   "   "   cleansing
                                                 outside of cup
3.   "   "   "   "   "   being like whitewashed
                                                 tombs
4.   "   "   "   scribes for imposing heavy burdens
5.   "   "   "   "   "   crossing land and sea to
                                                 make a proselyte
6.   "   "   "   "   "   shutting the kingdom of
                                                 heaven
7. Woe against scribes and Pharisees for building the
                                     tombs of the prophets.

Matthew on this view has reversed the order of the woes
against the Pharisees and scribes, putting the scribes first
because of the immediately preceding section of warning against
the scribes. (23:1ff.)/1/ He has in fact incorporated woe 4
into that section of warning (his 23:4), and so to keep the
structure intact he moves woe 6 forward into fourth position,
and then adds on an extra woe where woe 6 originally was. This
extra woe about oaths (Mt 23:16-22) is notable for being

/1/ Matthew obscures things for us by linking the Pharisees
with the scribes in his v 2. But Mark and Luke and the sense of
Matthew all suggest that the pre-synoptic tradition referred
only to 'scribes' at this point. See further below.

formally distinct from the other woes. The other major change
in Matthew is that he drops the distinction between the woes
directed to the scribes and those directed to the Pharisees,
lumping them all together.

Luke correctly has the woes against the Pharisees first,
but he brings woe 2 forward, because it was the link to his
preceding tradition - a debate with a Pharisee about hand-
washing./1/ (Note the especially good link with the Matthean
wording 'blind Pharisee'.) In being joined to the preceding
tradition, this woe loses its 'woe' form. Luke therefore has a
compensating woe 2, i.e. his woe on the Pharisees for wearing
long robes (drawn in fact from the preceding section of warning
against the scribes; cf. Mt 23:5-7, Mk 12:38,39/Lk 21:46 and see
further discussion below); he thus makes up the three woes
against the Pharisees. When he comes to the scribes he follows
the pre-synoptic tradition,/2/ but in writing for Gentiles he
omits woe 5 on Jewish proselytism and brings into its place woe
7, though chis is not quite so appropriate in the specifically
scribal setting.

The proposal about the pre-synoptic form of the woes makes
good sense of both Matthew and Luke, and it coheres well with
our earlier findings, particularly about Luke and the pre-
synoptic tradition, since he elsewhere manifests freedom so far
as the context of traditions is concerned, but reasonable
conservatism with regard to the contents of the traditions.
Also, the proposed pre-synoptic form has the same sort of
logical coherence as we observed in the concluding section of
the eschatological discourse (see pp. 95 - 97 above).

/1/ A less likely possibility is that Matthew reversed the
order of woes 1 and 2, so as to have the tithing woe after the
thematically similar oaths woe.
/2/ He may well have derived the lawyer's comment of 11:45 from
the pre-synoptic tradition; cf. Lk 12:41 and 17:37 and our
previous discussion on pp. 57-62, 167-70 and 301. Matthew
here again eliminates the narrative link.

1.4. A possible reconstruction of the pre-synoptic warning
     against the scribes

     To complete the picture, it is necessary to say something
about the warnings against the scribes (and Pharisees) that
precede the woes in Matthew 23 and that have parallels in
Mk 12:37-40/Lk 20:45-47.

     1.4.1. The sayings about seats, robes and greetings
     The crucial question for the reconstruction of the
pre-synoptic warning against the scribes concerns the
relationship of Mt 23:5-7, Mk 12:38,39, Lk 11:43 and 20:46.
The texts are as follows:

Mt 23:5b-7	Mk 12:38,39	Lk 20:46	Lk 11:43
πλατύνουσιν γὰρ	βλέπετε ἀπὸ τῶν	προσέχετε ἀπὸ	οὐαὶ ὑμῖν τοῖς
τὰ φυλακτήρια	γραμματέων τῶν	τῶν γραμματέων	Φαρισαίοις, ὅτι
αὐτῶν καὶ	θελόντων ἐν	τῶν θελόντων	ἀγαπᾶτε τὴν
μεγαλύνουσιν τὰ	στολαῖς καὶ	περιπατεῖν ἐν	πρωτοκαθεδρίαν
κράσπεδα,	ἀσπασμοὺς ἐν	στολαῖς καὶ	ἐν ταῖς
6. φιλοῦσιν δὲ	ταῖς ἀγοραῖς	φιλούντων	συναγωγαῖς καὶ
τὴν πρωτοκλισίαν	39. καὶ	ἀσπασμοὺς ἐν	τοὺς ἀσπασμοὺς
ἐν τοῖς δείπνοις	πρωτοκαθεδρίας	ταῖς ἀγοραῖς	ἐν ταῖς
καὶ τὰς	ἐν ταῖς	καὶ	ἀγοραῖς.
πρωτοκαθεδρίας	συναγωγαῖς καὶ	πρωτοκαθεδρίας	
ἐν ταῖς	πρωτοκλισίας ἐν	ἐν ταῖς	
συναγωγαῖς	τοῖς δείπνοις·	συναγωγαῖς καὶ	
7. καὶ τοὺς		πρωτοκλισίας	
ἀσπασμοὺς ἐν		ἐν τοῖς	
ταῖς ἀγοραῖς καὶ		δείπνοις.	
καλεῖσθαι ὑπὸ			
τῶν ἀνθρώπων			
ῥαββί. ὑμεῖς δὲ			
μὴ κληθῆτε ...			

     The following points are significant for the explaining of
the texts:

(1) Mt 23:6-7, Mk 12:38,39 and Lk 20:46 all have rather
cumbersome phraseology with a verb of wanting/liking followed
by four objects (or object clauses) linked by καί. Lk 11:43,
by contrast, has a simple balanced two-part object (cf. also
Mt 23:5b). (2) All four traditions agree on linking together
the phrases '(they love) the first seats in the synagogues and

the greetings in the market-places', though Mk 12:38,39/Lk 20:46
have the reverse order (i.e. greetings, seats). (3) Luke
has some notable agreements with Matthew against Mark:
(a) Lk 20:46 and Mt 23:6 have the verb φιλεῖν in common (contrast
Mark's θέλειν). (b) Lk 11:43 and Mt 23:6 have -i- rather
similar verbs, ἀγαπᾶν and φιλεῖν for Mark's θέλειν; -ii- they
both have the order 'first seat(s) in the synagogues, greetings
in the market places' (contrast the reverse order in Mark 12/
Luke 20); -iii- they have a verb of loving + articular objects
(Matthew τὴν πρωτοκλισίαν... τὰς πρωτοκαθεδρίας... τοὺς
ἀσπασμούς, Luke τὴν πρωτοκαθεδρίαν... τοὺς ἀσπασμούς), whereas
Mark 12 and Luke 20 have no comparable articles at the same
point. -iv- Mt 23:6 and Lk 11:43 agree in having the first
object singular (Matthew πρωτοκλισίαν/Luke πρωτοκαθεδρίαν),
whereas all the other objects in all the forms of the tradition are
plural (e.g. πρωτοκαθεδρίας, πρωτοκλισίας). (4) As has been
observed, Mark 12/Luke 20 have the sayings in question addressed
to the scribes, Lk 11:43 has the saying addressed to the
Pharisees. Arguably the references to people 'loving the first
seat(s) in the synagogues and greetings in the streets' fit the
scribes better than the Pharisees, especially if the 'first
seat' in the synagogue is the teacher's/preacher's seat and
certainly if the greeting in the market places was 'Rabbi' (as
Mt 23:7). (5) The reference to 'first seats in the dinners' is
absent from Lk 11:43 (despite the dinner context in Luke 11),
but is somewhat reminiscent of the later story in Lk 14:7-11, a
story also involving scribes and Pharisees. It is arguable that
the reference to 'first seats in the dinners' makes less good
sense in the context of Matthew 23/Mark 12/Luke 11/Luke 20,
where the emphasis is on religiosity rather than on social
conduct in general.

    Given these five observations, the probable conclusion is
(i) that originally the saying was as in Lk 11:43 '(They) love
the best seat in the synagogues and the greetings in the market
places'. But, although Luke has the most original form in his
11:43, his positioning of the verse within the woes against the
Pharisees is, as has already been suggested, probably
secondary; the saying is correctly located within the section
of warnings against the scribes, where Matthew and Mark (and
Luke 20) have it.
(ii) Although Mk 12:38,39/Lk 20:46 have the saying in the

correct context, the form of the saying has been modified. For
some reason the order of the clauses (best seats/greetings -
originally) has been reversed. Perhaps this was because the
reverse order fits better after Mark's preceding clause τῶν
θελόντων ἐν στολαῖς περιπατεῖν or because the author concerned
had it in mind to add the phrase 'and first seats in the
feasts'. This phrase is in any case added after the reference
to 'first seats in the synagogues', quite possibly under the
influence of the story preserved in Lk 14:1-11. The result is
a sentence rather overloaded with phrases joined by καί.
(iii) Mt 23:5-7 is a combination of the original form of Lk 11:43
and the modified form of Mk 12:38,39/Lk 20:46. Matthew has
taken over the additional reference to 'first seats in
dinners', but has moved it to the front of the sentence, using
the form ('love' + article + singular) of the first half of
Lk 11:43. This relocation of the 'first seat(s) in the dinners'
phrase enables him to keep the phrases 'first seats in the
synagogues and greetings in the market places' together in
their original order (of Lk 11:43), and then he is able to carry
on with the phrase καὶ καλεῖσθαι ὑπὸ τῶν ἀνθρώπων ῥαββί... /1/
(iv) One additional observation: it seems quite possible that
Mk 12:38 τῶν θελόντων ἐν στολαῖς περιπατεῖν is a less technical and
less Jewish equivalent of Matthew's more original πλατύνουσιν
γὰρ τὰ φυλακτήρια αὐτῶν καὶ μεγαλύνουσιν τὰ κράσπεδα, in which
case the original balanced form of the sayings may have been:

They broaden their phylacteries   and make large the
                                                  fringes
    They love the first seat in the synagogues   and the
                         greetings in the market-places./2/

/1/ Garland, *Matthew 23*, 14, explains that Matthew alters the
order of Mark 12/Luke 20 in order to lead into his vv 8-12, and
so he discounts the influence of the Lukan form. But the Lukan
form needs explanation, and it is probable that this has
influenced Matthew. Indeed it is possible that Matthew's
addition of v 7b and then of vv 8-12 is the result, not the
purpose,of his change of order!
/2/ This suggestion provokes the further interesting
speculation that Mark and Matthew may both have known and drawn
on an early 'translation' of these sayings, which spoke of the
scribes (θελόντων) περιπατεῖν ἐν στολαῖς (Mk 12:38/Lk 20:46)
καὶ καλεῖσθαι ὑπὸ τῶν ἀνθρώπων ῥαββί (Mt 23:7).

1.4.2. The whole section
Given the preceding argument it is a reasonable hypothesis
that the whole of the pre-synoptic section included
approximately the following:

A. Beware of the scribes.

B. They sit on Moses seat.

     All that they say to you do and keep
     but according to their deeds do not do,
     for they say and do not do.

C. All their deeds they do to be seen by men.

D. For they broaden their phylacteries and make large their
                                                        fringes.
     They love the first seat in the synagogues and the
                                 greetings in the market-places.

E. They eat the houses of widows and for pretence make
                                                   long prayers.

F. These shall receive greater condemnation.

         + the woes.

In favour of this, note: (1) Section A: We have seen other
examples of a pre-synoptic 'beware of' being rendered βλέπετε in
Mark and προσέχετε in Luke or Matthew (see pp. 120,229,230
above). (2) Section B: it is entirely consistent with earlier
observations that Mark and Luke omit this strongly Jewish
material. (3) Sections B and C: Matthew places between these
sayings the saying about the scribes putting burdens on people.
But Luke has this as a 'woe'; and that it is an interpolation in
the Matthean context is also suggested by the way it breaks the
flow from sections B to C. (4) On section D see previous
discussion. (5) Sections E and F: Mark and Luke retain these,
Luke even retaining the indicative tenses; Matthew omits them,
developing instead the thought of 'being called rabbi' with
material from another context. (6) As with our other
reconstructions of pre-synoptic tradition, the pre-synoptic
sequence is coherent and flows well.

1.5. The widow's mite (Mk 12:41-44, Lk 21:1-4)

It has been shown in the preceding two sections that much
of Matthew 23 has a possible pre-synoptic origin, and the
evidence of Lk 11:43 (where Luke incorporates a saying from the
warnings about the scribes into the woes) suggests that Luke
knew the warnings and the woes together - as Matthew has them.
But what then is to be said of the description of the widow
giving her two mites, which Mark and Luke have after the warning
against the scribes, but which Matthew omits altogether? The
probable answer to that is that this story was the narrative
bridge in the pre-synoptic tradition between the warning against the
scribes and the woes: it follows on very well from the description of
the scribes who 'devour widows' houses' and leads well into the first
woe against the Pharisees' hypocritical tithing. Matthew, not
untypically, has dropped the narrative bridge (and indeed the
preceding saying about the scribes devouring widows' houses/1/),
but he pays a price in that the transition from warning to woes
in his gospel is unexplained and slightly uncomfortable. The
situation is similar to that in Mt 24:23-28. (See above
pp. 167-70.)

1.6. Conclusions

The preceding discussion of the pre-synoptic form of the
sayings against the scribes and Pharisees has been dangerously
brief and has left many questions unanswered. But at least it
has suggested how the argument concerning the preceding context
of the eschatological discourse might go. If the argument is on
the right lines, then it points to Matthew, Mark and Luke all
having retained elements from a common pre-synoptic form of the
sayings against the scribes and Pharisees; and, since they all
put these sayings immediately before the eschatological
discourse, there must be a reasonable probability that this was
their pre-synoptic location.

If that seems rather a lame conclusion to a long argument,
it must be said that the main importance of the preceding
discussion of Matthew 23 and parallels for our overall thesis is
that it has shown how the idea of a pre-synoptic form of the
gospel tradition is fruitful in explaining one more of the
synoptic discourse sections.

/1/ His omissions may well be connected with his addition of his
23:8-12: he inserts these traditions (which have a parallel in
Jn 13:12-17) as commentary on 'being called rabbi' (23:7).

2. *THE LAMENTS OF MT 23:37-39/LK 13:34-35 AND OF LK 19:41-44*

The preceding discussion of Jesus' sayings against the
scribes and Pharisees left Jesus' lament over Jerusalem, which
Matthew has after the woes and before the eschatological
discourse (Mt 23:37-39), completely out of account. Luke has
the lament earlier in his gospel in 13:34-35. In the light of
our earlier findings about material that is differently located
in Matthew and Luke, the strong probability must be that
Matthew has retained the pre-synoptic location of the saying
immediately before the eschatological discourse, and that Luke
has located it in his chap. 13, because of the verbal or the
thematic link with the saying of Lk 13:33 .... ὅτι οὐκ
ἐνδέχεται προφήτην ἀπολέσθαι ἔξω 'Ιερουσαλήμ.

It is not possible to prove that this is what happened.
But it is just possible that Luke betrays his awareness of the
Matthean location of the lament in his own 19:41-44.

2.1. Observations about Lk 19:41-44

Various points are notable about Lk 19:41-44. (a) These
verses together with the preceding vv 39,40 stick out as a non-
Markan section in the middle of a block of material that is all
paralleled in Mark (Lk 19:28-20:47).

(b) Vv 39,40, which describe the Pharisees' complaining about
the disciples' shouts of enthusiasm, have some sort of a
parallel in Mt 21:14-16: there too the general context is that
of the triumphal entry, and Jewish leaders object to the
'hosannas' of Jesus' admirers. There too Jesus rejects the
Jews' objections with a succinct comment. This evidence may
point to an underlying common tradition (though there are
differences between Matthew and Luke); and if Luke's vv 39,40
are drawn from pre-Lukan tradition, then the same may well be
true of vv 41-44.

(c) Lk 19:41-44 contain some Lukan stylistic features, but it
is arguable that at least vv 43,44 contain non-Lukan elements./1/

(d) Vv 41-44 have definite similarity to the lament of Mt 23:37
-39/Lk 13:34,35. In Luke 19 Jesus weeps over the city of

/1/ So J. Dupont, *Biblica* 52 (1971) 310-14.

Jerusalem because of its failure to grasp its opportunity, and
he warns of resulting destruction; in Matthew 23/Luke 13 Jesus
laments Jerusalem's unresponsiveness to his loving initiatives
and warns 'Your house is forsaken'.

(e) The 'O Jerusalem, Jerusalem' saying of Matthew 23/Luke 13
ends with the words 'Blessed is he that comes in the name of
the Lord', words which recur in the triumphal entry story that
immediately precedes Lk 19:39-44.

(f) There is a verbal link between Lk 19:41-44 and the opening
of the eschatological discourse: compare Lk 19:43 ἥξουσιν
ἡμέραι with 21:6 ἐλεύσονται ἡμέραι (this being a Lukan turn of
phrase found elsewhere, e.g. 17:22) and especially 19:44 οὐκ
ἀφήσουσιν λίθον ἐπὶ λίθον with 21:6 οὐκ ἀφεθήσεται λίθος ἐπὶ
λίθῳ (cf. Mt 24:2/Mk 13:2). There is another link between
Lk 19:41-44 and the eschatological discourse, since both speak
of Jerusalem being 'surrounded' (19:43 περικυκλώσουσιν, 21:20
κυκλουμένην).

2.2. Possible explanations

The observations made about Lk 19:41-44 may prove nothing at
all. But it is possible that Luke knew a tradition in which his
19:41-44 preceded and introduced the eschatological discourse./1/
Alternatively, and perhaps more likely, Lk 19:41-44 could be a
Lukan substitute for the 'O Jerusalem' lament (which Luke had
used before), in which Luke uses some other traditional material.

Relevant to this suggestion may be the claim of J. Dupont
that (with the exception of the last phrase) Lk 19:43,44 is
probably pre-Lukan: he points to the marked paratactic style and
the strong OT flavour of the verses, and argues that the verses
may have been derived from the same source as the sayings of
Lk 23:29-31./2/ His suggestion is an attractive one; but by
itself it would leave unexplained the links that we noted between
Lk 19:41-44 and the eschatological discourse. Perhaps they need
no explanation: it may be a case of similar but distinct
traditions. However, another possibility is that Lk 19:43,44
should indeed be connected with 23:29,30 (though not with v 31)
and that both passages should be connected with the
eschatological discourse.

/1/ Cf. the tentative comments of Marshall in *Luke*, 717.
/2/ *Biblica* 52, pp. 315-19.

2.2.1. The argument for linking Lk 19:43,44, 23:29,30 and the eschatological discourse

In favour of this suggestion, apart from the links between Lk 19:43,44 and the eschatological discourse already noted, are the following points: (a) There is a good case for regarding Lk 23:29,30 as an interpolation in that context:/1/ the saying of Lk 23:28 would lead well into the ὅτι clause of 23:31, and it is easy to see how and why Luke slipped in the thematically relevant sayings of vv 29,30, using the ὅτι construction and his characteristic 'days are coming' phraseology. (b) It is possible to suggest how the sayings of Lk 19:43,44 and 23:29,30 might have fitted (together) in the section of the eschatological discourse describing the desolation of Jerusalem. The order of sayings could have been roughly as follows:

A. cf. Lk 21:20-22   ὅταν δὲ ἴδητε κυκλουμένην ὑπὸ στρατοπέδων
     & par.   'Ιερουσαλήμ ...... τότε οἱ ἐν τῇ 'Ιουδαίᾳ
                      φευγέτωσαν εἰς τὰ ὄρη. ὁ ἐπὶ τοῦ δώματος
                      .... ὁ εἰς τὸν ἀγρὸν μὴ ἐπιστρεψάτω ὀπίσω
                      ἆραι τὸ ἱμάτιον αὐτοῦ. ὅτι ἡμέραι
                      ἐκδικήσεως αὗται εἰσιν τῇ 'Ιερουσαλήμ.

B. cf. Lk 19:43,44   παρεμβαλοῦσιν οἱ ἐχθροί αὐτῆς χάρακα αὐτῇ/2/
                      καὶ περικυκλωσοῦσιν αὐτὴν καὶ συνέξουσιν
                      αὐτὴν πάντοθεν καὶ ἐδαφιοῦσιν αὐτὴν καὶ τὰ
                      τέκνα αὐτῆς.

C. cf. Lk 23:29   ἐν ἐκείναις ταῖς ἡμέραις ἐροῦσιν· μακάριαι
                      αἱ στεῖραι, καὶ αἱ κοιλίαι αἱ οὐκ ἐγέννησαν,
                      καὶ μαστοὶ οἱ οὐκ ἔθρεψαν.

D. cf. Lk 21:23 &   οὐαὶ δὲ ταῖς ἐν γαστρὶ ἐχούσαις καὶ ταῖς
     par.   θηλαζούσαις.

E. cf. Lk 23:30   ...... τότε ἄρξονται λέγειν τοῖς ὄρεσιν·

/1/ Cf. W. Käser, *ZNW* 54 (1963) 240-44. Despite Dupont's contrary claim (*Biblica* 52, p. 316) there is little difficulty in having Jesus respond to the tears of the women (23:28) with the proverbial saying of v 31. Cf. also Marshall, *Luke* 862,863.
/2/ Perhaps a second person plural could be read throughout instead of a third person singular. If these verses with their strong OT flavour were at this point in the eschatological discourse, this might lie behind Luke's 21:22b 'for everything written to be fulfilled'.

πέσατε .... /1/

This possible reconstruction hangs well together and would
fit in with our earlier observations about the relationship of
Matthew, Mark and Luke in this section of the discourse; Matthew
and Mark, it was suggested, omit overtly military material and
Luke omits material that he has already used earlier in his
gospel (i.e. the sayings of 19:43,44)./2/ The reconstruction
could perhaps also claim some support from Revelation 6, since
that chapter which has such strong links with the eschatological
discourse includes an equivalent of Lk 23:30, i.e. Rev 6:16
'They will say to the mountains and the rocks: fall on us and
hide us'.

2.2.2. Implications of the proposal
If the suggested reconstruction were correct, then Lk 19:41-44
could plausibly be regarded as a Lukan substitute for the
lament of Mt 23:37-39/Lk 13:34-35. Luke retains the thought of
that lament, but uses material from the eschatological discourse
(from the opening saying about no stone being left on another
and from the description of Jerusalem's desolation) to express
it. Luke could thus be said to attest indirectly, at least,
Matthew's location of the lament.

But even that is to oversimplify, since Luke does not agree
with Matthew in locating the lament immediately before the
eschatological discourse. He does indeed have it in the context
of Jesus' last visit to Jerusalem before his death, but earlier
than Matthew. So to sustain the thesis, we would have to argue
that Luke has brought the lament forward. This is by no means
impossible: Luke could have known a tradition like Matthew's
that described the triumphal entry, then later a controversy in
the temple over people shouting 'hosanna', and then later again
Jesus' lament over Jerusalem;/3/ but he could have moved these

---

/1/ This saying could have been located at a later point in the
discourse, perhaps in the section describing the parousia. See
above pp. 309-12.
/2/ Perhaps the saying of Lk 23:29 dropped out with those of 19:
43,44; but it was picked up again later. Compare Lk 22:28-30 and
our discussion above on pp. 129-34.
/3/ There is evidence that Matthew and Luke had access to a non-
Markan tradition in this section of their gospels. E.g. they
both have the cleansing of the temple following the triumphal
entry (without mentioning Mark's day in-between), and in the
story of the cleansing they have notable agreements against Mark

two non-Markan traditions into immediate proximity with the
story of the triumphal entry through association of ideas, since
that story has (a) people shouting hosanna (so in Matthew/Mark)
and (b) the greeting 'blessed is he that comes in the name of
the Lord', words found also in lament of Mt 23:37-39. Luke may
in any case have felt that the lament, which he rewords
extensively, fits well as an introduction to what follows.

2.2.3. Conclusions
If Lk 19:41-44 is a Lukan equivalent of Mt 23:37-39, then
it is possible that Luke has retained something of the
narrative context of that lament in his 19:41 and that this has
been eliminated (like other narrative links) by Matthew./1/
But it must be admitted that the whole hypothesis concerning Lk
19:41-44, which we have explored, is rather complicated and
also that the suggested reconstruction of the section of the
eschatological discourse describing the desolation of
Jerusalem is speculative (though attractive). Our conclusion
must then be that Lk 19:41-44 is uncertain support for the view
that Mt 23:37-39 is correctly located, though that view remains
probable.

(e.g. in omitting Mk 11:16 and in the wording of Jesus' saying
of 11:17 & par.)
/1/ It is possible that in the pre-synoptic tradition the
incident of the children in the temple came *after* the woes
against the scribes and Pharisees, that it was followed by
Jesus leaving the temple and Jerusalem (cf. Mt 21:17) and that
the lament came on the following morning as Jesus again 'neared
Jerusalem' (cf. Lk 19:41) - before the eschatological
discourse. Luke's combination of traditions in 19:39-44 would
be explicable thus, and perhaps also his failure to link the
eschatological discourse to Jesus' departure from the temple
(Lk 21:5, contrast Mt 24:1/Mk 13:1). But the question of the
relationship of the synoptic traditions in Matthew 21-23 & par.
is a complex one, though fascinating. Among other points to be
noted are Matthew's and Luke's agreements (a) in locating the
cleansing of the temple immediately after the triumphal entry,
(b) in the use of αὐλίζεσθαι in Mt 21:17, Lk 21:37.

3. THE EVIDENCE OF 1 THESS 2:14-16

The argument for considering the woes against the scribes
and Pharisees to have been part of the preceding context of the
eschatological discourse (see section 1.1 above) may receive
support from Paul.

We have already noted in passing (p. 203 above) that
1 Thess 2:14-16 may be echoing the sayings of Mt 23:29-38 (the
woe on those who build the tombs of the prophets). The evidence
for this is spelled out in an article by J. B. Orchard./1/
Orchard notes four words in common ἀποκτείνειν, προφήτης,
(ἐκ)διώκειν, (ἀνα)πληροῦν, and thinks it remarkable to find all
the four words together in two passages. More substantially he
notes a common thread of thought and similar development:
(i) Paul speaks of the Jews ἡμᾶς ἐκδιωξάντων (1 Thess 2:15);
and in Mt 23:34 Jesus says διώξετε ἀπὸ πόλεως εἰς πόλιν;
(ii) 1 Thess 2:16 εἰς τὸ ἀναπληρῶσαι αὐτῶν τὰς ἁμαρτίας πάντοτε
parallels Mt 23:32 ὑμεῖς πληρώσατε τὸ μέτρον τῶν πατέρων;
(iii) 1 Thess 2:15 τῶν καὶ τὸν κύριον ἀποκτεινάντων Ἰησοῦν καὶ
τοὺς προφήτας parallels Mt 23:34,37 (Jerusalem) ἀποκτείνουσα
τοὺς προφήτας; (iv) 1 Thess 2:16 ἔφθασεν δὲ ἐπ' αὐτοὺς ἡ ὀργὴ
εἰς τέλος parallels Mt 23:36 ἥξει ταῦτα πάντα ἐπὶ τὴν γενεὰν
ταύτην, v 38 ἰδοὺ ἀφίεται ὑμῖν ὁ οἶκος ὑμῶν ...

Although these parallels are not all very close and need
not be regarded as significant, it is impressive how much of
1 Thess 2:15,16 can be paralleled in Mt 23:29-38 (or even in the
shorter 23:32-36). Were the Lukan wording of the 'Q' passage to
be preferred, i.e. Luke 11:49 ἀποστελῶ εἰς αὐτοὺς προφήτας καὶ
ἀποστόλους, καὶ ἐξ αὐτῶν ἀποκτενοῦσιν καὶ διώξουσιν ...., this
would give an even closer parallel to Paul's τῶν..ἀποκτεινάντων
...τοὺς προφήτας καὶ ἡμᾶς ἐκδιωξάντων ... But it is only
Matthew who has the reference to 'filling up the measure of
your fathers', which is perhaps the most distinctive parallel
to 1 Thessalonians 2 'to fill up their sins'. This phrase is
often regarded as a Matthean addition to the 'Q' tradition./2/
But it is quite possible, even (in view of the Pauline evidence)
probable, that it was in the pre-synoptic tradition. Luke may
have omitted the phrase altogether; but it is probably
preferable to see his 'you approve the deeds of your fathers'

/1/ Biblica 19, pp. 20-23. Cf. also R. Schippers, NovT 8 (1966)
230-34, also my 'Paul and the Synoptic Apocalypse', 361-62.
/2/ E.g. E. Haenchen, Gott und Mensch (Tübingen: Mohr, 1965) 43.

(11:48) as a Lukan substitute for the more obscure Matthean
expression, and indeed to see the whole of Lk 11:47,48 as a
Lukan simplification of Mt 23:29-32.

In favour of seeing significance in the parallelism between
1 Thessalonians 2 and Matthew 23, apart from the overlap of
language and ideas, is the slight oddity of Paul's references in
1 Thess 2:14,15. E. Best discusses, in the first place, why
Paul picks on the churches of Judea as an example when writing
to Thessalonica./1/ This is quite simply explained, if there
is reason to think that Paul is here using the tradition that is
also found in Mt 23:29-38. Similarly, in verse 15, where Best
and others are mystified by the unparalleled violence of the
accusation against the Jews, if Paul is here quoting, then much
of his vehement language may be explicable. So may the unusual
use of ἀποκτείνειν in connexion with the death of Jesus, since
this hypothesis must presuppose that Paul added the reference
to 'the Lord Jesus' to the original simple reference to the
killing of 'the prophets'./2/

The significance of this argument concerning 1 Thess 2:14-16
for the question of the original context of the
eschatological discourse has to do with the fact that, as well
as echoing Mt 23:29-38, 1 Thess 2:16 can also be linked with
Lk 21:23,24, as was seen in chap. 5 above (pp. 199-204). Paul thus
seems to have blended together the tradition of the woes and
the tradition of the eschatological discourse. This does not
prove that those traditions were adjacent in the pre-synoptic
tradition, though it does show that both are primitive; but
what Paul has done is certainly the more readily intelligible
if the traditions were close to each other. Paul may,
therefore, lend support to the conclusion that has already been
argued on other grounds.

/1/ *Thessalonians*, 112-121.
/2/ It may possibly be significant that in 1 Thess 2:15,16
the verbs that have links with the synoptic tradition,
ἀποκτεινάντων, ἐκδιωξάντων, ἀναπληρωσαι, are all in the aorist,
whereas ἀρεσκόντων and κωλυόντων are in the present. Is this
something to do with a switch from citation to reflection on
present experience?

4. CONCLUSIONS

It has been seen in the preceding discussion that a number of strands of evidence all point to the conclusion that Matthew has preserved much of the preceding context of the eschatological discourse, though he omitted the story of the widow's mite. This is no surprise in view of our earlier findings about the discourse itself, but it is an interesting extension of those findings. It is very significant for our overall thesis that there is evidence that suggests that the traditions of Matthew 23 and parallels may be explicable in terms of a pre-synoptic tradition, such as we have already seen to lie behind the eschatological discourse. What could also be of considerable importance is the proposal made about Lk 19:43, 44 and 23:29,30: these sayings may have belonged in the pre-synoptic discourse, though the evidence was not such as to prove this.

CONCLUSION

1. *SUMMARY OF PRECEDING CHAPTERS*

The preceding chapters have been for the most part very
detailed and rather complicated analysis, and it is therefore
difficult to summarize the argument effectively. But an
attempt will be made.

Chapter 1 examined the traditions of Mk 13:34-36 and
Lk 12:36-38 and argued that a common parable of the watchman lies
behind the two passages. It was observed first that the
passages are indirectly linked through Matthew 24 (which has
connections with Mark 13 and Luke 12), and secondly that
Mk 13:33-37 contains slightly awkward elements that could perhaps be
explicable via the hypothesis that the Markan passage is an
amalgam of elements that are found in Matthew 24,25 and
Lk 12:35-48. The suggestions of Dupont, Weiser and Jeremias
concerning the history of the Markan and Lukan traditions were
then reviewed. Their suggestions that there was an underlying
parable about a watchman (singular - contrast Luke's plural) and
that Mk 13:34a belonged originally with the parable of the
talents not with the postulated parable of the watchman were
seen to be plausible. But some of their other proposals were
less plausible, and they failed to offer a convincing overall
explanation of the relationship of the traditions. However, a
fresh examination of the Markan and Lukan evidence and also of
Mt 24:42 led to a new proposal about an underlying parable of
the watchman, and it was claimed that this proposal made good
sense of all the synoptic texts in question. Significantly this
underlying form was known to each of the synoptic evangelists
independently.

Chapter 2 proceeded to argue that the 'pre-synoptic'
parable of the watchman was not alone, but belonged with the
other parables found in Mt 24:42-25:30, Mk 13:33-37, Lk 12:35-
48. The parable of the thief was examined first. Then the
sayings of Lk 12:41 and Mk 13:37 were discussed, and it was
argued that in the pre-synoptic tradition Peter's question of
Lk 12:41 'Are you saying this parable to us, or also to all?'
was answered by Jesus' saying of Mk 13:37 'What I say to you I
say to all, keep awake'. The parable of the steward was
considered, and then the parable of the talents: it was

concluded that the parable of the talents was followed in the
pre-synoptic tradition by the parable of the disobedient
servants (i.e. Lk 12:47,48), and also that Luke's parable of
the pounds may be a conflation of the parable of the talents
with a parable of the pretender to the throne. The parable of
the virgins was seen as part of the pre-synoptic tradition, and
Lk 12:35 'Let your loins be girded and your lamps burning' was
the pre-synoptic conclusion to the parable. The present
Matthean conclusion (Mt 25:13) belonged in fact with the parable
of the steward, but Matthew has moved the parable of the virgins
from its pre-synoptic position (reflected in Lk 12:35) and
placed it between the parable of the steward and the
exhortation that concluded that parable. The conclusion of
the argument was that there was a pre-synoptic collection of
eschatological parables known to all the synoptic evangelists
and quite possibly known also to Paul and to the author of
Revelation.

Chapter 3 took the argument a step further, and suggested
that the pre-synoptic tradition included the so-called 'Q'
sayings about Noah and Lot (Mt 24:37-44/Lk 17:26-35) and then
the Lukan exhortations of Lk 21:34-36. These exhortations,
which were known by Paul, led into the eschatological parables
discussed in chapter 2. Two additional notes explored the
Matthean sheep and goats section and the saying about the
twelve judging the tribes of Israel (Mt 19:28/Lk 22:28-30), and
argued that both traditions may have been part of the pre-
synoptic tradition, the saying preceding the description of the
sheep and the goats and both following the eschatological
parables. This last argument was of interest, but incidental
to the main thesis of the book.

Chapter 4 claimed that Lk 17:22-37 is an extract from the
pre-synoptic eschatological discourse, not a separate tradition
from the Markan discourse. This was suggested by the argument
in chapter 3 concerning the 'Q' sayings about Noah and Lot
(Mt 24:37-44/Lk 17:26-35), and by the overlap between Lk 17:20-23/
Mk 13:19-22. Luke has appended the extract to the saying about
the coming of the kingdom in Lk 17:20,21; Matthew has retained
the 'Q' material in question in its pre-synoptic context, and
Mark has for the most part omitted it. A detailed comparison of
the traditions in question substantiated this proposal, showing
how the Matthean and Lukan traditions in question are both
derived from a common original and how both retain some
original features. Luke retains the pre-synoptic reference to
the days of Lot and the comparison of the days of Noah and Lot

to the 'day(s) of the Son of man'; contrast Matthew's 'parousia
of the Son of man'. But in the preceding section Matthew is
more original in comparing 'the parousia' to lightning; contrast
Luke's 'the Son of man (in his day)'. And later Matthew's 'two
men in a field' is preferable to Luke's 'two in a bed'. Both
Matthew and Luke may have moved the saying about the 'body' and
the 'eagles' from its pre-synoptic position.

   Chapter 5 looked at the central section of the discourse
that describes the 'desolating sacrilege' or the 'desolation' of
Jerusalem. Paul's similar description of the advent of the man
of lawlessness in 2 Thessalonians 2 suggests that we are
dealing with primitive tradition in this section. But how are
the differences between the Matthew/Mark description of the
desolating sacrilege and the Lukan description of the
destruction of Jerusalem to be explained? Many scholars have
seen the Lukan version as Luke's redactional reworking of the
Matthew/Mark form of the tradition; on the other hand, not a
few scholars have maintained that Luke has retained a tradition
independent of that found in Matthew/Mark. The argument put
forward finds truth in both positions: Lk 21:20-23a is to be
explained largely as Lukan adaptation of the Matthew/Mark form;
but there is reason even here to think that Luke knew a non-
Markan form of the tradition that is used also in Matthew (cf.
Lk 17:31 with Mt 24:17/Mk 13:15). In the verses that follow
(Mt 24:21,22/Mk 13:19,20/Lk 21:23b,24) the case for Lukan
independence is even stronger, and it is argued that both the
Lukan reference to the destruction of Jerusalem and also the Matthew/
Mark description of unparalleled and universal distress belonged
together in the pre-synoptic tradition. This is suggested,
among other things, by evidence in Paul's letters and in the
book of Revelation pointing to the traditional origin of Luke's
tradition and by the fact that the slightly uneasy sequence of
thought in the Matthew/Mark form of the tradition is explicable
if they have omitted something like Luke's description of
Jerusalem's fall. It is possible that the pre-synoptic form
postulated is reflected in Revelation 13.

   Chapter 6 considered the sayings about appearing before the
authorities (Mt 10:17-20/Mk 13:9-11/Lk 12:11,12/Lk 21:12-15),
and argued that these sayings are correctly located by Matthew
in a mission discourse and that they were not part of the
eschatological discourse. The steps in this argument included
(a) demonstrating the existence of a non-Markan form of the
tradition in question and (b) showing the links between this
tradition and the difficult Matthean sayings of Mt 10:23 and

10:5 and 6. Some suggestions were made about the probable existence of a pre-synoptic tradition underlying the mission discourses of Matthew 10, Mark 6 and Luke 9 and 11.

Chapter 7 returned to the eschatological discourse and to the section describing the coming sufferings (Mt 24:9-14/ Mk 13:9-13/Lk 21:12-19). The previous chapter concluded that the sayings about appearing before the authorities, which Mark and Luke have here, belonged in fact in the mission discourse, and this chapter adds to that the observation that Mt 24:10-12 also appears to be an interpolation in the context. When the interpolated material is excluded from Matthew, Mark and Luke, then what is left is the pre-synoptic form of this section of the eschatological discourse: Matthew preserves the pre-synoptic tradition in his 24:9a; this was followed by the saying about brother handing over brother (Mt 10:21/Mk 13:12 cf. Lk 21:16), and then by the sayings concerning hatred and endurance (Mt 10:22/24:9b,13/Mk 13:13/Lk 21:17-19), and finally by the saying concerning the evangelization of the Gentiles (Mt 24:14/ Mk 13:10).

Chapter 8 attempted to tie up some loose ends. (1) Some remarks were made about the introduction to the discourse (Mt 24:1-3/Mk 13:1-3/Lk 21:5-7), and it was suggested that Luke may have retained some features of the pre-synoptic tradition that are not found in Matthew and Mark. (2) The opening warnings of the discourse were examined (Mt 24:4-8/Mk 13:5-8/Lk 21:8-11), and it seemed possible that the pre-synoptic tradition spoke of 'earthquakes .. plagues ... famines and disturbances', 'all these things' being 'the beginning of pangs'. Luke's intrusive 'Then he said to them' (21:10) could be a pre-synoptic element omitted by Matthew and Mark. (3) The description of the parousia itself differs in each of the synoptics (Mt 24:29-31/ Mk 13:24-27/Lk 21:25-28). Luke's reference to 'signs in heaven' may have been in the pre-synoptic tradition, as may his description of distress on earth. The evidence of Revelation 6 was cited in support of this proposal, but also led to the rather speculative suggestion that the pre-synoptic tradition may have included other elements (including the saying of Lk 23:30). Matthew's description of the 'sign of the Son of man' appearing in heaven and of the tribes mourning at his appearance was also tentatively assigned to the pre-synoptic tradition. The Matthew/Mark description of the gathering of the elect was seen as part of the pre-synoptic tradition, and so, much less certainly, was the Lukan exhortation to look up because of the nearness of 'your redemption'. (4) Finally the

parable of the fig tree and the sayings about the time of the
end were considered (Mt 24:32-36/Mk 13:28-32/Lk 21:29-33).
Matthew and Mark were considered more original in the wording of
the parable and in the inclusion of the saying about the
unknownness of the day and hour, but Luke may have retained the
pre-synoptic form in the opening 'And he spoke a parable to
them' and in the wording of the saying about all things
happening in a generation.

Chapter 9 looked at the context of the discourse in the
different gospels, concluding that the pre-synoptic context is
reflected in each of the synoptics, since it included sayings
against the scribes, the story of the widow's mite, the woes
against the Pharisees and scribes, and the lament over
Jerusalem. The possibility that Lk 19:41-44 is a version of the
lament that perhaps incorporates sayings that originally
belonged in the eschatological discourse was investigated.

2.   THE WHOLE PRE-SYNOPTIC TRADITION AS RECONSTRUCTED

Given the detailed analysis of earlier chapters, it is
now possible to suggest the form of the whole of the pre-
synoptic eschatological discourse, as far as we have
reconstructed it. But it is important to realise that parts
of this postulated pre-synoptic form can be reconstructed with
reasonable confidence, other parts only tentatively or
speculatively, and also that the reconstruction is quite
probably incomplete./1/ In the following proposed
reconstruction a very rough and ready attempt has been made to
differentiate those parts of the reconstruction that seem
relatively secure from those that seem less secure, but for
detailed discussion of the relative probability of the
different elements reference must be made to the preceding
chapters. The following distinctions have been made in the
reconstruction:
(1) Ordinary type: passages which have been discussed in detail
in the monograph and where it is possible to be reasonably
confident about most of the reconstruction (even if not about
all the detailed wording). *(2) Italic type: passages where*

_____

/1/ Some of the material included in the reconstruction is
found only in one of the synoptics and some is found in none
(but in the book of Revelation). It is quite probable that
other material which we have not identified, belonged in the
pre-synoptic eschatological discourse.

the discussion has been less conclusive and/or less detailed.
(3) Script type: passages where the proposal is quite
speculative.

(Context   *Sayings against scribes, story of widow's mite, woes*
                   against Pharisees and scribes, lament over Jerusalem)

Intro-   *And Jesus came out of the temple; and his disciples*
ductory   *came to him and showed him the buildings of the*
dialogue   *temple. And he said to them: 'Do you see these*
                   things? Truly I tell you one stone will not be left
                   on another that will not be pulled down'. And he
                   sat down on the Mount of Olives. And his disciples
                   said to him/asked him, saying: 'Teacher, tell us
                   when these things will be, and what will be the sign
                   when these things are going to happen?'

Opening   And he/Jesus said: 'See that no one leads you
warning   astray. For many will come in my name saying (that)
                   "I am (the Christ)", and will lead many astray. But
                   when you hear of wars and rumours of wars, do not be
                   disturbed. (For) it must happen, but the end is not
    ·   yet.

Beginnings   *(Then he said to them)*: Nation will rise
of pangs   against nation, and kingdom against kingdom. There
                   will be earthquakes in various places and famines,
                   there will be plagues and disturbances. But all
                   these things are the beginnings of pangs.

Coming   Then they will hand you over to tribulation,
tribulation and they will kill you. For brother will hand over
                   brother to death and father child, and children will
                   rise against parents and kill them. And you will be
                   hated by all the nations because of my name. But he
                   who endures to the end will be saved. And this
                   gospel of the kingdom will be preached for a
                   testimony to all the nations, and then the end will
                   come.

Desolation   When therefore you see *Jerusalem surrounded by*
of   *armies and* the desolating sacrilege *which was spoken*
Jerusalem   *of by Daniel the prophet* standing in the holy place,
                   let the reader understand. Then let those in Judea
                   flee to the mountains. He who is on the house let
                   him not go down to get the things from his house,

and he who is in the field let him not turn back to get his cloak. *For these are days of judgment on Jerusalem. Her enemies will cast up a ramp against her, and they will surround her and hem her in on all sides, and dash her and her children to the ground.* In those days they will say: *Blessed are the barren and the wombs which did not bear, and the breasts that did not give suck.* But woe to those with child and to those giving suck in those days. Pray that your flight may not be in winter *or on a sabbath.* For there will be great distress on the land and wrath on this people, and they will fall by the mouth of the sword and be taken captive into all nations, and Jerusalem will be trodden down by Gentiles until the times of the Gentiles are fulfilled.

Great
tribulation

And there will then be great tribulation as there has not been from the beginning of the world until now, nor will be. And if those days were not shortened, no flesh would have been saved. But for the sake of the elect those days will be shortened.

Warning of
deceivers

And if then anyone says to you: "Behold here is the Christ", or "there", do not believe it. For false Christs and false prophets will arise and will do great signs and wonders to deceive, if possible, even the elect. You be on your guard; I have told you beforehand.'

Visibility
of parousia

And they replying said to him: 'Where (then) Lord?'. And he said to them, 'Whereever the body is, there the eagles will be gathered together. So if they say to you, "Behold he is in the desert", do not go out; "behold he is in the chambers", do not pursue. For as the lightning goes from *the one end of heaven and shines to the other end of heaven,* so will be the parousia of the Son of man.

Signs of
parousia

And (Immediately after the tribulation of those days) there will be signs in heaven. The sun will be darkened, the moon will not give her light, the stars will fall from heaven, and the powers of the heavens will be shaken. And on earth *there will be a great earthquake. And every mountain and island will be moved from their places. There will be*

distress of nations at the roaring of the sea.
Men will tremble with fear and anticipation at the
things coming on the earth. They will begin to
say to the mountains "Fall on us" and to the hills
"Cover us". And then will appear the sign of the
Son of man in heaven. And then all the tribes of
the earth will mourn.

And they will see the Son of man coming on
the clouds (of heaven) with power and great glory.
And he will send his angels with a loud trumpet,
and they will gather his elect from the four winds
from one end of heaven to the other.

Recognizing   *When these things begin to happen, look up*
the signs   *and.lift up your heads, for your redemption is*
                   near.

And he told them a parable. See the fig
tree. When its branch becomes tender and puts out
leaves, you know that the summer is near. So you,
when you see these things happening, know that he
is near at the doors.

Time of the   Truly I tell you that this generation will
events   surely not pass away until *all things* happen.
                   Heaven and earth will pass away, but my words will
                   not pass away.

But of that day and hour knows no one, not
even the angels in heaven nor the Son, except the
Father.

The   For as it was in the days of Noah, so will it
unexpected   be in the day of the Son of man. They were eating
day   and drinking, marrying and giving in marriage
                   until the day when Noah entered the ark and the
                   flood came and destroyed all. Likewise as it was
                   in the days of Lot, so will it be in the day of
                   the Son of man. They were eating and drinking,
                   they were buying and selling, they were planting
                   and building, until the day when Lot went out of
                   Sodom and it rained fire and brimstone and
                   destroyed them all. *In that day there will be two*
                   in a field, one will be taken and one left; there

will be two at the mill, one will be taken and one
left.

Take heed therefore to yourselves, lest your
hearts be weighed down with carousing and
drunkenness and worldly cares, and that day comes
upon you suddenly like a snare. For it will come
upon all who dwell on the face of all the earth.

Keep awake   But keep awake at every moment praying that
at every   you may be able to escape all these things that
moment   are going to happen and to stand before the Son of
man.

Parables on   For the kingdom of God/heaven will be like
absent Lord   ten virgins ...... *(as in Matthew)* .... but he
coming at   answered: "Truly I tell you, I do not know you".
any moment   So you then let your loins be girded and your
lamps burning.

It is like a man awaiting his master, when he
will return from a feast, so that when he comes
and knocks he may immediately open to him.
Blessed is that servant whom the master shall find
awake when he comes. Truly I tell you, he will
gird himself and sit him down and serve him. So
then keep awake. For you do not know in which
watch the master of the house comes, whether in
the first, or in the second, or in the third, lest
coming suddenly he finds you sleeping.

Know this that if the householder knew in
what hour the thief was coming he would not have
allowed his house to be broken into. So you be
ready, for in an hour you do not expect the Son of
man comes.'

And Peter said: 'Lord, do you say this
parable to us or also to all?' And Jesus said:
'What I say to you I say to all: keep awake.

Parables on   Who is the faithful and wise servant whom the
serving   master appointed ...... *(as in Matthew/Luke)* ...
absent Lord   the lord of the servant will come in a day he does
responsibly   not expect and in an hour he does not know, and he
will punish him and put his part with the

faithless. So keep awake, for you do not know
the day nor the hour.

For as a man going away on a journey, he
called his servants and gave them his substance
to each according to his ability. To one he
gave five talents .... to one two, and to one
one. And he went away ..... (*as Matthew's
parable of talents*) ... for to everyone who has
will be given (and in abundance) and from him
who has not will be taken even what he has. *And
as for the useless servant cast him out* ....

That servant who knew his master's will and
did not prepare or do according to his will will
be beaten with many strokes. He who did not
know and did things worthy of strokes will be
beaten with few. But from everyone to whom much
is given will much be required, and from him to
whom they entrust much they will ask the more.'

The disciples'   *And Peter said to him in reply:* 'What about
reward   *us?'* And Jesus said: 'You who have followed me,
                   I promise to you, as my father promised me, a
                   kingdom. You will eat and drink at my table in
                   my kingdom, and you will sit on twelve thrones
                   judging the twelve tribes.

Judgment of   *But when the Son of man comes in his glory
the nations*   and all the angels with him, then he will sit on
                   the throne of his glory, and there will be
                   gathered before him all nations, and he will
                   separate .... (as in Matthew 25)'.

It must be reemphasized that some parts of the
reconstruction proposed above are uncertain. But other parts
have a high degree of probability, as has the general idea of
the pre-synoptic discourse form.

3. GENERAL CONCLUSIONS

3.1. A pre-synoptic tradition

Although it is almost impossible to summarize the detailed
argumentation of the book effectively, it is possible to

summarize its general conclusions. The main conclusion is that
there was an elaborate pre-synoptic form of the eschatological
discourse (or at least of major parts of the discourse), and
that this was known and used independently by Matthew, Mark and
Luke. This hypothesis has been seen to make sense of many
synoptic similarities, differences and peculiarities in a way
that other explanations do not. For example, it goes a long
way to answering the questions raised by Mk 13:33-37, by the
'Q' eschatological discourse (as it is usually regarded) of
Lk 17:22-37, by the considerable differences between the
Matthew/Mark and the Lukan descriptions of the desolation of
Jerusalem, and so on.   .

    Each of the evangelists has used the pre-synoptic tradition
differently. If anything, Matthew appears from our study as the
evangelist who most often and most fully reproduces the pre-
synoptic form of the tradition. Mark abbreviates it
substantially. Luke is the most free, so far as order is
concerned: although Matthew and Mark have some material out of
its pre-synoptic context (e.g. Mt 10:21,22 and perhaps 19:28-30,
Mk 13:9-11), Luke goes much further, using large sections of
the eschatological discourse out of the pre-synoptic context
for thematic or other reasons (notably Lk 12:35-48, 17:22-37,
cf. also 19:11-27, perhaps 19:41-44, 22:28-30, 23:29,30 etc.).
Luke also freely paraphrases the tradition, especially when he
is using a tradition for a second time, no doubt to avoid
sounding repetitious (e.g. Lk 21:12-19, 21:21, etc.). On the
other hand, his freedom is limited; and, when he does
paraphrase, he sometimes appears to check himself and to return
to the wording of the tradition that he has paraphrased
(cf. Lk 21:12-19; see pp. 226, 234-36, 267 and 268 above).

    It might appear to be a problem with the hypothesis
proposed that it presupposes that all the evangelists have
split up and in certain respects spoiled the coherence of the
postulated pre-synoptic tradition. It has frequently been
maintained in the course of the preceding discussion that
difficulties in the synoptic texts are to be explained on the
basis of a less difficult pre-synoptic text, and this could
seem unlikely. However, (a) it would be wrong to suggest that
the pre-synoptic tradition as reconstructed is always and in
all respects more coherent than all of the synoptic traditions.
The reconstructed version of the eschatological discourse is
usually similar to one or more of the synoptic versions, and
only at certain points is its structure evidently superior to
that of the synoptics. Occasionally the synoptic versions

are clearer than the pre-synoptic version (e.g. in Mt 24:3 and
Mk 13:30). (b) It would also be wrong to give the impression
that the synoptic versions are incoherent: their versions for
the most part make perfectly good sense. (c) They do, however,
contain some minor difficulties which need explanation and
which cannot be satisfactorily explained as quirks of style,
but which are explicable in the ways suggested. (d) Although
it would indeed be hard to imagine an editor working through a
coherent tradition trying to make it incoherent, it is not hard
to imagine an editor abbreviating a long tradition or editing a
tradition in line with his redactional interests and as a
result producing some minor editorial infelicities. (e) We may
still consider certain of the synoptists' modifications of the
pre-synoptic tradition surprising. But, as N. H. Palmer has
said, 'What we would do if we were the evangelists is just
irrelevant. What they would do can be discovered only by
inspecting what they did.'/1/ The case for the synoptic
evangelists' use of the pre-synoptic tradition rests on the
detailed examination of particular texts offered in the
monograph, and must be assessed accordingly.

*3.2. The pre-synoptic tradition in Paul's letters and other
church traditions*

      There is good reason to believe that Paul was familiar
with this pre-synoptic discourse form (or at least with major
parts of it). He knew the opening warning against deceivers
(see pp. 176-80, 295, 296 above), probably the warnings about
coming persecution and the saying about the preaching of the
gospel (see pp. 282-84 above), certainly the description of the
desolating sacrilege events and the description of the parousia
itself, including perhaps the Lukan call to 'lift up your
heads' because of the nearness of redemption (see pp. 176-80,
199-204, 304-06, 325, 326). He may have known the Matthew/
Mark saying about no one knowing the day or hour (see
pp. 121, 124 above), and he probably knew the exhortation of
Lk 21:34-36 and the following parables of the virgins, the
watchman, the thief and the steward (see pp. 54,55,63,89-91,
110-18 above). He draws on the discourse particularly in

/1/ *The Logic of Gospel Criticism* (London: Macmillan, 1968)
121. The modern critic must, of course, make some judgments
about whether an ancient author is likely or unlikely to have
done something; but extreme caution is needed in making such
judgments.

1 and 2 Thessalonians, but also echoes it elsewhere in his
writings (e.g. Rom 11:25, 13:11-14; perhaps 1 Cor 4:1-5,
7:26,29, 15:52, Eph 5:6-18, 6:10-18; 2 Tim 2:12). Not all of
possible echoes would be probable echoes taken by themselves;
but once it is established that Paul probably was familiar with
the eschatological discourse, evidence that would be
insignificant by itself assumes probable significance, and
there may well be more Pauline allusions to the discourse than
those we have noted.

There is also reason to believe that the author of
Revelation was familiar with the pre-synoptic discourse and that
he used it extensively. He was familiar with the opening woes
(see pp. 296, 297 above), with the warnings of persecution,
the call to endurance and the saying(s) about the preaching
of the gospel (see pp. 207-10, 284), with the description of
the desolating sacrilege and of the parousia (see pp. 205-13,
311-18), also with the parabolic exhortation at the end of the
discourse (see pp. 31, 55, 56, 79). Other early Christian
writings may also reflect the pre-synoptic tradition, notably
the Didache (see pp. 124, 125, 237, 238, 322, 323), perhaps James
and 1 Peter (see pp. 326, 328). Once again the list might be extended; no systematic attempt has been made in this book to track
down every possible allusion to the pre-synoptic discourse.

3.3. The nature of the pre-synoptic tradition

As for the nature of the postulated pre-synoptic tradition,
this has not been explored. But the conclusions reached seem to
point to some form of pre-synoptic gospel - a very early form of
the tradition, which was widely known and respected (e.g. by all
the evangelists) and which had a definite structure and order.
It may have been an oral or possibly a written source. The
evangelists probably knew a Greek form of the tradition (to
judge from verbal agreements, and, for example, from the
argument about οὐσία in chapter 2 above, pp. 44,45). The source
is not 'Q' in the normally understood sense, since it was known
to Mark and used by Mark, and there is no reason to suppose that
the source included only discourse, even though this has been
the primary object of this study./1/

/1/ It was suggested that the story of the widow's mite may
have been part of the pre-synoptic tradition (p. 345 above).
Perhaps the hosanna controversy (Mt 21:15,16; Lk 19:39,40) was
also. Other agreements of Matthew and Luke in the passion
narrative (e.g. in the stories of the cursing of the fig tree

To speculate about the nature of the pre-synoptic gospel is
probably unnecessary.   But it is not unlikely that J. A. T.
Robinson is correct in his view that there was a semi-official
form of the apostolic teaching known and taught in Jerusalem at
a very early date./1/ There may be more truth in the much-
discussed suggestions of H. Riesenfeld and B. Gerhardsson about
the apostolic role of passing on the gospel tradition than is
often recognized.

But it might be objected that it is premature to speak of a
pre-synoptic *gospel* on the basis of a study of one synoptic
discourse; perhaps it would be more prudent to speak of a
primitive tract of eschatological teaching material. However,
our preceding study of the eschatological discourse took us also
into the mission discourse (Matthew 10 and parallels) and into
the discourse against the scribes and Pharisees (Matthew 23 and
parallels), where the idea of a pre-synoptic form of the
tradition was also found fruitful. We have not here explored
the Sermon on the Mount (Matthew 5-7); but a similar sort of
explanation can be given of those traditions: Matthew may be
supposed to have retained the Sermon's framework and contents
most fully; Luke partially fragmented the discourse, though he
may retain some primitive elements; Paul and other NT writers
probably knew the pre-synoptic discourse./2/ A similar case
might be made out for the parable discourse (Matthew 13 and
parallels): Matthew retains the fullest pre-synoptic form, Mark
abbreviates,/3/ Luke is influenced by Mark, but shows some
knowledge of the pre-synoptic form and has some of the
traditions elsewhere (Lk 13:18-21)./4/ The idea, then, of a
_____
and the cleansing of the temple) may be similarly explained. Is
Paul drawing on the same pre-synoptic gospel, when he describes
the Last Supper (1 Cor 11:23-26) and the Lord's death and
resurrection (1 Cor 15:3-8)?

/1/ *Redating the New Testament* (London: SCM, 1976) pp.97,105 106.
/2/ See my review article on R. A. Guelich's *The Sermon on the
Mount* in the *Trinity Journal* vol. 4 (forthcoming).
/3/ Note his 'with many such parables' in 4:33. Cf. Chapman,
Matthew Mark and Luke, 5, 6.
/4/ My article 'The Interpretation of the Parable of the Sower',
NTS 20 (1974) 299-319 argues for a pre-synoptic form of the
interpretation. Cf. also my thesis, *The Composition of Mark 4:
1-34* (submitted to Manchester University in 1970) though I
suppose there that Mark knew Matthew.

pre-synoptic form of tradition is not fruitful in one passage
only, but in several. This is important for our overall
thesis, since otherwise it could be suggested that what appears
to work in the eschatological discourse does not work elsewhere;
and it means that the idea of a pre-synoptic gospel is not
far fetched.

3.4. The three synoptic accounts

The proposal of a pre-synoptic gospel (or at the very
least of substantial tracts of pre-synoptic gospel tradition)
does not exclude the possibility that our synoptic gospels are
also interdependent. Indeed the places where two of the
evangelists diverge from what seems to have been the pre-
synoptic tradition point to some interdependence - probably to
Luke's knowledge of Mark (hence, for example, his reproduction
of the mission discourse sayings within the eschatological
discourse in 21:12-14) and to Matthew's knowledge of Mark (see,
for example, his appending of 10:21,22 to the preceding
persecution sayings). But the dependence of Matthew and Luke
on Mark is much less than is usually supposed, and each of the
evangelists from time to time preserves the most primitive
pre-synoptic form of the tradition.

4. POSSIBLE IMPLICATIONS

4.1. The synoptic problem

The potential significance of our findings for the synoptic
problem is clearly considerable. To some the idea that
something like the old 'Ur Gospel' hypothesis should be
resurrected may seem depressing, since there are already enough
conflicting theories currently on offer in the scholarly market.
To others the suggestion that Matthew and Luke used Mark as well
as the pre-synoptic gospel tradition may sound a complicated
hypothesis, which is virtually unfalsifiable, since it allows
for so many possible explanations of any given text.

But neither of these reactions is justified: the fact of
scholarly discord on the question of the synoptic problem is an
indication that the problem is complex and that it has not yet
been solved, but it does not mean that there is no solution or
that the solution may not be discovered. It is not true that
the proposal we have made implies a very complicated solution to
the synoptic problem. To propose the existence of a

pre-synoptic gospel tradition known to all three evangelists
and the use of Mark by Matthew and Luke is hardly more complex
than the two-source hypothesis, and seems at least as likely -
it has never been plausible to suggest that Matthew and Luke
only knew (or used) the Markan version of the material that
they have in common with Mark. The fact that our proposal
allows greater flexibility in explaining synoptic relationships
in particular texts is a strength: it was the inability of the
two-source hypothesis to account easily for some original
features in Matthew and Luke and for some agreements of Matthew
and Luke against Mark that was its weakness. It is true that
the flexibility of ·the hypothesis proposed in this monograph
could appear to make it difficult either to prove or disprove;
but it is the argument of the book that the thesis of a
pre-synoptic tradition is demanded by the evidence of the texts
that have been studied. It has not been a case of devising a
catch-all hypothesis that cannot be disproved, but of being led
to one conclusion by a detailed examination of the evidence of
the texts and of different explanations of those texts.

It is not suggested that this monograph has comprehensively
'solved' the synoptic problem. But, if its arguments are
correct or even partially correct, then it provides significant
clues in the continuing search for a solution.

4.2.   *Form-critical ideas about the origins of the gospel*
tradition

The suggestion that there was an elaborate pre-synoptic
discourse form, quite possibly known to Paul, puts a question
mark against the common form-critical theory that the gospel
discourses are a compilation of originally separate traditions
that gradually came together over an extended period of time.
If there is anything in the theory, then the coalescing of the
traditions evidently happened very quickly and early; and what
we find in the gospels is not the building up of discourses
from smaller units, but rather the extracting of materials from
more elaborate pre-synoptic forms. Another common idea is
that the hortatory applications that frequently follow gospel
parables are secondary additions to the parables; but the
evidence considered (especially in chapter 2) suggests that the
applications go back to the early pre-synoptic stage of the
tradition.

It appears, then, that the gospel tradition took something
like its present form much earlier than is often supposed. Our

canonical gospels are not the freezing of a very fluid oral
tradition, but are to a considerable extent based on an already
well-established and respected tradition. If the pre-synoptic
tradition was oral, then our gospels may be seen as different
written versions of that tradition (though Matthew and Luke have
also utilized Mark).

4.3. The evangelists' redaction

The rediscovery of the pre-synoptic tradition introduces a
significant new factor into the discussion of the different
evangelists' redactional interests and methods, and so makes
very clear the continuing importance of source- and tradition-
critical questions for the interpretation of the gospels.

Very many elements in the different versions of the
eschatological discourse that have often been deemed redactional
have been shown to be traditional (e.g. Mk 13:37, Lk 12:41,44,
21:24, 34-36 etc.). And the evidence examined has suggested
that the evangelists have drawn quite strictly on tradition,
making relatively few modifications or additions of their own.
They have, on the other hand, been quite free in the selection
and rearrangement of the traditions. Luke in particular
exhibits such freedom with regard to the pre-synoptic context,
but Matthew and Mark also use some sayings out of context.
There seems to have been a tendency on occasions to bring
together or to assimilate similar material from differing
contexts.

The results of some of the evangelists' editorial work may
sometimes seem to be less than ideal: Luke in 12:41 has a
question without its immediate answer; in 17:31 Luke has an
exhortation that belonged in a context describing the fall of
Jerusalem in a context with no reference to the fall of
Jerusalem; Mark in 13:34 turns slightly awkwardly from one
parable to another, producing what seems to be a hybrid
parable. In none of these cases can it be said that the
evangelists have deliberately changed the meaning of the
tradition, and in each of the cases it can be explained why the
evangelist has made the change in question. But, if the
analysis is correct, it is true that the evangelists have
sometimes complicated the interpreter's task!

If the findings of this book are correct, they do suggest
that redaction critics have often exaggerated the redactional
element in the gospels. But they in no way undermine the

redaction-critical approach to the gospels. On the contrary,
if the suggestions made about the history of the traditions are
correct, then they are important data for the redaction critic.
Questions are immediately suggested: for example, if it is
correct that Matthew and Mark deliberately leave out the Lukan
(and pre-synoptic) description of the destruction of Jerusalem,
why do they do so? If Luke in Luke 12 deliberately avoids
calls to wakefulness, why does he do so? Such questions as
these are grist for the redaction critics' mill produced by our
study.

4.4. Paul, the early church, and the Jesus tradition

The findings of the book have obvious importance for the
much debated question of Jesus and Paul. Any suggestion that
Paul was unfamiliar with or uninterested in the Jesus tradition
must be considered improbable in view of the evidence
accumulated for Paul's use of the pre-synoptic eschatological
traditions. It appears on the contrary that Paul's teaching is
very heavily dependent on the teaching of Jesus, even though he
does not often explicitly acknowledge this dependence. The
Jesus-Paul question is, of course, a large one, which cannot be
discussed here. It has, however, been usefully discussed in
the recent article of D. C. Allison, 'The Pauline Epistles and
the Synoptic Gospels: The Pattern of the Parallels';/1/ the
arguments of this book would support, but also significantly
extend, the sort of case he presents.

The hypothesis of a firmly established pre-synoptic Jesus
tradition not only has relevance to the Jesus-Paul question,
but also for the whole understanding of the early church's
attitude to the Jesus tradition. The idea that the early
church, because of its eschatological and charismatic fervour,
was uninterested in the historical Jesus, is hardly tenable.
It is more probably the case that the early church's
eschatological fervour was the *result* of its familiarity with
the traditions of the eschatological discourse, since these
were known and received as authoritative dominical teaching
from a very early period.

The suggestion that the pre-synoptic tradition was known
to the author of the book of Revelation and to other early

/1/ *NTS* 28 (1982) 1-32.

Christian writers, such as the author of the Didache, has
significant implications not only for the general history of
the gospel traditions but also for the interpretation of the
writings concerned. And if Paul, the author of Revelation and
other early Christian writers have drawn on the pre-synoptic
tradition in the ways suggested, then this clearly raises big
and fascinating questions concerning the history and use of the
tradition in the early church, questions such as: why has Paul
interpreted the tradition religiously, not politically, in
2 Thessalonians? Why has the author of Revelation applied the
pre-synoptic references to Jerusalem and the Jews to the
church?/1/ This book has inevitably done little more than
raise these questions.

4.5. *The rediscovery of Jesus' eschatological discourse*

The findings of this book do not in themselves prove that
the pre-synoptic eschatological discourse goes back to Jesus.
If there was a pre-synoptic gospel, which included the
discourse but also included narrative (e.g. the story of the
widow's mite), this was presumably put together by the church,
perhaps as the apostolic version of Jesus' life and teaching.
And even if this version was current by or before AD 50, as
Paul's use of it suggests, this does not necessarily mean that
it is or was an unadulterated record of Jesus' life and
teaching.

On the other hand, it must be admitted that, if this
pre-synoptic tradition was well-known by the early 50s and if
the teaching in it was known by Paul and all the evangelists as
the authoritative teaching of Jesus, the onus of proof must be
on those who deny the teaching to Jesus, not on those who
affirm it. This is also suggested by the evidence that shows
(a) that Paul - and no doubt others - in the 50s were
interested in the tradition (contrary to the common assumption
of many scholars), (b) that the evangelists respected the
tradition and did not feel free to modify it substantially, and

---

/1/ It is notable that both Paul and the author of Revelation
appear to be much freer in the use of the traditions of the
eschatological discourse than are the synoptic evangelists,
which is probably because they are seeking to apply the
tradition, not to transmit it. The evangelists, while
interpreting the tradition, are seeking to preserve it and to
pass it on.

tradition and did not feel free to modify it substantially, and
(c) that some of the supposedly secondary features of the
gospel tradition (e.g. the hortatory conclusions of the
parables) go back at least to the pre-synoptic stage of
tradition. There is also the coherent order and arrangement of
the pre-synoptic tradition to be accounted for - with the
argument developing in a logical progression and with chiastic
and other patterns (e.g. in the parables at the end of the
discourse, see pp. 96,97 above, and in the seven woes of the
discourse against the scribes and Pharisees, see pp. 338-40
above). This could have been imposed on the Jesus tradition by
its earliest collators, though it has been lost to a
considerable extent by the synoptists. But it may well be that
Jesus himself was largely responsible for the logical and
systematic presentation of his teaching.

To say then that we have certainly rediscovered Jesus'
eschatological discourse is to go beyond the evidence. But it
is reasonable to claim that we have gone some way toward such a
rediscovery.

4.6. Conclusion

Although the possible implications of the argument of this
book for many important issues are of the greatest interest,
the issues in question are enormously complicated, and it would
be unwise to claim that our suggestions about implications are
more than possibilities that merit further study. A danger
with even mentioning the possibilities is that some readers may
be tempted to judge the book solely or primarily on the basis
of these possible implications, and may fail to come to grips
with the detailed arguments about the eschatological discourse
that are the substance of the book. It is the author's hope
that the book will be judged on the basis of its detailed
analysis of the traditions, and that, whatever the
implications, much of the analysis will be considered a useful
contribution to synoptic studies and to research into the
history of the traditions of Jesus' life and teaching.

BIBLIOGRAPHY AND INDICES

BIBLIOGRAPHY

D.C.Allison Jr.
'The Pauline Epistles and the Synoptic Gospels: The Pattern
of Parallels', *NTS* 28 (1982) 1-32.
A.M.Ambrozic
*The Hidden Kingdom: A Redaction-Critical Study of the
References to the Kingdom of God in Mark's Gospel*,
Washington: CBQ Association, 1972.
W.F.Arndt & F.W.Gingrich
*A Greek-English Lexicon of the New Testament and Other
Early Christian Literature*, Cambridge: UP, 1957.
E.H.Askwith
An Introduction to the Thessalonian Epistles, London:
Macmillan, 1902.
E.Bammel
'Matthäus 10,23', *ST* 15 (1961) 79-92.
C.K.Barrett
The Holy Spirit and the Gospel Tradition, London: SPCK, 1947.
R.J.Bauckham
'The Great Tribulation in the Shepherd of Hermas',
JTS 25 (1974) 27-40.
'The eschatological earthquake in the apocalypse of John'
NovT 19 (1977) 224-33.
'Synoptic Parousia Parables and the Apocalypse',
NTS 23 (1977) 162-76.
'Synoptic Parousia Parables Again', *NTS* 29 (1983) 129-34.
F.W.Beare
The Gospel according to Matthew A Commentary, Oxford:
Blackwell, 1981.
G.R.Beasley-Murray
*Jesus and the Future. An Examination of the Criticism of
the Eschatological Discourse, Mark 13, with Special
Reference to the Little Apocalypse Theory*, London:
Macmillan, 1954.
A Commentary on Mark 13, London: Macmillan, 1957.
The Book of Revelation, London: Oliphants, 1974.
E.Best
*A Commentary on the First and Second Epistles to the
Thessalonians*, London: A.& C. Black, 1972.
M.-E.Boismard
Synopse des Quatre Évangiles en Français (by P.Benoit &
M.-E.Boismard) Vol.II *Commentaire par M.-E.Boismard*,
Paris: Cerf, 1972.

D.Bosch
  *Die Heidenmission in der Zukunftsschau Jesu. Eine
  Untersuchung zur Eschatologie der synoptischen Evangelien,*
  Zürich: Zwingli, 1959.
W.Bousset
  'Antichrist' in *Encyclopedia of Religion and Ethics,* ed.
  J.Hastings, vol.1, Edinburgh: T.& T.Clark, 1908, pp.578-81.
G.Braumann
  'Die Lukanische Interpretation der Zerstörung Jerusalems',
  NovT 6 (1963) 120-27.
I.Broer
  'Das Gericht des Menschensohnes über de Völker. Auslegung
  von Mt 25,31-46', *BibLeb* 11 (1970) 273-95
J.P.Brown
  'Mark as Witness to an edited form of Q', *JBL* 80 (1961)
  29-41.
F.Brown, S.R.Driver, C.A.Briggs
  A Hebrew and English Lexicon of the Old Testament,
  Oxford: UP, 1907 (with corrections 1962).
R.E.Brown
  The Gospel according to John XIII-XXI, London: Chapman, 1971.
S.Brown
  'The Matthean Apocalypse', *JSNT* 4 (1979) 2-27.
R.Bultmann
  The History of the Synoptic Tradition, Oxford: Blackwells, 1972.
F.W.Burnett
  *The Testament of Jesus-Sophia: A Redaction-Critical Study of
  the Eschatological Discourse in Matthew,* Washington,
  UP of America, 1981.
  'Παλιγγενεσία in Matt. 19:28: A window on the Matthean
  Community?', *JSNT* 17 (1983) 60-72.
F.Busch
  *Zum Verständnis der synoptischen Eschatologie; Markus 13
  neu untersucht,* Gütersloh: Bertelsmann, 1938.
W.Bussmann
  Synoptische Studien, Halle: Waisenhauses, 1925-1931 (3 vols.)
B.C.Butler
  *The Originality of St Matthew. A Critique of the Two-
  Document Hypothesis,* Cambridge: UP, 1951.
D.Buzy
  '"L'Adversaire et l'Obstacle" (II Thess II 3-12)',
  RSR 24 (1934) 402-31.
  'Saint Paul et Saint Matthieu', *RSR* 28 (1938) 473-78.
M.Casey
  Son of Man   The interpretation and influence of Daniel 7,
  London: SPCK, 1979.

D.R.Catchpole
    'The Poor on Earth and the Son of Man in Heaven: A Re-
    Appraisal of Matthew XXV.31-46', *BJRL* 61 (1978-79) 355-97
J.Chapman
    *Matthew, Mark and Luke. A Study in the Order and
    Interrelation of the Synoptic Gospels,* London: Longmans,
    1937.
R.H.Charles
    *A Critical and Exegetical Commentary on the Revelation of
    St John,* Edinburgh: T.& T.Clark, 1920.
F.Christ
    Jesus Sophia. Die Sophia-Christologie bei den Synoptikern,
    Zürich: Zwingli, 1970.
R.F.Collins
    'Tradition, Redaction, and Exhortation in 1 Th 4,13-5,11'
    in J.Lambrecht, *L'Apocalypse johannique et l'Apocalyptique
    dans le Nouveau Testament,* Gembloux: Duculot, 1980,
    pp.325-43.
C.Colpe
    'ὁ υἱὸς τοῦ ἀνθρώπου', *TDNT* vol.8, pp.400-77.
H.Conzelmann
    'Geschichte und Eschaton nach Mc 13', *ZNW* 50 (1959) 210-21.
L.Cope
    'Matthew XXV:31-46 "The Sheep and the Goats" Reinterpreted',
    NovT 11 (1969) 32-44.
J.Coppens
    'Les logia du Fils de l'homme dans l'évangile de Marc' in
    L'Évangile selon Marc, ed. M.Sabbe, Gembloux: Duculot,
    1974, pp.487-528.
É.Cothonet
    'La IIe Épitre aux Thessaloniciens et L'Apocalypse
    Synoptique', *RSR* 42 (1954) 5-39.
    'Les prophètes chrétiens dans L'Évangile selon saint
    Matthieu' in *L'Évangile selon Matthieu,* ed. M.Didier,
    Gembloux: Duculot, 1972, pp.281-308.
A.C.Cotter
    'The Eschatological Discourse', *CBQ* 1 (1939) 125-32, 204-13.
C.B.Cousar
    'Eschatology and Mark's "Theologia Crucis". A Critical
    Analysis of Mark 13', *Int* 24 (1970) 321-35.
C.E.B.Cranfield
    'St Mark 13', *SJT* 6 (1943) 186-89, 287-303 & 7 (1954) 284-
    303.
    The Gospel according to Saint Mark, Cambridge: UP, 1955.
G.Dalman
    Arbeit und Sitte in Palästina V, Hildesheim: Olms, 1964.

P.H.Davids
   The Epistle of James   A Commentary on the Greek Text,
   Exeter: Paternoster, 1982.
F.Dewar
   'Chapter 13 and the Passion Narrative in St Mark',
   Theology 64 (1961) 99-107.
C.H.Dodd
   More New Testament Studies, Manchester: UP, 1968.
K.P.Donfried
   'The allegory of the ten virgins (Matt 25:1-13) as a
   summary of Matthean theology', *JBL* 93 (1974) 415-28.
D.L.Dungan
   *The Sayings of Jesus in the Churches of Paul   The Use of
   the Synoptic Tradition in the Regulation of Early Church
   Life,* Oxford: Blackwell, 1971.
J.Dupont
   '"Vous n'avez pas achevé les villes d'Israël avant que le
   Fils de l'Homme ne vienne" (Mat X 23)', *NovT* 2 (1958) 228-
   244.
   'Le logion des douze trônes (Mt 19,28; Lk 22,28-30),
   Bib 45 (1964) 355-92.
   'La Parabole du Figuier qui Bourgeonne (Mc,XIII,28-29 ET
   PAR.)', *RB* 75 (1968) 526-48.
   'Les épreuves des chrétiens avant la fin du monde Lc 21,5-
   19' in *Trente-troisième dimanche ordinaire* (Assemblées
   du Seigneur, 2e sêr, 64) Paris, 1969, pp.77-86.
   'La Parabole du Maître qui Rentre dans la Nuit (Mc 13, 34-
   36)' in *Mélanges Béda Rigaux,* Gembloux: Duculot, 1970,
   pp.89-116.
   'Il n'en sera pas laissé pierre sur pierre (Marc 13,2;
   Lk 19,44)', *Bib* 52 (1971) 301-20.
   'La portée christologique de l'évangélisation des nations
   d'après Luc 24:47' in *Neues Testament und Kirche* for
   R.Schnackenburg, Freiburg:Herder, 1974, pp.125-43.
   'La ruine du temple et la fin des temps dans le discours
   de Marc 13' in *Apocalypses et Theologie de l'Espérance,*
   LD 95, ed. L.Monloubou, Paris: Cerf, 1977, pp.207-69.
   'La Persécution comme Situation Missionnaire (Marc 13,
   9-11) in *Die Kirche des Anfangs* for H.Schürmann,
   Freiburg: Herder, 1978, pp.97-114.
E.E.Ellis
   The Gospel of Luke, London: Nelson, 1966.
J.Ernst
   Die Eschatologische Gegenspieler in den Schriften des N.T.,
   Regensburg: Pustet, 1967.

W.R.Farmer
> *The Synoptic Problem   A Critical Analysis,* London:
> Macmillan, 1964.

A.Farrer
> 'An Examination of Mark XIII.10', *JTS* 7 (1956) 75-79.

G.D.Fee
> 'A Text-Critical Look at the Synoptic Problem',
> *NovT* 22 (1980) 12-28.

A.Feuillet
> 'Le Discours de Jésus sur la Ruine du Temple D'Après
> Marc XIII et Luc XXl,5-36', RB 55 (1948) 481-502.
> 56 (1949) 61-92.
> 'Les Origines et la Signification de Mt 10,23',
> *CBQ* 23 (1961) 182-98.

P.Fiedler
> 'Die übergebenen Talente   Auslegung von Mt 25,14-30',
> *BibLeb* 11 (1970) 259-273.

F.Flückiger
> 'Die Redaktion der Zukunftsrede in Mark.13',
> *TZ* 26 (1970) 395-409.

D.Ford
> *The Abomination of Desolation in Biblical Eschatology,*
> Washington: UP of America, 1979.

R.T.France
> *Jesus and the Old Testament   His Application of Old
> Testament Passages to Himself and His Mission,*
> London: IVP, 1971.

G.Friedrich
> '1, Thessalonicher, 5,1-11, der apologetische Einschub
> eines Späteren', *ZTK* 70 (1973) 288-315.

J.Friedrich
> *Gott im Bruder,* Stuttgart: Calwer, 1977.

A.Fuchs
> *Sprachliche Untersuchungen zu Matthäus und Lukas,*
> Rome: Biblical Institute Press, 1971.

G.C.Fuller
> 'The Olivet Discourse: An Apocalyptic Timetable',
> *WTJ* 28 (1966) 157-63.

P.Gaechter
> *Das Matthäus Evangelium,* Innsbruck: Tyrolia, 1963.

D.E.Garland
> *The Intention of Matthew 23,* Leiden: Brill, 1979.

L.Gaston
> 'Sondergut und Markusstoff in Luk.21', *TZ* 16 (1960) 161-72.

L.Gaston
   *No Stone on Another. Studies in the Significance of the
   Fall of Jerusalem in the Synoptic Gospels.* Leiden:
   Brill, 1970.
R.Geiger
   Die Lukanischen Endzeitreden, Bern: Herbert-Lang, 1973.
B.Gerhardsson
   *Memory and Manuscript Oral Tradition and Written
   Transmission in Rabbinic Judaism and Early Christianity,*
   Uppsala: Gleerup, 1961.
R.Glover
   'The Didache's Quotations and the Synoptic Gospels',
   NTS 5 (1958-59) 12-29.
J.Gnilka
   Das Evangelium nach Markus, Zürich: Benziger, vol.2, 1979.
H.Gollinger
   '"Ihr wißt nicht, an welchem Tag euer Herr kommt" Auslegung
   von Mt 24,37-51', *BibLeb* 11 (1970) 238-47.
M.D.Goulder
   Midrash and Lection in Matthew, London: SPCK, 1974.
E.Gräßer
   *Das Problem der Parusieverzögerung in den synoptischen
   Evangelien und in der Apostelgeschichte,*
   Berlin: de Gruyter, 1977[3].
K.Grayston
   'The Study of Mark XIII', *BJRL* 56 (1973-74) 371-87.
W.Grundmann
   Das Evangelium nach Matthäus, Berlin: Evangelische, 1968.
R.A.Guelich
   The Sermon on the Mount A Foundation for Understanding,
   Waco: Word, 1982.
R.H.Gundry
   Matthew A Commentary on His Literary and Theological Art,
   Grand Rapids: Eerdmans, 1982.
E.Haenchen
   Gott und Mensch Gesämmelte Aufsatze, Tübingen: Mohr, 1965.
F.Hahn
   Mission in the New Testament, London: SCM, 1965.
   'Die Rede von der Parusie des Meschensohnes Markus 13',
   in *Jesus und der Menschensohn für A Vögtle,*
   Freiburg: Herder, 1975, pp.240-60.
A.Harnack
   The Sayings of Jesus, London: Williams & Norgate, 1908.

L.Hartman
     Testimonium Linguae, Lund: Gleerup, 1963.
     *Prophecy Interpreted The Formation of Some Jewish
     Apocalyptic Texts and of the Eschatological Discourse
     Mark 13 Par.*, Uppsala: Gleerup, 1966.
     'La Parousie du Fils de l'homme Mc 13, 24-32', in
     Trente-troisième dimanche ordinaire (Assemblées du
     Seigneur, 2ᵉ sér, 64) Paris, 1969, pp.47-57.
E.Hatch and H.A.Redpath
     A Concordance to the Septuagint, Oxford: UP, 1897.
W.Haupt
     Worte Jesus und Gemeindeüberlieferung, Leipzig:
     Hinrichs'sche, 1913.
A.J.B.Higgins
     'The Sign of the Son of Man (Matt.XXIV.30)',
     NTS 9 (1963) 380-82.
P.Hoffmann
     'Πάντες έργάται άδικίας Redaktion und Tradition in
     Lc 13 22-30', *ZNW* 58 (1967) 188-214.
C.L.Holman
     'The Idea of an Imminent Parousia in the Synoptic Gospels',
     Studia Biblica et Theologica III (1973) 15-31.
     *Eschatological Delay in Jewish and Early Christian
     Apocalyptic Literature*, University of Nottingham
     PhD thesis, 1982.
M.D.Hooker
     Review of Hartman's *Prophecy Interpreted* in
     JTS 19 (1968) 263-65.
R.Hummel
     *Die Auseinandersetzung zwischen Kirche und Judentum
     im Matthäusevangelium*, München: Kaiser, 1966.
H.G.Jameson
     The Origin of the Synoptic Gospels, Oxford: Blackwells,
     1922.
J.Jeremias
     Jesus' Promise to the Nations, London: SCM, 1958.
     The Parables of Jesus, London: SCM, 1963.
     The Eucharistic Words of Jesus, London: SCM, 1964.
     'Lampades in Matthew 25:1-13' in *Soli Deo Gloria New
     Testament Studies in Honor of William Childs Robinson*,
     Richmond: John Knox, 1968, pp.83-87.
     Jerusalem in the Time of Jesus, London: SCM, 1969.
     *Die Sprache des Lukasevangeliums Redaktion und Tradition
     im Nicht-Markusstoff des dritten Evangeliums*,
     Göttingen: Vandenhoeck & Ruprecht, 1980.

P.Joüon
    'La Parabole du *Portier qui doit veiller* (Marc, 13,33-37)
    et la Parabole des *Serviteurs qui doivent veiller* (Luc,
    12,35-40)', *RSR* 30 (1940) 365-68.
W.Käser
    'Exegetische und Theologische Erwägungen zur Seligpreisung
    der Kinderlosen Lc 23 29b', *ZNW* 54 (1963) 240-54.
J.M.Kik
    Matthew Twenty-Four An Exposition, Swengel: Bible Truth
    Depot, 1948.
G.D.Kilpatrick
    'The Gentile Mission in Mark and Mark 13[9-11]' in
    Studies in the Gospels for R.H.Lightfoot, ed. D.E.Nineham,
    Oxford: Blackwells, 1955, pp.145-158.
    'Mark XIII.9-10', *JTS* 9 (1958) 81-86.
J.S.Kloppenborg
    'Didache 16 6-8 and Special Matthean Tradition',
    ZNW 70 (1979) 54-67.
W.L.Knox
    The Sources of the Synoptic Gospels, Cambridge:
    UP, vol.1, 1953, vol.2, 1957.
W.G.Kümmel
    'Die Weherufe über die Schriftgelehrten und Pharisäer
    (Matthäus 23,13-36)' in *Antijudaismus im Neuen Testament,*
    ed. W.P.Eckert, etc., München: Kaiser, 1967, pp.135-47.
M.J.Lagrange
    Évangile selon Saint Matthieu, Paris: Gabalda: 1948[7].
J.Lambrecht
    'Die Logia-Quellen von Markus 13', *Bib* 47 (1966) 321-60.
    *Die Redaktion der Markus-Apokalypse Literarische Analyse
    und Strukturuntersuchung,* Rome: Pontifical Institute, 1967.
    'Die "Midrasch-Quelle" von Mk 13' (review of Hartman,
    Prophecy Interpreted), *Bib* 49 (1968) 254-70.
    'The Parousia Discourse Composition and Content in
    Mt.,XXIV-XXV' in *L'Évangile selon Matthieu Rédaction et
    Théologie,* Gembloux: Duculot, 1972, pp.309-42.
    Parables of Jesus Insight and Challenge, Bangalore:
    Theological Publications in India, 1978.
E.Linnemann
    Parables of Jesus Introduction and Exposition,
    London: SPCK, 1966.
E.Lövestam
    Spiritual Wakefulness in the New Testament, Lund:
    Gleerup, 1963.

E.Lövestam
'The ἡ γενεὰ αὔτη Eschatology in Mk 13,30 parr.', in
*L'Apocalypse johannique et l'Apocalyptique dans le Nouveau
Testament,* ed. J.Lambrecht, Gembloux: Duculot, 1980,
pp.403-13.

D.Lührmann
Die Redaktion der Logienquelle, Neukirchen: Neukirchener,
1969.
'Noah und Lot (Lk 17 26-29) - ein Nachtrag', *ZNW* 63 (1972)
130-32.
'Markus 14:55-64: Christologie und Zerstörung des Tempels
im Markusevangeliums', *NTS* 27 (1981) 457-74.

A.H.McNeile
The Gospel according to St Matthew, London: Macmillan, 1915.

I.Maisch
'Das Gleichnis von den klugen und törichten Jungfrauen
Auslegung von Mt 25,1-13', *BibLeb* 11 (1970) 247-59.

T.W.Manson
The Sayings of Jesus, London: SCM, 1949.

I.H.Marshall
'The Resurrection of Jesus in Luke', *TynB* 24 (1973) 55-98.
The Gospel of Luke, Exeter: Paternoster, 1978.

W.Marxsen
Mark the Evangelist, Nashville: Abingdon, 1969.

E.Massaux
*Influence de l'Évangile de saint Matthieu sur la
litterature chrétienne avant saint Irênêe,* Gembloux:
Duculot, 1950.

M.Meinertz
'Die Tragweite des Gleichnisses von den zehn Jungfrauen'
in *Synoptische Studien für A. Wikenhauser,* München:
Karl Zink, 1953, pp.94-104.

W.Michaelis
Die Gleichnisse Jesu Eine Einführung, Hamburg: Furche,1956

A.L.Moore
The Parousia in the New Testament, Leiden: Brill, 1966.

W.F.Moulton and A.S.Geden
A Concordance to the Greek New Testament, Edinburgh:
T.& T.Clark, 1926[3].

R.H.Mounce
'Pauline Eschatology and the Apocalypse', *EvQ* 46 (1974) 164-66

J.Munck
Paul and the Salvation of Mankind, London: SCM, 1959.

F.Neirynck
'Le discourse anti-apocalyptique de Mc,XIII',
ETL 45 (1969) 154-164.

F.Neirynck
'Marc 13 Examen critique de l'interpretation de R.Pesch'
in *L'Apocalyse johannique de l'Apocalyptique dans le
Nouveau Testament*, ed. J.Lambrecht, Gembloux: Duculot,
1980, pp.369-401 (first appeared in *ETL* 53 and 54).
P.Nepper-Christensen
'Das verborgene Herrnwort. Eine Untersuchung über
1.Thess. 4,13-18', *ST* 19 (1965) 136-154.
A.Oepke
'λάμπω .. etc.', *TDNT* 4, pp.16-28.
G.E.Okeke
'1 Thessalonians 2.13-16: The Fate of the Unbelieving
Jews', *NTS* 27 (1980-81) 127-36. ·
T.Onuki
'Die johanneischen Abschiedsreden und die synoptische
Tradition... eine traditionskritische und
traditionsgeschichtliche Untersuchung', *Annual of the
Japanese Biblical Institute* 3 (1977) 157-268.
J.B.Orchard
'Thessalonians and the Synoptic Gospels', *Bib* 19 (1938)
19-42..
W.Ott
*Gebet und Heil Die Bedeutung der Gebetsparänese in der
Lukanischen Theologie*, München: Kösel, 1965.
N.H.Palmer
The Logic of Gospel Criticism, London: Macmillan, 1968.
N.Perrin
Rediscovering the Teaching of Jesus, London: SCM, 1967.
C.Perrot
'Essai sur le discours eschatologique (Mc.XIII, 1-37;
Mt.XXIV,1-36; Lc.XX1,5-36)', *RSR* 47 (1959) 481-514.
R.Pesch
Naherwartungen Tradition und Redaktion in Mk 13,
Düsseldorf: Patmos, 1968.
'Eschatologie und Ethik Auslegung von Mt 24, 1-36'
BibLeb 11 (1970) 223-38.
Das Markusevangelium, Freiburg: Herder, vol.1, 1976,
vol.2, 1977.
'Markus 13' in *L'Apocalypse johannique et l'Apocalyptique
dans le Nouveau Testament*, ed. J.Lambrecht, Gembloux:
Duculot, 1980, pp.355-368.
W.Pesch
'Theologische Aussagen der Redaktion von Matthäus 23',
in *Orientierung an Jesus... Für Josef Schmid*,
ed. P.Hoffmann, Freiburg: Herder, 1973, pp.286-99.

E.Peterson
    'Die Einholung des Kyrios', *ZST* 7 (1929-30) 682-702.
J.Plevnik
    '1 Thess 5,1-11: Its Authenticity, Intention and Message',
    Bib 60 (1979) 71-90.
E.J.Prycke
    Redactional Style in the Marcan Gospel, Cambridge: UP, 1978.
A.Rahlfs,
    ed. *Septuaginta,* Stuttgart: Württembergische Bibelanstalt,
    8th edition, 1965.
F.Rehkopf
    Die Lukanische Sonderquelle Ihr Umfang und Sprachgebrauch,
    Tübingen: Mohr, 1955
K.Rengstorf
    'σημεῖον', *TDNT* 7, pp.200-61.
B.Rigaux
    *L'Antéchrist et l'Opposition au Royaume Messianique dans
    l'Ancien et le Nouveau Testament,* Gembloux: Duculot, 1956.
    Saint Paul Les Épitres aux Thessaloniciens, Gembloux:
    Duculot, 1956.
    'ΒΔΕΛΥΓΜΑ ΤΗΣ ΕΡΗΜΩΣΕΩΣ Mc 13,14; Mt 24,15',
    Bib 40 (1959) 675-83.
    'La petite apocalypse de Luc (XVII, 22-37)' in *Ecclesia a
    Spiritu Sancto edocta.... à Mgr Gérard Philips,* Gembloux:
    Duculot, 1970, pp.407-38.
D.M.Roarck
    'The Great Eschatological Discourse', *NovT* 7 (1964-65) 122-27.
J.A.T.Robinson
    'The "Parable" of the Sheep and the Goats', *NTS* 2 (1955-56)
    225-37.
    Redating the New Testament, London: SCM, 1976.
F.Rousseau
    'La structure de Marc 13', *Bib* 56 (1975) 157-72.
W.Schenk
    'Auferweckung der Toten oder Gericht nach den Werken.
    Tradition und Redaktion in Mattäus xxv 1-13',
    NovT 20 (1978) 278-99.
R.Schippers
    'The Pre-Synoptic Tradition in 1 Thessalonians II 13-16',
    NovT 8 (1966) 223-34.
A.Schlatter
    Das Evangelium des Lukas aus seinen Quellen erklärt,
    Stuttgart: Calwer, 1931.
    Der Evangelist Matthäus, Stuttgart: Calwer, 1959.

J.Schmid
   Das Evangelium nach Matthäus, Regensburg: Pustet, 1959.
   Das Evangelium nach Lukas, Regensburg: Pustet, 1960.
R.Schnackenburg
   'Der eschatologische Abschnitt Lk 17, 20-37' in *Mélanges
   Bibliques ... au R.P.Béda Rigaux,* Gembloux: Duculot, 1970,
   pp.213-34.
   *Schriften zum Neuen Testament Exegese in Fortschritt
   und Wandel,* München: Kösel, 1971.
T.Schramm
   Der Markus-Stoff bei Lukas, Cambridge: UP, 1971.
S.Schulz
   Q Die Spruchquelle der Evangelisten, Zürich:
   Theologischer, 1972.
H.Schürmann
   Jesu Abschiedsrede Lk 22, 21-38, Münster: Aschendorsche,
   1957.
   'Sprachliche Reminiszenzen an abgeänderte oder
   ausgelassene Bestandteile der Spruchsammlung im Lukas-
   und Matthäusevangelium', *NTS* 6 (1959/60) 193-210.
   'Das Thomasevangelium und das lukanische Sondergut',
   BZ 7 (1966) 236-60.
   *Traditionsgeschichtliche Untersuchungen zu den
   synoptischen Evangelien,* Düsseldorf: Patmos, 1968.
E.Schweizer
   The Good News according to Mark, London: SPCK, 1971.
   The Good News according to Matthew, London: SPCK, 1976.
D.P.Senior
   *The Passion Narrative according to Matthew A Redactional
   Study,* Leuven: UP, 1975.
R.H.Shaw
   'A Conjecture on the Signs of the End', *ATR* 47 (1965)
   96-102.
J.S.Sibinga
   'The Structure of the Apocalyptic Discourse, Matthew 24
   and 25', *ST* 29 (1975) 71-80.
R.H.Smith
   'The Household Lamps of Palestine in New Testament Times',
   BA 29 (1966) 2-27.
R.Sneed
   '"The Kingdom of God is within you" (Lk 17,21)',
   CBQ 24 (1962) 363-82.
H.F.D.Sparks
   'St. John's Knowledge of Matthew: The Evidence of John
   13, 16 and 15,20', *JTS* 3 (1952) 58-61.

D.M.Stanley
    'Pauline Allusions to the Sayings of Jesus', *CBQ* 23 (1961)
    26-39.
O.H.Steck
    Israel und der gewaltsame Geschick der Propheten,
    Neukirchen: Neukirchener, 1967.
E.Stommel
    'Σημεῖον ἐκπετάσεως (Didache 16,6)', *RQ* 48 (1953) 21-42.
M.J.Suggs
    Wisdom, Christology and Law in Matthew's Gospel,
    Harvard: UP, 1970.
H.B.Swete
    The Gospel according to St Mark, London: Macmillan, 1909[3].
V.Taylor
    The Gospel according to St Mark, London: Macmillan, 1952.
W.G.Thompson
    'An Historical Perspective in the Gospel of Matthew',
    JBL 93 (1974) 243-62.
C.M.Tuckett
    *The Revival of the Griesbach Hypothesis   An analysis and
    appraisal*, Cambridge: UP, 1983.
A.Vögtle
    'Exegetische Erwägungen über das Wissen und
    Selbstbewußtsein Jesus', in *Gott in Welt... für Karl
    Rahner*, Freiburg: Herder, 1964.
    Das Neue Testament und die Zukunft des Kosmos,
    Düsseldorf: Patmos, 1970.
N.Walter
    'Tempelstörung und synoptische Apokalypse', *ZNW* 57 (1966)
    38-49.
A.Weiser
    Die Knechtsgleichnisse der Synoptischen Evangelien,
    München: Kösel, 1971.
D.Wenham
    The Composition of Mark 4:1-34, Manchester University
    PhD thesis, 1970
    'The Synoptic Problem Revisited: Some New Suggestions
    about the Composition of Mark 4:1-34', *TynB* 23 (1972) 3-38.
    'The Resurrection Narratives in Matthew's Gospel',
    TynB 24 (1973) 21-54.
    'The Interpretation of the Parable of the Sower',
    NTS 20 (1974) 299-319.
    'Recent study of Mark 13', *TSF Bulletin* 71 (1975) 6-15
    & 72 (1975) 1-9.
    'A Note on Matthew 24:10-12', *TynB* 31 (1980) 155-62.

D.Wenham

    'Paul and the Synoptic Apocalypse', in *Gospel Perspectives Studies of History and Tradition in the Four Gospels,* vol.II, ed. R.T.France & D.Wenham, Sheffield: JSOT, 1981.

    'A Note on Mark 9:33-42/Matt.18:1-6/Luke 9:46-50', *JSNT* 14 (1982) 113-18.

    '"This generation will not pass..." A study of Jesus' future expectation in Mark 13', in *Christ the Lord Studies in Christology presented to Donald Guthrie,* ed. H.H.Rowdon, Leicester: IVP, 1982.

    'Review Article   Guelich on the Sermon on the Mount: A Critical Review', *Trinity Journal* 4 (1983) forthcoming.

E.M.Wilson

    'The Second Coming in the Discourse of the Last Things', *PTR* 26 (1928) 65-79.

J.Winandy

    'Le Logion de l'Ignorance (Mc,XIII,32; Mt.,XXIV,36)', *RB* 75 (1975) 63-79.

M.Zerwick

    Untersuchungen zum Markus-Stil, Rome: Pontifical Biblical Institute, 1937.

    'Die Parabel vom Thronanwärter', *Bib* 40 (1959) 654-74.

J.Zmijewski

    Die Eschatologiereden des Lukas-Evangeliums   Eine traditions- und redaktionsgeschichtliche Untersuchung zu Lk 21,5-36 und Lk 17,20-37, Bonn: Peter Hanstein, 1972.

INDICES

1. BIBLICAL REFERENCES & CITATIONS FROM OTHER ANCIENT AUTHORS

*Where a passage or group of verses is referred to, references to
individual verses within the passage have not always been given*

APOCRYPHA AND OTHER WORKS

2. MODERN AUTHORS

3. SUBJECTS

This is a selective index, not a complete list of references